MCDBA SQL Server 7

Test Yourself

Practice Exams

(Exams 70-028 and 70-029)

Syngress Media, Inc.

Osborne/McGraw-Hill

Berkeley New York St. Louis San Francisco Auckland Bogotá Hamburg London Madrid Mexico City
Milan Montreal New Delhi Panama City Paris São Paulo Singapore Sydney Tokyo Toronto

Osborne/**McGraw-Hill**
2600 Tenth Street
Berkeley, California 94710
U.S.A.

For information on translations or book distributors outside the U.S.A., or to arrange
bulk purchase discounts for sales promotions, premiums, or fund-raisers, please contact
Osborne/**McGraw-Hill** at the above address.

MCDBA SQL Server 7 Test Yourself Practice Exams

1234567890 AGM AGM 019876543210

ISBN 0-07-212181-5

Publisher
Brandon A. Nordin

**Associate Publisher and
Editor-in-Chief**
Scott Rogers

Acquisitions Editor
Gareth Hancock

Editorial Management
Syngress Media, Inc.

Project Editor
Mark Karmendy

Acquisitions Coordinator
Tara Davis

Series Editor
Robert Aschermann

Technical Editors
Lauri Bryant
Robert Patton

Copy Editors
Nancy Hannigan
Nancy Faughnan

Proofreaders
John Gildersleeve
Carol Burbo

Computer Designers
Mickey Galicia
Jim Kussow

Illustrators
Beth Young
Robert Hansen
Brian Wells

Series Design
Roberta Steele

Cover Design
Regan Honda

This book was composed with Corel VENTURA™ Publisher.

From Global Knowledge

At Global Knowledge we strive to support the multiplicity of learning styles required by our students to achieve success as technical professionals. In this series of books, it is our intention to offer the reader a valuable tool for successful completion of the MCDBA and MCSE certification exams.

As the world's largest IT training company, Global Knowledge is uniquely positioned to offer these books. The expertise gained each year from providing instructor-led training to hundreds of thousands of students worldwide has been captured in book form to enhance your learning experience. We hope that the quality of these books demonstrates our commitment to your lifelong learning success. Whether you choose to learn through the written word, computer-based training, Web delivery, or instructor-led training, Global Knowledge is committed to providing you the very best in each of those categories. For those of you who know Global Knowledge, or those of you who have just found us for the first time, our goal is to be your lifelong competency partner.

Thank you for the opportunity to serve you. We look forward to serving your needs again in the future.

Warmest regards,

Duncan Anderson
President and Chief Operating Officer, Global Knowledge

The Global Knowledge Advantage

Global Knowledge has a global delivery system for its products and services. The company has 28 subsidiaries, and offers its programs through a total of 60+ locations. No other vendor can provide consistent services across a geographic area this large. Global Knowledge is the largest independent information technology education provider, offering programs on a variety of platforms. This enables our multi-platform and multi-national customers to obtain all of their programs from a single vendor. The company has developed the unique CompetusTM Framework software tool and methodology which can quickly reconfigure courseware to the proficiency level of a student on an interactive basis. Combined with self-paced and on-line programs, this technology can reduce the time required for training by prescribing content in only the deficient skills areas. The company has fully automated every aspect of the education process, from registration and follow-up, to "just-in-time" production of courseware. Global Knowledge, through its Enterprise Services Consultancy, can customize programs and products to suit the needs of an individual customer.

Global Knowledge Classroom Education Programs

The backbone of our delivery options is classroom-based education. Our modern, well-equipped facilities staffed with the finest instructors offer programs in a wide variety of information technology topics, many of which lead to professional certifications.

Custom Learning Solutions

This delivery option has been created for companies and governments that value customized learning solutions. For them, our consultancy-based approach of developing targeted education solutions is most effective at helping them meet specific objectives.

Self-Paced and Multimedia Products

This delivery option offers self-paced program titles in interactive CD-ROM, videotape and audio tape programs. In addition, we offer custom development of interactive multimedia courseware to customers and partners. Call us at 1 (888) 427-4228.

Electronic Delivery of Training

Our network-based training service delivers efficient competency-based, interactive training via the World Wide Web and organizational intranets. This leading-edge delivery option provides a custom learning path and "just-in-time" training for maximum convenience to students.

ARG

American Research Group (ARG), a wholly-owned subsidiary of Global Knowledge, one of the largest worldwide training partners of Cisco Systems, offers a wide range of internetworking, LAN/WAN, Bay Networks, FORE Systems, IBM, and UNIX courses. ARG offers hands on network training in both instructor-led classes and self-paced PC-based training.

Global Knowledge Courses Available

Network Fundamentals

- Understanding Computer Networks
- Telecommunications Fundamentals I
- Telecommunications Fundamentals II
- Understanding Networking Fundamentals
- Implementing Computer Telephony Integration
- Introduction to Voice Over IP
- Introduction to Wide Area Networking
- Cabling Voice and Data Networks
- Introduction to LAN/WAN protocols
- Virtual Private Networks
- ATM Essentials

Network Security & Management

- Troubleshooting TCP/IP Networks
- Network Management
- Network Troubleshooting
- IP Address Management
- Network Security Administration
- Web Security
- Implementing UNIX Security
- Managing Cisco Network Security
- Windows NT 4.0 Security

IT Professional Skills

- Project Management for IT Professionals
- Advanced Project Management for IT Professionals
- Survival Skills for the New IT Manager
- Making IT Teams Work

LAN/WAN Internetworking

- Frame Relay Internetworking
- Implementing T1/T3 Services
- Understanding Digital Subscriber Line (xDSL)
- Internetworking with Routers and Switches
- Advanced Routing and Switching
- Multi-Layer Switching and Wire-Speed Routing
- Internetworking with TCP/IP
- ATM Internetworking
- OSPF Design and Configuration
- Border Gateway Protocol (BGP) Configuration

Authorized Vendor Training

Cisco Systems

- Introduction to Cisco Router Configuration
- Advanced Cisco Router Configuration
- Installation and Maintenance of Cisco Routers
- Cisco Internetwork Troubleshooting
- Cisco Internetwork Design
- Cisco Routers and LAN Switches
- Catalyst 5000 Series Configuration
- Cisco LAN Switch Configuration
- Managing Cisco Switched Internetworks
- Configuring, Monitoring, and Troubleshooting Dial-Up Services
- Cisco AS5200 Installation and Configuration
- Cisco Campus ATM Solutions

Bay Networks

- Bay Networks Accelerated Router Configuration
- Bay Networks Advanced IP Routing
- Bay Networks Hub Connectivity
- Bay Networks Accelar 1xxx Installation and Basic Configuration
- Bay Networks Centillion Switching

FORE Systems

- FORE ATM Enterprise Core Products
- FORE ATM Enterprise Edge Products
- FORE ATM Theory
- FORE LAN Certification

Operating Systems & Programming

Microsoft

- Introduction to Windows NT
- Microsoft Networking Essentials
- Windows NT 4.0 Workstation
- Windows NT 4.0 Server
- Advanced Windows NT 4.0 Server
- Windows NT Networking with TCP/IP
- Introduction to Microsoft Web Tools
- Windows NT Troubleshooting
- Windows Registry Configuration

UNIX

- UNIX Level I
- UNIX Level II
- Essentials of UNIX and NT Integration

Programming

- Introduction to JavaScript
- Java Programming
- PERL Programming
- Advanced PERL with CGI for the Web

Web Site Management & Development

- Building a Web Site
- Web Site Management and Performance
- Web Development Fundamentals

High Speed Networking

- Essentials of Wide Area Networking
- Integrating ISDN
- Fiber Optic Network Design
- Fiber Optic Network Installation
- Migrating to High Performance Ethernet

DIGITAL UNIX

- UNIX Utilities and Commands
- DIGITAL UNIX v4.0 System Administration
- DIGITAL UNIX v4.0 (TCP/IP) Network Management
- AdvFS, LSM, and RAID Configuration and Management
- DIGITAL UNIX TruCluster Software Configuration and Management
- UNIX Shell Programming Featuring Kornshell
- DIGITAL UNIX v4.0 Security Management
- DIGITAL UNIX v4.0 Performance Management
- DIGITAL UNIX v4.0 Intervals Overview

DIGITAL OpenVMS

- OpenVMS Skills for Users
- OpenVMS System and Network Node Management I
- OpenVMS System and Network Node Management II
- OpenVMS System and Network Node Management III
- OpenVMS System and Network Node Operations
- OpenVMS for Programmers
- OpenVMS System Troubleshooting for Systems Managers
- Configuring and Managing Complex VMScluster Systems
- Utilizing OpenVMS Features from C
- OpenVMS Performance Management
- Managing DEC TCP/IP Services for OpenVMS
- Programming in C

Hardware Courses

- AlphaServer 1000/1000A Installation, Configuration and Maintenance
- AlphaServer 2100 Server Maintenance
- AlphaServer 4100, Troubleshooting Techniques and Problem Solving

About Syngress Media

Syngress Media creates books and software for Information Technology professionals seeking skill enhancement and career advancement. Its products are designed to comply with vendor and industry standard course curricula, and are optimized for certification exam preparation. You can contact Syngress via the Web at www.syngress.com.

Contributors

Robert A. Patton (MCDBA, MCSD, MCSE+Internet, MCP+Internet) is a software engineer specializing in client-server development with SQL Server as the back-end platform. He is currently a Senior Applications Developer at the Midland Life Insurance Company in Columbus, Ohio and has done work for First Union National Bank, Corporate Strategic Services and Sykes Enterprises. He attended the University of Chicago, where he studied Public Policy and played varsity football. Robert earned his Bachelor of Science degree in Software Engineering from The Ohio State University and is an avid fan of Buckeye athletics. He lives in Dublin, Ohio with his wife Jenny and their son Michael, and is anxiously awaiting the birth of Michael's little brother.

Mike Martone is an MCSD, MCSE, MCP+Internet, and LCNAD. In 1995, Mike became one of the first thousand MCSDs and is certified in SQL Server 6.5 and 7.0. Since graduating from Bowling Green State University with degrees in Computer Science and Psychology, he has specialized in developing Visual Basic, Internet, and Office applications for corporations and government institutions. He is currently working for an electronics distributor in Cleveland, and working towards his Masters in MIS at Case Western Reserve University. Mike lives in Lakewood, Ohio.

Michael Cross (MCSE, MCPS, MCP+Internet) is a computer programmer and network support specialist. He works as an instructor at private colleges, teaching courses in hardware, software, programming, and networking. He is the owner of KnightWare, a company that provides consulting, programming, network support, Web page design, computer training, and various other services. In his spare time, he has been a freelance writer for several years, in genres of fiction and non-fiction. He currently lives in London, Ontario.

Jennifer Watson is a consultant in the Atlanta metro area. She is an MCSE and is currently working on datawarehousing ERP systems. She specializes in analyzing and optimizing SQL databases for ERP clients.

R.W. (Bob) Reimer (MCP, MCSD) is a systems architect with AXIA Solutions Inc., a Waterloo, Ontario, Canada Microsoft Certified Solution Provider. Bob's interest in computers began in high school in 1969, programming an IBM1130 using Fortran IV. After some of the worst advice ever in 1972, "They are graduating far too many programmers, you'll never get a job when you graduate," Bob worked as a weather observer for the Canadian Government. In 1981, Bob attended the University of Waterloo and eventually finished his BMath part time in 1988. During that time Bob joined the insurance industry and worked in various capacities for some of Canada's top insurance companies developing insurance valuation and sales illustration systems for mainframes and PCs using APL, COBOL, IDMS, SAS, Lotus 1-2-3, and Excel. Bob's current technological focus is on Visual Basic, SQL Server, and Office Visual Basic for Applications. With a strong belief in continuing education, Bob holds the life insurance industry designation, FLMI/M (Master Fellow of the Life Management Institute), as well as his MCSD. He is currently working towards obtaining his MCDBA and MCSE. Bob also enjoys baseball, both real and virtual, and avidly follows sumo wrestling. I want to thank my wife, Barbara, and son, Aaron, for putting up with me during this writing assignment and in the past as I extended my skillsets through study at home.

Series Editor

Robert Aschermann (MCP, MCSE, MCT, MBA) has been involved with information systems as an IS professional for nearly 10 years. During his career he has worked in technical support, systems design, consulting, and training. Robert has been an MCSE for almost five years now and has passed more than 15 Microsoft certification exams. Currently Robert works for a large computer manufacturer based in Austin, Texas. His job responsibilities include systems engineering, project management, and business analysis. As a project manager he has lead large Windows NT and Windows 95 operating system migrations and many small to medium size client/server development projects. As a systems engineer and architect his responsibilities include identifying business processes that need improvement, drafting design specifications for solutions, and building systems that meet those design specifications. He routinely works with Microsoft development tools such as SQL Server 7.0, Access, IIS 4.0, Visual InterDev, Visual Basic, and the Microsoft Solutions Framework.

Technical Review by:

Lauri M. Bryant (MCT, MCSD, NCI) is the principal owner of LM Bryant and Associates, a small consulting firm located in Chicago, Illinois. Her firm focuses on providing support and training for Microsoft's visual tools. She has been programming for the past 15 years. Lauri's training career began 10 years ago providing end-user training for the Fortune 100. Five years ago she became certified to deliver Microsoft training. Lauri attended Rutgers University and has a background in English and graphical design.

ACKNOWLEDGMENTS

We would like to thank the following people:

- Richard Kristof of Global Knowledge for championing the series and providing us access to some great people and information.

- To all the incredibly hard-working folks at Osborne/McGraw-Hill: Brandon Nordin, Scott Rogers, and Gareth Hancock for their help in launching a great series and being solid team players; in addition, Tara Davis and Mark Karmendy for their help in fine-tuning the book.

- To Karen Croner at Microsoft Corp., for being patient and diligent in answering all our questions.

CONTENTS

Part I
SQL Server 7.0 Administration (Exam 70-028)

Part II
SQL Server 7.0 Designing and Implementing Databases (Exam 70-029)

Part III
Practice Exams

Wbuilt this book for a specific reason. Every time we asked MCDBAs and MCSEs and MCDBA certification candidates what they wanted in their study materials, they answered "More questions!" Based on that request, we built a book full of over 700 new questions on the MCDBA core SQL Server 7.0 exams so you can test yourself to your heart's content. You'll find full coverage of Administering Microsoft SQL Server 7.0 (Exam 70-028), and Designing and Implementing Databases with Microsoft SQL Server 7.0 (Exam 70-029).

In This Book

This book is organized in parts or modules, around the topics covered within the Microsoft exams administered at Sylvan Testing Centers. We cover each of the exams in a separate section and we also have a separate "Test Yourself" module. Microsoft has specific objectives for the MCDBA/MCSE exams: we've followed their list carefully, so you can be assured you're not missing anything.

The Q & A Modules

You will find two Q & A modules for each of the two exams—Administration and Design, followed by an answer section that has full explanations of both the correct and incorrect choices.

Each module is divided into categories, so you will cover every topic tested by Microsoft. Each topic is a heading within the chapter, so you can study by topic if you like. Should you find you need further review on any particular topic, you will find that the topic headings correspond to the chapters of Osborne/McGraw-Hill's MCDBA Study Guides. Want to simulate an actual exam? The section "The Test Yourself Modules" explains how.

In addition, throughout the Q & A modules, we have sprinkled helpful notes in the form of Exam Watches and Q & A scenarios:

- Exam Watch notes call attention to information about, and potential pitfalls in, the exam. These helpful hints are written by authors who have taken the exams and received their certification—who better to tell you what to worry about? They know what you're about to go through!

- Q & A sections lay out problems and solutions in a quick-read format:

QUESTIONS AND ANSWERS

Jesse needs to be able to manage logins for the SQL Server...	Add Jesse to the securityadmin fixed server role.
Mike wants to have the database he is responsible for accessed only with a password...	Create an Application user-defined database role and distribute an application that has the password hardcoded in it.

The Test Yourself Modules

If you have had your fill of exam questions, answers, and explanations, the time has come to test your knowledge. Or maybe, you want to start with a practice exam in the Test Yourself module to see where your strengths and weaknesses are, and then review only certain topics. Either way, turn to Part III of the book, the Test yourself Practice Exams. In this section we actually simulate the exams. We have given you two practice tests per exam. Lock yourself in your office or clear the kitchen table, set a timer, and jump in.

The Global Knowledge Web Site

Check out the Web site. Global Knowledge invites you to become an active member of the Access Global Web site. This site is an online mall and an information repository that you'll find invaluable. You can access many types of products to assist you in your preparation for the exams, and you'll be able to participate in forums, on-line discussions, and threaded discussions. No other book brings you unlimited access to such a resource. You'll find more information about this site in Appendix A.

MCDBA and MCSE Certification

Although you've obviously picked up this book to study for a specific exam, we'd like to spend some time covering what you need to complete in order to attain MCDBA or MCSE status. Because this information can be found on the Microsoft Web site, http://www.microsoft.com/mcp/, we've repeated only some of the more important information. You should review the train_cert site and check out Microsoft's information, along with their list of reasons to become an MCDBA or MCSE, including job advancement.

As you probably know, to attain MCSE status, you must pass a total of six exams—four requirements and two electives. For MCDBA status, one elective is required. For the MCDBA Windows 2000 track, you must pass three core exams and one elective. One required exam is on networking basics, one on NT Server (or Windows 2000 Server for the Windows 2000 track), one on NT Server in the Enterprise, and one on a client (either Windows NT Workstation or Windows 95 or 98). There are several electives from which to choose—and many of these electives also count toward Microsoft's MCSE+Internet (MCSE+I) certification. The following table lists the exam names, their corresponding course numbers, and whether they are required or elective. We're showing you the NT 4.0 track, and some information is included on the new MCDBA Windows 2000 track (for the latest information, check http://www.microsoft.com/mcp /certstep/mcdba.htm).

Exam Number	Exam Name	Required or Elective
70-58	Networking Essentials	Required for MCSE
70-64 or 70-98	Implementing and Supporting Microsoft Windows 95 or 98	Required for MCSE (either 70-63, 70-64, 70-98, or 70-73)

Exam Number	Exam Name	Required or Elective
70-67	Implementing and Supporting Microsoft Windows NT Server 4.0	Required for MCDBA and MCSE (candidates who haven't passed this and two other Windows NT 4.0 exams may take 70-215 instead, for the Windows 2000 track).
70-68	Implementing and Supporting Microsoft Windows NT Server 4.0 in the Enterprise	Required for MCDBA and MCSE (candidates who haven't passed this and two other Windows NT 4.0 exams may take 70-215 instead, for the Windows 2000 track).
70-73	Implementing and Supporting Microsoft Windows NT Workstation 4.0	Required for MCSE (either 70-73, 70-64 or 70-98)
70-13	Implementing and Supporting Microsoft SNA Server 3.0	Elective for MCSE (either 70-13 or 70-85)
70-14	Supporting Microsoft System Management Server 1.2	Elective for MCSE
70-15	Designing and Implementing Distributed Applications with Microsoft Visual C++ 6.0	Elective for MCDBA
70-18	Implementing and Supporting Microsoft Systems Management Server 1.2	Elective for MCSE (either 70-18 or 70-86)
70-19	Designing and Implementing Data Warehouses with Microsoft SQL Server 7.0	Elective for MCDBA and MCSE
70-59	Internetworking with Microsoft TCP/IP on Windows NT 4.0	Elective for MCDBA and MCSE
70-81	Implementing and Supporting Microsoft Exchange Server 5.5	Elective for MCSE (either 70-81 of 70-76)
70-85	Implementing and Supporting Microsoft SNA Server 4.0	Elective for MCSE (either 70-85 or 70-13)
70-86	Implementing and Supporting Microsoft Systems Management Server 2.0	Elective for MCSE (either 70-86 or 70-18)

Exam Number	Exam Name	Required or Elective
70-87	Implementing and Supporting Microsoft Internet Information Server 4.0	Elective for MCDBA and MCSE and Required for MCSE+I
70-88	Implementing and Supporting Microsoft Proxy Server 2.0	Elective for MCSE
70-28	Administering Microsoft SQL Server 7.0	Elective for MCDBA and MCSE
70-29	Designing and Implementing Databases with Microsoft SQL Server 7.0	Elective for MCDBA, MCSE and MCSD
70-76	Implementing and Supporting Microsoft Exchange Server 5	Elective for MCSE (either 70-76 or 70-81)
70-79	Implementing and Supporting Microsoft Internet Explorer 4.0 by Using the Internet Explorer Administration Kit	Elective for MCSE and Required for MCSE+I
70-175	Designing and Implementing Distributed Applications with Microsoft Visual Basic 6.0	Elective for MCDBA
70-215	Installing, Configuring and Administering Microsoft Windows 2000 Server	Required for MCDBA Windows 2000 track, *if* you have not passed exams 70-67, 70-68 and 70-73 (if you have, take 70-240)
70-240	Microsoft Windows 2000 Accelerated Exam for MCPs Certified on Microsoft Windows NT 4.0	Required for MCDBA Windows 2000 track *if* you have passed exams 70-67, 70-68 and 70-73

How to Take a Microsoft Certification Examination

If you are new to Microsoft certification, we have some good news and some bad news. The good news, of course, is that Microsoft certification is one of the most valuable credentials you can earn. It sets you apart from the crowd, and marks you as a valuable asset to your employer. You will gain the respect of your peers, and Microsoft certification can have a wonderful effect on your income.

The bad news is that Microsoft certification tests are not easy. You may think you will read through some study material, memorize a few facts, and pass the Microsoft examinations. After all, these certification exams are just computer-based, multiple-choice tests, so they must be easy. If you believe this, you are wrong. Unlike many "multiple guess" tests you have been exposed to in school, the questions on Microsoft certification examinations go beyond simple factual knowledge. The purpose of this introduction is to teach you how to take a Microsoft certification examination. To be successful, you need to know something about the purpose and structure of these tests. We will also look at the latest innovations in Microsoft testing. Using *simulations* and *adaptive testing*, Microsoft is enhancing both the validity and security of the certification process. These factors have some important effects on how you should prepare for an exam, as well as your approach to each question during the test.

We will begin by looking at the purpose, focus, and structure of Microsoft certification tests, and examining the effect these factors have on the kinds of questions you will face on your certification exams. We will define the structure of examination questions and investigate some common formats. Next, we will present a strategy for answering these questions. Finally, we will give some specific guidelines on what you should do on the day of your test.

Why Vendor Certification?

The Microsoft Certified Professional program, like the certification programs from Lotus, Novell, Oracle, and other software vendors, is maintained for the ultimate purpose of increasing the corporation's profits. A successful vendor certification program accomplishes this goal by helping to create a pool of experts in a company's software and by "branding" these experts so that companies using the software can identify them.

We know that vendor certification has become increasingly popular in the last few years because it helps employers find qualified workers, and because it helps software vendors like Microsoft sell their products. But why vendor certification rather than a more traditional approach like a college degree in computer science? A college education is a broadening and enriching experience, but a degree in computer science does not prepare students for most jobs in the IT industry.

A common truism in our business states, "If you are out of the IT industry for three years and want to return, you have to start over." The problem, of course, is *timeliness*; if a first-year student learns about a specific computer program, it probably will no longer be in wide use when he or she graduates. Although some colleges are trying to integrate Microsoft certification into their curriculum, the problem is not really a flaw in higher education, but a characteristic of the IT industry. Computer software is changing so rapidly that a four-year college just can't keep up.

A marked characteristic of the Microsoft certification program is an emphasis on performing specific job tasks rather than merely gathering knowledge. It may come as a shock, but most potential employers do not care how much you know about the theory of operating systems, networking, or database design. As one IT manager put it, "I don't really care what my employees know about the theory of our network. We don't need someone to sit at a desk and think about it. We need people who can actually do something to make it work better."

You should not think that this attitude is some kind of anti-intellectual revolt against "book learning." Knowledge is a necessary prerequisite, but it is not enough. More than one company has hired a computer science graduate as a network administrator, only to learn that the new employee has no idea how to add users, assign permissions, or perform the other day-to-day tasks necessary to maintain a network. This brings us to the second major characteristic of Microsoft certification that affects the questions you must be prepared to answer. In addition to timeliness, Microsoft certification is also job task oriented.

The timeliness of Microsoft's certification program is obvious, and is inherent in the fact that you will be tested on current versions of software in wide use today. The job task orientation of Microsoft certification is almost as obvious, but testing real-world job skills using a computer-based test is not easy.

Computerized Testing

Considering the popularity of Microsoft certification, and the fact that certification candidates are spread around the world, the only practical way to administer tests for the certification program is through Sylvan Prometric testing centers. Sylvan Prometric provides proctored testing services for Microsoft, Oracle, Novell, Lotus, and the A+ computer technician certification. Although the IT industry accounts for much of Sylvan's revenue, the company provides services for a number of other businesses and organizations, such as FAA pre-flight pilot tests. In fact, most companies that need secure test delivery over a wide geographic area use the services of Sylvan Prometric. In addition to delivery, Sylvan Prometric also scores the tests and provides statistical feedback on the performance of each test question to the companies and organizations that use their services.

Typically, several hundred questions are developed for a new Microsoft certification examination. The questions are first reviewed by a number of subject matter experts for technical accuracy, and then are presented in a beta test. The beta test may last for several hours, due to the large number of questions. After a few weeks, Microsoft Certification uses the statistical feedback from Sylvan to check the performance of the beta questions.

Questions are discarded if most test takers get them right (too easy) or wrong (too difficult), and a number of other statistical measures are taken of each question. Although the scope of our discussion precludes a rigorous treatment of question analysis, you should be aware that Microsoft and other vendors spend a great deal of time and effort making sure their examination questions are valid. In addition to the obvious desire for quality, the fairness of a vendor's certification program must be legally defensible.

The questions that survive statistical analysis form the pool of questions for the final certification examination.

Test Structure

The kind of test we are most familiar with is known as a *form* test. For Microsoft certification, a form usually consists of 50–70 questions and takes 60–90 minutes to complete. If there are 240 questions in the final pool for an examination, then four forms can be created. Thus, candidates who retake the test probably will not see the same questions.

Other variations are possible. From the same pool of 240 questions, *five* forms can be created, each containing 40 unique questions (200 questions) and 20 questions selected at random from the remaining 40.

The questions in a Microsoft form test are equally weighted. This means they all count the same when the test is scored. An interesting and useful characteristic of a form test is that you can mark a question you have doubts about as you take the test. Assuming you have time left when you finish all the questions, you can return and spend more time on the questions you have marked as doubtful.

Microsoft may soon implement *adaptive* testing. To use this interactive technique, a form test is first created and administered to several thousand certification candidates. The statistics generated are used to assign a weight, or difficulty level, for each question. For example, the questions in a form might be divided into levels one through five, with level one questions being the easiest and level five the hardest.

When an adaptive test begins, the candidate is first given a level three question. If it is answered correctly, a question from the next higher level is presented, and an incorrect response results in a question from the next lower level. When 15–20 questions have been answered in this manner, the scoring algorithm is able to predict, with a high degree of statistical certainty, whether the candidate would pass or fail if all the questions in the form were answered. When the required degree of certainty is attained, the test ends and the candidate receives a pass/fail grade.

Adaptive testing has some definite advantages for everyone involved in the certification process. Adaptive tests allow Sylvan Prometric to deliver more tests with the same resources, as certification candidates often are in and out in 30 minutes or less. For Microsoft, adaptive testing means that fewer test questions are exposed to each candidate, and this can enhance the security, and therefore the validity, of certification tests.

One possible problem you may have with adaptive testing is that you are not allowed to mark and revisit questions. Since the adaptive algorithm is interactive, and all questions but the first are selected on the basis of your response to the previous question, it is not possible to skip a particular question or change an answer.

Question Types

Computerized test questions can be presented in a number of ways. Some of the possible formats are used on Microsoft certification examinations, and some are not.

True/False

We are all familiar with True/False questions, but because of the inherent 50 percent chance of guessing the correct answer, you will not see questions of this type on Microsoft certification exams.

Multiple Choice

The majority of Microsoft certification questions are in the multiple-choice format, with either a single correct answer or multiple correct answers. One interesting variation on multiple-choice questions with multiple correct answers is whether or not the candidate is told how many answers are correct.
    EXAMPLE:

Which two files can be altered to configure the MS-DOS environment? (Choose two.)

OR

Which files can be altered to configure the MS-DOS environment? (Choose all that apply.)

You may see both variations on Microsoft certification examinations, but the trend seems to be toward the first type, where candidates are told explicitly how many answers are correct. Questions of the "choose all that apply" variety are more difficult, and can be merely confusing.

Graphical Questions

One or more graphical elements are sometimes used as exhibits to help present or clarify an exam question. These elements may take the form of a network diagram, pictures of networking components, or screen shots from the software on which you are being tested. It is often easier to present the concepts required for a complex performance-based scenario with a graphic than with words.

Test questions known as *hotspots* actually incorporate graphics as part of the answer. These questions ask the certification candidate to click on a location or graphical element to answer the question. As an example, you might be shown the diagram of a network and asked to click on an appropriate location for a router. The answer is correct if the candidate clicks within the *hotspot* that defines the correct location.

Free Response Questions

Another kind of question you sometimes see on Microsoft certification examinations requires a *free response* or type-in answer. An example of this type of question might present a TCP/IP network scenario and ask the candidate to calculate and enter the correct subnet mask in dotted decimal notation.

Knowledge-Based and Performance-Based Questions

Microsoft Certification develops a blueprint for each Microsoft certification examination with input from subject matter experts. This blueprint defines the content areas and objectives for each test, and each test question is created to test a specific objective. The basic information from the examination blueprint can be found on Microsoft's Web site in the Exam Prep Guide for each test.

Psychometricians (psychologists who specialize in designing and analyzing tests) categorize test questions as knowledge-based or performance-based. As the names imply, knowledge-based questions are designed to test knowledge, while performance-based questions are designed to test performance.

Some objectives demand a knowledge-based question. For example, objectives that use verbs like *list* and *identify* tend to test only what you know, not what you can do.

EXAMPLE:

Objective: Identify the MS-DOS configuration files.

Which two files can be altered to configure the MS-DOS environment? (Choose two.)

A. COMMAND.COM
B. AUTOEXEC.BAT
C. IO.SYS
D. CONFIG.SYS
   Correct answers: B, D

Other objectives use action verbs like *install, configure,* and *troubleshoot* to define job tasks. These objectives can often be tested with either a knowledge-based question or a performance-based question.

EXAMPLE:

Objective: Configure an MS-DOS installation appropriately using the PATH statement in AUTOEXEX.BAT.

Knowledge-based question:

What is the correct syntax to set a path to the D:directory in AUTOEXEC.BAT?

A. SET PATH EQUAL TO D:
B. PATH D:
C. SETPATH D:
D. D:EQUALS PATH
   Correct answer: B

Performance-based question:

Your company uses several DOS accounting applications that access a group of common utility programs. What is the best strategy for configuring the computers in the accounting department so that the accounting applications will always be able to access the utility programs?

A. Store all the utilities on a single floppy disk, and make a copy of the disk for each computer in the accounting department.
B. Copy all the utilities to a directory on the C: drive of each computer in the accounting department, and add a PATH statement pointing to this directory in the AUTOEXEC.BAT files.
C. Copy all the utilities to all application directories on each computer in the accounting department.
D. Place all the utilities in the C: directory on each computer, because the C: directory is automatically included in the PATH statement when AUTOEXEC.BAT is executed.
   Correct answer: B

Even in this simple example, the superiority of the performance-based question is obvious. Whereas the knowledge-based question asks for a single fact, the performance-based question presents a real-life situation and requires that you make a decision based on this scenario. Thus, performance-based questions give more bang (validity) for the test author's buck (individual question).

Testing Job Performance

We have said that Microsoft certification focuses on timeliness and the ability to perform job tasks. We have also introduced the concept of performance-based questions, but even performance-based multiple-choice questions do not really measure performance. Another strategy is needed to test job skills.

Given unlimited resources, it is not difficult to test job skills. In an ideal world, Microsoft would fly MCP candidates to Redmond, place them in a controlled environment with a team of experts, and ask them to plan, install, maintain, and troubleshoot a Windows network. In a few days at most, the experts could reach a valid decision as to whether each candidate should or should not be granted MCDBA or MCSE status. Needless to say, this is not likely to happen.

Closer to reality, another way to test performance is by using the actual software, and creating a testing program to present tasks and automatically grade a candidate's performance when the tasks are completed. This *cooperative* approach would be practical in some testing situations, but the same test that is presented to MCP candidates in Boston must also be available in Bahrain and Botswana. Many Sylvan Prometric testing locations around the world cannot run 32-bit applications, much less provide the complex networked solutions required by cooperative testing applications.

The most workable solution for measuring performance in today's testing environment is a *simulation* program. When the program is launched during a test, the candidate sees a simulation of the actual software that looks, and behaves, just like the real thing. When the testing software presents a task, the simulation program is launched and the candidate performs the required task. The testing software then grades the candidate's performance on the required task and moves to the next question. In this way, a 16-bit simulation program can mimic the look and feel of 32-bit operating systems, a complicated network, or even the entire Internet.

Microsoft has introduced simulation questions on the certification examination for Internet Information Server 4.0. Simulation questions provide many advantages over other testing methodologies, and simulations are expected to become increasingly important in the Microsoft certification program. For example, studies have shown that there is a very high correlation between the ability to perform simulated tasks on a computer-based test and the ability to perform the actual job tasks. Thus, simulations enhance the validity of the certification process.

Another truly wonderful benefit of simulations is in the area of test security. It is just not possible to cheat on a simulation question. In fact, you will be told exactly what tasks you are expected to perform on the test. How can a certification candidate cheat? By learning to perform the tasks? What a concept!

Study Strategies

There are appropriate ways to study for the different types of questions you will see on a Microsoft certification examination.

Knowledge-Based Questions

Knowledge-based questions require that you memorize facts. There are hundreds of facts inherent in every content area of every Microsoft certification examination. There are several keys to memorizing facts:

- **Repetition**   The more times your brain is exposed to a fact, the more likely you are to remember it.

- **Association**   Connecting facts within a logical framework makes them easier to remember.

- **Motor Association**   It is often easier to remember something if you write it down or perform some other physical act, like clicking on a practice test answer.

We have said that the emphasis of Microsoft certification is job performance, and that there are very few knowledge-based questions on Microsoft certification exams. Why should you waste a lot of time learning filenames, IP address formulas, and other minutiae? Read on.

Performance-Based Questions

Most of the questions you will face on a Microsoft certification exam are performance-based scenario questions. We have discussed the superiority of these questions over simple knowledge-based questions, but you should remember that the job task orientation of Microsoft certification extends the knowledge you need to pass the exams; it does not replace this knowledge. Therefore, the first step in preparing for scenario questions is to absorb as many facts relating to the exam content areas as you can. In other words, go back to the previous section and follow the steps to prepare for an exam composed of knowledge-based questions.

The second step is to familiarize yourself with the format of the questions you are likely to see on the exam. You can do this by answering the questions in this study guide, by using Microsoft assessment tests, or by using practice tests. The day of your test is not the time to be surprised by the convoluted construction of Microsoft exam questions.

For example, one of Microsoft Certification's favorite formats of late takes the following form:

Scenario: You have a network with…

Primary Objective: You want to…

Secondary Objective: You also want to…

Proposed Solution: Do this…

What does the proposed solution accomplish?

A. Satisfies the primary and the secondary objective

B. Satisfies the primary but not the secondary objective

C. Satisfies the secondary but not the primary objective

D. Satisfies neither the primary nor the secondary objective

This kind of question, with some variation, is seen on many Microsoft Certification examinations.

At best, these performance-based scenario questions really do test certification candidates at a higher cognitive level than knowledge-based questions. At worst, these questions can test your reading comprehension and test-taking ability rather than your ability to use Microsoft products. Be sure to get in the habit of reading the question carefully to determine what is being asked.

The third step in preparing for Microsoft scenario questions is to adopt the following attitude: Multiple-choice questions aren't really performance-based. It is all a cruel lie. These scenario questions are just knowledge-based questions with a little story wrapped around them.

To answer a scenario question, you have to sift through the story to the underlying facts of the situation, and apply your knowledge to determine the correct answer. This may sound silly at first, but the process we go through in solving real-life problems is quite similar. The key concept is that every scenario question (and every real-life problem) has a fact at its center, and if we can identify that fact, we can answer the question.

Simulations

Simulation questions really do measure your ability to perform job tasks. You must be able to perform the specified tasks. There are two ways to prepare for simulation questions:

1. Get experience with the actual software. If you have the resources, this is a great way to prepare for simulation questions.

2. Use official Microsoft practice tests. Practice tests are available that provide practice with the same simulation engine used on Microsoft certification exams. This approach has the added advantage of grading your efforts.

Signing Up

Signing up to take a Microsoft certification examination is easy. Sylvan operators in each country can schedule tests at any testing center. There are, however, a few things you should know:

1. If you call Sylvan during a busy time period, get a cup of coffee first, because you may be in for a long wait. Sylvan does an excellent job, but everyone in the world seems to want to sign up for a test on Monday morning.

2. You will need your social security number or some other unique identifier to sign up for a Sylvan test, so have it at hand.

3. Pay for your test by credit card if at all possible. This makes things easier, and you can even schedule tests for the same day you call, if space is available at your local testing center.

4. Know the number and title of the test you want to take before you call. This is not essential, and the Sylvan operators will help you if they can. Having this information in advance, however, speeds up the registration process.

Taking the Test

Teachers have always told you not to try to cram for examinations because it does no good. Sometimes they lied. If you are faced with a knowledge-based test requiring only that you regurgitate facts, cramming can mean the difference between passing and failing. This is not the case, however, with Microsoft certification exams. If you don't know it the night before, don't bother to stay up and cram.

Instead, create a schedule and stick to it. Plan your study time carefully, and do not schedule your test until you think you are ready to succeed. Follow these guidelines on the day of your exam:

1. Get a good night's sleep. The scenario questions you will face on a Microsoft certification examination require a clear head.

2. Remember to take two forms of identification—at least one with a picture. A driver's license with your picture and social security or credit cards are acceptable.

3. Leave home in time to arrive at your testing center a few minutes early. It is not a good idea to feel rushed as you begin your exam.

4. Do not spend too much time on any one question. If you are taking a form test, take your best guess and mark the question so you can come back to it if you have time. You cannot mark and revisit questions on an adaptive test, so you must do your best on each question as you go.

5. If you do not know the answer to a question, try to eliminate the obviously wrong answers and guess from the rest. If you can eliminate two out of four options, you have a 50 percent chance of guessing the correct answer.

6. For scenario questions, follow the steps we outlined earlier. Read the question carefully and try to identify the facts at the center of the story.

Finally, we would advise anyone attempting to earn Microsoft MCDBA and MCSE certification to adopt a philosophical attitude. Even if you are the kind of person who never fails a test, you are likely to fail at least one Microsoft certification test somewhere along the way. Do not get discouraged. If Microsoft certification were easy to obtain, more people would have it, and it would not be so respected and so valuable to your future in the IT industry.

Part I

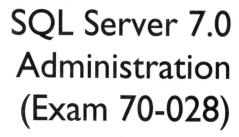

SQL Server 7.0
Administration
(Exam 70-028)

EXAM TOPICS

Microsoft SQL Server 7.0 Overview

Capacity and Growth Planning for a SQL Database

Planning Database and Server Security

Planning for Installation

Installing SQL Server

Configuring SQL Server

Monitoring and Tuning SQL Server

Managing Database Files

Managing Security

Automating Administrative Tasks

Backing Up Databases

Methods of Restoring Databases

Transferring Data

Replication

Implementing Replication Scenarios

Setting Up Replication

MICROSOFT CERTIFIED DATABASE ADMINISTRATOR

SQL Server 7.0 Administration Questions

Q & A

This section is designed to help you prepare for Exam #70-28, Administering Microsoft SQL Server 7.0. After completing this exam successfully, you will be one step closer to your MCDBA certification. The following questions mirror the types of questions presented on Microsoft certification tests. Take your time and read each question carefully. Read all the answer choices carefully, as there may be more than one correct answer. Choose all correct answers for each question.

Microsoft SQL Server 7.0 Overview

1. You have just successfully installed a dedicated SQL Server 7.0 database server for the sales department of your company on a Windows 98 machine. The sales department client workstations are a mix of Windows 95 and Windows 98, connected by a Windows NT network. After installing the SQL Server client software on the sales staff workstations, you find that the workstations cannot make a connection to the new SQL Server database. Your first instinct is to verify physical connections, and you find that they are all physically connected properly. What is the most probable cause for this problem, and what SQL Server tool is used to provide a resolution?

   A. Each machine connected to the new server must reboot in order to make the first connection.

   B. Both the SQL Server and the client workstations need to be configured to use the correct protocol, which is TCP/IP. You can use the Client Network Utility to select the appropriate protocol.

   C. Both the SQL Server and the client workstations need to be configured to use the correct protocol, which is NWLink. You can use the Client Network Utility to select the appropriate protocol.

   D. The Windows 9x machines must be configured to use Named Pipes as their default protocol. Use the Client Network Utility to make this setting.

2. You are the database administrator for a SQL Server being used by your company's in-house application developers. Because there are many

different testing applications being built that need databases created, you are allowing the developers to create databases on the server as they are needed. Because this server is for application design, though, hard drive space is at a premium. You have asked the developers to limit the maximum size of these test databases to 10MB, but you haven't been getting much cooperation, mainly due to forgetfulness. As a result the server is constantly running out of disk space. What steps could you take to alleviate this problem?

A. Use the Model database to establish the desired default settings for all newly created databases.

B. Use the Enterprise Manager options settings to restrict the size of newly created databases.

C. Set users, permissions to restrict the creation of databases larger than 10MB.

D. Use the Master database to establish the desired default settings for all newly created databases.

---

exam
Ⓦatch

Make sure you know the operating systems and which service packs are required in order for SQL to run.

---

3. Recently your team migrated data for an application from flat text files into SQL Server. The application had originally been designed for a small number of users, using a small data set. As the application's usage grew, so did the data files. The decision was made to migrate the data to a relational database solution using SQL Server as the backend. After simply importing the text files into the newly created database, the users have not noticed any significant performance gains when accessing the data. Sorting and querying the data is still a slow process. In addition, the users would like to see the data sorted by the record's CustomerID field. The CustomerID also happens to be the primary key for the Customers table. What steps can be taken to immediately improve your data access performance and satisfy the users' need to see their data ordered by the CustomerID? (Choose all that apply.)

    A. Create nonclustered indexes for the table fields that are being used in joins, as criteria in SQL Select where clauses, and in SQL Select Order By clauses.

    B. Create a clustered index on each field, for each of the tables.

    C. Combine the data from multiple tables into one table for better access.

    D. Create a clustered index based on the CustomerID field so that the records will be ordered based on the CustomerID.

4. You are the database administrator for a department of many users that have SQL Server installed on their workstations to serve as stand-alone database servers. The databases that are being stored locally should not be allowed to become larger than 25MB in file size. When they do, a decision needs to be made to determine if that database should be placed on a network server. You want to be able to take advantage of SQL Server's ability to dynamically reconfigure itself; however, you must control the maximum size of the user databases. How can you accomplish both of your goals?

    A. Use the Database Configuration Wizard to configure the databases for dynamic file growth in megabytes, but set the maximum file size setting to 25MB.

    B. Use the Enterprise Manager to configure the databases for dynamic file growth in megabytes, but set the maximum file size setting to 25MB.

    C. Use the SQL Server Agent to configure the databases for dynamic file growth in megabytes, but set the maximum file size setting to 25MB. Also create an Agent job that notifies you when a database has reached 25MB.

    D. Create a trigger that sends the database administrator a message when a database reaches 25MB.

5. Your company has recently installed SQL Server 7.0, and the corporate developers are beginning to design their first client/server applications. You have installed SQL Server 7.0 Desktop Edition on each of the developer's desktops. Each development team is using the development tool of its choice to build the client applications. Many of the developers have no experience writing SQL Select statements and are having difficulty building the statements necessary to return the required data to the client applications. Writing and testing the SQL statements in their development tools are becoming tedious and time-consuming tasks. What can you do to help facilitate the process of generating the correct SQL statements? (Choose all that apply.)

A. Tell the developers to use the Enterprise Manager to create their SQL statements. From within the Enterprise Manager you can select table and field names without having to type them.

B. Teach the developers to use the SQL Server Query Analyzer to interactively develop and test their SQL statements. Once they have generated the correct syntax in the Query Analyzer, they can save the SQL statement into a view that can be reused, or the SQL statement can be copied directly into the client application as embedded SQL in locations that support embedded SQL.

C. Determine which of the data sets being derived are from static SQL statements and create views or stored procedures on the server, instead of having the developers use embedded SQL in the client application.

D. Instruct the developers to use stored procedures instead of writing SQL statements. Because stored procedures are easier to write, this should speed up the process.

e x a m
ⓦa t c h   *Understand the protocols supported by SQL Server. The protocol of choice is TCP/IP, due to the popularity of the Internet.*

6. The staff developers at your company are in the process of planning a new client/server application for the accounting department. Everyone agrees that there isn't enough storage space or bandwidth on any of the existing servers to accommodate the new database and application. Therefore a new SQL Server will need to be configured. There are no more Windows NT licenses available to bring up another NT server, so the developers are considering installing SQL Server on a Windows 98 machine, even though all of the existing SQL

Servers have been installed on NT machines. Why would you caution against installing the new SQL Server on a Windows 98 machine?

A. When SQL Server is installed on a Windows 9x server, you can't connect to its services remotely. Therefore all users will have to be physically connected to the same LAN as the Windows 9x server.

B. When SQL Server is installed on a Windows 9x server, you can use only Named Pipes as the network protocol. Using Named Pipes only would severely restrict the developers from creating high-performance applications.

C. There are no issues to consider when installing SQL Server 7.0 on a Windows 9x server. SQL Server 7.0 is not limited by any of the operating systems that it supports.

D. When SQL Server is installed on a Windows 9x server, it cannot support Windows NT Authentication Mode. Therefore users will have to be logged into the Windows 98 SQL Server explicitly, using a valid SQL Server login ID. This might prove confusing and distracting to users because they will prompted to log in to the SQL Server databases stored on the Windows 98 server every time they need to access its resources.

7. Your network environment consists of Windows 9x machines connected by a Windows NT Server. All corporate databases are SQL Server-based servers on Windows NT Servers. A small department-level database needs to be added to your environment. This small database will be accessed only by a limited number of users. The decision is made to install SQL Server on a Windows 9x machine. You follow the same installation and setup procedures that have been successfully used to install all of your other SQL Servers. You know that when SQL Server is running a Windows 9x-based server, it cannot use Named Pipes as the Net-Library. Named Pipes is, however, the Net-Library being used for all of your other servers; therefore you cannot universally configure all the client machines to use a different Net-Library. How can you accommodate the new Windows 9x server?

  A. Use the front-end applications being built for the new database to handle any special login needs.

  B. Use the Enterprise Manager to define a server alias for the new Windows 9x server that specifies the appropriate protocol to use when accessing this server.

  C. Use the Service Manager to define a server alias for the new Windows 9x server that specifies the appropriate protocol to use when accessing this server.

  D. Use the SQL Server Client Configuration utility to define a server alias for the new Windows 9x server that specifies the appropriate protocol to use when accessing this server.

8. How will SQL Server's ability to provide "server-enforced data integrity" assist developers in enforcing data integrity rules and reduce redundancy of integrity handling?

  A. SQL Server provides the ability to control data access using the most appropriate security mode. This allows you to limit the users to those that understand how to use the databases.

  B. SQL Server permissions allow you to control what each user can do to each database.

  C. SQL Server provides the ability to store all rules on the server with the data. This provides a single control point for data consistency. As a result, there is no need to embed these rules in each front-end application.

  D. SQL Server allows you to create database rules using the Query Analyzer. The Query Analyzer can be used to create rules and triggers to control data modifications.

9. During the database design phase you want to ensure support for entity integrity, to preserve the uniqueness of table entities. How can you achieve entity integrity? (Choose all that apply.)

  A. Create views to help enforce integrity by embedding them with database rules.

  B. Entity integrity can be enforced by creating primary keys.

  C. Unique indexes can be used to enforce entity integrity.

  D. Constraints can be used to enforce entity integrity.

10. In designing a table that will contain employee information, you want to ensure domain integrity for certain values. Domain integrity enforces valid entries at the field/column level. What techniques could be used to achieve domain integrity? (Choose all that apply.)

A. Restrict data entry through a field's data type.

B. Use each field's normal value attribute to establish the type of value expected for each column.

C. Specify data formats.

D. Restrict the range of values accepted by a field/column.

11. You have just designed your first database, and you want to make sure that it is a logical database design. To ensure that your design meets the basic rules of normalization, which of the following rules would you want to verify are enforced? (Choose all that apply.)

A. Verify that you don't have repeating groups or multivalue columns in your tables.

B. Make sure that each nonkey field/column in a table is dependent on the entire primary key.

C. Ensure that nonkey fields/columns in your tables do not depend on other nonkey fields/columns in that same table.

D. Make sure that each field has a unique index defined to ensure entity integrity.

12. The database design team has just presented you with the tables and relationships for a new SQL Server database that they need implemented. As you scan the table schema you have been given, you notice that normalized design produces several four-way join relationships. Why would this fact concern you?

A. SQL Server has a three-way relationship limitation. Therefore you will not be able to implement the database design that has been given to you.

B. The rules of normalization prohibit the use of four-way relationships.

C. The joins necessary to create whole entity data sets will require complicated queries that may impede the database's performance.

D. SQL Server views will not support displaying data involved in four-way relationships.

13. The database design team has just presented you with the tables and relationships for a new SQL Server database that they need implemented. As you scan the table schema you have been given, you notice that normalized design produces several four-way join relationships. This fact concerns you, and you discuss your concerns with the design team leader. What could you suggest that would assist the team in eliminating some of the four-way join relationships?

A. Suggest that the team replace some of the tables with views. Views do not require relationships.

B. Suggest that the team perform some level of denormalization on the tables in the database design. They could eliminate primary keys on some of the tables. Tables without primary keys will not require joins.

C. Suggest that the team replace some of the tables with stored procedures. Stored procedures do not require relationships.

D. Suggest that the team perform some level of denormalization on the tables in the database design. They could use a combination of adding duplicate columns and adding derived columns to some of the database tables.

14. Current situation: You are building queries for a SQL Server database. You are only vaguely familiar with the database tables, and you often don't remember the exact spelling of the tables and fields.

Desired result: You need to be able to see the database tables and fields while writing your queries.

Optional desired result: You want to be able to see a schema of the table relationships.

Proposed solution: Start the Enterprise Manager (EM). On the EM menu bar choose Tools | SQL Server Query Analyzer.

What is the result of the proposed solution?

A. The proposed solution satisfies the desired result but not the optional desired result.

B. The proposed solution satisfies both the desired result and the optional desired result.

C. The proposed solution satisfies the optional desired result but not the desired result.

D. The proposed solution satisfies neither the desired result nor the optional desired result.

15. Your SQL Server is set to use integrated security. You are in the Enterprise Manager adding a new user to the Payroll's database server. You receive the error shown here. What is the problem, and how can you resolve it?

A. The login name that you supplied is not a member of any NT group. Only NT users that have been added to group accounts can be added to SQL Server's list of valid logins.

B. The login name that you supplied is only a guest account on the NT server specified. NT guest accounts cannot be added to SQL Server's list of valid logins.

C. The login name that you supplied is a system administrator account on NT. NT system administrator accounts cannot be added to SQL Server as valid login accounts.

D. The login name that you supplied is not a valid name on the NT Server that was specified. Validate the spelling of the user's login name on the NT Server, then go back to the Enterprise Manager and attempt adding the user again.

---

exam
Ⓦatch   *If using Windows NT 4.0 only mode, the user does not have to enter in a separate database user name since the user names are the same in Windows NT 4.0 and SQL Server.*

---

16. In developing a client interface for the corporate SQL Server database, the developers have found that there are five groups of records that must always be acquired. The SQL needed to produce these five data sets is complicated. They would like a way of retrieving those five data sets quickly and easily, as well as the ability to use the five data sets in SQL statements embedded in their applications. As the database administrator, what will you do to bring this functionality about?

A. Create replicated tables on the client desktops, then synchronize the data overnight.

B. Create triggers that will produce the data sets needed. The triggers can then be invoked from within the client applications.

C. Create SQL Server views on the database that represent each of the five required data sets.

D. Show the developers how to use the Query Analyzer to write Transact SQL statements that can be embedded in the applications.

17. You have installed a new device on your server that is running SQL Server. You need to reboot the machine to complete the installation process. It's late afternoon, and most employees have gone home for the day. You are already in the Enterprise Manager and want to check database activity before you shut down the server. If you see any users on the server, you would like to send them a message asking them to log off within the next 10 minutes. How can you accomplish this from within the Enterprise Manager?

A. From the Enterprise Manager menu bar choose Tools | Current Activity. In the Current Activity dialog box you can view a list of all server activity. You can select a user's name and send the user a message using the Send Message command button.

B. From the SQL Agent menu bar choose Tools | Current Activity. In the Current Activity dialog box you can view a list of all server activity. You can select a user's name and send the user a message using the Send Message command button.

C. From the Services Manager menu bar choose Tools | Current Activity. In the Current Activity dialog box you can view a list of all server activity. You can select a user's name and send the user a message using the Send Message command button.

D. From the MSDTC Administrative Console menu bar choose Tools | Current Activity. In the Current Activity dialog box you can view a list of all server activity. You can select a user's name and send the user a message using the Send Message command button.

18. You want to become familiar with using the Query Analyzer to test SQL statements. You want to use the Pubs sample database that ships with SQL Server to write your SQL statements. You enter the statement seen in the following illustration, and you receive the error message displayed. What is the problem and how can you correct your mistake?

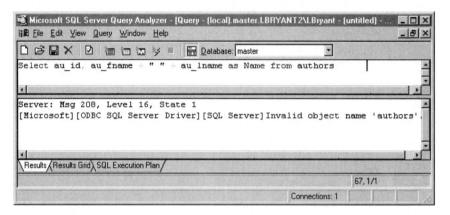

A. You have incorrectly typed the name of the table. SQL statements are case sensitive, so retype the table name with a capital "A".

B. You have the Query Analyzer loaded, but you are not connected to the server; therefore the table can't be found.

C. You have incorrectly spelled the name of the table. Use the Enterprise Manager to verify the table name.

D. You have the wrong database selected in the Query Analyzer. Use the drop-down list for the database selection to choose the Pubs database instead of the Master database.

19. You are using the Query Analyzer to write and test SQL statements for a very large database table. Your main concern is that your statements are retrieving the necessary fields, outputting them correctly, and using the appropriate joins. It is not necessary for you to view all rows that your statements return; a sample of the return data set will suffice. What can you do to speed the execution of your statements?

A. From the Query Analyzer menu bar choose Query | Configure Options. In the Configure Options dialog box specify an adequate number of sample rows to be returned. This is accomplished by specifying a "Row Count" value.

B. From the Query Analyzer menu bar choose Query | Properties. In the Properties dialog box specify an adequate number of sample rows to be returned. This is accomplished by specifying a "Row Count" value.

C. From the Query Analyzer menu bar choose Query | Set Properties. In the Query Properties dialog box specify an adequate number of sample rows to be returned. This is accomplished by specifying a "Row Count" value.

D. From the Query Analyzer menu bar choose Query | Set Options. In the Query Options dialog box specify an adequate number of sample rows to be returned. This is accomplished by specifying a "Row Count" value.

20. You have just used the SQL Server Service Manager to pause the MSSQLServer service. What is the result of this action?

A. Pausing the server prevents new users from logging into the service while users currently connected to the service remain connected. Now that you have prevented new users from logging in, you can send current users a message to complete their tasks and log off the service.

B. Pausing the server allows everyone currently connected 10 minutes to log off before being disconnected. The amount of time allotted is set using the Service Manager.

C. Pausing the server prevents new users from logging into the service. It will also hang the connections of users already logged in. You should use the Enterprise Manager to send a message asking users to log off before pausing or stopping a server.

D. Pausing the server will send a message to users currently connected that all services have been paused. New users will be prevented from logging into the service once it has been paused.

21. You are planning a SQL Server 7.0 installation. You have installed several SQL Server 6.5 servers. As you are looking through the notes of previous installations, you see a section on configuring the server after installation. You know that SQL Server 7.0 will now dynamically configure many of its settings, based on its environment. Which settings will you not have to set manually after installing your new SQL Server 7.0 server? (Choose all that apply.)

A. Net-Libraries

B. Connections

C. Locks

D. Open objects

22. In your company's enterprise there are many replicated databases that require a minimum amount of management. You have users at the locations where these replicated databases exist who are capable of carrying out a small set of administrative tasks. You feel, however, that the learning curve of using the Enterprise Manager is too great. Instead you would like a custom interface that exposes only the functionality necessary to a small list of predefined tasks. How can this be accomplished?

A. Use SQL-DMO to build a custom application that exposes only the functionality required.

B. Create a group account with permissions set to expose only the functionality required for these administrators to carry out their duties.

C. Use the Enterprise Manager to develop a custom application. You can control which tools are available in the Tools menu, so that you can restrict the access to certain functionality.

D. Create a series of stored procedures that can be executed from a custom application.

23. You are participating in a team meeting to discuss developing a front-end application for a new SQL server that was recently installed. Many of the developers are new to developing applications for SQL Server. When asked their data access choices for developing the front-end applications, which methods will you suggest? (Choose all that apply.)

A. Microsoft Query

B. DAO

C. Jet

D. RDO

QUESTIONS AND ANSWERS

My programmers need to write client-side software, what API can they use?	Use OLE DB, ODBC, and DB-Library.
I am running the Novell Client 32 on my Windows 95 system...	Install NWLink on the client. NWLink is Microsoft's version of Novell's IPX/IPX.
I am unable to connect to SQL Server, what can I do?	Run the MAKEPIPE and READPIPE commands to test the connection.
Why do my client and server need to use the same Net-Library DLL?	They must use the same IPC DLL from the Net-Library in order to communicate.

Capacity and Growth Planning for a SQL Database

1. You are determining how much space will be needed to store a specific number of rows in a table. Which of the following would you use to calculate such an estimate?

A. SQL Server Agent

B. SQL Server Enterprise Manager

C. sp_spaceused

D. sp_estspace

2. You are determining the total size of a user database. Which of the following elements will you consider in making your calculations? (Choose all that apply.)

    A. The amount of data in each user table

    B. Space allocated for the transaction log

    C. The time users will spend working with user tables

    D. Space used by system tables

3. You have determined that your database will need to store 100,000 rows of data. Each row of your database averages 150 bytes in length. Based on this information, how many data pages will be needed to store this number of rows of data?

    A. 150

    B. 1886

    C. 8060

    D. 100,000

4. You are preparing to create several user databases, and you are trying to determine the amount of disk space that will be needed on the SQL Server 7.0 computer. Initially, what will be the amount of disk space consumed by the default set of system tables for each database that's created?

    A. 8KB

    B. .5MB

    C. 2MB

    D. It will vary from table to table

5. You are determining the size of a database, and you decide to check how much space is currently being used. Which of the following can you use to calculate this? (Choose all that apply.)

    A. SQL Server Agent

    B. SQL Server Enterprise Manager

    C. sp_spaceused

    D. sp_estspace

6. You are concerned about losing data should the system or network fail or a natural disaster occur. Which of the following would be used to recover data in such an event?

A. Primary data files
B. Secondary data files
C. Transaction logs
D. System tables

7. You have created a SQL Server 7.0 database. As the database is filled, it begins to exceed its initial size. What will happen?

A. The database will grow beyond its initial size.
B. SQL Server 7.0 databases cannot grow beyond their initial size.
C. The database will split itself into two databases automatically.
D. An error will occur, and a message will automatically be sent to the administrator informing him or her of the database exceeding its initial size.

8. You are planning the physical placement of files making up a SQL Server 7.0 database. In doing so, you realize that you need to know what role a file plays in a database based on the default extension of a database file. Which of the following file extensions would hold all transaction log information that's used to recover a database?

A. .MDF
B. .LDF
C. .MDB
D. .NDF

9. You have created a SQL Server 7.0 database. The database appears to work fine, but when you check the files making up the database, you find that there are no .NDF files. What is most likely the reason for this?

A. There are no log files for this database containing transactional log information.

B. This database doesn't require a primary data file because there is no data in the database yet.

C. The database you created doesn't require a secondary data file.

D. .NDF files are used only with Microsoft Access databases. They aren't used with SQL Server databases.

10. Current situation: You are running SQL Server 7.0 on an NT Server computer. You are using the new feature in SQL Server 7.0 that allows databases to grow beyond their initial size. You are concerned that as the database grows, the hard disk will at one point run out of space.
Required result: You want a message sent to you—the administrator—when space is running low on the hard disk.
Optional desired result: You want real-time monitoring of the disk space; as space becomes low, you want the hard disk to be automatically compressed.
Proposed solution: Use the Alerter Service.
Which of the following results will the proposed solution produce?

A. The proposed solution produces the required result and produces both of the optional results.

B. The proposed solution produces the required result and produces only one of the optional results.

C. The proposed solution produces the required result and produces none of the optional results.

D. The proposed solution doesn't produce the required result.

exam
ⓦatch   *In prior versions of SQL Server, it was critical to assign the transaction log to a separate operating system file in order to back it up separately. In version 7.0, SQL Server forces the log onto a separate file by default.*

11. Current situation: You have a large database consisting of a primary data file, two secondary data files, and a log file. The database runs on an NT Server that has four hard disks on it. Due to the number of reads and writes

to this database, performance is beginning to slow down on the NT Server running SQL Server 7.0.

Required result: Increase the performance of the SQL Server database.

Optional desired results: The data should be fault tolerant; the solution should not adversely affect the user's ability to access the data.

Proposed solution: Implement RAID level 5 so that the hard disks use disk striping with parity distributed on all hard drives in the stripe set.

Which of the following results will the proposed solution produce?

A. The proposed solution produces the required result and produces both of the optional results.

B. The proposed solution produces the required result and produces only one of the optional results.

C. The proposed solution produces the required result and produces none of the optional results.

D. The proposed solution doesn't produce the required result.

12. You have created file groups. You now want to use a file located in another file group for a new database you've created. When you attempt to do so, what will happen?

A. It will fail because a file or file group can be used by only one database.

B. It will succeed. You can have more than one database using the same file or file groups.

C. It will succeed; however, the two databases can't be accessed at the same time. This is because a file or file group can be used by only one database at a time.

D. It will succeed. File groups are completely unrelated to databases created with SQL Server.

13. You are planning the use of file groups, and you are determining their placement on the computer. Which of the following will not be part of any file group you create?

A. Primary data files

B. Secondary data files

C. Log files

D. .MDF files

14. Current situation: You have a large database consisting of a primary data file, two secondary data files, and a log file. The database runs on an NT Server that has four hard disks on it. Due to the number of reads and writes to this database, performance is beginning to slow down on the NT Server running SQL Server 7.0.

Required result: Increase the performance of the SQL Server database.

Optional desired results: The data should be fault tolerant; the solution should not adversely affect the user's ability to access the data.

Proposed solution: Put each of the data and log files on a different hard disk.

Which of the following results will the proposed solution produce?

A. The proposed solution produces the required result and produces both of the optional results.

B. The proposed solution produces the required result and produces only one of the optional results.

C. The proposed solution produces the required result and produces none of the optional results.

D. The proposed solution doesn't produce the required result.

15. You are concerned about the performance of a SQL Server database running on an NT Server computer. You decide to use NTFS file compression on the partition containing this large SQL Server database. What effect will this have?

A. The database and log files will be compressed, but performance won't improve.

B. The database and log files will be compressed, and performance will improve.

C. The database and log files won't compress, as SQL databases and log files can't be compressed. Because of this, there will be no improvement in performance.

D. This will not work because SQL Server cannot read compressed files.

16. A SQL Server database is running on an NT Server with an 8GB hard drive. There is 4.5GB of free disk space, and 250MB of data is being added to the database each month. Purchasing tells you that if you order a new hard disk, it will take 2 months total to approve the requisition, order it, and have it delivered so that you can install it. How many months will it be until a new hard disk should be purchased?

A. 2 months

B. 6 months

C. 18 months

D. 16 months

17. You are planning the physical hardware system for a computer that will run SQL Server 7.0. In doing so, there are four main areas that will be of primary concern. Which of the following are they?

A. Processor, RAM, disk subsystem, network

B. Processor, network, printing, disk subsystem

C. RAM, disk subsystem, virtual memory, sound card

D. Disk subsystem, RAM, network, Internet.

18. You are planning the physical hardware to be used for a computer running SQL Server 7.0. Which of the following processors can you use? (Choose all that apply.)

A. Intel

B. MIPS

C. Alpha

D. PowerPC

19. You are planning the physical hardware to be used for a computer running SQL Server 7.0. At any given time, 25 users will be connected to SQL Server 7.0. What is the total amount of RAM these users will consume when all 25 users are connected?

A. 1MB

B. 2MB

C. 32MB

D. 23MB

20. You are concerned with the performance of a SQL Server for which you're planning the physical hardware. A major concern is available RAM. Which of the following does SQL Server use RAM for?

A. Procedure cache, virtual memory, configurable overhead, static server overhead

B. Procedure cache, RAID, virtual memory, configurable overhead

C. Procedure cache, data and index page caching, configurable overhead, static server overhead

D. Data and dynamic HTML page caching, configurable overhead, static server overhead, processor cache

21. You are planning the physical hardware system for a computer that will run SQL Server 7.0. In doing so, you want to use the fastest hard disk controller. Which of the following will you use?

A. RAID

B. SCSI

C. IDE

D. EIDE

22. You are planning the physical hardware system for a computer that will run SQL Server 7.0. You estimate that at any given time, 25 locks will prevent users from reading data that isn't yet written to the database. How much RAM will these 25 locks consume?

A. 2.4KB

B. 24KB

C. 1MB

D. 2MB

23. 225 users are going to be using a SQL Server database at any given time. During this time, a considerable number of locks will be on data. What will happen when the lock is released?

A. The memory used by the locks will continue to be consumed. This memory won't be released until the computer is rebooted.

B. The memory used by the locks will continue to be consumed. While SQL Server can consume more memory needed by locks, it can't release it.

C. RAM is allocated dynamically, so the memory is released when the lock is released.

D. The memory used by the locks will continue to be consumed. SQL Server can't release memory automatically. This needs to be released manually.

24. You are using SQL Server 7.0 on a Windows NT computer with 200MB of RAM. At any given time, there seems to be at least 40MB of free RAM. Approximately, how much memory will SQL Server attempt to keep free?

A. 5MB

B. 10MB

C. 20MB

D. 40MB

Planning Database and Server Security

1. You are running SQL Server on an NT Server machine. You are determining which login authentication mode you will use with SQL Server on this computer. When users log in, you want security to be based solely on the permissions that have been set in User Manager for Domains. Which of the following login authentication modes will you use?

A. Windows NT authentication mode

B. Windows User authentication

C. Mixed authentication

D. SQL authentication mode

2. You are running SQL Server on an NT Server machine. You are determining which login authentication mode you will use with SQL Server

on this computer. You want to use an authentication mode that will rely on SQL Server authentication if the user logs into SQL Server. If the user doesn't log in, then SQL Server will rely on Windows NT as its source of authenticating the user. Which mode will you use?

A. Windows NT authentication mode

B. Windows User authentication mode

C. Mixed authentication

D. SQL authentication

3. A new user has logged into a SQL Server. The user doesn't have any permissions set to use databases on the server. This server has a guest account setup, but the user has logged in using his own username and password. What will happen?

A. The user will have access to all databases on the SQL Server.

B. The user will have access to all primary and secondary data files.

C. The user won't have access to anything.

D. The user will have select permission to system tables, plus guest account access and rights.

4. You are the administrator of a SQL Server database used to store criminal records at a police station. Users of this database input information on people who have been charged with various crimes. Recently users have been getting promoted due to the retirement of older users. In doing so, their security levels need to be upgraded. You need to determine what level of security privileges will be afforded to users of this database.

A. Give users as many security privileges as possible. This way, the user's account won't need to be upgraded in the future.

B. Give users slightly more security privileges than they currently need. This way, there is less chance that you'll need to upgrade the account in the near future.

C. Give users only the security privileges they need to do their work.

D. Give users fewer security privileges than they need so they can be better monitored.

5. After assessing security models, you decide to use the standard security model. Which of the following benefits will you gain by using this model? (Choose all that apply.)

    A. Each user will need to have logins and passwords set for each database that will be used.

    B. Each user won't need to have logins and passwords set, as Windows NT does authentication.

    C. High level of security.

    D. Less administration is required than with the integrated security model.

---

exam
ⓦatch
Fixed server, fixed database, and public roles are built-in roles and cannot be dropped.

---

6. You are using SQL Server on a Novell NetWare network. SQL Server is installed on a Windows 95 computer. Which of the following security models will you use?

    A. Standard

    B. Integrated

    C. Both of the above

    D. None of the above

7. You have 10 users who need access to a SQL Server database running on an NT Server computer. You are pressed for time and need to use the quickest method possible for assigning these users access to the database. This database is used for customer information, and it is needed by all 10 of the users in the sales department. Which of the following will you do to give these users access to the database?

    A. In SQL Server Enterprise Manager, individually provide each user with access.

    B. In SQL Server Enterprise Manager, give the local or global group these users are members of access to the database.

    C. In User Manager, give the local or global group these users are members of access to the database.

    D. Create a transaction log with a listing of users, and apply it to the database.

8. You have created several user-defined database roles for users, but you have yet to add any users to these roles. Despite this, each of the users in Finance has access to a financial database, and users in Sales are using a customer database. To which of the following roles would these users already belong?

   A. Each of the users of the database would automatically belong to the user-defined roles that you've set up for a database.
   B. All users will belong to the fixed server role.
   C. All users of a database will belong to the fixed database role.
   D. All users of a database will belong to that database's public role.

9. You are cleaning up the roles used on a SQL Server. Certain user-defined and built-in roles aren't being used. When dropping some of these roles from the SQL Server, which of the following roles will you not be able to drop? (Choose all that apply.)

   A. Fixed server
   B. Public server
   C. Public database
   D. Fixed database

10. Current situation: You have set up SQL Server on an NT Server, and you are now in the process of applying user accounts to fixed server roles. You need to apply users in the correct roles so that they don't have more access than they need to do their jobs. Any access beyond what's required to do their job will be considered a security threat.
    Required result: The user must have permissions on all databases on the server.
    Optional desired result: The user must be able to create and alter all of the databases on the server; the user must be able to shut down and set all server-related options.
    Proposed solution: Add the user to the role of Serveradmin.
    Which of the following results will the proposed solution produce?

   A. The solution fulfills the required result and both of the desired results.

   B. The solution fulfills the required result but only one of the desired results.

   C. The solution fulfills the required result but doesn't fulfill either of the desired results.

   D. The solution doesn't fulfill the required result.

11. A user needs to have full access to all disk files and also needs to be able to create and modify all databases on the server. The user should get access to perform these functions only through fixed server roles. Any access beyond this will be considered a potential security threat. Which of the following will you do?

   A. Add the user to the Sysadmin and Setupadmin roles.

   B. Add the user to the db_accessadmin and db_owner roles.

   C. Add the user to the Sysadmin role.

   D. Add the user to both the Diskadmin and Dbcreator roles.

---

exam
ⓦatch

Though SQL Server can scale from Windows 95/98 to Windows NT, Microsoft SQL Server services only run on Windows NT platforms because Windows 95/98 does not support services. Windows 95/98 simulates services. You do not have to create user accounts for them.

---

12. You are adding users to fixed database roles. One of these users needs to have full access to the database to which you're assigning access levels. To which of the following fixed database roles will you apply this user's account?

   A. db_owner

   B. db_ddladmin

   C. db_securityadmin

   D. db_datadmin

13. You are adding users to fixed database roles. One of these users needs the ability to manage permissions, ownerships, and roles. Despite the fact that this user helps in administering the database, you don't want to give the user full access to the database. To which of the following fixed database roles will you apply this user's account?

A. db_owner

B. db_accessadmin

C. db_securityadmin

D. db_datareader

14. A group of users needs to perform tasks that aren't covered in either the fixed server roles or the fixed database roles. What will you do?

A. Add the user to both fixed database and fixed server roles.

B. Create a user-defined database role, then add the group of users as members.

C. Create a new fixed server role, then add the group of users as members.

D. Create a new fixed database role, then add the group of users as members.

15. You have set up a new SQL Server database on an NT Server. You don't have time to set up access and permissions for users of this database, but it is crucial that this database is used immediately. What will you do? (Choose all that apply.)

A. Add each of the users of this database to groups in Windows NT. Once this is done, map the groups to the database so that users can access it.

B. Add each of the users of this database to groups in Windows NT. Once this is done, map the groups to roles so that they have permissions at a server or database level.

C. Set up permissions and access to the database for each individual user through Windows NT User Manager.

D. Set up permissions and access to the database for each individual user through SQL Server Enterprise Manager.

16. You have set up SQL Server 7.0 on a Windows NT machine. You are now setting up SQL services to run as NT services by setting up each service to run under a Windows NT account. These services will run only on the local machine, and they won't access or communicate with other SQL Servers on the network. Which of the following Windows NT accounts will you use? (Choose all that apply.)

A. Local System Account

B. Local User Account

C. Domain User Account

D. Guest Account

17. You have set up SQL Server 7.0 on a Windows NT machine. You are now setting up SQL services to run as NT services by setting up each service to run under a Windows NT account. These services will communicate with other SQL Servers in your network. Which of the following Windows NT accounts will you use? (Choose all that apply.)

A. Local System Account

B. Local User Account

C. Domain User Account

D. Guest Account

18. You have set up SQL Server 7.0 on a Windows NT machine. After setting up SQL Server services to run as NT services by running under a Windows NT account, you find that it still can't fully access the necessary local and network resources. Which of the following must you do to ensure that SQL Server services have the necessary access to function properly? (Choose all that apply.)

A. Add the Local User or Local System account that's used by SQL Server services to the Administrators local group, then configure it to log on as a network service.

B. By using a Local System account, you would only need to configure it to log on as a network service.

C. Add the Domain User account used by SQL Server services to the Administrators local group.

D. Add the Domain User account used by SQL Server services to the Administrators local group, then configure it to log on as a network service.

19. You are planning an n-tier application security strategy to control access of components in the application. In doing so, you should understand how n-tier applications are set up. Which of the following is true of the client logic of such applications? (Choose all that apply.)

A. The client is used only to display data.

B. The business logic runs on the server.

C. The business logic runs on the client.

D. The components don't run on the server but are distributed to all clients.

20. You are planning the security requirements for linked databases. In order for the SQL Server on your computer to connect with a database or linked server, what must be done?

A. The database you're connecting to must send a login name and password.

B. The linked server you're connecting to must send a login name and password.

C. The SQL Server connecting to the linked database or server must send a login name and password.

D. The SQL Server connecting to the linked database or server must send a login name and password. The linked server or database then sends a countersign—its own login name and password—back to the SQL Server.

21. In order to send login and password information between SQL Servers and linked servers and databases, login mappings need to be created. How will the login mappings be created, and what will they do? (Choose all that apply.)

A. sp_setaddrole is a stored procedure used to allow users to use the same permissions as their login or to emulate the permissions of another user.

B. sp_addlinkedsrvlogin is a stored procedure used to allow users to use the same permissions as their login or to emulate the permissions of another user.

C. Windows NT passes the security information to the SQL Server account.

D. A SQL Server authenticated account is used to connect to the linked server with a user's credentials to impersonate another user.

22. A user attempts to access a database without a valid account. The SQL Server database has SA, Guest, and DBO accounts. What will occur?

A. The user will be refused any access.

B. The user will default to a guest account.

C. The user will default to the SA account.

D. The user will default to the DBO account.

23. A user with a DBO user account for the customer database attempts to administer the sales database. Upon attempting this, the user finds she doesn't have full access to all operations and rights in the sales database. Why?

A. The user needs an SA account to have full access at the database level.

B. DBO accounts administer database servers. The sales database must exist on another server.

C. DBO accounts exist at the database level.

D. A DBO user account never has full access to operations and rights.

24. A user transfers DBO to another user. Which of the following is true?

A. The SA account can still control the database as owner.

B. The original DBO user can still control the database as owner.

C. The original DBO user and the SA account won't be able to control the database as owner.

D. The original DBO, the new DBO, and the SA account will be able to control the database as owner.

25. A user wants to transfer DBO to another user. Which of the following needs to be executed for this to happen?

A. Exec sp_adduser

B. Exec sp_changedowner 'login id'

C. Exec sp_changebowner 'login id'

D. Exec sp_changedbowner 'login id'

Planning for Installation

1. You have installed SQL Server, and you want users to have the ability to enter questions like "How many people at Microsoft were born at a hospital?" without entering any code. Which of the following will you use?

   A. Microsoft English Query Interface
   B. DTC Client Support
   C. Query Analyzer
   D. Transact SQL

2. A SQL Server is being used to store product and customer information, which users can access over the World Wide Web. Which of the following best describes what SQL Server is being used for?

   A. Business application
   B. Analysis of historical data
   C. Electronic commerce
   D. Data-warehousing

3. You are planning to install SQL Server on several computers in your department. Each of the computers is running different operating systems. Onto which of the following operating systems can you install SQL Server 7.0?

   A. Windows 95
   B. Windows NT Workstation with no service packs installed
   C. Windows NT Workstation with Service Pack 4
   D. Windows NT Server with Service Pack 3

4. You are planning to install SQL Server on a computer running Windows NT Server. The computer has 32MB of RAM, an Intel Pentium II processor, CD-ROM, and 100MB of free hard disk space. Based on this

information, will you be able to perform a minimum installation of SQL Server 7.0 on this computer?

A. No, because there isn't enough hard disk space
B. No, because there isn't enough RAM
C. No, because the processor isn't powerful enough
D. Yes, you will be able to install on this computer.

exam
ⓦatch   *Microsoft exams commonly include questions regarding the minimum hardware requirements.*

5. You are planning to install SQL Server 7.0 on several computers in your department. The type of installation you're planning is a typical installation. Each of these computers has a method of accessing the installation files. Which of the following computers meets the minimal requirements to install SQL Server 7.0?

A. DEC Alpha AXP with 32MB of RAM, 200MB of free hard disk space
B. Intel Pentium II with 32MB of RAM, 150MB of free hard disk space
C. 486/33 computer with 64MB of RAM, 190MB of free hard disk space
D. Intel Pentium 133 with 24MB of RAM, 170MB of free hard disk space

6. You have 100 computers that need to have SQL Server 7.0 installed. How will you install SQL Server 7.0 on these computers in the fastest manner possible?

A. Use the Installation Wizard in SQL Server 7.0 to install on each of these computers at once over the network.
B. Use the Installation Wizard on each and every computer on which you want to install SQL Server.
C. Perform an automated installation using the AUTORUN.EXE program on the SQL Server 7.0 installation CD.
D. Perform an automated installation by creating and editing files that will be used to automatically install SQL Server.

7. You are planning to install SQL Server on a computer running Windows NT Workstation. The operating system is a fresh install, and no service packs have been installed. The computer has 32MB of RAM, an Intel Pentium II processor, no CD-ROM, 170MB of free hard disk space, and a connection to a network. You want to perform a typical install of SQL Server 7.0 on this computer, but you find that you cannot. Why?

   A. There isn't enough RAM.
   B. The processor isn't powerful enough.
   C. There is a problem with the operating system.
   D. There isn't enough hard disk space.

8. You are planning to install SQL Server on a computer running Windows NT Workstation. The computer has 32MB of RAM, an Intel Pentium PRO processor, no CD-ROM, 150MB of free hard disk space, and a connection to a network. You want to perform a full install of SQL Server 7.0 on this computer, but you find that you cannot. Why?

   A. There isn't enough hard disk space.
   B. There isn't enough RAM.
   C. There is no CD-ROM.
   D. The processor isn't powerful enough.

9. One of the computers you want to upgrade is running SQL Server 4.2. You want to upgrade this to SQL Server 7.0. How will you do this?

   A. Use the Upgrade Wizard to upgrade SQL Server 4.2 to SQL Server 7.0.
   B. Use the Upgrade Wizard to upgrade data in SQL Server 4.2 to a schema that can be used by SQL Server 7.0.
   C. Upgrade SQL Server 4.2 to SQL Server 6.5. Once this is done, upgrade SQL Server 6.5 to SQL Server 7.0.
   D. Perform a full install of SQL Server 7.0. SQL Server 7.0 will automatically detect the database belonging to the previous version and convert it.

10. You are planning to install SQL Server 7.0 on a Windows NT Server that already has SQL Server 6.5 installed on it. You don't want to upgrade SQL Server 6.5, but you want to have both available for use. Which of the following is true?

A. SQL Server 6.5 and SQL Server 7.0 can coexist on the same server. You will need to switch between the running version of SQL Server, so that only one SQL Server is available at any given time.

B. SQL Server 6.5 and SQL Server 7.0 can't be installed separately on the same server. During installation, you will be forced to upgrade the previous version.

C. SQL Server 6.5 and SQL Server 7.0 can't be installed separately on the same server. During installation, SQL Server will automatically upgrade the previous version to SQL Server 7.0.

D. SQL Server 7.0 will install normally on the server, and it will be able to run at the same time as the previous version. This will allow users to have access to both database systems.

11. You are upgrading SQL Server 6.5 on your network to SQL Server 7.0. The import computer is SQL Server 7.0, and the export computer is SQL Server 6.5. You check your hard disk requirements for performing the installation of SQL Server 7.0, and you find that there is enough free space. How much additional disk space will be required by the import computer during the upgrade?

A. None

B. Twice the size of the SQL Server 6.5 database being imported

C. 1.5 times the size of the SQL Server 6.5 database being imported

D. The size of the SQL Server 6.5 database being imported

12. You are preparing to upgrade from SQL Server 6.0 to SQL Server 7.0. You want to keep both versions on your computer, so that both versions are maintained. Which of the following methods will you use to perform the upgrade?

A. Computer-to-computer

B. Side-by-side

C. Standalone-to-server

D. Network-to-network

13. You are planning to migrate data from other data sources on your network into a SQL Server 7.0 database. Which of the following would you use to import data from Access, Excel, and Visual FoxPro into this database?

A. Bulk Copy Program

B. Data Transformation Services

C. BCP

D. You can't migrate this data. SQL Server allows data migration only from text files and SQL Server 4.2, 6.x, 7.0, and Sybase databases.

14. You are planning to migrate data from ODBC data sources on your network into a SQL Server 7.0 database. Which of the following would you use to import the data, and what will need to be installed prior to using this tool?

A. Bulk Copy Program would be used, with ActiveX installed on the computer.

B. Data Transformation Program would be used, with ODBC drivers installed on the computer.

C. Data Migrator would be used, with drivers for each database system being accessed installed on the computer.

D. Data Transformation Program would be used, with drivers for each database system being accessed installed on the computer.

15. You are installing SQL Server on a computer running Windows 95 Server. The computer has 64MB of RAM, an Intel Pentium II processor, and

100MB of free hard disk space. When you reach the point where you install network libraries, you decide to install network libraries and you accept each of the choices so that all communications are supported. After SQL Server is installed, you notice that performance is sluggish. What is most likely the reason for this?

A. There isn't enough RAM.

B. Network libraries are consuming more resources than needed.

C. The network libraries that are installed haven't been configured properly.

D. The processor is too slow.

16. You are installing and configuring network libraries on a SQL Server that's running on a Windows NT Workstation computer. After installing and configuring TCP/IP on this system, you find that the client is unable to communicate with the SQL Server on this computer. Which of the following might be the reason for this? (Choose all that apply.)

A. A different network library is installed on the client.

B. A different name has been given to the pipe.

C. The server and client are configured to use different ports.

D. A different name has been given to the port.

17. You are installing and configuring network libraries on a SQL Server that's running on a Windows NT Workstation computer. You want to use encryption to protect data being passed between clients and servers on your network. Which of the following will you install and configure?

A. TCP/IP

B. NWLink

C. Multiprotocol

D. Named pipes

18. You are installing and configuring network libraries on a SQL Server that's running on a Windows NT Workstation computer. After installing and configuring named pipes on this system, you find that the client is unable to communicate with the SQL Server on this computer. Why?

A. The default pipe has been changed.

B. The default port number has been changed.

C. An entry hasn't been made in the registry.

D. SQL Server doesn't support named pipes on this computer.

19. By default, SQL Server creates a number of server roles. Which of these roles would you use if you wanted a user to be able to grant the ability to create a database? (Choose all that apply.)

A. Database creator

B. Security administrator

C. System administrator

D. Server administrator

20. You have installed TCP/IP on a SQL Server running on NT Server. You decide to change a client using a different port number to use the port number that the newly installed SQL Server uses. What is the default port that you will reconfigure TCP/IP to use?

A. 1433

B. 1

C. 1344

D. There is no default port number for TCP/IP.

21. You have installed SQL Server 7.0 on a Windows NT machine, and you attempt to use the SQL Server Upgrade Wizard. When you attempt to start this wizard, it fails. What is most likely the reason for this?

A. Named pipes haven't been installed so the client and server can't communicate.

B. The default named pipe has been changed.

C. The client is using a different name for the named pipe.

D. The default port has been changed.

22. By default, SQL Server creates a number of server roles. Which of these roles would you use if you wanted a user to be able to add and drop devices and create mirroring? Security is an issue, so you don't want the user to be able to do more than this. (Choose all that apply.)

A. System administrator

B. Disk administrator

C. Security administrator

D. Process administrator

23. You have set up Multiprotocol as a network library to be installed on SQL Server 7.0. Even though Multiprotocol encryption has been selected, communication isn't encrypted. Which of the following will you do to ensure that communication is encrypted and to fix this problem?

A. In HKEY_LOCAL_MACHINE\SOFTWARE\Microsoft\ MSSQLServer\Client of the Registry, add a new key called RPCNetLib and enter the value REG_SZ (String) data type. Name the new value "Security" and set the value to "Encypt".

B. In HKEY_SQL_MACHINE\SOFTWARE\Microsoft\MSSQLServer\ Client of the Registry, add a new key called RPCNetLib and enter the value REG_SZ (String) data type. Name the new value "Security" and set the value to "Encypt".

C. Reinstall the network library.

D. Multiprotocol doesn't offer encryption.

Installing SQL Server

1. You are preparing to install NT Server on a Windows NT machine. Before installing SQL Server 7.0, which of the following will you want to ensure is installed on the computer? (Choose all that apply.)

A. SQL Server 6.x

B. Internet Explorer 4.01 or higher

C. Windows NT Service Pack 3 or higher

D. DTC Client Support

2. You have decided not to upgrade a SQL Server 6.x database to SQL Server 7.0 when first starting the SQL Server setup program. Instead, you decide that you will later migrate the SQL Server 6.0 database to SQL Server 7.0. When you reach the Select Components screen of the Custom installation, which of the following will you install to migrate the data?

A. Upgrade Tools from the Server components

B. Upgrade Tools from the Management Tools components

C. DTC Client Support from the Management Tools components

D. Virtual Device Interface from the Development Tools components

3. You are choosing the character set to use for a server that will occasionally have data restored from European and South American branches of your company. The character set you need to use will require English characters for your own office. Which of the following character sets will you choose? (Choose all that apply.)

A. Central European code page 1250

B. The default code page 1252

C. The U.S. English code page 437

D. The Multilingual code page 850

4. You are creating a SQL Server database for a travel book company. Data will be entered into the database in a dozen different languages. Which of the following will you do to support the different characters that will be used in the database?

A. Use a character set for each language in this database.

B. Create one database for each language. Use a character set for each language in the databases, then link the databases together.

C. Use the default code page for SQL Server, and use Unicode equivalent data types for front-end development.

D. SQL Server doesn't have multilanguage support, so it can't be done.

5. You have to restore data from a machine that is using a case-sensitive dictionary order onto a machine that uses the default sort order. When you attempt restoring the data, what will happen?

A. The default sort order is the case-sensitive dictionary order, so no problem will result.

B. The sort order of the data will be automatically changed to the default sort order of the new machine.

C. You won't be able to restore the data.

D. You will be able to restore the data, as sort order has no effect on a restore.

6. A user is complaining that the result set being returned from a database is being returned in a strange order. Capital letters are being returned in the order of Z-A, while lowercase letters are being returned in the order of a-z. For example, the result set is yielding results that are sorted as follows: Zebra, Yak, apple, banana
What is most likely the reason for this?

A. The character set of a foreign language is being used.

B. The Unicode Collation Sequence is set to a certain locale that sorts in this way.

C. The server is using a binary sort order.

D. The server is using a case-insensitive, uppercase preference dictionary order.

7. You are preparing to install SQL Server on an NT Server, and you need to establish an NT user account. The type of account you choose will allow SQL Server to perform heterogeneous joins across remote sources. Which of the following types of accounts could you use to enable SQL Server to use this functionality?

A. LocalSystem account

B. Machine account

C. Domain account

D. Any of the above

8. You have set up a Windows NT user account for SQL Server Services. A month later, you find that SQL Server is no longer able to use SQL Mail. Which of the following might be a reason for this?

   A. The SQL Mail that comes with SQL Server isn't the full version, and it will expire after a one-month period.

   B. The wrong type of Windows NT account was assigned to SQL Server services.

   C. The "User must change password at next login" was checked.

   D. The "Password never expires" was not checked.

9. Your company has a policy that each SQL Server and SQL service is to have separate NT accounts. Because of this, you have a significant number of accounts to set up in your domain, and you decide to use a script to automate the process. Which of the following would you use to set up each of these accounts through a script? (Choose all that apply.)

   A. User Manager for Domains

   B. The NET USER command

   C. The NET GROUP command

   D. SQL Server

10. You are performing a Custom setup of SQL Server 7.0. Which of the following would you select to install to trace and record database activity, and under which component would you find it?

   A. SQL Server, under Server Components

   B. Enterprise Manager, under Server Components

   C. Enterprise Manager, under Management Tools

   D. Profiler, under Management Tools

11. You have reached the point in the setup program of SQL Server where you must choose the Character Set/Sort Order/Unicode Collation. If you don't

enter the settings you're certain you want to use on this screen, what will happen if you attempt to change them after SQL Server is installed?

A. You won't be allowed to change these settings.

B. Changing these settings will cause the master database to be rebuilt, and you will lose the database currently being worked on.

C. Changing these settings will cause the master database to be rebuilt, and you will lose all databases on the server.

D. You will be able to change the sort order, but not the Unicode collation or character set.

12. You are preparing to perform an unattended setup that will install SQL Server 7.0 on a number of computers in your department. You already have SQL Server 6.5 computers in your company and the .ini files used for their automated installation. Which of the following would you do to specify the settings to be used when doing an unattended installation of SQL Server 7.0?

A. Use the command SetupSQL.exe k=rc.

B. Use the command SetupSQL.exe –fl followed by the name and path of the initialization file to create.

C. Use the command SetupSQL.exe.

D. Use the existing .ini files for the unattended installation of SQL Server 6.5.

13. You are ready to perform an unattended installation of SQL Server 7.0 on a number of computers in your department. You already have SQL Server 6.5 computers in your company and the .ini files used for their automated installation. Which of the following would you do to start an unattended installation of SQL Server 7.0?

A. Use the command SetupSQL.exe k=rc.

B. Use the command SetupSQL.exe –fl followed by the name and path of the initialization file to use.

C. Use the SetupSQL.exe command.

D. Use the existing .ini files for the unattended installation of SQL Server 6.5.

14. You have a SQL Server 6.x database on a Windows NT server. You want to upgrade this to SQL Server 7.0. How will you convert the existing data in the SQL Server 6.x database to version 7.0?

A. Run the SQL Server Upgrade Wizard by starting UPGRADE.EXE on the installation disk.

B. Run the SQL Server setup program from the installation disk. Once started, the setup program will detect the older database and ask if you want to run the SQL Server Upgrade Wizard.

C. Run the SQL Server setup program from the installation disk. Select "Upgrade" as the Setup Type.

D. Run the SQL Server setup program from the installation disk. Select "Custom" as the Setup Type.

15. You are upgrading a SQL Server 6.x database to SQL Server 7.0, and you have reached the point where you need to determine the method in which data will be transferred between servers. Which of the following methods can you choose to transfer the data? (Choose all that apply.)

A. Named pipe

B. Network

C. FTP

D. Tape

16. While upgrading SQL Server 6.x to SQL Server 7.0, you choose to use the tape method to transfer the data. What else must be installed for the upgrade to succeed?

A. Named pipes

B. A Windows NT tape driver

C. Nothing. Selecting Tape is the only thing you need to select and configure.

D. Nothing. Tape isn't an option for transferring the data.

17. After installing SQL Server 7.0 on your machine, several SQL Server services are installed on your machine. Which of the following is the only service that is necessary to the basic operation of SQL Server?

A. MSDTC

B. MSSQL Server

C. SQLServer Agent

D. Service Manager

18. After installing SQL Server 7.0 on your machine, several SQL Server services are installed on your machine. Which of the following services can be configured to respond to on-demand activities raised by SQL Alerter?

A. MSDTC

B. MSSQL Server

C. SQLServer Agent

D. Service Manager

19. You have finished installing SQL Server; upon completion, a number of directories are created under the MSSQL7 directory (or the directory in which SQL Server 7.0 was installed). Under which directory will you find the executables for the SQL Server 7.0 environment?

A. Binn

B. Bin

C. Exe

D. SQL

20. You run an unattended installation, and error code 0 is returned. What is the problem?

A. A general error has occurred.

B. An invalid option has been selected.

C. File does not exist.

D. The installation was successful.

21. You are installing SQL Server 7.0 on a Windows 95 computer. The installation fails, but no message appears stating what the problem was.

Which of the following will you use to determine what is the installation problem? (Choose all that apply.)

A. Application log and Systems log, using EventView

B. SQLstp.log in the Windows directory

C. Cnfgsvr.out in the MSSQL\Install directory

D. Files left in the MSSQL\Log directory

22. You are preparing to install SQL Server client utilities on computers in your department. On which of the following will you need to install these utilities?

A. Windows 9x computers

B. Windows NT Workstations

C. Windows NT Servers

D. All computers that will connect to SQL Server

23. You are setting up SQL Server 7.0 to store and process orders that users enter online over the Internet. Users will enter their orders through a Web page, which will then be stored on a SQL Server located on that server. NWLink is set up on the server, but users are unable to access this database. Why?

A. The network address is wrong.

B. The IP address is wrong.

C. The port number is wrong.

D. The wrong protocol is being used.

Configuring SQL Server

1. You have decided to create a workstation that will allow you to manage all of the SQL servers in your environment. After evaluating the options, you have decided to register all of the servers in the SQL Enterprise Manager tool. Furthermore, because of the number of servers that must be registered,

you decide to use the registration wizard. Which of the following is something that you need to remember when using the Registration Wizard?

A. You can't register SQL servers in other domains.

B. You can't register a SQL server that participates in replication.

C. You can only register one SQL server at a time.

D. You cannot view the system databases of a server registered through the wizard.

2. You need to configure the minimum range of dynamic memory allocation for one of your SQL servers. Furthermore, you would like to do this with a script so that you have some documentation of the change. Which of the following sets of commands will accomplish your goal?

A.
```
USE MASTER
GO
EXEC sp_configure 'min server memory (MB)', 128
RECONFIGURE
```

B.
```
USE MASTER
sp_configure 'memory', 128
RECONFIGURE
```

C.
```
xp_configure 'min server memory (MB)', 128
```

D.
```
sp_reconfigure 'memory', 128
```

3. Which of the following are things that you should keep in mind when determining how to configure user connections on your SQL Server?

A. SQL Server allows a maximum of 32,767 user connections.

B. The user connections option is a dynamic, self-configuring option, and SQL Server adjusts the maximum number of user connections automatically as needed, up to the maximum value allowable.

C. Each connection takes approximately 40KB of overhead, regardless of whether the connection is being used.

D. All of the above

4. How should SQL Server process queries that have been mailed to the MAPI mailbox associated with the MSSQL Server Service account?

A. SP_PROCESSMAIL
B. XP_GETMAIL
C. XP_READMAIL
D. XP_NEXTMSG

5. Consider the following statements about database and connection options. Select the statement that is incorrect.

A. Server-wide options are set using the SP_CONFIGURE system-stored procedure.
B. Database options are set by the SP_DBOPTIONS system-stored procedure and override server-wide options.
C. Connection-level options are the lowest-level options and are set using the SET <option> syntax. They override any database options.
D. Statement-level options override connection-level options.

6. Under certain circumstances, you might want to restrict SQL Server to a subset of the processors available on a multiprocessor system. What are the benefits of restricting SQL Server to a specific processor or set of processors?

A. You can keep SQL Server from consuming all of the processing resources on a system that is shared between SQL Server and other applications.
B. Under the right circumstances, you can increase the performance of SQL Server by allowing SQL Server exclusive use of one or more processors.
C. You can simulate the effects of a large processing load on the system by restricting the number of processors available.
D. None of the above

7. You are evaluating the benefits of using full-text indices. Which of the following should you consider as part of your evaluation?

A. Full-text indices are repopulated synchronously and therefore must be updated on a scheduled basis.

B. Full-text indices are repopulated asynchronously, therefore they must be updated on a scheduled basis.

C. Full-text indices are repopulated synchronously and therefore the indices are updated automatically as the data changes.

D. Full-test indices are repopulated asynchronously and so the indices are updated automatically as the data changes.

8. The Microsoft search service is running. You have used the Full-Text Indexing Wizard to create a full-text index. The population of the index has not yet been scheduled. When you run a query using the CONTAINS clause, what will your result set look like?

A. The warning: "Cannot use a CONTAINS or FREETEXT predicate on table Suppliers because it does not contain a full-text index."

B. The query will execute, automatically creating the full-text indices as needed.

C. The CONTAINS operator will automatically be converted to a LIKE operator.

D. The query will execute without errors, but no data will be returned.

9. You are trying to determine whether to use FREETEXTTABLE or CONTAINSTABLE. Which of the following is an advantage of using FREETEXTTABLE?

A. FREETEXTTABLE can be used to rank the results by how well they match.

B. FREETEXTTABLE can automatically parse the search parameters into words and phrases that can be individually searched for in the destination table.

C. FREETEXTTABLE doesn't require the Microsoft search service to be running.

D. FREETEXTTABLE allows you to search for tense variants of nouns and verbs.

10. You have been asked to provide a variety of querying capabilities for a database. You are thinking about implementing full-text searches, but the setup is more complicated than you are comfortable with. Your primary goal is to determine whether or not a string exists in a field, and you must be able to support phrase searches. Secondarily, you would like to rank and sort the quality of the matches from high to low and also to support proximity searches.

You propose to meet your goals by not implementing full-text searches at this time and relying on the wildcard and LIKE operators for searching capabilities.

A. The proposed solution meets the primary goal and both secondary goals.

B. The proposed solution meets the primary goal and only one of the secondary goals.

C. The proposed solution meets the primary goal and neither of the secondary ones.

D. The proposed solution doesn't meet the primary goal.

11. Your users are overwhelming you with requests for queries. You would like to just give them the Query Analyzer, but you know that they are not knowledgeable enough to use the tool effectively. Instead, you decide to use full-text searches. Your primary goal in doing this is to enable users to type a question and have that question result in a search against the table for which you have established the full-text index. Secondarily, you wish to use the ISABOUT...WEIGHT syntax to determine terms that should have more influence in calculating which records represent the best matches. Also, you use the NEAR operator to search all the matching terms and how closely the matching terms appear to one another.

To meet your goals, you propose developing a Web-based application that allows a user to enter a question into a form, then uses the SQL FREETEXT operator to query the database with the question as the search parameter.

A. The proposed solution meets the primary goal and both secondary goals.

B. The proposed solution meets the primary goal and only one of the secondary goals.

C. The proposed solution meets the primary goal and neither secondary one.

D. The proposed solution doesn't meet the primary goal.

12. When using free-text searches, if you need a rowset that contains a ranking column, which of the operators listed below would you use?

A. CONTAINS

B. CONTAINSTABLE

C. FREETEXT

D. FREETEXTTABLE

13. You are trying to explain to a user the benefits of using full-text searches. At present, the user is responsible for generating reports from a database that has very little data validation in the data-entry programs. As a result, the same information may be entered using a number of slight variations. As a demonstration, you pick the phrase Full Text. Which of the following would be equivalent to Free Text?

A. Full-Text

B. full text

C. full! Text

D. All of the above

Monitoring and Tuning SQL Server

1. You want to monitor activity on your SQL Server, and poor query performance in particular. Which monitoring tool should you use?

A. Performance Monitor

B. SQL Server Profiler

C. Enterprise Manager

D. Query Analyzer

2. You have a large OLTP database with frequent INSERT operations on the SALES table. Performance for the SALES report has degraded. You run DBCC SHOWCONTIG and the Scan Density is 60. What should you do?

A. Rebuild the clustered index on the SALES table.

B. Rebuild the clustered index on the database.

C. Create a new non-clustered index.

D. Nothing. This setting is normal.

3. You are examining a query in Query Analyzer with the graphical SHOWPLAN. You notice that the query is using a table scan on a large table. What does this indicate you need to do?

A. Examine indexes and determine a better index.

B. Use an INDEX_HINT on the query.

C. Create a clustered index.

D. Nothing

4. Performance on your SQL Server is poor. You decide to use Performance Monitor to determine where the bottleneck is. The system processor queue length counter is consistently above 10. You have two processors on your system and 1GB of RAM. What does this indicate?

A. You need to add more RAM.

B. You need to add more processors.

C. You need to add more disk drives.

D. Nothing. This is the optimal processor queue value.

5. How can you monitor poorly performing queries in your SQL 7.0 database?

A. Run Create Trace Wizard and find the worst performing queries option in Profiler.

B. Use Performance Monitor to monitor poorly performing queries.

C. Use SP_MONITOR to monitor processes exceeding a time limit.

D. Set the Query Governor Cost Limit.

6. Your SQL Server is tight on disk space. You have allowed for automatic growth, but set a restriction on size to prevent filling up the disk. You want to monitor all database file sizes, and have an alert sent to you when a certain size is reached. How can you accomplish this?

A. Performance Monitor

B. SP_MONITOR

C. SQL Profiler

D. Query Analyzer

7. SQL Server Agent periodically shuts down unexpectedly. You want to automatically restart the agent. What is the best way you can accomplish this?

A. Create a program to restart the service.

B. Create a job to restart the agent.

C. Set the startup value to automatic.

D. You do not need to do anything. SQL Server Agent will restart itself.

8. You want to look at disk activity generated by T-SQL statements. What option can you use to return this information?

A. SQL Profiler RPC: Completed

B. Query Analyzer Set statistics I/O ON

C. Query Analyzer Set statistics time ON

D. SQL Profiler SQL: BatchCompleted

9. You have a high frequency of deadlocks on your server. You need to find the cause. What utility can you use?

A. Enterprise Manager

B. Performance Monitor

C. Create Trace Wizard

D. SP_MONITOR

---

exam
Watch
Since the query governor cost limit option is an advanced option, it can only be set when show advanced options is set to 1.

---

10. A table without a clustered index receives a high number of INSERTS and DELETES. Performance has degraded on the table, and you suspect that it is fragmented. How can you check this?

A. DBCC SHOWCONTIG

B. Performance Monitor

C. SQL Server Profiler

D. SP_MONITOR

11. You are receiving messages that SQL has exceeded the number of locks. How can you resolve this?

    A. Increase the amount of memory (RAM).

    B. Add more processors.

    C. Add more disks.

    D. Increase the Locks configuration option.

12. You've limited growth of the transaction log. You want to be sure that the log is dumped when it reaches 70-percent full, and you want to be notified. Which is the best, automated way to accomplish this?

    A. Create an alert to notify you when the log is 70-percent full, and run a job to back up the log.

    B. Use Performance Monitor to monitor log file size.

    C. Use Profiler to monitor and send an alert.

    D. Use SP_MONITOR.

13. You are running the Microsoft Search service on your SQL Server machine. What option do you need to set manually?

    A. Locks

    B. Fill factor

    C. Max server memory

    D. Min server memory

---

exam

ⓦatch

Both Statistics I/O and Showplan are options within the SQL Server Query Analyzer that analyze the efficiency of your queries.

---

14. When do you need to manually run UPDATE STATISTICS?

    A. When a table has been truncated and refreshed

    B. On a daily basis

    C. When a large number of records have been inserted

    D. When there is a significant change in key values of an index

15. Users are complaining that a particular query is running very slowly. The query was created recently, and you know there are indexes on the tables it is running against. What utility optimizes the query?

A. Performance Monitor

B. Client Network Utility

C. Enterprise Manager

D. Query Analyzer

16. You are not sure what the correct size of tempdb should be for your database. You decide to use Performance Monitor to monitor the server. What counter can you use to determine the optimal size of tempdb?

A. Percent log used

B. Transactions/sec

C. Data file size

D. Active transactions

---

exam
ⓦatch
Understand and remember the differences between the reports, alerts, logs, and charts for the Performance Monitor. In certain situations, some methods are preferred over others.

---

17. You need to upgrade to SQL 7.0 for performance and administrative purposes. You have a mirrored drive on which your applications resides and a data drive on which your SQL files reside. The application that runs on your SQL Server was written for SQL 4.2. You are concerned that the application will not work as designed, especially in regards to NULLS.
Your primary goal is to upgrade to SQL 7.0. You have two secondary goals. You would like to ensure the NULL operations of 7.0 will not affect application and you would like to ensure point-of-failure recovery if the data file is corrupted. To achieve your objectives, you upgrade your database to 6.5, then upgrade to 7.0.

A. Your solution achieves the primary and both secondary goals.

B. Your solution achieves the primary and the first secondary goal.

C. Your solution achieves the primary, but neither secondary goal.

D. Your solution does not achieve the primary goal.

18. You have a server on which you run SQL Server and Exchange. There are a lot of performance problems with Exchange. SQL Server was installed with all defaults, and you have made no changes to configuration values. How can you ensure Exchange can continue to operate?

A. Lower min server memory

B. Lower max server memory

C. Increase min server memory

D. Increase max server memory

19. You've added a second controller and disk drive to your machine. The current configuration is a mirrored C:/ drive, which holds the OS and application files, and an 18GB D:/ drive, on which reside all SQL data files. The new disk is drive E:/. Your primary goal is to provide point-of-failure recovery. Your two secondary goals are to optimize query performance and to optimize disk I/O. You propose to meet these goals by creating a primary data file and placing it on the mirrored drive, creating two file groups and placing one on D and one on E. You place the indexes on D and the data on E.

A. Both primary and secondary goals are met.

B. The primary and first secondary goal are met.

C. The primary and second secondary goal are met.

D. The primary goal is not met.

---

exam
Ⓦatch   *You can configure timeouts to also prevent deadlocks.*

---

20. You need to implement full-text search. You want to minimize overhead associated with maintenance of the catalogs. What should you do?

A. EXEC sp_fulltext_catalog 'Cat_text', 'start_full'

B. EXEC sp_fulltext_catalog 'Cat_text', 'start_incremental'

C. EXEC sp_fulltext_catalog 'Cat_text', 'rebuild'

D. Enable auto-update statistics on the Full Text index.

21. You want to view a snapshot of system statistics, such as CPU usage, I/O usage, and time idle. How can you accomplish this?

A. SQL Server Profiler

B. Enterprise Manager

C. SP_MONITOR

D. SP_WHO

22. You've created a trace and identified a problem. After resolving the issue, you want to make sure the error has been fixed. How can you best accomplish this?

A. Replay the trace.

B. Monitor the server.

C. Use SP_WHO to monitor usage.

D. Use SP_MONITOR.

---

exam

ⓦatch

Do not confuse the time slice for either the operating system or the SQL Server. The SQL Server kernel controls the time slice for SQL Server.

---

23. You are replicating a table to another server. You aren't sure of the space needed to store the table on the new server. You have 1500 tables in your database. What is the best way to view the size information for a single table?

A. Enterprise Manager

B. SP_SPACEUSED 'TABLEA'

C. SP_MONITOR

D. Performance Monitor

---

exam
ⓦatch   *Traces can be saved and re-executed later on. There are also predefined traces.*

Managing Database Files

1. You have a sales force that periodically needs an updated copy of the products database. The sales force is not connected to the corporate network so the decision is made to distribute a copy of the database once a month on removable media. Which option of the system-stored procedure sp_dboption would you use to distribute the database on removable media?

   A. Offline

   B. Distribute

   C. Read Only

   D. Subscribed

2. You need to create a database that will grow to one megabyte, at most. You want to script the creation of this database because it is a task that you perform on a regular basis. Your primary goal is to create a database that will not grow beyond one megabyte. Secondarily, you would like to restrict the log file size to half of the data file size and to restrict the growth increment of the log and data files to 5KB. You execute the following script.

```
USE master
GO
CREATE DATABASE Sales
ON
( NAME = Sales_dat,
  FILENAME = 'c:\mssql7\data\saledat.mdf',
  SIZE = 10,
  MAXSIZE = 1024,
  FILEGROWTH = 5 )
LOG ON
( NAME = 'Sales_log',
  FILENAME = 'c:\mssql7\data\salelog.ldf',
  SIZE = 512,
  MAXSIZE = 512,
  FILEGROWTH = 5 )
GO
```

A. The script achieves the primary goal and both secondary goals.

B. The script achieves the primary goal and only one secondary goal.

C. The script achieves the primary goal and neither secondary goal.

D. The script does not achieve the primary goal.

3. You have a very small database. The data file is only one megabyte in size with 512KB in use. At this point, the transaction log is also one megabyte in size with about 10KB being used on a regular basis. You decide that there would be some benefit to having this database or a 1.44MB floppy disk. How should you size the files to fit them on the floppy disk?

A. Reduce the size of the database file to 512KB and the log file to 512KB.

B. Reduce the size of the log file to 20KB.

C. Let the system automatically shrink the files to their minimum size.

D. You will not be able to fit this database on a floppy disk.

exam
ⓦatch

Although there may be more than one, there must be at least one log file for each database. The minimum size for each log file is 512KB.

4. You are trying to attach a database. The database has a primary data file, two additional data files, and a log file. You receive an error when you execute the following script. What is the problem?

```
EXEC sp_attach_db @dbname = N'pubs',
     @filename1 = 'c:\mssql7\data\pubs1.mdf',
     @filename2 = 'c:\mssql7\data\pubs_log.ldf',
     @filename3 = 'c:\mssql7\data\pubs2.mdf',
     @filename4 = 'c:\mssql7\data\pubs3.mdf'
```

A. All of the data files must be specified before the log file is specified.

B. The log file must be specified before the data files.

C. The non-primary data files should have a file extension of .NDF.

D. All files should have the file extension of .DBF.

5. You are the system administrator of a heavily used database. At least once a day you are paged because the database is almost out of space and needs to be extended. You decide that letting the data files grow automatically does not represent any significant risk and would certainly make your life easier. Which of the approaches could you use to configure the system to grow the files?

A. Set the database to grow in increments of 4096KB.

B. Set the database to grow by five percent.

C. Set the database to grow by 4MB.

D. Database files do not grow. They must be extended manually.

6. Recently one of the DBAs at your company left under questionable circumstances. Even though you have changed the SA password and disabled the person's account, you feel that they may still represent a security risk. You decide that changing the ownership of the master

database would provide an additional level of security. What method would you use to change the ownership of the master database?

A. You can only change the ownership of the master database by using the TRANSACT SQL command.

B. The master database owner can only be changed by an administrator through SQL Enterprise Manager.

C. There is a wizard for changing the ownership of the master database and it is the only way that ownership can be changed.

D. Ownership of the master database cannot be changed.

7. Over the past few days, you have noticed that hard-drive activity on your SQL Server has increased dramatically. You think that a possible cause for this increased activity is data fragmentation. Which command would you choose to investigate your concerns?

A. SET SHOWPLAN_TEXT ON

B. SET SHOWFRAGEMENTATION ON

C. DBCC SHOWCONTIG

D. DBCC SHOWFRAGMENTS

8. You have a database with two data files that are both 50-percent used. You are planning for considerable growth, and decide to add a third database file. There are 50MB of data in the first two data files. Next you import 350MB of data. What are the file sizes of your three data files after the import?

A. 50MB, 50MB, 350MB

B. 150MB, 150MB, 150MB

C. 100MB, 100MB, 250MB

D. 200MB, 200MB, 50MB

9. You are planning on implementing filegroups in your databases as part of your migration from SQL Server 6.5 to SQL Server 7.0. There are many things to consider when implementing filegroups. Which of the following is something that you should NOT consider?

A. The primary filegroup contains the primary data file and any other files that are not put into another filegroup. The primary filegroup holds all the pages for the system pages.

B. User-defined filegroups are specified using the following: FILEGROUP keyword in a CREATE DATABASE or ALTER DATABASE statement, or on the database property page within SQL Server Enterprise Manager.

C. The default filegroup contains the pages for all tables and indices that do not have a filegroup specified when they are first created. Each database can have only one filegroup at a time that is the default filegroup. If a default filegroup is not specified, then it automatically defaults to the primary filegroup.

D. Filegroups cannot be backed up as a unit. When defining a backup strategy you must be sure to design your backup strategy around individual databases so that you capture the data files as a unit.

---

exam
ⓦatch

When a database is created, all the files that comprise the database are filled with zeros to overwrite any existing data left on the disk by previously deleted files. Although this means that the files take longer to create, it prevents Windows NT from clearing out the files when data is written to the files for the first time during normal database operations. This increases the performance of your database.

---

10. You have a heavily used database, and developers are constantly creating new objects such as tables and indices. The data file in the primary filegroup is not set to grow automatically, and periodically the file is filled and no additional objects can be created. Your primary goal is to prevent the collision of user table and indices with the system tables to prevent normal operations from being interrupted. Secondarily, you want to configure the system to be able to back up all of the user objects separately from all of the system objects. You also would like to configure the system in a way that allows you to quickly detach the user objects from one server and attach

them to another. You propose meeting these goals by creating a user-defined filegroup and assigning it as the default for the database.

A. The proposed method achieves the primary and both secondary goals.

B. The proposed method achieves the primary goal and only one of the secondary goals.

C. The proposed method achieves the primary goal and neither secondary goal.

D. The proposed solution does not achieve the primary goal.

e x a m

ⓦatch

It is impossible to move files to a different filegroup once the files have been added to the database.

11. In today's world, companies are merging left and right. Having the capability to detach and attach databases is useful if you need to move a database from one company's server to another company's server. This alleviates the need to manually re-create the database and then restore the database. Which procedure would you use to move a database from one server to another?

A. EXEC sp_detach_db accounts, true
   EXEC sp_attach_single_file_db @dbname = 'accounts'
   @physname = 'd:\mssql7\data\accounts.mdf'

B. EXEC sp_detach_db accounts, false
   EXEC sp_attach_db @dbname = 'accounts'
   @filename1 = 'd:\mssql7\data\accounts.mdf'
   @filename2 = 'd:\mssql7\data\accounts_log.ldf'

C. EXEC sp_detach_db accounts, true
   EXEC sp_attach_single_file_db @dbname = 'accounts'
   @filename1 = 'd:\mssql7\data\accounts.mdf'

D. EXEC sp_detach_db accounts, true
   EXEC sp_attach_db @dbname = 'accounts'
   @physname1 = 'd:\mssql7\data\accounts.mdf'
   @physname2 = 'd:\mssql7\data\accounts_log.ldf'

12. As the database owner, you decide that the transaction log file for the database should not be larger than 5MB. You set a primary goal of making sure the database does not have a single transaction log that exceeds 5MB; however, the database may require more than 5MB of transaction log space. You set two secondary goals: prevent the use of more than 5MB of transaction log space and automatically clear out any unnecessary information in the transaction log. Your method of achieving these goals is to add additional 5MB transaction log files to take over when the existing log is close to being full.

    A. The proposed solution achieves the primary goal and both secondary goals.
    B. The proposed solution achieves the primary goal and only one of the secondary goals.
    C. The proposed solution achieves the primary goal and neither secondary goal.
    D. The proposed solution doesn't achieve the primary goal.

---

exam
ⓦatch   *You cannot change ownership of any of the system databases, such as master, model, or tempdb.*

---

13. You need to mark a database as Read Only in order to perform some maintenance tasks. Which of the following methods will allow you to do this?

    A. Use the Read Only option of the SP_DBOPTION command.
    B. Select the Read Only box from the options tab of the database properties page of the SQL Server Enterprise Manager.
    C. Set the user connections value to zero for the database.
    D. Pause the SQL Server service using the control panel services application.

QUESTIONS AND ANSWERS

The Sales database is rapidly running out of room...	Manually expand it or set it to automatically grow.
You need to close the database down cleanly after the last user exits....	Use the autoclose option for sp_dboption from a Transact-SQL statement.
Martha is the owner of the Sales database and has been replaced in the sales department by Bill...	Use sp_changedbowner to make Bill the new Sales database owner.
The database owner doesn't want the transaction log file to be bigger than 5 megabytes...	Add additional 5MB transaction log files to take over when the existing file is full.
You need to make sure that no one modifies any data in the Sales database...	Use the read only option for sp_dboption from a Transact-SQL statement or select the Read Only box from the Option tab of the database properties page of SQL Server Enterprise Manager.

Managing Security

1. You have Novell, Unix, and Windows clients on your network. All clients need to access SQL Server databases. Your primary goal is to implement security, while your first optional goal is allowing all clients access to SQL Server. As a second optional goal, you would also like to encrypt data transmission between server and client and restrict user access to data. You propose accomplishing these goals by implementing mixed mode security, using the TCP/IP network library, and by implementing roles, creating views, and assigning permissions to the views.

   Which of the following results does the proposed solution achieve?

   A. The proposed solution achieves your primary and both optional goals.

   B. The proposed solution achieves your primary and the first optional goal.

   C. The proposed solution achieves your primary and the second optional goal.

   D. The proposed solution does not achieve your primary goal.

2. A role was created to allow contractors access to the Accounting database. The contract is over and you now need to remove the role. You are a member of the db_owner role, and you attempt to drop the role and fail. You used Query Analyzer and entered SP_DROPROLE CONTRACT. What is the most likely cause of this failure?

A. The role has existing users.

B. You entered the command incorrectly.

C. You do not have permission to drop a role.

D. The role is a fixed-server role.

3. You need to create a foreign key between the Orders and Customers tables. The customer_id should exist in the Customers table before inserting a record in the Orders table so that every order has a valid customer_id. What permissions do you need to create the foreign key?

A. Reference permission on Customer

B. Reference permission on Orders

C. Select permission on Customers

D. Select permission on Orders

exam
ⓦatch
Windows NT Authentication Mode is not available when SQL Server is running on Windows 95 or Windows 98. It is available when Windows 95 and Windows 98 clients access SQL Server on Windows NT.

4. You need to change the owner of a database. The new owner already has a login and a user account in the database. What must you do to change the owner?

A. SP_DROPUSER

B. SP_CHANGEDBOWNER

C. SP_ADDUSER

D. SP_CHANGE_USERS_LOGIN

5. You are the DBO of the accounting table. You give only User1 the select and create view right and User1 creates a view. User1 then gives permission to the view to User2. User2 tries to execute view, but an error message is returned. Why was an error message returned?

A. User2 did not have permission to the view.

B. User1 did not have permission to the view.

C. User1 did not have permission to the table.

D. User2 did not have permission to the table.

6. You want to establish security on your database. You want to allow users access to the HR table, but you don't want users to see two confidential columns. How can you best accomplish this?

A. Apply DENY permission to the two columns.

B. Create a role that does not have access to the two columns.

C. Create a view that does not show the two columns.

D. None of the above

7. You remove an NT group from the Accounting database. Julie has created a table in the database and is a member of the NT group that was removed. What can Julie access when you remove the NT group?

A. You cannot remove the group.

B. You can remove the group, but Julie can still access the database.

C. You can remove the group, and Julie cannot access the database.

D. You can remove the group after you create a login for Julie.

8. All access to the SQL database will be through custom application. You have two groups that require different types of access. What is the best way to set up access?

A. Create an application role for the application.

B. Create two application roles, one for each group.

C. Create a login for each user.

D. Create a single login for everyone to use.

9. You are a member of fixed server role, serveradmin. You create a job that backs up the database and copies the backup file to a network drive. When you run the SQL statements in Query Analyzer, the backup succeeds. When you execute the job, the backup succeeds but fails to copy the file to the network drive. Why?

A. SQL Server Agent is not running.

B. The account used for SQL Server Agent does not have permission to the network drive.

C. The browser service is not running.

D. You can't copy backup files to a different server.

10. You want your assistant to see all the data in the database, but you don't want her to be able to change any information. What roles should you assign her?

A. Db_datareader

B. Db_datawriter

C. Db_denydatareader

D. Db_denydatawriter

11. An employee moves to another department and you delete his SQL Server user account. You later discover that the employee is still accessing the database. How is this possible?

A. He created a table.

B. His account was a member of a role.

C. He created a view.

D. Login account still exists.

12. You've been assigned a new assistant. You want her to help you administer the SQL server, but you only want her to manage users and logins. How can you do this?

A. Assign her to the setupadmin role.

B. Assign her to the db_accessadmin role.

C. Assign her to the securityadmin role.

D. Assign her to the processadmin role.

13. You are the administrator for a SQL server. You are required to implement security.

Primary goal: Finance should only be allowed to access the ACCOUNTING table and HR should only be allowed to access the EMPLOYEES table.

First optional goal: a custom application should be implemented.

Second optional goal: employees should not be able to access the database directly.

Proposed solution: implement application roles. Create one role for Finance, and another for Employees. The custom application is modified to verify users and set the role based on the user.

Which of the following results does the proposed solution achieve?

A. The proposed solution meets the primary and both optional goals.

B. The proposed solution meets the primary and first optional goal.

C. The proposed solution meets the primary goal, but neither optional goal.

D. The proposed solution does not meet the primary goal.

---

14. You wish to deny access to a limited number of employees to a specific table. You have granted db_datareader permission to the Company role, of which everyone is a member. How can you best deny access without affecting their other permissions?

A. Create a role, add individual users to the role, and deny access to that role.

B. Remove the users from the Company role.

C. Use sp_grantdbaccess.

D. Use sp_revokelogin.

15. You've added a guest account to the model database. Users are gaining access to all new databases created, and you need to find out why. How are they gaining access?

    A. Logins provide access to all databases.

    B. All users are able to create user accounts in databases.

    C. Guest accounts exist in all databases by default.

    D. Guest accounts exist in all databases created since you added the guest account.

16. You are using SQL Server authentication and you need to grant Select permission to 40 users, Insert permission to 50 users, and Update permission to all 90 users. How can you best accomplish this?

    A. Apply each permission to each user account.

    B. Create two NT groups and apply permissions to the groups.

    C. Create two views and grant users permission to the view.

    D. Create two roles and apply permissions to the roles.

exam
ⓦatch

Any Windows NT user that belongs to the BUILTIN\Administrators group is automatically added as a member of the sysadmin fixed server role.

17. A user has forgotten his SQL login password. How can you change it?

    A. Login properties in Enterprise Manager

    B. SP_PASSWORD

    C. Delete login and re-create.

    D. User properties in Enterprise Manager

18. You have UNIX, NT, and NetWare clients. How should you configure security?

A. Create SQL logins for Unix clients.

B. Create SQL logins for Netware clients.

C. Create NT logins for NT clients.

D. Create NT logins for Netware clients.

19. You want to add a user account to your database. Which system-stored procedure should you use?

A. SP_ADD_OPERATOR

B. SP_ADDALIAS

C. SP_GRANTLOGIN

D. SP_GRANTDBACCESS

20. John is a member of Finance, HR, and Accounting. The roles have the following permissions in the Customers database. Finance has SELECT and UPDATE permission, HR has INSERT, and Accounting has DENY permission to the Customers database. What are John's permissions on the Customers database?

A. INSERT, SELECT, AND UPDATE

B. SELECT AND UPDATE

C. INSERT

E. None

21. You want to assign permission to add, modify, and drop objects in your database to your assistant. How should you do this?

A. Assign her to the db_ddladmin role.

B. Assign her to the sysadmin role.

C. Grant her the specific permissions.

D. Give her your user ID and password.

22. Alan is given the SELECT permission WITH GRANT option on the ACCOUNTING table. He gives permission to three other users. You use SQL standard security. Alan leaves the company and you need to delete his account. How can you delete his account?

    A. SP_DROPDBACCESS *Alan*

    B. SP_REVOKELOGIN *Alan*

    C. REVOKE SELECT ON ACCOUNTING TO *Alan* CASCADE
       SP_DROPDBACCESS *Alan*

    D. REVOKE SELECT ON ACCOUNTING TO *Alan* CASCADE
       SP_DROPDBACCESS *Alan*
       SP_REVOKELOGIN *Alan*

23. You add a new login using SQL Server Enterprise Manager, but you forget to specify the default database. To which database do the new SQL Server login properties apply?

    A. MSDB

    B. MASTER

    C. PUBS

    D. None

24. A user is a member of the Finance, HR, and Management roles. Finance has INSERT permission to the Accounting table, HR has UPDATE permission and Management has SELECT permission. What are the user's effective permissions to the Accounting table?

    A. SELECT

    B. UPDATE

    C. INSERT

    D. All of the above

25. Julie is a member of the Sales group. You are using NT authentication to access your SQL server. The Sales group has access to the SQL server. You want to prevent Julie from accessing the SQL database. How can you do this?

A. SP_DENYLOGIN *domain/julie*

B. SP_REVOKELOGIN *domain/julie*

C. SP_DENYLOGIN *domain/sales*

D. SP_REVOKELOGIN *domain/sales*

QUESTIONS AND ANSWERS

Management has formed a team from different offices to temporarily study specific portions of the sales database…	Create a Standard user-defined database role that can access the specific portions of the sales database and place the members of the team in it.
Jesse needs to be able to manage logins for the SQL Server…	Add Jesse to the securityadmin fixed server role.
Mike wants to have the database he is responsible for accessed only with a password…	Create an Application user-defined database role and distribute an application that has the password hardcoded in it.
Franklin needs to be able to back up a single database …	Add Franklin to the db_backup operator fixed database role.
David needs the capability to perform any activity on the company SQL Server…	Add David to the sysadmin fixed server role.

Automating Administrative Tasks

1. You have recently configured SQL Server to alert you when one of your databases is full. Before relying on this functionality, you decide to test it by sending yourself a test e-mail and a test page. After waiting a few minutes, you realize that something must not be configured properly. Which of the following is a likely reason for your not receiving your test messages?

   A. The MSDTC service is not running.

   B. The SQLServer Agent service is not running.

   C. The MSSQL Service is not running.

   D. The Windows NT NetLogon Service is not running.

2. There are a number of different ways that the SQL Agent can notify an operator of an alert. Assume that the environment that you are working in has a MAPI-compliant e-mail system. Also assume that you can page an operator by dialing that operator's pager number and typing in a phone number. Which of the following methods do you have available for alert notification?

   A. E-mail

   B. Page

   C. Net send

   D. IRC

3. There are a number of tools available to an administrator for automating common tasks. These tools also help in managing a server. What are the tools that SQL Server provides for automation and management?

   A. Administrators

   B. Operators

   C. Alerts

   D. Jobs

4. John is a Windows NT Domain Administrator. He is also a DBA and a member of the Network Administrators group. Recently one of the SQL Servers that he is responsible for crashed. He can't understand why he did not receive a notification or alert. He knows that alerts were generated because some of the other DBAs were alerted. He does not ever remember receiving an alert from that server. What is a likely cause for his not receiving an alert?

A. The e-mail server must have been down because domain administrators receive alerts by default when there is a significant SQL Server error.

B. John must not be configured as an operator.

C. John's account must have been removed from the DBA group because DBAs receive alerts by default whenever there is a significant SQL Server error.

D. John must not be set up as the default operator for the system.

---

exam
Ⓦatch *Adding a delay between responses for a recurring alert helps to prevent multiple notifications for the same error.*

---

5. Current situation: Your boss seems to be receiving every error message that your SQL Server generates as a pop-up message on his workstation. He is not pleased, and he would like the situation rectified as soon as possible. Required result: Eliminate any possibility of your boss receiving pop-up notifications.

Optional results: Provide a way for your boss to be notified in the event of a serious problem with the SQL Server. Log all error messages to the Windows NT Event Log.

Proposed solution: Remove his account or workstation name from the "Error message pop-up recipient" box found on the general tab of the SQL Agent properties dialog. Then create an operator account for your boss and have him notified by e-mail.

A. The proposed solution produces the required result and both of the optional results.

B. The proposed solution produces the required result and only one of the optional results.

C. The proposed solution produces the required result and neither of the optional results.

D. The proposed solution doesn't produce the required result.

6. You would like to create a custom tool to automate some of the common management activities you are performing on your server. You would like to use Visual Basic to do your development. What do you need to do start developing your tool?

A. Nothing. The SQL-DMO DLL is installed as part of a client or server install of SQL Server.

B. You need to install the SQL-DMO package from your SQL Server CD.

C. You need to install the SQL-DMO header files from your SQL Server CD.

D. Nothing. Visual Basic provides everything you need to develop tools for SQL Server.

7. You have a multiserver environment and you routinely create jobs that run on multiple servers. Recently, your company has become a multinational company. Each country is a site. Each site has its own Windows NT master domain, its own file and print servers, and its own SQL Servers. All of the countries still share some resources. You have a development SQL Server that everyone shares. This server is set up as a target server for the master server in the United States. When the European countries try to use this server as a target server, they are unsuccessful. What is the problem?

A. All master servers must be using the same service account, so they must all be in the same Windows NT domain.

B. Master and target servers must be connected by a high-speed connection.

C. A target server can have only one master server.

D. A master server can have only one target server.

8. If you have a job with multiple steps, you must order the steps. You can alter the order of steps, add steps, or delete steps at any time. Changes take effect the next time the job is run. The following illustration shows a job with multiple steps. Which steps must complete successfully for the job to report success?

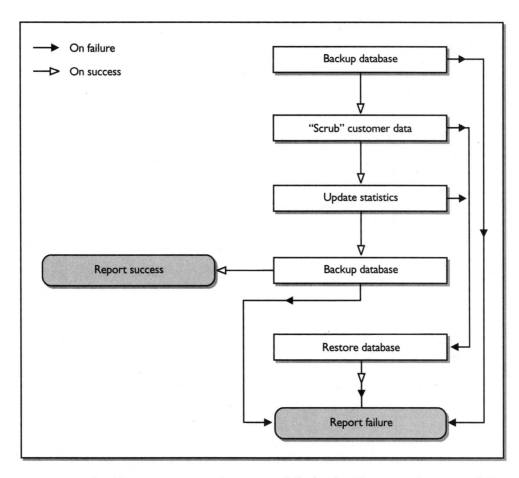

A. All steps must complete successfully for the job to complete successfully.

B. The backup database step must complete successfully for the job to complete successfully.

C. All steps prior to and including the backup database step must complete successfully for the job to complete successfully.

D. As long as the database is not being restored, the job will report success.

exam
Ⓦatch   *It might be easier to remember that Job options are for success status.*

9. You are creating a multiserver job using the explicit method of configuration. If you issue the following command, where is the job definition stored?

```
EXECUTE msdb.dbo.sp_post_msx_operation 'INSERT', 'JOB',
'<job id>'
```

A. SYSDOWNLOADLIST table in the MSDB database
B. SYSDOWNLOADLIST table in the MASTER database
C. SYSDOWNLOADLIST table in the TEMPDB database
D. SYSDOWNLOADLIST table in the user database that is the target of the job

10. You have a multiserver job that is set to run once a minute. You are concerned that you are not getting the job results uploaded to the master server for every run of the job. What could be the problem?

A. The job's execution frequency is probably set higher than the polling interval of the server.
B. The server's polling interval is probably set higher than the job's execution frequency.
C. The servers are probably suffering from a lack of bandwidth due to a low-speed connection.
D. None of the above

11. You have a master server with one target server. This configuration has been in operation for approximately three months. As part of a naming standards project, some of the servers in the environment have been renamed. The target server was one of the servers that were renamed. There haven't been any job results uploaded to the master server since the rename. What procedure would have facilitated a target server name change without any service interruption?

ADMINISTRATION
QUESTIONS

A. You should have changed the target server's name in the MSDB database before changing the name of the system.

B. You should have run the sp_update_target system stored procedure before making the name change on the target server.

C. You should have defected the target server before making the name change, then reenlisted the target server with the new name.

D. There must be some other problem in the system as master and target servers keep track of each other through SIDs, and the name change on the target server would not have changed the server's SID.

exam
Ⓦatch

MAPI must be installed for SQL Server Agent Mail to work. There are many ways to obtain it, including Windows Messaging, Microsoft Exchange, and Microsoft Outlook.

12. You have a number of options available to you for scheduling either local or multiserver jobs. Which of the following represent options that you can use to develop a job scheduling system? (Choose all that apply.)

A. Whenever CPU utilization of the computer is at a level you have defined as idle

B. One time, at a specific date and time

C. On a recurring schedule

D. In response to an alert

Backing Up Databases

1. A natural disaster strikes a rival company's building containing servers that store various databases. How can you keep a similar event from affecting data stored on the servers of your company? (Choose all that apply.)

   A. Perform regular backups, and store all backups in a location on the premises.

   B. Perform regular backups, and store all backups in a location separate from where the server's reside.

   C. Perform regular backups. Store one copy of backups on the premises, and store a separate copy in an off-site storage facility.

   D. Perform backups only when the possibility of a disaster is foreseen. Store one copy of backups on the premises, and store a separate copy in an off-site storage facility.

2. You are concerned with preventing data loss on servers containing information that's vital to your company. In preparing methods to deal with this, which of the following will you consider as a potential cause of data loss in a database? (Choose all that apply.)

   A. Hard disk failures

   B. Errors caused by users

   C. Errors caused by applications

   D. Server loss

3. You have made several backups of a SQL Server database and transaction logs. When you restore the database, what portion of the transaction log will be restored from the current backup?

A. All transactions that have occurred since the first backup of the database will be restored.

B. Only transactions that have occurred since the last backup will be included in the backup. When the database is restored, only the transactions that occurred between the previous and current backup will be restored.

C. None of the transactions will be restored with data. You need to restore transaction logs as a separate process from restoring data.

D. Backing up a database doesn't copy portions of the transaction log. As only data is backed up, no portion of the transaction log is backed up.

4. You have limited storage space and very little time to perform a backup of a database on a SQL Server computer. What will you do?

A. Perform a full backup.

B. Perform a differential backup.

C. Perform a complete backup.

D. Perform a decremental backup.

5. You are in the process of restoring a database from a backup. In restoring the database, what will happen when SQL Server reads through the transaction log?

A. SQL Server will roll forward all of the transactions.

B. SQL Server will roll back all of the transactions.

C. All completed transactions will be rolled forward, and all incomplete transactions will be rolled back.

D. All completed transactions will be rolled back, and all incomplete transactions will be rolled forward.

6. Current situation: A virus has infected the hard disk of a network server running SQL Server, and it has destroyed the database containing customer and ordering information. After removing the virus, reformatting the hard disk, and reinstalling the operating system and programs used on this computer, you are ready to restore the lost data.

Required result: All data must be restored so that the database is in the same condition previous to the failure.

Optional desired result: Data must be restored as quickly as possible; all successful transactions need to be restored with the data, while unsuccessful ones will need to be undone.

Proposed solution: Restore the last differential backup, and restore all of the transactional log backups that have been created since the last differential backup was done.

Which of the following will be the result of the proposed solution?

A. The proposed solution produces the required result and produces both of the optional results.

B. The proposed solution produces the required result and produces only one of the optional results.

C. The proposed solution produces the required result and produces none of the optional results.

D. The proposed solution doesn't produce the required result.

---

exam
ⓦatch

If you use file and filegroup backups then you must also use transaction log backups so that when you perform a restore procedure, you can bring the database to a consistent state.

---

7. Your department has several mission-critical databases. If the NT Server running SQL Server and containing these databases goes down for any length of time, and if users are unable to access the data, it could mean tens or even hundreds of thousands of dollars in losses. Which of the following could you implement so that users are able to access data with little to no downtime? (Choose all that apply.)

A. Implement a regimen of regular backups. When the server goes down, restore from the backups.

B. Implement a standby server. The data from the primary server would be synchronized with the standby server.

C. Implement a cluster server so that data is available if one server goes down.

D. Use mirroring so that data contained on one hard disk on the server is copied onto another hard disk on the server.

8. The primary server has gone offline for a while, and a standby server has been used in the interim. Upon restarting the primary server, what must be done to ensure that the information on the primary server is identical to that on the standby server?

A. You will need to synchronize the databases so that the data in each database is identical.

B. You will need to restore a backup of the data in the primary server's database to the standby server's database.

C. Nothing. The standby server and the primary server are accessed through a virtual server. The database is the same regardless of which physical server is being used.

D. Nothing. Upon restarting the standby server, the primary server's database will be automatically synchronized with the database on the standby server.

9. Current situation: A SQL Server database is being used for 911 calls. This database is used for storing mission-critical data. Any downtime is critical, and data needs to always be available.

Required result: Develop a solution that will have data available 24 hours a day, 7 days a week. If a server goes down, the data will still be available.

Optional desired result: If the server goes down, users won't be aware that a problem exists; no data is lost when the server goes down.

Proposed solution: Implement a standby server.

Which of the following will be the result of the proposed solution?

A. The proposed solution produces the required result and produces both of the optional results.

B. The proposed solution produces the required result and produces only one of the optional results.

C. The proposed solution produces the required result and produces neither of the optional results.

D. The proposed solution doesn't produce the required result.

10. You want to implement failover support so that data is available even in the event of a failure. Which of the following would you need to implement failover support? (Choose all that apply.)

A. Windows NT Server

B. Microsoft Cluster Server

C. Windows NT Workstation

D. SQL Server 7.0

11. A colleague has set up failover support to ensure that data is available when a server goes down. If the primary server fails, the administrator must change the control of the SQL Server to the secondary server. What type of failover support has been implemented?

A. Active

B. Passive

C. Active/Passive

D. Active/Active

12. A colleague has set up failover support to ensure that data is available when a server goes down. The configuration of failover support uses two virtual servers and two copies of SQL Server 7.0 on shared hard disks. What type of failover support has been implemented?

A. Active

B. Passive

C. Active/Passive

D. Active/Active

13. You have set up SQL Server 7.0 failover support on your network so that users can still access data in the event of a failure. You now want to administer failover and failback policies, and you want to move services and resources between servers used in the failover support. Which of the following will you use to administer these areas?

A. MSCS Cluster Administrator

B. SQL Server Enterprise Manager

C. SQL Server Profiler

D. SQL Server Agent

14. You want to implement SQL Server 7.0 failover support as a data availability solution. In using clustering, what is the lowest number of physical servers required to implement failover support?

A. One

B. Two

C. Three

D. No minimum number of servers is required to implement failover support.

15. You attempt backing up a SQL Server database to a tape device that's physically connected to another NT Server on your local area network. When you attempt to do this, you find that you cannot. Why?

A. The named pipe used to back up the data hasn't been configured properly.

B. To back up to a tape device, the tape device needs to be physically connected to the computer running SQL Server.

C. The tape backup device is full.

D. SQL Server doesn't support tape devices.

16. You are using a third-party backup device and application to back up a SQL Server 7.0 database. This device and application use backup media that are directly supported in SQL Server. Which of the following would be used under these circumstances to back up the database?

A. Disk backup

B. Named pipes

C. Unnamed pipes

D. Tape backup

17. Your supervisor instructs you to perform a complete backup of a database to a tape backup device. During the backup, the tape becomes full. What will happen?

A. The backup will fail. Replace the tape with a blank one, then restart backing up the database.

B. The backup will fail. Replace the tape with a blank one, then perform a differential backup of the data.

C. Replace the tape with the existing one that's full. Backup will continue by putting the remaining data over existing data on the tape.

D. Replace the tape with another one, then continue with the backup.

---

exam
ⓦatch

During a failover, SQL Server Failover Support may not function correctly if it runs short of memory. To ensure the failover is successful and that the clients have satisfactory response times, make sure you have sufficient memory for your cluster.

---

18. You are planning to completely back up a SQL Server 7.0 database. Which of the following programs can you use to back up this data? (Choose all that apply.)

A. SQL Server Enterprise Manager

B. Transact-SQL Enterprise Manager

C. Transact-SQL

D. The Create Backup Wizard

19. You plan on backing up a database using Transact-SQL. Which of the following would you use to back up a database called Sales to a backup device called Sale_Bak so that the database can later be restored when needed?

A. BACKUP Sales TO Sale_Bak

B. BACKUP DATABASE Sales TO Sale_Bak

C. BACKUP DATABASE Sales TO Sale_Bak WITH RESTART

D. BACKUP DATABASE Sales TO Sale_Bak WITH RESTORE

20. You are performing a backup of a SQL Server 7.0 database when another user attempts to create a new database file. What will happen?

A. The backup will fail, and the database will be created.

B. The database will be created, and the backup will continue as normal.

C. The database won't be created, and the backup will continue as normal.

D. The database won't be created, and the backup will fail.

21. You plan on backing up a database using Transact-SQL. While you are backing up a database called Sales to a backup device called Sale_Bak, a power outage occurs. When the power returns, you want the backup to continue where it left off before the failure. Which of the following would you use to resume the backup?

A. BACKUP Sales TO Sale_Bak

B. BACKUP DATABASE Sales TO Sale_Bak

C. BACKUP DATABASE Sales TO Sale_Bak WITH RESTART

D. BACKUP DATABASE Sales TO Sale_Bak WITH RESTORE

22. You are preparing to back up a SQL Server 7.0 database. When you attempt to start the backup, another user is already creating an index. What will happen?

A. The backup will abort, and the index will be created.

B. The index will be created, and the backup will continue as normal.

C. The index won't be created, and the backup will continue as normal.

D. The index won't be created, and the backup will abort.

23. A colleague wants to back up the master database of a SQL Server but he is unsure under what conditions this database should be backed up. Under which of the following conditions will you tell him to back up the master database? (Choose all that apply.)

A. Any time a user database is added or deleted

B. Any time a user database is backed up

C. Any time server-wide or database configuration options are changed

D. Any time that data is added or changed since the last full backup of a user database

24. You are preparing to back up a record of changes made to the database. You need the active portion of the log used to record these changes backed up. Which kind of backup will you perform using the options available in the Create Backup Wizard? (Choose all that apply.)

A. Database backup

B. Differential database

C. Transaction log

D. Full backup

25. You are planning to perform a differential backup on a SQL Server 7.0 database. Which of the following methods can you use to back up this data? (Choose all that apply.)

A. SQL Server Enterprise Manager

B. Transact-SQL Enterprise Manager

C. Transact-SQL

D. The Create Backup Wizard

exam
ⓦatch   *Database and differential database backups contain the active*
portion of the transaction logs automatically.

26. You are preparing to do a differential backup on a database using Transact-SQL. You are backing up a database called Customer to a backup device called Cust_Bak. Which of the following would you use to perform such a backup?

A. DIFFERENTIAL BACKUP Customer TO Cust_Bak

B. BACKUP DATABASE Cust_Bak TO Customer WITH DIFFERENTIAL

C. BACKUP Customer TO Cust_Bak WITH DIFFERENTIAL

D. BACKUP DATABASE Customer TO Cust_Bak WITH DIFFERENTIAL

27. You are preparing to back up a SQL Server database. Which of the following backups will not back up a transaction log? (Choose all that apply.)

A. File or filegroup backup

B. Full or complete backup

C. Differential backup

D. Transaction log

28. You want to automate backups of SQL Server 7.0 databases used by your department. Which of the following programs will you use to configure SQL Server to automatically perform backups at regular intervals?

A. SQL Server Enterprise Manager

B. Database Maintenance Plan Wizard

C. Transact-SQL

D. The Create Backup Wizard

29. You want to back up a SQL Server 7.0 database, but you have experienced problems with corrupt databases on restoring them. Which of the following backup methods can you use to verify the integrity of a database once it has been backed up? (Choose all that apply.)

A. SQL Server Enterprise Manager
B. Database Maintenance Plan Wizard
C. SQL Verify Agent
D. The Create Backup Wizard

QUESTIONS AND ANSWERS

The employee database does not change very often...	Use a database backup on a weekly basis.
The company depends on the financial database...	Use a combination of full database backups, differential backups, and transaction log backups to ensure that you have backups of the most current data. The transaction log backups need to be scheduled based upon the amount of time that you can afford to lose any data.
The database has grown so big that there is not enough time to back it up completely during the night...	Perform file or filegroup backups on it nightly. For example you may need to split it over two or three nights to completely back up the entire database. You could also perform a differential backup if you already had a complete backup of the database. Another option is to perform a full backup on weekends and differentials nightly.
You have added two databases to SQL Server ...	Perform a full backup of the master database.
Marissa is a new database administrator in your company and she is nervous about backing up databases...	Have her use the Backup Database Wizard until she is comfortable with other methods of performing backup operations.

Methods of Restoring Databases

1. You are restoring your database from a multiple tape volume, and you have a power outage, interrupting your restore. How can you continue the restore operation?

A. RESTORE DB1 FROM BACKUP1

B. RESTORE DB1 FROM BACKUP1 WITH RESTART

C. RESTORE DB1 FROM BACKUP1 WITH UNLOAD

D. RESTORE DB1 FROM BACKUP1 WITH REPLACE

2. You've split the Accounting table indexes on to two filegroups, Index1 and Index2, to enhance performance. You back up Accounting and Index1 on Tuesday, and Index2 on Wednesday. You need to restore the database on Friday. How do you restore it?

A. RESTORE DATABASE db1 FILE = 'db1',
   FILEGROUP = 'accounting',
   FILE = 'db1_index', FILEGROUP = 'index1',
   FILE = 'db1_index2', FILEGROUP = 'index2' from db1_bu1

B. RESTORE DATABASE db1 FROM db1_bu

C. LOAD DATABASE db1 FROM db1_bu WITH RECOVERY

D. Restore the tables, and recreate the indexes.

---

exam

ⓦatch   *Tape backup devices must be physically attached to the server. It is not possible to use tape backup devices on remote computers.*

---

3. You have a standby server. A full database backup of the ACCOUNTING database is performed every night. The transaction log is not backed up during the day. The ACCOUNTING database on the production server fails. How should you bring the standby server online? (Choose the correct order.)

A. Execute RESTORE DATABASE WITH RECOVERY on the standby server.

B. Restore the active transaction log to the standby server.

C. Back up the active transaction log on the production server.

D. None of the above

4. Current situation: You are required to implement a recovery disaster plan.
   Required result: Have the database available to users with the shortest downtime.
   Optional results: Offload some reporting functions from the production server. Reports produced are prior day's sales. Minimize the backup process.
   Proposed solution: Purchase and maintain a standby server. Backups will be performed nightly, and restored to the standby server.
   What does the proposed solution provide?

   A. The proposed solution meets the required result and both optional results.

   B. The proposed solution meets the required result and one optional result.

   C. The proposed solution meets the required result but neither of the optional results.

   D. The proposed solution does not meet the required result.

5. You need to restore a database with a different name for developers to work on. How would you accomplish this? (Choose all that apply.)

   A. Copy and rename the .MDF and .LDF files and use sp_attach_db.

   B. Restore the database with the REPLACE switch.

   C. Restore the database with the RENAME switch.

   D. You cannot restore a database with a different name.

6. The MASTER database is corrupted, but you can start SQL server. You haven't made any system changes, and you backed up MASTER last weekend. What is the best way to recover?

A. Run REBUILDM.EXE.

B. Restart SQL in single-user mode, and restore the MASTER backup.

C. Reinstall SQL Server.

D. Execute sp_resetstatus.

exam
Ⓦatch

Omitting the FROM clause can be used to attempt recovery of a non-suspect database that has been restored with the NORECOVERY option, or to switch over to a standby server. If the FROM clause is omitted, either NORECOVERY, RECOVERY, or STANDBY must be specified or you will receive error messages and no action will be taken by the server.

7. An application performed an invalid update. Your database is marked suspect, and you want to recover to the point in time right before the application performed the update. What would you do? (Choose the best answer.)

A. Back up the active log, restore the database, and reapply the transaction log with the TIME option.

B. Back up the active log, restore the database, and reapply the transaction log using the STOPAT option.

C. Restore the database, and reapply all transaction log backups.

D. You cannot recover to a point in time.

8. The ACCOUNTING database fails Friday afternoon. A full backup is performed on Sunday and Wednesday, and transaction logs are backed up every four hours. You must restore the database to point of failure. How do you restore the database?

A. Restore Wednesday's backup.

B. Back up the active transaction log, restore Wednesday's backup, and restore each transaction log.

C. Restore Wednesday's backup, then each transaction log backup in the order backed up.

D. Restore Sunday's backup, restore Wednesday's backup, and restore each transaction log.

9. The ACCOUNTING database has a media failure on Friday at 2 p.m. A full backup is performed every Saturday at 7 p.m., and a differential backup is performed every Wednesday at 7 p.m. Transaction logs are backed up at 12 p.m. and 4 p.m. every day. You need to restore the database to point of failure. With which backup do you use the RECOVERY option?

A. The full backup

B. The differential backup

C. The transaction log on Friday, 12 p.m.

D. The active transaction log backup

10. A full database backup of the database was performed on Wednesday and restored to the standby server. The database on the production server fails on Thursday. No transaction log backups have been performed since Wednesday. You bring the standby server online. How do you recover the database on the production server?

A. Back up the database and log on the standby server, restore to the production server with the RECOVERY option.

B. Execute RESTORE DATABASE WITH RECOVERY.

C. Back up the log on the standby server, restore to the production server.

D. Rename the production server.

exam
Ⓦatch

When performing a Restore Database command, the sp_dboption settings are reset to the settings that were in use when the database backup was executed. When other restore commands are executed, these database settings are not affected.

11. You have a primary and a secondary filegroup on separate drives. A database backup is performed at 3 a.m. A differential backup is performed at 12 p.m. A secondary filegroup backup is performed at 9 a.m. and 2 p.m.

Transaction logs are backed up every hour. All data resides in the secondary filegroup, and the primary filegroup is rarely modified. The disk on which the secondary filegroup resides fails at 2:30, and you know the primary file has not been modified. How can you recover to the point of failure?

A. Restore the database backup, the differential backup, and each transaction log backup up until 2 p.m.

B. Back up the active transaction log, and restore the secondary filegroup backup and each transaction log backup.

C. Restore the database backup, the filegroup backup, and each transaction log backup.

D. Restore the differential backup and each transaction log backup.

12. You have Merge replication set up, with a single publisher and multiple subscribers. The Distributor is on a separate server. You back up the Publisher, Distributor, and all subscribers nightly. The Publisher fails. How can you recover?

A. Restore the Publisher database.
   Synchronize each subscribing database.

B. Restore the Publisher database.
   Restore the Distribution database and snapshot folder.
   Synchonize each subscribing database.

C. Restore the Publisher database.

D. Restore the Publisher database.
   Restore the Distributor database.

13. You create a full backup and three log backups every day.
   Full backup at 3 a.m.
   Log backup at 9 a.m.
   Log backup at 1 p.m.
   Log backup at 4 p.m.

Your database gets corrupted after one of the employees updates a table at 3:30 p.m.

How can you restore your database to a point before the update?

A. Restore the full backup of 3 a.m. with NORECOVERY option.
   Restore the Log backup of 9 a.m. with NORECOVERY option.
   Restore the Log backup of 1 p.m. with NORECOVERY option.
   Restore the Log backup of 4 p.m. with RECOVERY option,
   STOPAT 3:29 p.m.

B. Restore the full backup of 3 a.m. with NORECOVERY option.
   Restore the Log backup of 9 a.m. with NORECOVERY option.
   Restore the Log backup of 1 p.m. with NORECOVERY option.
   Restore the Log backup of 4 p.m. with NORECOVERY option,
   STOPAT 3:29 p.m.

C. Restore the full backup of 3 a.m. with NORECOVERY option.
   Restore the Log backup of 4 p.m. with RECOVERY,
   STOPAT 3:29 p.m.

D. Restore the full backup of 3 a.m. with NORECOVERY option.
   Restore the Log backup of 4 p.m. with NORECOVERY,
   STOPAT 3:29 p.m.

---

exam
Ⓦatch   *It is not possible to restore a partial transaction log backup using the Enterprise Manager interface.*

---

14. The following sequence of events occurs:
    10:00 Transaction 1 begins
    10:05 Transaction 2 begins
    10:10 Database backup begins
    10:12 Transaction 2 is committed
    10:14 Transaction 3 begins
    10:15 Transaction 2 is committed
    10:16 Database backup completes

10:17 Transaction 1 is committed
10:18 Transaction 3 is committed
10:25 Media failure
To what point can you recover the database?

A. Transaction 3 is committed.

B. Transactions 1 and 3 are committed.

C. Transaction 2 is committed.

D. Transactions 1, 2, and 3 are committed.

15. You back up the database as follows:
Sunday 12 p.m. full backup
Monday and Wednesday 5 p.m. differential backup
Every day at 2 p.m. transaction log backup
The transaction log and primary data file are located on a mirrored drive.
The secondary database files are located on an array. The array fails on
Thursday at 1 p.m. How do you recover?

A. Restore Wednesday's backup and the active transaction log.

B. Restore Sunday's backup, Wednesday's backup, and the active
transaction log.

C. Restore Sunday's backup, restore Monday's backup, and restore
Wednesday's backup.

D. Restore Sunday's backup.

16. You've added a database file since your last full backup. Your database
fails, and you begin a restore operation. What must you do to restore the
database?

A. Nothing, restore as normal.

B. Add an ALTER DATABASE statement to the restore script.

C. You cannot restore the database.

D. Delete the file in Explorer.

17. You upgraded a SQL 6.5 database to SQL 7.0, and you've installed a new server. You decide to use the old server as the standby server and the new server as the production server. You back up the database on the new production server, and you attempt to restore to the standby server using RESTORE with STANDBY. Why does the restore fail?

A. You should use the NORECOVERY option.

B. You cannot restore backups to a different server.

C. You should use the RECOVERY option.

D. The standby server is set to 6.5 compatibility mode.

18. The SALES database has three filegroups: a primary filegroup stored on a mirrored drive with the transaction log, a SALES filegroup containing the ORDERS table and indexes, and a CUSTOMERS filegroup containing the CUSTOMER table and indexes. A full backup is performed on the SALES database every Friday at 9 p.m. A CUSTOMERS filegroup backup is performed every Tuesday and Thursday at 9 p.m. A SALES filegroup backup is performed every Monday and Wednesday at 9 p.m. Transaction logs are backed up every day at 12 p.m. and 6 p.m. At 9 a.m. on Thursday morning, a user runs a DELETE statement on the ORDERS table and deletes all the orders. What is the best way to recover the table?

A. Back up the active transaction log.
   Restore the Wednesday SALES filegroup backup.
   Restore the active transaction log with the STOPAT option.

B. Restore the Wednesday SALES filegroup backup.

C. Restore Friday's backup.
   Restore Tuesday's backup.
   Restore Wednesday's backup.

D. Run a ROLLBACK operation.

19. You need to perform a one-time restore from the production server to the development server. The production server has two tape drives and the development server has one. What is the best way to restore the database to the development server?

A. Back up the production database using one tape drive, and restore to development.

B. Copy the .MDB files to the development server and use sp_attach_db.

C. Use Snapshot replication to copy the data from production to development.

D. Back up the production database using both tape drives, restore to development using one tape drive.

20. You have a production DEC Alpha SQL 7.0 server. You want to implement a standby server on an Intel server. How can you best accomplish this?

A. Use DTS to move data to the Intel server.

B. Back up the DEC server, and restore to the Intel server using the STANDBY option.

C. Use bcp to move the data to the Intel server.

D. Copy the database files to the Intel server.

21. You need to restore the backup shown here to a different database as a standby server.

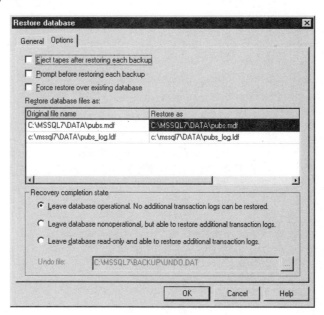

What options do you need to select?

A. Select "Leave database read-only and able to restore additional transaction logs".

B. Select "Leave database operational. No additional transaction logs can be restored".

C. Select "Leave database nonoperational, but able to restore additional transaction logs".

D. None of the above

22. A full backup is performed on the FINANCE database every Sunday. On Wednesday at 9 p.m. a differential backup is performed. Transaction logs are backed up every day at 5 p.m. On Friday the database fails; however, you are missing the tape from Thursday's transaction log backup. What is the last point you can restore to?

A. Friday

B. Thursday

C. Wednesday

D. Sunday

23. You are restoring a database from the following backup scenario:
Sunday full backup
Tuesday 6 p.m. differential backup
Thursday 6 p.m. differential backup
Every day at 12 p.m. transaction log backup
Failure occurred Friday at 1 p.m.
You are restoring the Thursday differential backup, and you accidentally use the RECOVER option. How do you proceed?

A. Begin the restore again, and apply Sunday's full backup, Thursday's differential backup, and Friday's log backup.

B. Continue restoring Friday's log backup.

C. Reapply Thursday's differential backup with the NORECOVERY option.

D. Nothing; leave the point of restore at Thursday.

Transferring Data

1. You are the DBA for a sports statistics service. You have created a DTS package that imports data from several different information providers into your SQL Server database. During the football season, you need to update the statistics 15 minutes after the last game of the day, but because you do not know when the last football game will be completed, you cannot schedule this process ahead of time. You want to give Tom, your intern, the ability to execute the package, but not make changes to it. How could you do this?

A. Give Tom the operator password but not the owner password.

B. Give Tom the owner password but not the operator password.

C. In User Manager, assign Tom to the DTSOwner group, but not the DTSOperator group.

D. In User Manager, assign Tom to the DTSOperator group, but not the DTSOwner group.

2. You are using Data Transformation Services to move content into a SQL Server table. You step through the Data Import Wizard, and you define the source of the table to import. You then select the "Advanced" button on the Transformations tab, to define the field mapping for the new table. The source field can store decimal values but not nulls, while the destination field can store only integers though it can store nulls. Under the "Advanced" button of the Transformations tab, what flags would you have to set to enable this conversion?

A. "Allow data type promotion"

B. "Allow data type demotion"

C. "Allow null conversion"

D. "Default Transformation Flags—all possible conversions are allowed"

3. You need to combine content from a supplier's Web page and an internal Oracle database into a SQL Server table. The conversion process will be complex, requiring more functionality than you could put in a single query. How could you use DTS to do this?

A. Create Connection Objects that use DataPump tasks to move the content from one OLEDB object to another, and then create Task Objects to sequence these Connection Objects.

B. Create Connection Objects that use DataPump tasks to move the content from one OLEDB object to another, and then create Step Objects to sequence these Connection Objects.

C. Create Step Objects that use DataPump tasks to move the content from one OLEDB object to another, and then create Task Objects to sequence these Step Objects.

D. Create Task Objects that use DataPump tasks to move the content from one OLEDB object to another, and then create Step Objects to sequence these Task Objects.

4. You need to export your Authors table into a text file for a user who needs to import it into a Lotus 1-2-3 spreadsheet. You create a DTS package to create this text file, and the format of the output is defined as shown below:

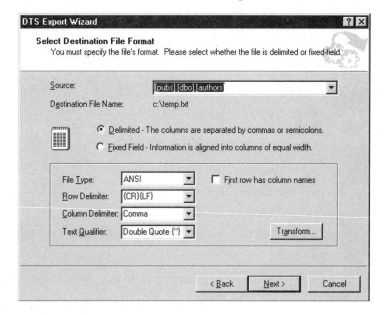

After the text file is created, you open the resulting file in Wordpad. What should you expect to see on the first line?

A. au_id, au_lname, au_fname, phone, address, city, state, zip, contract

B. "172-32-1176", "White", "Johnson", "408 496-7223", "10932 Bigger Rd.", "Menlo Park", "CA", 94025, -1

C. au_id, au_lname, au_fname, phone, address, city, state, zip, contract {CR}{LF}

D. "172-32-1176", "White", "Johnson", "408 496-7223", "10932 Bigger Rd.", "Menlo Park", "CA", 94025, -1 {CR}{LF}

5. Situation: Your company, which has standardized on SQL Server 7.0, has recently purchased a company that uses Oracle databases for its mission-critical applications and Access databases for some specialized needs. You want to provide this content to your SQL Server users. Required results: Have all the data from Oracle, Access, and SQL Server available in real-time to users with SQL Server accounts. Optional desired results: Minimize the maintenance required; allow all the data sources to be referenced and combined in a single query. Proposed solution: Use the DTS Import Wizard and DTS Export Wizard to define how the content should be provided to SQL Server. Which of the following results does the proposed solution produce?

A. The proposed solution produces the required result and both of the optional results.

B. The proposed solution produces the required result and only one of the optional results.

C. The proposed solution produces the required result and neither of the optional results.

D. The proposed solution doesn't produce the required result.

6. Every morning at 3 a.m. for the last six months, your system has downloaded a data file containing pricing information from a vendor's FTP site and called BCP from a batch file to import it into a SQL Server table named "Prices." There are three INT fields in this table: PARTNUMBER, PRICE, and INSTOCK. This week, your vendor has informed you that it

will be changing the format of its FTP file to now be in the following format: DISCOUNT, PARTNUMBER, PRICE. (The vendor is eliminating the INSTOCK field because it has vertically integrated with its main supplier, so all products are always "in stock.") If you do not need this new DISCOUNT field, which of the following is the best approach to import these new fields?

A. Add the DISCOUNT field to your pricing table and import as usual.

B. Create a new format file to map the new fields appropriately.

C. Write a batch file to modify the input text file before the import, deleting the extra column and adding a fixed blank field at the end of each line.

D. Create a new table for the new import format, and use the SELECT INTO statement to copy only the needed columns into your Prices table.

7. The budget director has constructed the annual corporate budgets manually in Access and provided a text export ("budg.txt") from this database for you to import into a SQL Server table ("budget"). The table is properly formatted with a tab separating the fields and a newline separating the records. In the Access table he created every field as a text field, including the date fields. For employees for whom there was no available start date, he entered "9/99/9999." There are 207 records in the text file, and of these records 16 have a "9/99/9999" value in this field. You need to map this field to STARTDATE (a datetime field) in your SQL Server table. All of the other fields in these 16 records are properly populated. What will happen when you try to execute the following BCP file?
bcp "pubs corporate..budget" in budg.txt -c -U"correctusername" -P"correctpassword"

A. No records will be loaded.

B. All the records will be loaded, but the STARTDATE will be NULL in these 16 records.

C. The records with a valid STARTDATE will be imported, and the records with invalid STARTDATES will not be imported.

D. The records with a valid STARTDATE will be imported, and the records with invalid STARTDATES will be written to a log file.

8. A user informs you that he has accidentally made inappropriate changes to a table, and he does not remember what the values used to be. He wants to know if you can restore the whole table to the content it had a week ago. The table definition is as follows:

```
CREATE TABLE dbo.Patient (
    PatientID int IDENTITY (1, 1) NOT NULL ,
    LastName varchar (16) NOT NULL ,
    FirstName varchar (16) NULL ,
    BloodType varchar (2) NOT NULL
)
```

Fortunately, you have a copy of the old data in an Excel spreadsheet, and after a little manipulation, you are able to use BCP to import this content back to SQL Server. Now the views that reference the table are returning unusual results. Some of the views return no records, and other views return information for the wrong patients. Of the following, which is the most likely to fix the situation?

A. Add the "k" flag to the BCP import.

B. Add the "Usa" parameter to the BCP import.

C. Add the "E" flag to the BCP import.

D. Add the "F" flag to the BCP import.

9. You have just used BCP to import 180,000 records into your PARTS table. You wanted to use fast bulk copy mode, so you turned on the "Select Into / Bulk Copy Files" flag, and you dropped the table indexes before importing the data. Assuming you want the new data to have the same restrictions as the existing data, which of the following actions should you take now?

A. Populate default values for columns omitted from the field list.

B. Convert imported data to the appropriate data type.

C. Delete records that violate table constraints.

D. Re-create the indexes for that table.

10. You receive information from a vendor in a single BCP file. In SQL Server, though, you store this content in two separate tables, and both of these tables need to be updated by this import. You have created a view that selects columns from your two tables, to simulate the layout of the vendor file. Of the following, which is the best way to import this content?

A. BCP the file directly into the view.
B. BCP the file into a global temporary table, and then loop through record by record to populate tables.
C. BCP the file into a global temporary table, and then use two INSERT statements to populate both tables.
D. BCP the file into a global temporary table, and then use INSERT INTO to populate the view.

11. You are exporting data from your employee table using BCP. If the BCP operation yields the results illustrated here, which of the following statements are true?

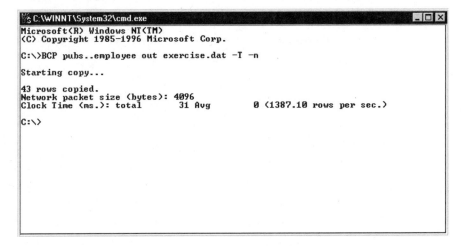

A. The "exercise.dat" file can be imported into SQL Server 6.5.
B. The "exercise.dat" file can be imported into Excel.
C. BCP logged in as SA to export the data.
D. BCP overwrote any existing text file named "exercise.dat".

12. You need to assign 10 new employees to offices. The definition of the table is as follows:

```
CREATE TABLE dbo.Offices (
   EmpId int IDENTITY (1, 1) NOT NULL ,
   LastName varchar (32) NOT NULL ,
   FirstName varchar (32) NOT NULL ,
   OfficeID int NOT NULL
)
```

You do not have the administrative tools on your own machine. Rather than using T-SQL, you much prefer to use Access to link to SQL Server and then edit the table like a spreadsheet. You want to insert all the needed blank records using T-SQL and then edit the content in Access. What happens when you execute the following statement?

```
INSERT Offices DEFAULT VALUES
```

A. In the new record, LastName will be NULL and OfficeID will be a zero.

B. In the new record, LastName will be a zero-length string and OfficeID will be 0.

C. In the new record, LastName will be a zero-length string and OfficeID will be NULL.

D. The new record will not be inserted.

13. Every week, you need to create a report describing the total sales generated that week from each state. Because you do not want this data to change during the week, you want to use SELECT INTO instead of a view. You create a destination table with the following definition:

```
CREATE TABLE dbo.StateSales (
   State varchar (2) NOT NULL ,
   TotalSales real NOT NULL
)
```

You know that some of the fields in the AllSales table are sometimes unpopulated, so you create the following query to test the integrity of the data:

```
SELECT STATE, Sum(Sales) AS TOTALSALES FROM ALLSALES GROUP BY STATE
```

The results of this query are as follows:

```
STATE              TOTALSALES
(null)             11
Ohio               16
Pennsylvania       22
Kentucky           9
```

Satisfied, you then use the INSERT INTO command to use this query to populate the SALESREPORT table. What happens when this statement is run?

A. No rows will be added to the table.

B. One row will be added to the table.

C. Three rows will be added to the table.

D. Four rows will be added to the table.

14. Situation: You are responsible for maintaining a facilities database. You need to perform INSERT INTO statements on this table. You learn that your database administrator plans to change the design of the tables frequently. Required result: Your SQL statement must still work if the DBA adds a column to the base table.

Optional desired results: Your SQL statement should still work if a field is renamed by the DBA; it should still work if the table is recreated with columns in a different order.

Proposed solution: Create a view that references only the needed columns, and perform the insert into this view instead of the base table. Omit the column list from the Insert statement.

Which of the following results does the proposed solution produce?

A. The proposed solution produces the required result and both of the optional results.

B. The proposed solution produces the required result and only one of the optional results.

C. The proposed solution produces the required result and none of the optional results.

D. The proposed solution doesn't produce the required result.

15. Your company has recently purchased another company, and you need to add several records to your SalesPerson table. The table has the following definition:

```
CREATE TABLE dbo.SalesPeople (
    EmpNumber int IDENTITY (1, 1) NOT NULL ,
EmpUnique UNIQUEIDENTIFIER
    DateHired datetime NOT NULL,
    HomeOffice varchar (20) NULL
)
```

To save time, you want to omit the field list in your INSERT INTO statements. How many parameters do you need to include in the column list?

A. 4

B. 3

C. 2

D. 1

16. Your DBA prefers people to use views instead of tables, and she has provided you with a simple view that returns all the records from a table, while excluding unneeded columns. The DBA then noticed that there was some redundancy in this table, so she normalized the table into two tables, and then created a new view that joined these two tables. The new view and old view return identical results when you use Select, but how will this affect updates?

A. You cannot insert a new record, regardless of how many tables are referenced in the field list.

B. You can insert a new record, but only if fields from only one table are referenced in the field list.

C. You can insert a new record, even if fields from both tables are referenced in the field list, but only one of the tables will be updated.

D. You can insert a new record, even if fields from both tables are referenced in the field list, and both tables will be updated.

17. You are creating summary tables to analyze the growth of your franchises. You create the following query:

```
SELECT state, Count(state) AS StateCount FROM stores GROUP BY state
```

This query outputs the following results:

```
state StateCount
----- -----------
CA    3
OR    1
WA    2
(3 row(s) affected)
```

What would happen if you execute the following query?

```
SELECT state, Count(state) AS StateCount
INTO #temptable
FROM stores
WHERE state < "AK"GROUP BY state
ORDER BY state
COMPUTE COUNT(STATE) by state
```

A. The query will fail, but it would succeed if the WHERE clause were replaced with a HAVING clause.

B. The query will fail, but it would succeed if the WHERE clause were removed.

C. The query will fail, but it would succeed if the COMPUTE BY clause were removed.

D. The query will succeed.

18. You have four servers in branch offices. You want to make sure that the ID fields in the tables do not duplicate each other, so you have carefully chosen your seeds and increments for your identity fields so they do not overlap. For example, these are the ID fields for the first five records in each of your four branches:

- Cleveland: 1000, 1004, 1008, 1012, 1016

- New York: 1001, 1005, 1009, 1013, 1017

- Los Angeles: 1002, 1006, 1010, 1014, 1018

- Chicago: 1003, 1007, 1011, 1015, 1019

You are performing some data maintenance on the Cleveland table. If the first line in the following sequence returns "26,500", what value does the last line in the following sequence return?

```
SELECT max(ID) FROM Sales
SELECT * into #tempdelme from Sales
INSERT #tempdelme DEFAULT VALUES
SELECT max(ID) FROM #tempdelme
```

A. 1

B. 4

C. 26500

D. 26504

19. You want to insert content into the PUBS table using fast BCP. You view
the options associated with this database, as displayed in this illustration:

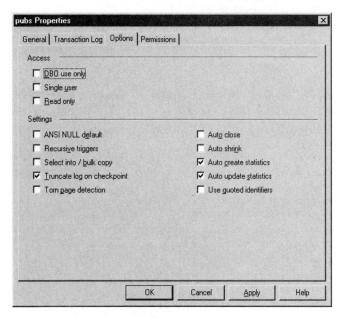

Which of the following changes should you make?

A. Set "DBO use only" to checked.

B. Set "Read only" to checked.

C. Set "Select Into/ Bulk Copy" to checked.

D. Set "Truncate log on checkpoint" to unchecked.

20. You are performing data migration that will take several steps. You have combined the first several needed tables into a temporary table named "#temporarynames". You perform queries on this temporary table and are satisfied with the content in it. You then realize that to populate the final column in your temporary table, however, you need to reference an additional table. You do not have permissions to this table. When you track down the table's owner and log on as her, you can see that additional table you need but not the temp table you just created. If you go back to your own account, what statement could you run to fix this?

A. Select * into #pubs.temporarynames2 from #temporarynames.

B. Select * into #temporarynames2 from #temporarynames with public option.

C. Select * into ##temporarynames2 from #temporarynames.

D. Select * into @temporarynames2 from #temporarynames.

21. You are creating a new user account for an individual who will have to maintain his own very large tables. Which one of the roles shown in the following illustration must this user be in to use BULK INSERT?

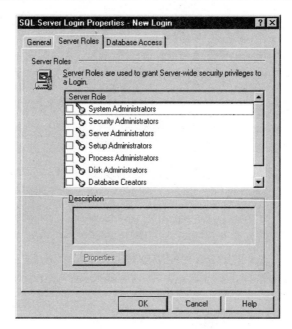

A. System Administrators

B. Security Administrators

C. Server Administrators

D. Setup Administrators

22. Your payroll data is stored on an IBM System/360. You do not need real-time access to this data because it is updated only twice a month, but your users do want to be able to reference this data in their SQL Server queries. Assuming that the System/360 records are never deleted but are updated, which of the following would be the best option for using Host Data Replication (HDR) to get the most recent content from DB2 to SQL Server?

A. Maintain a timestamp field in your DB2 tables, and configure HDR to use Snapshot replication to retrieve the changed records.

B. Maintain an identity field in your DB2 tables, and configure HDR to use Snapshot replication to retrieve the new records.

C. Use Incremental replication to copy only the records that have changed since the last update.

D. Use Incremental replication to copy only the records that have been created since the last update.

23. You need to retrieve order inventory. The actual order fulfillment is maintained on a mainframe database. Your salespeople need to know if they can make a shipment while they are on the phone with potential customers, so they need to view real-time inventory data. Which of the following solutions could provide what is needed?

A. Use the ODBC Driver for SNA.

B. Use the ODBC Driver for DB2.

C. Use HDR Replication for the needed vertical subset.

D. Use HDR Replication for the needed horizontal subset.

24. Current situation: You are moving your SQL Server database from a 7.0 server with a single processor to a 7.0 server with a dual processor. Your users want to have both servers available for a few months until they have confidence in the reliability and accessibility of the new machine.

Required result: Migrate all the records in all the tables from the old server to the new.

Optional desired results: Migrate all the table constraints on the new server; migrate the table security rights on the new server.

Proposed solution: Create a linked server connecting through OLE DB to the new database from the old database, and use SELECT INTO statements to copy over the tables one at a time.

Which of the following results does the proposed solution produce?

A. The proposed solution produces the required result and both of the optional results.

B. The proposed solution produces the required result and only one of the optional results.

C. The proposed solution produces the required result and none of the optional results.

D. The proposed solution doesn't produce the required result.

25. You are moving your home office from Chicago to New York, and you need to move the content and accounts on your Chicago SQL 7.0 server to an identically configured server in New York. Which of the following would be the best solution?

A. Use Transfer Manager to move the data and accounts.

B. Use Transfer Manager to move the data, and then create the needed accounts manually on the destination server.

C. Use DTS to move the data and accounts.

D. Use DTS to move the data, and then create the needed accounts manually on the destination server.

Replication

1. You are implementing snapshot replication to provide lookup tables to remote sites. You create a destination database at each Subscriber. You use the Push Subscription Wizard to create a push subscription. You create a

job to start the Distribution Agent for the subscription. Which server does the Distribution Agent run on?

A. Publisher

B. Subscriber

C. Distributor

D. Publisher and Distributor

2. You have a traveling sales force that needs copies of the Product database on their laptops. The database is 2GB. They will not be modifying data, and they will need to update their local copy of the database when they dial in. Which is the best type of replication for the sales force?

A. Snapshot

B. Transactional with pull subscriptions

C. Transactional with Immediate Updating Subscribers

D. Merge

3. SQL uses the publisher/subscriber metaphor to implement replication design. As a publisher, you have made several articles available within several publications. What can be subscribed to?

A. Publisher

B. Articles

C. Publications

D. None of the above

exam
ⓦatch

The primary difference between immediate and latent guaranteed consistency is timing. Despite that, time is not the only significant difference between two-phase commit and replication. It is important to understand that two-phase commit transactions must be coded as such and are therefore a design time decision. Replication services are a server-based solution. They can be added at any time without changing the application or its parameters. Remembering this difference will help you to eliminate multiple options on exam questions.

4. You have set up replication from a single publisher to multiple subscribers. When changes are made at the Publisher, these changes are made at all the subscribers within seconds. The subscribers do not modify data, and transactional consistency is high. What type of replication is this?

A. Transactional replication

B. Snapshot replication

C. Merge replication

D. Transactional replication with Immediate Updating Subscribers

5. You have snapshot replication scheduled to run at 9 a.m. every day. Your users are complaining that they cannot modify the data between 9 and 10 a.m. How can you resolve this?

A. Schedule update statistics for 8 a.m.

B. Configure replication to not lock the table.

C. Schedule the replication for off-peak hours.

D. Do not allow users in the database between 9 and 10 a.m.

6. You have a PERSONNEL table in your HR database that a remote site needs to read on a daily basis. The remote site should not see the Social Security nor the Salary information. How would you implement this?

A. Merge replication

B. Transactional replication with horizontal filtering on the table

C. Transactional replication with vertical filtering on the table

D. Snapshot replication with vertical filtering on the table

7. You are implementing snapshot replication. You have a 25GB database, and you are replicating the entire database to a second SQL server. The Publisher and Distributor are on the same server. You have a 45GB array on your source server, with 20GB free. The second server is on a different subnet. Why wouldn't you be able to replicate?

A. You can't replicate 25GB of data.

B. You can't replicate 25GB of data to a server on a different subnet.

C. You don't have enough disk space.

D. None of the above

8. You have a separate Publisher, Distributor, and multiple Subscribers, and you are using transactional replication. Where does the Log Reader Agent execute?

A. Publisher

B. Distributor

C. Subscriber

D. Publisher and Distributor

exam
ⓦatch

SQL Server does not implement any technology to stop users from making updates to a destination database. This must be handled in the application. All changes made directly to a subscribing database are overwritten when the next snapshot is applied.

9. The central SQL database is located in Texas. There is a 128KB line to New York, and four branches are located in the New England area. The branches are connected to the New York office with 56KB lines. How would you implement replication?

A. Publisher/Distributor in Texas, Publishing Subscriber in New York, and Subscribers at the branches

B. Publisher/Distributor in Texas, Subscribers at all other locations

C. Publisher in Texas, Distributor in New York, and Subscribers at the branches

D. Subscriber in Texas, Publishers at all other locations

10. You are in the initial stages of planning for replication. There are three design elements you need to consider while designing your replication strategy. What are these elements? (Choose all that apply.)

A. Data consistency

B. Site autonomy

C. Partitioning data to avoid conflicts

D. Types of replication

11. You have three sites connected to your corporate headquarters by T1 lines. All sites need access to the CUSTOMER database. All sites will be modifying the database and will require the best degree of data consistency possible, with little autonomy. Data consistency is more important than latency. What type of replication should you implement?

A. Transactional replication with Immediate Updating Subscribers

B. Merge replication

C. Snapshot replication

D. Transactional replication

12. Your company has 75 retail locations, linked by 128KB lines. Your product database is located at headquarters. The main table, PRODUCTS, is updated frequently. The retail locations need a copy of the PRODUCTS table to ensure accurate sales, but you need to minimize network traffic. Which type of replication should you implement?

A. Transactional replication with a corporate Publisher/Distributor and each location as a Subscriber

B. Transactional replication with a corporate Publisher, and a Distributor and Subscriber at each location

C. Snapshot replication with a corporate Publisher/Distributor, and each location as a Subscriber

D. Merge replication

13. You have implemented merge replication. Each Subscriber is a local subscription. Subscriber A changes the PRICE column to 3.00, Subscriber B changes the PRICE column to 4.00, and Subscriber C changes the PRICE column to 4.50 on the same record. Subscriber A merges with the Publisher first, C is second, and B is last. What is the PRICE column's value?

A. 3.00

B. 4.00

C. 4.50

D. 3.83

14. Current situation: Corporate headquarters has a SALES database that reflects a high volume of updates. The Accounting office needs access to the SALES database to run reports. The three retail sites need to update the SALES database with orders. The Accounting office is connected with a 56KB line to corporate headquarters. The three retail sites are connected with a 256KB connection to corporate headquarters. You need to set up a replication strategy.

    Required result: Achieve a high degree of data consistency between Corporate and the retail sites while allowing all sites to modify data.

    Optional results: Maintain a read-only database for the Accounting Office. Minimize network traffic.

    Proposed solution: Implement transactional replication with Immediate Updating Subscribers between Corporate and the three retail sites, with Corporate as the Publisher and the sites as Subscribers. Implement snapshot replication between Corporate and the Accounting Office.

    Which of the following results does the proposed solution produce?

    A. The proposed solution meets the required result and all optional results.

    B. The proposed solution meets the required result and the first optional result.

    C. The proposed solution meets the required result and the second optional result.

    D. The proposed solution does not meet the required result.

It is important to understand that merge replication is the only type of replication that will generate conflicts and thus require conflict resolution. There are no priority issues for snapshot or transactional replication. Merge replication is the greatest replication change in SQL Server 7.0. You will most likely see multiple questions on this topic in the exam.

15. Your company's offices are all over the world. You need to replicate a SQL 7 database from your headquarters in Dallas to all offices, as shown in the following diagram. What replication strategy should you implement?

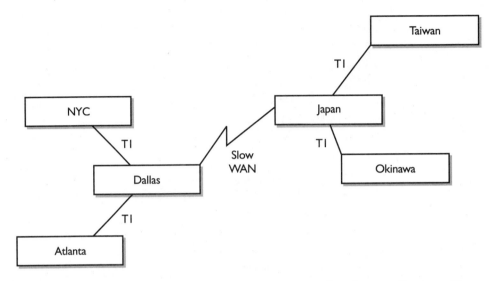

   A. Publisher in Dallas, Distributor in Japan, Subscribers in all other offices

   B. Publisher/Distributor in Dallas, Publishing Subscriber in Japan, Subscribers in all other offices

   C. Publisher/Distributor in Dallas, Subscribers in all other offices

   D. Publisher in Japan, Distributor in Dallas, and Subscribers in all other offices

16. You want to enable your database for Internet replication. You want to allow push subscriptions only. You've set up TCP/IP on the server. What else do you need to do? (Choose all that apply.)

   A. Set the @enabled_for_internet property of the publication to TRUE.

   B. Install IIS on the Distributor.

   C. Set up the MSSQL7\REPLDATA\FTP directory as an FTP site.

   D. Set up the Publisher inside the firewall and the Distributor outside the firewall.

17. Your company has five warehouses. Each warehouse has a SQL sever and tracks only its own inventory. The corporate sales office needs all the inventory information for reporting. What type of replication will enable the corporate office to access all the inventory information?

A. Snapshot with warehouses as Subscribers, sales office as Publisher/Distributor

B. Transactional with warehouses as publishers, sales office as distributor/Subscriber

C. Transactional with warehouses as Publishers/Distributors, sales office as Subscriber

D. Merge with warehouses as Subscribers, sales office as Publisher

18. The performance on your Publisher/Distributor is poor, and you have decided to move the distribution database to a different server. What do you have to do to move it?

A. Configure the current Publisher to use the distribution database on the new server.

B. Disable the current publication and enable a new publication to use the distribution database on the remote server. Re-create all publications and subscribers.

C. Back up the current distribution database and restore to the new server.

D. Drag and drop the publications to the new distribution database in Enterprise Manager.

19. You want to enable this publication for Internet replication:

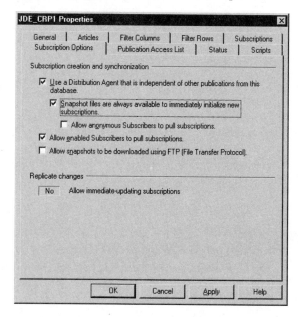

You will have a large number of subscribers, and security is not a concern. Which of the following changes should you make?

A. Set "Use a Distribution Agent that is independent of other publications from this database" to unchecked.

B. Set "Allow snapshots to be downloaded using FTP" to checked.

C. Set "Allow anonymous Subscribers to pull subscriptions" to checked.

D. None of the above

20. You have an Oracle database you want to publish to a SQL Server 7 publication. You are using ODBC drivers. What type of replication can you use?

A. Pull subscription

B. Both push and pull subscriptions

C. Push subscription

D. None of the above

21. You want to view the replication history of a subscriber. You have a separate Publisher, Distributor, and Subscriber. Which server would you look at to view the history of the subscriber?

A. Publisher

B. Distributor

C. Subscriber

D. You can install the Replication Monitor on your workstation.

22. Your company has 150 stores. Each store needs to modify the SALES_ORDER database on a frequent basis. Not all stores have permanent connections to Corporate, where the SALES_ORDER database is located. What type of replication should you use?

A. Transactional

B. Snapshot

C. Merge

D. Transactional with Immediate Updating Subscribers

23. You've set up merge replication between four sites. Site A has been assigned a conflict priority of 99.99, Site B has been assigned a conflict priority of 95, Site C has a conflict priority of 5, and Site D has a conflict priority of 50. Sites B, C, and D update the same row simultaneously. Who wins the conflict?

A. Site B

B. Site C

C. Site D

D. Site A decides the conflict.

24. Current situation: You have a central SQL 7.0 server. Your sales force needs to update the SALES database, but they are not always in the office to modify the data. The laptops they are using are a couple of years old, and they won't be getting new ones until next year, but they are using Access 2000.
Required result: Enable the sales force to update the central SALES database with sales orders.
Optional results: Minimize software costs. Minimize installation time.
Proposed solution: Set up merge replication with SQL 7 and Access 2000.
Which of the following results does the proposed solution produce?

A. The proposed solution meets the required result and both optional results.

B. The proposed solution meets the required result and the first optional result.

C. The proposed solution meets the required result and the second optional result.

D. The proposed solution does not meet the required result.

Implementing Replication Scenarios

1. Your company has a sales database that is distributed across a number of regions. You have decided to start replicating this information to the individual sales representatives. In order to keep the data manageable, you have decided to replicate only the data that pertains to customers of that sales representative in the sales representative's region. This is an example of what type of filtering?

A. Vertical

B. Geographical

C. Horizontal

D. Zone

---

2. SQL Server is acting as a replication publisher. This system is somewhat overused, and your replication requirements only demand an update of your branch offices once a week. You would like to set up a replication model that will produce the least demand on your publishing server on an ongoing basis. Which replication model should you choose?

A. Transactional

B. Snapshot

C. Two-phase commit protocol

D. Merge

3. Transactions are a basic component of replication. A transaction is defined through a set of criteria commonly referred to as the ACID test. Which of the following is not an element of the ACID test for transactions?

A. Atomicity

B. Consistency

C. Isolation

D. Distribution

4. You are implementing merge replication between your Los Angeles office and your Hong Kong office. Your CIO informs you that decisions in these locations will be made based on this data on a regular basis, so the data must always be the same. Is there a problem with your replication scheme?

A. No. Merge replication will meet all the requirements. It will be the least bandwidth-intensive form of replication and provide the best performance for applications in both offices.

B. No. Merge replication will provide the best method of replication because it is the only one that meets the requirements you have been given.

C. Yes. Merge replication requires that all servers be synced. The differences in time zones will generate an inordinate amount of validation at each site and will adversely affect the performance of the applications.

D. Yes. Merge replication does not provide immediate, guaranteed consistency.

5. You are configuring an environment for merge replication. You know that the table that needs to be replicated needs a mechanism to uniquely identify every row in every copy of the table. This mechanism provides a unique row identifier. You decide to add a column to the table for this purpose. What attribute should you set for the column?

A. UNIQUE

B. CLUSTERED

C. ROWGUIDCOL

D. TIMESTAMP

6. Site autonomy refers to the effect of one site's operations on another. There is complete site autonomy if one site's ability to do its normal work is independent of its connectivity to another site. Which replication option provides the most site autonomy?

A. Merge

B. Transactional

C. Snapshot

D. Two-phase commit protocol

7. What option can be used with snapshot replication to allow subscribers to make updates to data, thereby increasing the site autonomy of the subscriber?

   A. Two-phase commit
   B. Immediate Updating Subscribers
   C. Immediate Merging Subscribers
   D. Temporary merge replication

8. You are configuring merge replication and are having trouble. You keep checking the subscriber for signs that the replication process has begun, but the new tables haven't yet been created. You determine that there is probably a problem with one of the agents. Which agent would you troubleshoot first?

   A. Merge
   B. Snapshot
   C. Log Reader
   D. Distribution

9. If you experience difficulties with merge replication after the initial snapshot has been successfully delivered to the subscriber, there is one particular agent that you should focus on. Which agent moves and reconciles incremental data changes that occurred after the initial snapshot was created?

   A. Merge
   B. Snapshot
   C. Log Reader
   D. Distribution

exam
Ⓦatch *When running a SQL Server database in read-only mode, it is critical to understand that the database cannot be in read-only mode during the replication period. For this reason, it works best with snapshot replication.*

10. You are concerned about your Publisher being inundated with replication requests from Subscribers during peak hours of operation. This could potentially bring down the Publisher and the databases on the system. In order to let the Publisher control when replication occurs, what type of replication would you set up?

   A. Pull

   B. Push

   C. Merge

   D. Transactional

11. In a pull subscription, who is responsible for initiating the replication process?

   A. Publisher

   B. Distributor

   C. Subscriber

   D. User

12. Replication does not seem to be functioning properly in your environment. You suspect agent problems, but have not been able to determine which agent or agents may be malfunctioning. Which tools would you use to monitor the overall performance of all of the agents:

   A. Performance Monitor

   B. Task history

   C. Replication Monitor

   D. SQL Enterprise Manager

exam
Ⓦatch

In both a multipublisher and a multimaster model, data is being edited on multiple servers, but they are different configurations. A multimaster environment has multiple servers (one publisher and one or more subscribers) that may edit the same data. In a multipublisher environment, there are multiple servers editing different data.

13. Replication data validation routines use two values to determine whether data at the publisher and data at the subscriber have diverged. If the data has diverged, then replication needs to occur. What values are used to detect data divergence?

A. Timestamp

B. Checksum

C. Row count

D. ROWGUID

Setting Up Replication

1. Each replication agent supports a set of run-time parameters. The parameters can be set through the command line of the agent job. When a replication agent is created, it is associated with an agent profile, maintained at the distributor. The agent profile contains a set of parameters to be used each time the agent runs. During the startup process, each agent logs into the distributor and queries for the parameters in its profile. Using Enterprise Manager, in which of the following locations can you manage these profiles?

A. Create Distributor Wizard

B. Pull Subscription Wizard

C. Configure Publishing and Distribution Wizard

D. Create Publication Wizard

2. You are using the Pull Subscription Wizard to create a subscription. You are somewhat concerned that you were not prompted for any type of login or security-related information. You are concerned that your data may be open to anyone who can use the wizard. You discuss your concerns with another DBA and he assures you that the data is secure. What does the other DBA know that you don't?

A. The replication service is not properly installed.

B. The SQL Server Agent is running as a user in the publication access list.

C. The SQL Server Service is running as a user in the publications access list.

D. The other DBA has removed rights to the database for all user accounts except for the replication service account.

3. You need to create a publication, and you do not have SQL Enterprise Manager or any of the wizards available. You remember that all of the tasks that can be accomplished through the Create Publication Wizard can be accomplished through stored procedures. Which of the following stored procedures will NOT be used to create your publication?

A. SP_SCHEDULE_PUBLICATION

B. SP_GRANT_PUBLICATION_ACCESS

C. SP_ADDARTICLE

D. SP_ADDPUBLICATION

4. When designing your replication strategy you discover that you are required to limit the rows that are replicated to subscribers. For example, the sales office in London has no use for the sales data belonging to the sales office in Sydney. You were planning to use the wizards to configure replication. Is this still an option?

A. No. It isn't supported.

B. You must meet the requirement with user-written SELECT statements.

C. You must meet the requirement with user-written WHERE clauses.

D. Yes. Just use the GUI to select the records to publish.

5. When using the Create Publication Wizard, how do you specify which articles will be a part of the replication? Choose the most accurate statement.

A. Articles are added using the Add Article Wizard.

B. Articles must be added later using the sp_addarticle system-stored procedure.

C. The wizard allows you to configure one article per table.

D. The wizard creates one article per table and you must add any filters using the sp_addfilter system-stored procedure.

6. You have users in five locations that need a database solution that will allow them to edit their data in all five locations. They also need to have weekly data available from all offices in one location for reporting. Which replication configuration would you recommend?

A. Single publisher
B. Multisubscriber
C. Central subscriber
D. Anonymous subscriber

7. There are many advantages to allowing anonymous subscriptions. However, there is one big disadvantage. Which of the following is not an advantage of supporting anonymous subscriptions?

A. Facilitated administration
B. Lower overhead
C. Security
D. Internet subscribers

8. You have two offices that share data back and forth. Each office edits its own data locally and publishes it for read-only use by the other office. Are you in a multimaster configuration?

A. Yes. Whenever two sites move data back and forth between each other, each site is the master of its own data.
B. Yes. Anytime a database is segmented between two locations, even if one location only uses the data in read only form, there must be a master for each segment.
C. No. The data is only edited in one location.
D. No. Two or more sites can be controlled with a single master.

9. Site A updates accounts receivable information and replicates it to Site C. Sites A and C are connected by Site B, which contains a distribution database. What is the role being played by Site B?

A. Remote subscriber
B. Remote distributor
C. Publisher
D. Re-publisher

10. Site A and Site C are connected through Site B. Both A and C manage and publish data for subscription to one another. Site B contains the distribution database. Which of the following roles is the server in Site A NOT playing?

A. Subscriber

B. Publisher

C. Distributor

D. Database server

exam
⚠atch *It is important to remember that even when using the wizard, you must still enter the SQL Server syntax for the where clause to perform horizontal filtering. The wizard does not provide the graphical tools that are available with Microsoft Access.*

11. If you are using a roll-up server in your replication architecture so that all of your remote sites publish their data to a central roll-up server, which scenario does NOT describe the type of replication you are using?

A. Single subscriber

B. Multisubscriber

C. Central subscriber

D. Multipublisher

12. Your company is moving to a client-server architecture using SQL Server. Your company is convinced that it can save money and become more responsive to its customers by moving its orders database from the mainframe to Windows NT servers running SQL Server. To allow for scheduled maintenance and to provide fault tolerance, two SQL Servers will be configured. Both boxes should always contain the most up-to-date data. If one were to fail, the other would be put into production and no transactions should be lost. Which distributed data solution would you implement?

A. Transaction replication

B. Two-phase commit

C. Merge replication

D. Multisubscriber

13. Which server contains the master database?

A. Publisher

B. Distributor

C. Subscriber

D. Gateway

SQL Server 7.0 Administration Answers

Q & A

The answers to the questions are in boldface, followed by a brief explanation. Some of the explanations detail the logic you should use to choose the correct answer, while others give factual reasons why the answer is correct. If you miss several questions on a similar topic, you should review the corresponding section in the *MCDBA SQL Server 7 Administration Study Guide* before taking the test.

Microsoft SQL Server 7.0 Overview

1. ☑ **B.** When using Windows 95/98 clients, client applications must be configured to use TCP/IP as the default protocol because Named Pipes is not support by Windows 9*x*.

   ☒ **A,** each machine connected to the new server must reboot in order to make the first connection, is wrong because rebooting the machine won't do anything to help make a connection to the server. **C,** both the SQL Server and the client workstations need to be configured to use the correct protocol, NWLink, and **D,** the Windows 9*x* machines must be configured to use Named Pipes as their default protocol, are wrong because they are using the wrong protocol for a Windows NT-based SQL Server being accessed by Windows 9*x* clients.

2. ☑ **A.** Use the Model database to establish the desired default settings for all newly created databases. The Model database is one of SQL Server's system databases. It is used as the template for all newly created databases. Any settings established on the Model database will be reflected in all new databases.

   ☒ **D,** use the Master database to establish the desired default settings for all newly created databases, is wrong because it specifies the wrong database to use. The Master database is another of SQL Server's system databases. It contains information on the database server's content, and it contains administrative stored procedures and extended stored procedures that can be used to carry out many of the server's administrative tasks. **B,** use the Enterprise Manager options settings to restrict the size of newly created databases, is wrong because the Enterprise Manager itself has no way of making settings for new databases. **C,** set user's permissions to restrict the creation of databases larger than 10MB, is also incorrect because there are no security permissions that will restrict the user's ability to create databases of certain sizes.

3. ☑ **A, D.** Create nonclustered indexes for the table fields that are being used in joins, as criteria in SQL Select Where clauses, and in SQL Select Order By clauses. In addition, create a clustered index based on the CustomerID field so that the records will be ordered based on the CustomerID. Creating indexes improves the database's ability to retrieve rows. Indexes act as pointers to row data, and they eliminate the need for the entire row to be accessed. Nonclustered indexes should be created for fields that are referred to frequently. Each table can be assigned only one clustered index. The clustered index also controls the order in which the rows in a table will appear. Clustered indexes are generally made against a table's primary key.

☒ **B,** create a clustered index on each field, for each of the tables, is incorrect because you can have only one clustered index per table. **C,** combine the data from multiple tables into one table for better access, is incorrect because in designing relational databases, we don't combine all the tables into one table. This would do nothing to increase data retrieval, but it would open up a host of data integrity problems.

4. ☑ **B.** Use the Enterprise Manager (EM) to configure the databases for dynamic file growth in megabytes, but set the maximum file size setting to 25MB. The EM can be used to configure your database size—its ability to grow dynamically and to maximum size. The database properties dialog box can be accessed by right-clicking the database you want to configure and selecting Properties from the shortcut menu displayed.

☒ **A,** use the Database Configuration Wizard to configure the databases for dynamic file growth in megabytes, but set the maximum file size setting to 25MB, is wrong because there is no such thing as the Database Configuration Wizard. **C,** use the SQL Server Agent to configure the databases for dynamic file growth in megabytes, but set the maximum file size setting to 25MB, and create an Agent job that notifies you when a database has reached 25MB, is incorrect because the SQL Agent can't be used to configure database settings. **D,** create a trigger that sends the database administrator a message when a database reaches 25MB, is also incorrect. Triggers can be used to carry out tasks when certain events/ actions have occurred, but they can't be used to restrict a database's size.

5. ☑ **B, C.** Teach the developers to use the SQL Server Query Analyzer to interactively develop and test their SQL statements. Once they have generated the correct syntax in the Query Analyzer, they can save the SQL statement into a view that can be reused, or the SQL statement can be copied directly into the client application as embedded SQL in locations that support embedded SQL. By determining which statements can be reused by the client applications, you can reduce the redundancy of embedding the same SQL statements in different locations of a client application, as well as improve performance with using stored procedures.
☒ **A,** tell the developers to use the Enterprise Manager to create their SQL statements, is incorrect because the Enterprise Manager can't be used to generate SQL statements. **D,** instruct the developers to use stored procedures instead of writing SQL statements, is also incorrect because stored procedures are not easier to create than embedded SQL. If they create stored procedures, they are likely to run into the same problems of attempting to learn the syntax and check the accuracy of the returned data sets.

6. ☑ **D.** When SQL Server is installed on a Windows 9x server, it cannot support Windows NT Authentication Mode. Users will have to log into the SQL Server explicitly.
☒ **A,** when SQL Server is installed on a Windows 9x server, you can't connect to its services remotely, is wrong because no remote connection limitations are presented by using a Windows 9x server. **B,** when SQL Server is installed on a Windows 9x server, you can use only Named Pipes as the network protocol, is the opposite of what is true concerning

Windows 9*x* as a server for SQL Server. Windows 9*x* can't support Named Pipes; therefore B is incorrect. **C,** SQL Server 7.0 is not limited by any of the operating systems that it supports, is incorrect because there are authentication issues when using Windows 9*x.*

7. ☑ **D.** Use the SQL Server Client Configuration utility to define a server alias for the new Windows 9*x* server that specifies the appropriate protocol to use when accessing this server. Creating aliases allows you to customize the connection parameters used to access a database.
☒ **A,** use the front-end applications being built for the new database to handle any special login needs, is incorrect because the front-end application wouldn't have the ability to change to the appropriate Net-Library. **B,** use the Enterprise Manager to define a server alias for the new Windows 9*x* server that specifies the appropriate protocol to use when accessing this server, and **C,** use the Service Manager to define a server alias for the new Windows 9*x* server that specifies the appropriate protocol to use when accessing this server, are both incorrect because they are using the wrong SQL Server utility to create database aliases.

8. ☑ **C.** SQL Server provides the ability to store all rules on the server with the data. This provides a single control point for data consistency. As a result, there is no need to embed these rules in each front-end application.
☒ **A,** SQL Server provides the ability to control data access using the most appropriate security mode, is incorrect because security modes determine only how users are authenticated when logging into your server. Although SQL Server permissions will allow you to control what users can do to database components, permissions cannot be used to preserve database integrity. Therefore, **B,** SQL Server permissions allow you to control what each user can do to each database, is wrong. **D,** SQL Server allows you to create database rules using the Query Analyzer, is wrong because it specifies the wrong tool. The Query Analyzer is used to create ad hoc queries and execute Transact SQL statements. It is not used to define rules.

9. ☑ **B, C, D.** Entity integrity can be enforced by creating primary keys; unique indexes can be used to enforce entity integrity; constraints can be used to enforce entity integrity. Primary keys are used to preserve the uniqueness of a record within a database table. Unique indexes make sure that there are no duplicate values within the columns specified by an index. Constraints can be used to enforce that a value already exists in one table before that value can be used in another table.

☒ **A,** create views to help enforce integrity by embedding them with database rules, is incorrect because views are used to define virtual data sets for viewing or modification data, and they are not used to ensure your data's integrity.

10. ☑ **A, C, D.** Restrict data entry through a field's data type, specify data formats, and restrict the range of values accepted by a field/column. All of these techniques can be used to control data entry at the field level.

☒ **B,** use each field's normal value attribute to establish the type of value expected for each column, is incorrect because there is no normal value attribute for controlling field-level values.

11. ☑ **A, B, C.** Verify that you don't have repeating groups or multivalue columns in your tables; make sure that each nonkey field/column in a table is dependent on the entire primary key; and ensure that nonkey fields/columns in your tables do not depend on other nonkey fields/columns in that same table. These rules specified satisfy the basic rules of normalization.

☒ **D,** make sure that each field has a unique index defined to ensure entity integrity, is wrong because creating a unique index on each field in a table has nothing to do with the rules of normalization.

12. ☑ **C.** The joins necessary to create whole entity data sets will require complicated queries that may impede the database's performance. When normalizing a database design, we regard many four-way relationships with hesitation. The SQL statements necessary to use data from this type of design will be complicated, and they always involve joins and multiple relationships to present the data. In this type of situation, it is better to review the database design again and consider denormalizing some of the tables.

☒ **A,** SQL Server has a three-way relationship limitation, is incorrect because SQL Server has no limitation on the number of relationships to which a table can be a member. **B,** the rules of normalization prohibit the use of four-way relationships, is incorrect because the rules of normalization suggest against many four-way relationships but do not prohibit them. **D,** SQL Server views will not support displaying data involved in four-way relationships, is also incorrect because views do not have join limitations.

13. ☑ **D.** Suggest that the team perform some level of denormalization on the tables in the database design. They could use a combination of adding duplicate columns and adding derived columns to some of the database tables. Adding duplicate columns across some of the tables can make some of the primary information needed for an entity available in single tables. Instead of multifield primary keys, using derived keys can also help to reduce some of the fields required in the join relationships.

☒ **A,** suggest that the team replace some of the tables with views because views do not require relationships, is wrong because views do not attribute to the joins needed at the table level. **B,** suggest that the team perform some level of denormalization on the tables in the database design to eliminate primary keys on some of the tables, is incorrect because whether a table has a primary key has nothing to do with its involvement in a relationship. It is true, however, that primary key fields are most often involved in relationships with foreign key fields of another table. Eliminating primary keys would also degrade entity integrity. **C,** suggest that the team replace some of the tables with stored procedures because stored procedures do not require relationships, is incorrect because the addition of stored procedures has nothing to do with the relationships required at the table level.

14. ☑ **B.** The proposed solution satisfies both the desired result and the optional desired result. By using the Enterprise Manager, you will be able to select the tables from the database you are working on at any time. You will

also be able to open the folder of the necessary database and see the database schema. The schema is a visual rendering of the tables and relationships that exist for a given database. You can then launch the Query Analyzer from the Tools menu so that you can write your SQL statements.

☒ **A, C,** and **D** are incorrect because the proposed solution does satisfy all requirements.

15. ☑ **D.** The login name that you supplied is not a valid name on the NT Server that was specified. Validate the spelling of the user's login name on the NT Server, then go back to the Enterprise Manager and attempt to add the user again. With integrated security, all users and groups that are added to SQL Server must be valid NT accounts or groups.

☒ **A,** the login name that you supplied is not a member of any NT group, is incorrect because any valid NT user account can be added to SQL Server as a login ID. It doesn't have to be a member of an NT group. **B,** the login name that you supplied is only a guest account on the NT server specified, is incorrect because a NT user account with only guest privileges can still be added to SQL Server. **C,** the login name that you supplied is a system administrator account on NT, is incorrect because an administrator's account from NT is not restricted from being added to SQL Server as a valid login.

16. ☑ **C.** Create SQL Server views on the database that represent each of the five required data sets. Views can be used to produce frequently required data sets. Views are transact SQL that have been stored for future use. The data within a view can be modified. Views can also be referenced in SQL statements as though there were a base table.

☒ **A,** create replicated tables on the client desktops, then synchronize the data overnight, is incorrect because replicating the database tables on the client desktops would not provide easy access to the data required. **B,** create triggers that will produce the data sets needed and then invoke the triggers from within the client applications, is incorrect because triggers can't be called on to produce data sets; they are stored procedures that are automatically invoked when data has been modified. **D,** show the developers how to use the Query Analyzer to write Transact SQL statements that can be embedded in the applications, would work to produce the complicated SQL statements necessary to initially produce the data sets, but the objective was not to embed the SQL into that application.

17. ☑   **A.** From the Enterprise Manager menu bar choose Tools | Current Activity. In the Current Activity dialog box you can view a list of all server activity. You can select a user's name and send the user a message using the Send Message command button. The Enterprise Manager can be used to view server activity and will display a list of the users that are currently logged on.
☒   **B,** from the SQL Agent menu bar choose Tools | Current Activity, **C,** from the Services Manager menu bar choose Tools | Current Activity, and **D,** from the MSDTC Administrative Console menu bar choose Tools | Current Activity, are all incorrect because they are stating the wrong tool.

18. ☑   **D.** You have the wrong database selected in the Query Analyzer. Use the drop-down list for the database selection to choose the Pubs database instead of the Master database. The SQL statements that are executed in the Query Analyzer are executed against the currently selected database. Before testing your statements, you need to make sure that you are connected to the correct database.
☒   **A,** SQL statements are case sensitive and you have incorrectly typed the name of the table, is incorrect because the entity names in Transact SQL are not case sensitive. **B,** you have the Query Analyzer loaded, but you are not connected to the server, is wrong because the Query Analyzer immediately asks you to connect to a server if no connection is present when the Query Analyzer is loaded. **C,** you have incorrectly spelled the name of the table; use the Enterprise Manager to verify the table name, is highly possible, and if you received that message while having the correct database selected, that would be the most obvious error. The most glaring error in this example, however, is not having the correct database selected.

19. ☑   **D.** From the Query Analyzer menu bar choose Query | Set Options. In the Query Options dialog box specify an adequate number of sample rows

to be returned. This is accomplished by specifying a "Row Count" value, as shown in the following illustration. Setting a "Row Count" value will allow you to sample the returned data set. Specify just enough rows to satisfy your needs. This will also speed up your testing process because it will shorten the time needed for your SQL statement to return the data set.

☒ **A**, from the Query Analyzer menu bar choose Query | Configure Options, **B**, from the Query Analyzer menu bar choose Query | Properties, and **C**, from the Query Analyzer menu bar choose Query | Set Properties, are all incorrect because they use the wrong menu selections.

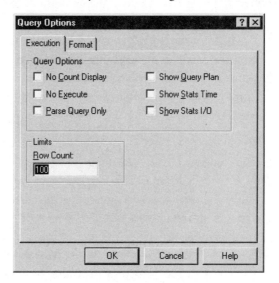

20. ☑ Pausing the server prevents new users from logging into the service while users currently connected to the service remain connected. Now that you have prevented new users from logging in, you can send current users a message to complete their tasks and log off the service. Pausing the server is a good precursor to shutting the server down. This allows users currently connected time to complete their tasks. You can view a list of the users currently connected using the Enterprise Manager. If you are in a hurry to shut the server down, from the Enterprise Manager you can send a message asking the current users to log off.

☒ **B,** pausing the server allows everyone currently connected 10 minutes to log off before being disconnected, is incorrect because there is no way to set a grace period in which users can log off the server. **C,** pausing the server prevents new users from logging into the service but hangs the connections of users already logged in, is incorrect because although pausing will prevent new users from logging on, it does not hang current user connections. **D,** pausing the server will send a message to users currently connected that all services have been paused, is incorrect because pausing will not automatically send any messages; you will need to do that yourself. New users, though, will be prevented from logging on.

21. ☑ **B, C, D.** Connections, locks, and open objects will be automatically configured by the server. SQL Server will increase and decrease the resources it exposes and consumes based on its current working environment.
☒ **A,** Net-Libraries, is incorrect because you will need to make sure yourself that each client machine is configured to use the correct protocol to communicate with the SQL Server.

22. ☑ **A.** Use SQL-DMO to build a custom application that exposes only the functionality required. SQL-DMO contains COM interfaces that expose the functionality found in the Enterprise Manager. This allows independent software developers to build custom front-end applications to manage servers.
☒ **B,** create a group account with permissions set to expose only the functionality required for these administrators to carry out their duties, is incorrect because limiting permissions will not assist in learning the Enterprise Manager. **C,** use the Enterprise Manager to develop a custom application to control which tools are available in the Tools menu, is incorrect because although you can add external tools to the Tools menu, you can't remove the default tools available. **D,** create a series of stored procedures that can be executed from a custom application, is incorrect because building a custom application using SQL-DMO would be preferred. You could conceivably create an application that did nothing more than execute stored procedures, but it would not be the preferred method.

23. ☑ **A, B, C, D.** SQL Server can use any of these methods of data access. Microsoft Query can be used to access SQL Server data using a graphical front-end. Data Access Objects (DAO) is a programmable interface into data that can be utilized to access data stored in SQL Server. Jet (Joint Engine Technology) is the Microsoft Access database engine. The Jet can communicate with SQL Server databases. Remote Data Objects (RDO) can also be used to access SQL Server databases. Like DAO, RDO is a programmable interface into data.

Capacity and Growth Planning for a SQL Database

1. ☑ **D.** sp_estspace is a utility that's used to estimate how much space will be needed to store a certain number of rows in a table.
   ☒ **A**, SQL Server Agent, is wrong because it is used for scheduling tasks and alerts. **B**, SQL Server Enterprise Manager, is also wrong because SQL Server Enterprise Manager is used to manage SQL Server objects from a single location. **C**, sp_spaceused, is wrong because sp_spaceused is a stored procedure that can be executed through SQL Server Query Analyzer to determine required disk space by seeing the space used by a table.

2. ☑ **A, B, and D.** In determining the total size of a user database, you will need to look at the amount of data in each user table, space allocated for use by the transaction log, and the space used by the system tables.
   ☒ **C**, the time users will spend working with user tables, is wrong because time won't necessarily affect the total size of a user database. The amount of data that's put into a database will affect its total size. As such, time that users spend working with user tables isn't a consideration when determining the total size of a database.

3. ☑ **B.** Because we know that there is an average of 150 bytes required for each row, and that there are 8060 bytes available for data on each page, we start by dividing the 8060 by 150. This gives us the number of rows that fit

on a page, which is 53.73. We then use the following formula to find the number of data pages needed:

Number of Rows in Table / Number of Data Rows per Page = Number of Data Pages

By dividing the number of rows needed (which is 100,000) by the 53 rows that will fit on each page, we find that we'll need 1886 data pages.

☒ **A**, 150, is wrong because 150 is the average number of bytes stated in the question used in each row. **C**, 8060, is wrong because 8060 is the number of bytes available for use in a data page. **D**, 100,000, is wrong because 100,000 is the number of rows needed to store data, as stated in the question.

4. ☑ **B.** The amount of disk space initially consumed by the system tables created for a user database is .5MB. As objects are added to the database, the size of the system tables will grow as more rows are written to it.

☒ **A, C,** and **D** are wrong because the initial size of system tables is 0.5MB. 8K is the size of a data page but not the initial size of system tables. 2MB is also wrong. Although system tables rarely exceed 2MB, their initial size is .5MB. The initial size is fixed at .5MB, so **D**, the size will vary from table to table, is also incorrect.

5. ☑ **B, C.** SQL Server Enterprise Manager is used to manage SQL Server objects from a single location. By selecting the database name from the Databases folder, you can use Enterprise Manager to display the database size. sp_spaceused is a stored procedure that can be executed through SQL Server Query Analyzer to view the size of a table. By adding the values of each table together, you can use sp_spaceused to determine the size of a database.

☒ **A**, SQL Server Agent, is wrong because SQL Server Agent is used for scheduling tasks and alerts. **D**, sp_estspace, is wrong because sp_estspace is a utility that's used to estimate how much space will be needed to store a certain number of rows in a table.

6. ☑ **C.** Transaction logs are serial records of modifications made to a database. The records contained in these log files document the start of every transaction made over a period of time, what changes were made to the data, and information on how to undo (i.e., roll back) the modifications.

☒   **A, B,** and **D** are wrong because system tables and primary and secondary data files aren't used to restore data. Primary data files contain pointers to other files in the database and are starting points of databases. Secondary data files consist of all data files other than primary and log files. System tables are created whenever you create a database.

7. ☑   **A.** A new feature in SQL Server 7.0 is its ability to grow beyond its initial size. When this feature is used, SQL Server 7.0 databases can continue to grow until the hard drive(s) used by the database become full.
☒   **B,** SQL Server 7.0 databases cannot grow beyond their initial size, is wrong because they can grow beyond their initial size. Previous versions of SQL Server did not allow this. **C,** the database will split itself into two databases automatically, is wrong because the database won't be split into two. It will expand itself until no more space is available on the hard disk(s). **D,** an error message will be sent to the system administrator, is also wrong because SQL Server won't send such an error message.

8. ☑   **B.** Files with the .LDF extension are log files that contain transaction log information, which is used to recover a database. Transaction logs in these files show changes made to a database. Each SQL Server database has such a log file, and it can also have multiple log files.
☒   **A,** .MDF, is wrong because .MDF files are the primary data files, which contain pointers to other files in a database. **C,** .MDB, is wrong because .MDB files are Microsoft Database files, which contain data but not transaction log information. **D,** .NDF, is also wrong because .NDF files are secondary data files and don't contain transaction log information.

9. ☑   **C.** SQL Server 7.0 databases may not require secondary data files, which by default have the extension .NDF. Secondary data files consist of all other data files, other than the primary data file. As this database works fine, it is most likely that only a primary data file is being used for this database.
☒   **A,** there are no log files for this database containing transactional log information, is wrong because .NDF files are log files containing transactional log information. Files with the extension .LDF are used for this. **B,** this

database doesn't require a primary data file because there is no data in the database yet, is also wrong; when you create a new database, a primary data file with the default extension .MDF is created. Every database has a primary data file, regardless of whether it has yet been filled with any data. **D**, .NDF files are used only with Microsoft Access databases, is also wrong because .NDF files aren't used with Microsoft Access databases; they are used with SQL Server databases.

10. ☑ **B.** The proposed solution produces the required result and produces only one of the optional results. The Alerter Service provides real-time monitoring of disk space, and it will send a message (i.e., an alert) when hard disk space becomes low.

☒ **A**, the proposed solution produces the required result and produces both of the optional results, is wrong; while the proposed solution produces the required result, it doesn't produce both of the optional results. You can't set the Alerter Service to automatically compress a drive once it starts getting full. **C**, the proposed solution produces the required result and produces none of the optional results, is incorrect because the proposed solution does produce the required result and one of the optional results. **D**, the proposed solution doesn't produce the required result, is wrong because the required result is met. The Alerter Service can be used to monitor the hard disk and send a message when hard disk space is getting low.

11. ☑ **A.** By implementing disk striping with parity, performance is improved and fault tolerance is established. Although RAID 5 offers fewer performance benefits than RAID 0 (disk striping without parity), it still provides performance benefits. As data is read from and written to the disk, separate read/write heads on each of the hard disks will read and write the data. This means that data is accessed faster. This is invisible to the user and thereby won't adversely affect the user's ability to access data. The additional bonus is that if one of the hard disks fails, data can be restored from parity information stored on other disks in the array.

☒ **B, C,** and **D** are incorrect because the proposed solution produces the required result and both of the optional results. As all of the results are achieved, each of the other choices is incorrect.

12. ☑ **A.** It will fail because a file or file group can be used by only one database. File groups allow you to group data files together and to determine where these files will be placed on physical disk(s). Files and file groups, however, can't be used by more than one database. For example, if a secondary data file is being used by one database, it can't be used by another database.
☒ **B,** it will succeed, is wrong because you can't have more than one database using the same file or file group. **C,** it will succeed, is wrong because it doesn't matter if only one of the two databases is attempting to access the file or file group. A file can be a member of only one file group and can be used by only one database. **D,** it will succeed, is wrong because file groups are related to databases created with SQL Server. File groups are used with SQL Server databases.

13. ☑ **C.** Log files are never a part of any file groups. They are always separate from data files making up a file group. Because of this, it is often beneficial to place log files on separate hard disks from data files. As each hard disk reads and writes log and data files on different disks, the read and write time to these files improves.
☒ **A,** primary data files, and **D,** .MDF files, are wrong because primary data files—which have the default extension .MDF—are part of file groups. **B,** secondary data files, is also wrong because secondary data files are also part of file groups.

14. ☑ **B.** The proposed solution produces the required result and produces only one of the optional results. By spreading the different data files over several hard disks, it will improve the performance of the database. As data is read from and written to the disk, separate read/write heads on each of the hard disks will read and write the data. This means that data is accessed faster. This is invisible to the user and thereby won't adversely affect the user's ability to access data.

☒ **A,** the proposed solution produces the required result and produces both of the optional results, is incorrect because it doesn't produce both of the optional results. Spreading the data files across four different hard disks won't provide fault tolerance, unless the NT Server's hard disks are using RAID level 5. **C,** the proposed solution produces the required result and produces none of the optional results, is incorrect because the proposed solution does produce the required result and one of the optional results. **D,** the proposed solution doesn't produce the required result, is wrong because the required result is met. Spreading the data files across several hard disks will improve performance.

15. ☑ **A.** The database and log files will be compressed, but performance won't improve. NTFS compression should be used if free disk space becomes an issue. Compression, however, will reduce the performance of the database, as the data is compressed and will take more time to read and modify.
☒ **B,** the database and log files will be compressed and performance will improve is wrong, because performance won't improve. **C,** the database and log files won't compress, as SQL databases and log files can't be compressed, is wrong because SQL Server databases and log files can be compressed. Despite this, the compression won't enhance the performance of the database. **D** is wrong, because SQL Server can read compressed files.

16. ☑ **D.** It will be 16 months before a new hard disk needs to be purchased. To determine this you first need to determine the projected number of months before the disk space will be used up. This is calculated by dividing the free disk space (4.5GB) by the estimated growth per month (250MB). This will give you 18 months. You then need to subtract the number of months it will take for the purchase order to go through. It takes 2 months to approve a request, order it, and have it delivered for installation. This brings the number of months to 16 months (18 months – 2 months).
☒ **A,** 2 months, is wrong because at two months there will be 4GB of free disk space. **B,** 6 months, is wrong because at 6 months there will still be 3GB of free hard disk space. **C,** 18 months, is wrong because this is the projected number of months before the disk space will be used up.

17. ☑ **A.** The primary concerns for hardware planning are processor power, RAM, disk subsystem, and network. These areas can affect the performance and overall ability of SQL Server to function on a computer.

☒ **B,** processor, network, printing, disk subsystem, is wrong because printing isn't a vital concern in planning the physical hardware system of a computer running SQL Server. Printers won't have an effect on performance, and any printer compatible with the operating system on which SQL Server runs will work with SQL Server. **C,** RAM, disk subsystem, virtual memory, sound card, is also wrong. Virtual memory is where disk space is used to mimic RAM. As such, there are only there areas specified here, and the question calls for four. In addition, SQL Server doesn't require a sound card to function. **D,** disk subsystem, RAM, network, Internet, is wrong because SQL Server doesn't require access to the Internet to function.

18. ☑ **A, C.** SQL Server 7.0 can run on computers with Alpha and Intel processors. These are the only two processor platforms available for SQL Server 7.0.

☒ **B,** MIPS, and **D,** PowerPC, are wrong because SQL Server 7.0 won't run on computers with MIPS and PowerPC processors. While previous versions of SQL Server could run on computers with these processors, version 7.0 of SQL Server cannot.

19. ☑ **A.** Each user connection consumes 40K of RAM. As there are 25 user connections at any given time, you would multiply 40K by 25, to come up with 1000K, which is roughly 1MB.

☒ **B,** 2MB, **C,** 32MB, and **D,** 23MB, are all wrong, as each of these figures exceeds the amount that 25 user connections would take up. Each user connection uses 40K of RAM. This means that when 25 users are connected, 1MB would be consumed.

20. ☑ **C.** SQL Server uses RAM for its procedure cache, data and index page caching, configurable overhead, and static server overhead. Without sufficient RAM, SQL Server's performance will suffer.

☒ **A,** procedure cache, virtual memory, configurable overhead, static server overhead, is wrong because virtual memory is where disk space is used to mimic RAM. **B,** procedure cache, RAID, virtual memory, configurable overhead, is wrong because SQL Server doesn't require RAID. Although virtual memory may improve performance, it isn't necessary if sufficient memory is available. **D,** data and dynamic HTML page caching, configurable overhead, static server overhead, processor cache, is wrong because there is no such thing as dynamic HTML caching or processor cache.

21. ☑ **A.** RAID provides the best performance with SQL Server 7.0. In using RAID controllers, you will also be able to implement fault tolerance and enhanced performance. In planning the physical hardware system, you should attempt to use the fastest controllers available.

    ☒ **B,** SCSI, is wrong. RAID controllers provide the fastest performance, but SCSI will offer better performance than each of the other choices mentioned here. **C,** IDE, and **D,** EIDE, are wrong. EIDE will provide lower speed than RAID or SCSI. Being the oldest, IDE will provide the slowest of the choices offered.

22. ☑ **A.** Each lock uses 96 bytes of RAM. A lock occurs when data has been changed but isn't yet written to the database. This prevents concurrent users (users who are using SQL Server databases at the same time) from reading unwritten data. By multiplying 96 bytes by 25, you come up with 2400 bytes. 1000 bytes is roughly one kilobyte, which translates to 2.4K.

    ☒ **B,** 24K, is wrong, as this would be 24000 bytes, which is considerably more than the 25 locks at 96 bytes apiece. **C,** 1MB, is wrong, as this would be the result of calculating 25 user connections by 40K. This would relate to the amount of RAM consumed by the user connections but not the locks. **D,** 2MB, is wrong, as the amount is far too high.

23. ☑ **C.** RAM is allocated dynamically, so the memory is released when the lock is released. When the lock is released, the RAM is freed up, so it can be used for other purposes or applications.

    ☒ **A** and **B** are both wrong, as each choice states that RAM isn't released once a lock is released. This isn't true. **D,** the memory used by the locks will continue to be consumed because SQL Server can't release memory automatically, is wrong because SQL Server releases the consumed memory automatically.

24. ☑ **A.** SQL Server increases or shrinks its buffer cache to keep (plus or minus 200K) 5MB of RAM free. It does this to keep NT from using paging. This lowers performance, as NT will need to read and write to the hard disk as an alternative to using RAM.

☒ **B,** 10MB, **C,** 20MB, and **D,** 40MB, are wrong. SQL Server uses memory dynamically. It checks the system to see how much free physical memory is available. If there is less than 5MB, then SQL Server will shrink its buffer cache. If there is more than 5MB, then it will recommit RAM to the buffer cache.

Planning Database and Server Security

1. ☑ **A.** With Windows NT authentication mode, SQL Server bases authentication on the permissions set for a user's account through User Manager for Domains (on NT Server) or User Manager (on NT Workstations). SQL Server plays no part in authenticating the user when this security mode is selected.

☒ **B,** Windows User authentication, is wrong because there is no such thing as Windows User authentication. **C,** Mixed authentication, is wrong because Mixed authentication uses NT permissions and SQL Server authentication. **D,** SQL authentication mode, is wrong because SQL authentication mode doesn't exist. Although SQL Server can be used for authentication, selecting Mixed as the security mode will force SQL Server to rely on NT authentication and SQL Server authentication.

2. ☑ **C.** With Mixed authentication, SQL Server authentication is used when the user logs into SQL Server. If the user doesn't log in, then SQL Server will rely on Windows NT as its source of authenticating the user.

☒ **A,** Windows NT authentication mode, is wrong because when Windows NT authentication is used, SQL Server isn't used to authenticate users. **B,** Windows User authentication mode, is wrong because there is no such authentication mode as Windows User authentication. **D,** SQL authentication, is wrong because SQL authentication mode doesn't exist. Although SQL Server can be used for authentication, selecting Mixed as the security mode will force SQL Server to rely on NT authentication and SQL Server authentication.

3. ☑ **D.** The user will have select permission to system tables, plus guest access and rights. Because a guest account is available, SQL Server will allow the user the same access and rights as if he had logged in with the guest account.
☒ **A,** the user will have access to all databases on the SQL Server, is wrong because the user will have only select permissions to system files, and he will have the access and rights assigned to the guest account. **B,** the user will have access to all primary and secondary data files, is wrong for the same reason. If the user had access to all of the primary and secondary data files, then he would have access to all databases, which is the choice provided in A. **C,** the user won't have access to anything, is also wrong. As a guest account is available, the user will have the same permissions as this account, and he will be afforded a minimal level of access.

4. ☑ **C.** You should give users only the security privileges they need to do their work. Any access beyond what's needed by a person to do his or her job could become a security risk. As a user's needs change, and more access is required, give the user additional privileges.
☒ **A,** give users as many security privileges as possible, is wrong because doing so could result in users getting into areas where they don't belong and possibly modifying or corrupting data that they don't need. **B,** give users slightly more security privileges than they currently need, is also wrong for this same reason. Providing users with even slightly more access than they need could become a security problem. **D,** give users fewer security privileges than they need, s wrong for different reasons. If a user has fewer privileges than he or she needs, it will keep the user from being able to do his or her job properly.

5. ☑ **A, C.** When the standard security model is used, each user needs to have logins and passwords set for each database that will be used. This makes the standard security model more secure than the integrated security model, where authentication is controlled solely through the NT operating system.

☒ **B,** each user won't need to have logins and passwords set, as Windows NT does authentication, is wrong because it is the integrated security model—not the standard security model—that has Windows NT authenticating users. When the standard security model is used, authentication is done through both SQL Server and Windows NT. **D,** less administration is required than with the integrated security model, is wrong, as standard security model requires more administration when SQL Server is used to set logins and passwords for each database a user will use.

6. ☑ **A.** The standard security model uses SQL Server authentication to control access to databases. As this is a Novell NetWare network, and as SQL Server resides on a Windows 95 computer, NT authentication isn't an option here. As such, authentication must be done through the SQL Server.

☒ **B,** integrated, is wrong because this is a non-Windows NT environment. As Windows NT isn't being used, the integrated security model isn't an option. **C,** both of the above, is wrong because you would use the standard or the integrated security model, not both. As the standard security model uses both standard and integrated security, standard is the correct answer. **D,** none of the above, is wrong because you would use the standard security model in a non-Windows NT environment. With the integrated security model, Windows NT provides authentication.

7. ☑ **B.** In SQL Server Enterprise Manager, give the local or global group these users are members of access to the database. To do this, you would expand the SQL Server groups. After expanding the server and right-clicking on Login, you would click Windows NT Authentication and add a Windows NT group.

☒ **A,** in SQL Server Enterprise Manager, individually provide each user with access, is wrong because the question asks for the quickest method of providing these users with access. Individually providing each user account with access is considerably more time-consuming than assigning access to a group. **C,** in User Manager, give the local or global group these users are members of access to the database, is wrong, as User Manager is the program used on Windows NT Workstations, not NT Servers. It is also wrong because you would assign access for the local or global group with SQL Enterprise Manger. **D,** create a transaction log with a listing of users and apply it to the database, is wrong, as transaction logs aren't used to provide users with access.

8. ☑ **D.** All users of a database will belong to that database's public role. This means that in Finance, users will belong to the public role of the financial database, and users in Sales who use the customer database will belong to the public role of the customer database.
☒ **A,** each of the users of the database would automatically belong to the database's user-defined roles, is wrong because users aren't automatically added to user-defined roles. The users you want to belong to a certain role must be added. **B,** all users will belong to the fixed server role, and **C,** all users of a database will belong to the fixed database role, are wrong because all users of a database may not necessarily belong to the fixed server or fixed database roles. Users need to be added to these roles.

9. ☑ **A, C, D.** Fixed server, public database, and fixed database are all built-in roles. In SQL Server 7.0, these built-in roles cannot be dropped. Although you're not forced to use them and you can manage databases using user-defined roles, you can't drop them.
☒ **B,** public server, is wrong because—unless you created a user-defined role called Public Server—there is no such role built into SQL Server. If you did have a user-defined role with this name, it would still be wrong because user-defined roles can be dropped.

10. ☑ **B.** The solution fulfills the required result but only one of the desired results. Any of the fixed server roles has permissions on all databases in a server. Therefore, the required result has been met. The Serveradmin has the ability to shut down and set all server-related options. Because of this, one of the desired results has also been met.
☒ **A,** the solution fulfills the required result and both of the desired results, is wrong because the solution meets only one of the desired results. **C,** the solution fulfills the required result but doesn't fulfill either of the

desired results, is wrong, as one of the desired results has been met. The only desired result that hasn't been fulfilled is that of the user being able to create and alter all of the databases on the server. This is attributed to the Securityadmin role, not the Serveradmin fixed server role. **D**, the solution doesn't fulfill the required result, is wrong because the required result has been fulfilled.

11. ☑ **D.** The Diskadmin role gives a member user the ability to access all disk files. The Dbcreator role gives a member user the ability to create and modify all databases. By adding the user to each of these roles, only the access required for the user to perform her duties is given.
☒ **A**, add the user to the Sysadmin and Setupadmin roles, and **C**, add the user to the Sysadmin role, are wrong because the Sysadmin role allows the user to have full access to all database objects and to perform any task. This is more power than the user needs so it could become a security threat. **A** is also wrong as the Setupadmin role is used to allow the user to set login and CREATE DATABASE permissions. Finally, **B**, add the user to the db_accessadmin and db_owner roles, is wrong because these roles aren't fixed server roles. They are fixed database roles that give a user access at the database level. db_owner gives a user full access to a specific database, while db_accessadmin allows the user to manage user IDs.

12. ☑ **A.** db_owner. The db_owner fixed database role allows members to have full access to a database.
☒ **B**, db_ddladmin, is wrong because db_ddladmin gives the user the ability to issue ALL DDL. DDL is the "Database Definition Language" and is used to define and declare database objects. **C**, db_securityadmin, is also wrong because db_ddladmin is a role that allows members to manage permissions, ownerships, and roles in a database. **D**, db_datadmin, is wrong because db_datadmin isn't a real fixed database role. As it doesn't actually exist, a user can't be added to it.

13. ☑ **C.** db_securityadmin. This fixed database role is used to allow a member to manage permissions, ownerships, and roles. It doesn't give the user full access, but it is used to administer the database.

☒ **A,** db_owner, is wrong because the question states that the user isn't to get full access to the database. Although db_owner would be able to manage permissions, ownerships, and roles, it would give the member full access. **B,** db_accessadmin, is wrong because db_accessadmin gives the member the ability to manage user IDs. **D,** db_datareader, is wrong because db_datareader gives a member the ability to give read (i.e., SELECT) permissions to any database object.

14. ☑ **B.** Create a user-defined database role, then add the group of users as members. User-defined database roles are used if there isn't a fixed server or fixed database role that applies to tasks that need to be performed.
☒ **A,** Add the user to both fixed database and fixed server roles is wrong, because the tasks the users need to perform aren't covered by fixed server or fixed database roles. **C,** create a new fixed server role and add the group of users as members, and **D,** create a new fixed database role and add the group of users as members, are both wrong. Fixed server roles and fixed database roles are—as their names state—fixed. You can't add new roles.

15. ☑ **A, B.** Add each of the users of this database to groups in Windows NT. Once this is done, map the groups to the database so that users can access it. You can also add each of the users of this database to groups in Windows NT. Once this is done, map the groups to roles so that they have permissions at a server or database level.
☒ **C,** set up permissions and access to the database for each individual user through Windows NT User Manager, and **D,** set up permissions and access to the database for each individual user through SQL Server Enterprise Manager, are both wrong. You don't need to set permissions and access to the database for each user, as you can map Windows NT groups into a database or to a role. **C** is also wrong because the program used to set user account permissions is User Manager for Domains.

16. ☑ **A, B, C.** SQL Server services can be run under a Local System Account, Local User Account, or Domain User Account. Although local accounts will run only on the local machine and domain accounts can

access other SQL Servers on the network, each of these has the ability to access local resources.

☒   **D,** Guest Account, is wrong because a Guest Account is on most NT machines (and by default) an account with minimal access to resources. This means that the guest account wouldn't have the necessary permissions to access needed resources, or the guest account would need to be modified to allow guest users to have considerably more power than they should.

17. ☑   **C.** SQL Server services that need to access resources or communicate with other SQL Servers in your domain need to run under a Domain User Account. Local accounts will run only on the local machine, and domain accounts can access other SQL Servers on the network.

☒   **A,** Local System Account, is wrong because a Local System Account runs only on a local system. It is for this same reason that **B,** Local User Account, is wrong, as a Local User Account also runs only on the local machine. **D,** Guest Account, is wrong because a Guest Account is on most NT machines (and by default) and has minimal access to resources. This means that the guest account wouldn't have the necessary permissions to access needed resources, or the guest account would need to be modified to allow guest users to have considerably more power than they should.

18. ☑   **D.** Domain user accounts require full access to local and network resources, and it is for that reason that a Domain User account being used to run SQL Server services needs to be added to the Administrator group. It also needs to be configured to log on as a network service, so that it can log in automatically.

☒   **A,** add the Local User or Local System account that's used by SQL Server services to the Administrators local group, then configure it to log on as a network service, is wrong. The Local System and Local User accounts are used to access resources on the local computer. It would need to be a Domain User account to access network resources. As the Local System account wouldn't be able to access the resources on the domain network, **B,** by using a Local System account, you would only need to configure it to log

on as a network service, is also wrong. **C**, add the Domain User account
used by SQL Server services to the Administrators local group, is wrong
because it hasn't been configured to log in as a network service.

19. ☑ **A, B.** In n-tier or multitier systems, the client is used only to display
data, while the business logic runs on the server. This allows the client logic
to be split into two places and run more efficiently.
☒ **C**, the business logic runs on the client, is wrong because business logic
runs on the server and not on the client portion of the n-tier application. **D**,
the components don't run on the server but are distributed to all clients, is
wrong because components run on the server, so that the components
making up the application don't need to be distributed to all clients.

20. ☑ **C.** To connect to a linked database or server, the SQL Server that's
connecting needs to send a login name and password to the database or
server to which it's connecting. This confirms that the connecting SQL
Server actually has access to the information it's attempting to access.
☒ **A**, the database you're connecting to must send a login name and
password, is wrong because the database being connected to doesn't send
the password; the SQL Server that's connected to the database sends login
and password information. **B**, the linked server you're connecting to must
send a login name and password, is wrong for the same reason, as the linked
server being connected to doesn't send the login name and password. **D**, the
SQL Server connecting to the linked database or server must send a login
name and password; the linked server or database then sends a login name
and password back to the SQL Server, is wrong. Only the SQL Server
connecting to the linked server or database sends a login name and
password. The linked server or database does not send a login name and
password back to the connecting server.

21. ☑ **B, D.** sp_addlinkedsrvlogin is a stored procedure used to allow users to
use the same permissions as their login or to emulate the permissions of
another user. When sp_addlinkedsrvlogin is used, login mappings are
created. Windows NT doesn't allow security information to be passed from

the NT account to the SQL Server account, so a SQL Server authenticated account is used. A SQL Server authenticated account is used to connect to the linked server with a user's credentials to impersonate another user.
☒ **A,** sp_setaddrole is a stored procedure used to allow users to use the same permissions as their login or to emulate the permissions of another user, is wrong because sp_addlinkedsrvlogin—not sp_setaddrole—allows users to use their login permissions or emulate another user's permissions. **C,** Windows NT passes the security information to the SQL Server account, is wrong because NT won't allow you to pass security information from the Windows NT account to the SQL Server account.

22. ☑ **B.** The user will default to the guest account. The guest account has a lower level of access, which gives the user minimal access to the database.
☒ **A,** the user will be refused any access, is wrong. Because the guest account exists, the user will automatically default to using that account. **C,** the user will default to the SA account, and **D,** the user will default to the DBO account, are wrong because the SA (System Administrator) and DBO (Database Owner) accounts are high-level accounts. SQL Server wouldn't default to these accounts because doing so would give any user without a valid account considerable access and would be a security threat.

23. ☑ **C.** DBO accounts are database owner user accounts. When a user is the database owner, they have full access to all operations and rights to that database. Because this works at the database level, though, the DBO of one database won't have full access to all operations and rights on another database, unless the user is DBO of that database as well.
☒ **A,** the user needs an SA account to have full access at the database level, is wrong because the system administrator (SA) account works at the server level. If the user is the DBO of a database, the user will have full access. **B,** DBO accounts administer database servers; the sales database must exist on another server, is also wrong. DBO accounts are database owner accounts, and they allow full access on the database to which a user is the owner. DBO accounts aren't used to administer database servers, but the individual databases themselves. **D,** a DBO user account never has full access to

operations and rights, is wrong because a DBO user account has full access to operations and rights if the user is using the database that he or she owns.

24. ☑ **A.** The SA account can still control the database as owner. The system administrator account (SA) works at the server level. It allows an SA user account to administer databases and control the database as an owner. This is true regardless of whether the SA is DBO of that particular database.
☒ **B,** the original DBO user can still control the database as owner, is wrong because the original DBO user won't have control over the database. The user has transferred ownership and is thereby not the owner anymore. **C,** the original DBO user and the SA account won't be able to control the database as owner, is wrong because the SA account will still be able to control the database. The original DBO owner, however, will not. **D,** the original DBO, the new DBO, and the SA account will be able to control the database as owner, is wrong. The original DBO user won't be able to control the database; the SA account and new DBO will have control.

25. ☑ **D.** Exec sp_changedbowner 'login id' is used to transfer DBO (Database Ownership) to another user. By executing this, the current DBO loses ownership, and the new DBO gains ownership.
☒ **A,** Exec sp_adduser, is wrong because this would be used to add a user account to a database. For example, to add a guest user account, you would enter "Exec sp_adduser guest". **B,** Exec sp_changedowner 'login id', and **C,** Exec sp_changebowner 'login id', are wrong because the command is sp_changedbowner (i.e., change db owner), not sp_changedowner or sp_changebowner.

Planning for Installation

1. ☑ **A.** Microsoft English Query Interface allows you to enter queries without having to enter any lines of Transact SQL code. This means you can enter natural language queries and obtain results.
☒ **B,** DTC Client Support, is wrong because DTC Client Support is used to extend transactions across multiple servers. **C,** Query Analyzer, is wrong

because Query Analyzer is a utility that's used to enter and evaluate TSQL statements. **D,** Transact SQL, is wrong because the question states that you don't want the user to have to enter code. Transact SQL is used to perform actions and return results by entering statements of code.

2. ☑ **C.** Electronic commerce involves companies being able to do business and sell products over the World Wide Web. Using SQL Server 7.0, you can store product and customer information, which can be used to process sales.
☒ **A,** business application, is wrong because business applications are programs that are developed to deal with a specific business need. **B,** analysis of historical data, and **D,** data-warehousing, are wrong because data warehousing and analysis of historical data give users the ability to store data, allowing data to be rolled up and complex queries to be performed on it.

3. ☑ **A, C, D.** SQL Server 7.0 can be installed on computers running Windows 9x operating systems (i.e., Windows 95 and 98), Windows NT Workstation, and Windows NT Server. If you are installing on Windows NT machines, then you must have Service Pack 3 or higher installed as well.
☒ **B,** Windows NT Workstation with no service packs installed, is wrong because this computer doesn't have Service Pack 3 or higher installed. Without the Service Pack installed, SQL Server 7.0 won't be able to install or run properly.

4. ☑ **D.** Yes, you will be able to install on this computer. SQL Server 7.0 requires a minimum of 32MB of RAM, Intel Pentium 133 or higher processor, a CD-ROM or connection to a network share containing installation files, and at least 74MB of hard disk space for a minimum install.
☒ **A,** no because there isn't enough hard disk space, is wrong; there is enough hard disk space. For a minimum installation, at least 74MB of free hard disk space is required. Since this computer has 100MB, more than enough hard disk space is available. **B,** no because there isn't enough RAM, is wrong; SQL Server 7.0 requires a minimum of 32MB of RAM. **C,** no because the processor isn't powerful enough, is wrong because the processor is powerful enough. As the installation also requires the computer to have a

minimum Intel Pentium 133 or higher processor—and this computer has an Intel Pentium II—the processor is powerful enough.

5. ☑ **A, D.** Of the computers listed, these are the only two that meet the minimal requirements for a typical installation. SQL Server 7.0 requires a DEC Alpha AXP or compatible system, Intel Pentium 133 or higher processor, 32MB of RAM, and 190MB of free hard disk space.
☒ **B,** Intel Pentium II with 32MB of RAM, 150MB of free hard disk space, is wrong because this computer doesn't have enough free disk space. For a typical installation, there must be at least 163MB of available disk space. **C,** 486/33 computer with 64MB of RAM, 190MB of free hard disk space, is wrong because the processor isn't powerful enough.

6. ☑ **D.** Perform an automated installation by creating and editing files that will be used to automatically install SQL Server. System Management Users can use the .PDF files included with this product to save the step of creating the files used in automated setups. Once the files are created, you can then use them to script the automated installation of SQL Server 7.0 on multiple computers.
☒ **A,** use the installation wizard in SQL Server 7.0 to install on each of these computers at once over the network, is wrong; the SQL Server 7.0 installation wizard doesn't provide the functionality to perform multiple installations over the network. Although **B,** use the installation wizard on each and every computer on which you want to install SQL Server, would get SQL Server 7.0 onto the 100 different computers, it is not the fastest manner of installing SQL Server. **C,** perform an automated installation using the AUTORUN.EXE program on the SQL Server 7.0 installation CD, is wrong because you don't use AUTORUN.EXE to perform an automated installation. This is the program that starts the SQL Server installation wizard when the CD is inserted into the CD-ROM and closed.

7. ☑ **C.** There is a problem with the operating system. The question mentions that this is a fresh install of Windows NT Workstation and that no service

packs have been installed. If Service Pack 3 hasn't been installed, SQL Server 7.0 won't be able to install or run properly. It's for this reason that you need to install the Windows NT Service Pack 3 or higher on the computer.

☒ **A**, there isn't enough RAM, is wrong because 32MB of RAM is required to install and run SQL Server 7.0. **B**, the processor isn't powerful enough, is wrong because SQL Server requires a minimum Intel Pentium 133 processor or higher. As this computer is using a Pentium II, this requirement has been met. **D**, there isn't enough hard disk space, is wrong because a typical install of SQL Server requires at least 163MB of free disk space. As this computer has 170MB of free disk space, this requirement has been met.

8. ☑ **A.** There isn't enough hard disk space. To perform a full install of SQL Server 7.0, you need a minimum of 190MB of free hard disk space. As only 150MB of free hard disk space is available on this computer, you won't be able to install SQL Server.

☒ **B**, there isn't enough RAM, is wrong because 32MB of RAM is the minimum amount of memory required to install and run SQL Server 7.0. **C**, there is no CD-ROM, is wrong because although the computer has no CD-ROM, it is connected to a network. By having the installation files available on a network share, you will still be able to install SQL Server. **D**, the processor isn't powerful enough, is wrong because SQL Server 7.0 can use a minimum Intel Pentium 133 or higher processor, such as Pentium PRO processors.

9. ☑ **C.** Upgrade SQL Server 4.2 to SQL Server 6.5. Once this is done, upgrade SQL Server 6.5 to SQL Server 7.0. This is the only way to upgrade the server and its data, as Microsoft currently doesn't offer a way to upgrade SQL Server 4.2 to SQL Server 7.0.

☒ **A**, use the Upgrade Wizard to upgrade SQL Server 4.2 to SQL Server 7.0, is wrong because the Upgrade Wizard won't work on such older versions. Although it will upgrade SQL Server 6.x, it won't upgrade SQL Server 6.x servers or data. For this reason, **B**, use the Upgrade Wizard to upgrade data in SQL Server 4.2 to a schema that can be used by SQL Server 7.0, is also wrong. **D**, perform a full install of SQL Server 7.0, which will automatically detect the database belonging to the previous version and convert it, is wrong, because performing a full install of SQL Server 7.0 also won't upgrade the version 4.2 server or its data.

10. ☑ **A.** SQL Server 6.5 and SQL Server 7.0 can't coexist on the same server. You will need to switch between the running version of SQL Server, so that only one SQL Server is available at any given time. By using the *switch* function, you will be able to switch between the running version of SQL Server.

☒ **B,** SQL Server 6.5 and SQL Server 7.0 can't be installed separately on the same server; during installation, you will be forced to upgrade the previous version, is wrong. SQL Server 6.5 and SQL Server 7.0 can be installed separately on the same server. During installation, you will have the option of upgrading the previous version. **C,** SQL Server 6.5 and SQL Server 7.0 can't be installed separately on the same server; during installation, SQL Server will automatically upgrade the previous version to SQL Server 7.0, is wrong. SQL Server 6.5 and SQL Server 7.0 can be installed separately on the same server; they just can't run and be available to users at the same time. It is also wrong because during installation of SQL Server 7.0, you're given the option of upgrading. If you choose not to, you can switch between running versions or migrate the previous version's data to SQL Server 7.0. **D,** SQL Server 7.0 will install normally on the server, and it will be able to run at the same time as the previous version, allowing will users to have access to both database systems, is wrong. Although SQL Server 7.0 will install normally on the server, it won't be able to run at the same time as the previous version. It is also wrong because users won't have access to both database systems at the same time.

11. ☑ **C.** 1.5 times the size of the SQL Server 6.5 database being imported. In addition to the free disk space needed to install SQL Server 7.0, it will need disk space for the SQL Server 6.5 database being imported. In addition to this, it will need the additional space to convert the database to a SQL Server 7.0 schema.

☒ Each of the other choices is wrong because they either exceed or don't have enough free disk space to convert the data being imported. **A,** none, is wrong because the import computer will need 1.5 times the size of the SQL Server database being imported. For this same reason, **B**, twice the size of the SQL Server 6.5 database being imported, is also wrong. **D**, the size of the SQL Server 6.5 database being imported, is wrong because the SQL Server 7.0 computer will need free space for the SQL Server 6.5 database, plus free space to convert the data.

12. ☑ **B.** When a side-by-side installation is performed, two versions of SQL Server are maintained on your system. This may be versions 6.0 and 7.0 or 6.5 and 7.0. Although the two versions are on the computer, you can't use them at the same time, unless you use the switch utility to switch between the two existing versions on the computer.

☒ **A**, computer-to-computer, is wrong because a computer-to-computer installation has a copy of SQL Server on two separate servers. The administrator must specify a source and destination system for this type of upgrade, which is commonly used when performing a hardware upgrade simultaneous to installing SQL Server. **C**, standalone-to-server, and **D**, network-to-network, are both wrong because there are no installation methods called "standalone-to-server" and "network-to-network." These terms were made up for the purpose of this question.

13. ☑ **B.** Data Transformation Services (DTS) allows you to import nonnative SQL data into SQL Server 7.0 databases. Using DTS, you can import data from Access, Excel, FoxPro, Dbase, Oracle, Paradox, Site Server, Index Server, or ODBC data sources.

☒ **A**, Bulk Copy Program, is wrong because Bulk Copy Program, or BCP, is a utility that's left over from previous versions of SQL Server. It enables you to migrate data into SQL Server databases from text files. Because BCP is the Bulk Copy Program, **C**, BCP, is also wrong. **D**, you can't migrate this data because SQL Server allows data migration only from text files and SQL Server 4.2, 6.x, 7.0, and Sybase databases, is wrong. Data Transformation Services allows you to migrate data from a wide variety of sources. In previous versions of SQL Server, you were allowed data migration only from text files and SQL Server 4.2, 6.x, and Sybase databases. This has changed in version 7.0 of SQL Server.

14. ☑ **B.** Data Transformation Program would be used, with ODBC drivers installed on the computer. Data Transformation Program allows you to import nonnative SQL data sources, such as ODBC data sources, into a SQL Server 7.0 database. ODBC drivers would need to be installed on your computer so that the data can be accessed.

☒ **A,** Bulk Copy Program would be used, with ActiveX installed on the computer, is wrong because Bulk Copy Program isn't able to access ODBC data sources, and ActiveX wouldn't be needed to use this program. **C,** Data Migrator would be used, with drivers for each database system being accessed installed on the computer, is wrong because there is no such program called Data Migrator. **D,** Data Transformation Program would be used, with drivers for each database system being accessed installed on the computer, is wrong because you would need ODBC drivers installed to access ODBC data sources. You wouldn't need drivers for each and every database system being accessed, only a version of ODBC drivers used for SQL Server.

15. ☑ **B.** Network libraries are consuming more resources than needed because you have installed more network libraries than you need. Network libraries each consume system resources, and you should choose only the ones needed for the client and server to communicate. If more than are required are installed and configured, then a considerable amount of resources will be used for nothing.

☒ **A,** there isn't enough RAM, is wrong because SQL Server requires a minimum of 32MB of RAM with 64MB recommended. This computer meets not only the minimal requirements but meets the recommended ones. **C,** the network libraries that are installed haven't been configured properly, is wrong because even if all of the network libraries installed were configured properly, they would still consume a considerable amount of resources. **D,** the processor is too slow, is wrong because SQL Server requires a minimum of a Pentium 133 processor to run, and this computer has a Pentium II that is more powerful.

16. ☑ **A, C.** Because TCP/IP is being used, the only choices that apply here are that the server and client are configured to use different ports and that a different network library is installed on the server. To use TCP/IP, the TCP/IP network library needs to be installed. In addition to this, the server and client must be configured to use the same port.

☒ **B**, a different name has been given to the pipe, is wrong because names are given to pipes only when named pipes are installed. **D**, a different name has been given to the port, is wrong because names aren't given to ports in TCP/IP. They are given numbers that the port listens to.

17. ☑ **C.** Multiprotocol. Of the different network libraries listed here, the only one that provides encryption is Multiprotocol. Using Multiprotocol enhances the security of the SQL Server using it.

☒ Each of the other protocols listed here does not support encryption. It is for that reason that **A**, TCP/IP, **B**, NWLink, and **D**, named pipes, are wrong.

18. ☑ **A.** The default pipe has been changed. For a client and server machine to communicate using named pipes, both computers must be running named pipes, and both must be configured to use the same pipe name.

☒ **B**, the default port number has been changed, is wrong because named pipes don't use a default port number. This is something that's used when TCP/IP is installed. **C**, an entry hasn't been made in the registry, is wrong because when configuring named pipes, you shouldn't have to go into the Windows Registry and make new entries or change existing ones. **D**, SQL Server doesn't support named pipes on this computer, is wrong because SQL Server does support named pipes on computers running Windows NT.

19. ☑ **B, C.** Security administrator and system administrator have the power to grant the right of creating databases to other users. System administrators have full access to the system, while security administrators can add and drop logins, read the audit log, and grant the ability to create a database.

☒ **A**, database creator, is wrong because database creators have the ability to alter, create, extend, and rename a database. They don't have the power to allow other users to do this. **D**, server administrator, is wrong because there is no default server role called server administrator.

20. ☑ **A.** The default port number that TCP/IP uses is 1433. TCP/IP listens to this port and detects whether a client is attempting to communicate with the server. If the client or server is using different ports, then they won't be able to communicate.

☒ **B,** 1, is wrong because 1 is not the default port number used by TCP/IP. **C,** 1344, is wrong because TCP/IP uses 1433, not 1344. **D,** there is no default port number for TCP/IP, is wrong because there is a default port number that TCP/IP uses. If the client and server aren't using the same port number, then they won't be able to communicate.

21. ☑ **B.** The default named pipe has been changed. Because named pipes haven't been installed, certain utilities like SQL Server Upgrade Wizard—which depends on the default pipe name—can't communicate. This means that the wizard won't be able to run properly, and it will fail when attempts are made to use it.

☒ **A,** named pipes haven't been installed so the client and server can't communicate, is wrong because in this case, it doesn't matter if the client and server can't communicate. The problem is that SQL Server can't communicate with other processes on the system. For this reason, **C,** the client is using a different name for the named pipe, is also wrong. **D,** the default port has been changed, is wrong because default ports are used with TCP/IP and not named pipes. Programs like SQL Server Upgrade Wizard depend on named pipes being installed properly and using the default pipe name.

22. ☑ **B.** Disk administrators have the ability to add and drop devices and configure mirroring on SQL Server 7.0. This is a default role that's created when SQL Server is installed.

☒ **A,** system administrator, is wrong because this role gives full access on the system. This is more power than you want to give a user when security is an issue. **C,** security administrator, is wrong because security administrators can add and drop logins, read the audit log, and grant the ability to create a database. **D,** process administrator, is wrong because—although it too is a default role created when SQL Server 7.0 is installed—it only has the power to KILL processes.

23. ☑ **A.** In the Registry, you will need to make changes before Multiprotocol encryption is active. Until the changes are made, encryption will not be available between client and server communications. Encryption is enabled through the HKEY_LOCAL_ MACHINE\SOFTWARE\Microsoft\ MSSQLServer\Client of the Registry. Here, add a new key called RPCNetLib and enter the value REG_SZ (String) datatype. Name the new value "Security" and set the value to "Encypt".

☒ **B,** in HKEY_SQL_MACHINE\SOFTWARE\Microsoft\ MSSQLServer\Client of the Registry, add a new key called RPCNetLib, enter the value REG_SZ (String) datatype, name the new value "Security", and set the value to "Encypt", is wrong; there is no HKEY_SQL_MACHINE in the Registry. **C,** reinstall the network library, is wrong because without making changes to the registry, encryption won't be active. This happens regardless of how many times you reinstall the network library. **D,** Multiprotocol doesn't offer encryption, is wrong because Multiprotocol is the only network library that offers encrypted communication.

Installing SQL Server

1. ☑ **B, C.** Before installing SQL Server 7.0, you will need Internet Explorer 4.01 (or higher) and the Windows NT Service Pack 3 (or higher) on your Windows NT computer. The Service Pack upgrades files in Windows NT, which may cause problems when running NT. Without the Service Pack, SQL Server won't install and run properly. Internet Explorer is a Web browser used by various tools in SQL Server for displaying help files and other screens.

☒ **A,** SQL Server 6.x, is wrong because SQL Server 6.x isn't required unless you are upgrading to SQL Server 7.0 from a previous version. **D,** DTC Client Support, is wrong because DTC Client Support is installed with the management tools component of SQL Server. It is used to extend database transactions across multiple servers.

2. ☑ **A.** Upgrade Tools from the Server Components installs tools that are used to migrate data from SQL Server 6.x databases to SQL Server 7.0. If you choose not to upgrade the database when first starting SQL Server setup, you can use these tools to migrate the data afterward.

☒ **B,** Upgrade Tools from the Management Tools component, is wrong because Upgrade Tools is found under Server Components on the Select Components screen. **C,** DTC Client Support from the Management Tools components, is wrong because DTC Client Support is used to extend database transactions across multiple servers. **D,** Virtual Device Interface from the Development Tools components, is wrong because Virtual Device Interface under Development Tools installs dynamic link libraries (DLLs) that are required to back up and restore data.

3. ☑ **D.** The multilingual character set (code page 850) contains English characters and also contains special characters used in most European and South American languages. No other character sets would be used because you can have only one character set on each server, which all databases on the server must use.

☒ **A,** Central European code page 1250, is wrong because the Central European character set wouldn't have the characters used by the South American branches of your company, nor would it have the English characters used by your office. **B,** the default code page 1252, is wrong. The SQL Server default code page is 1252, which is compatible with Windows NT and 9x programs, and it is the one generally used by SQL Servers. As it doesn't contain characters used in other languages, it wouldn't be used for this situation. **C,** the U.S. English code page 437, is wrong because the U.S. English code page wouldn't have the characters used by the other branches of your company. This would result in errors when you attempt restoring data.

4. ☑ **C.** Use the default code page for SQL Server, and use Unicode equivalent data types for front-end development. Microsoft recommends this, as applications use the Unicode equivalent data types, which are able to store characters used in most languages.

☒ **A,** use a character set for each language in this database, is wrong because you can use only one character set per database. **B,** create one database for each language and use a character set for each language in the databases, then link the databases together, is wrong because you can use only one character set on each server. All databases on that server must use the same code page. **D,** SQL Server doesn't have multilanguage support, so it can't be done, is wrong because SQL Server does support multiple languages.

5. ☑   **C.** You won't be able to restore the data. You can't restore data on another SQL Server unless both machines use the same sort order. What you would need to do in such a situation is change the sort order by destroying all databases, re-creating them, and using the BCP/DTS utilities to restore them.

   ☒   **A,** the default sort order is the case-sensitive dictionary order, so no problem will result, is wrong because you can't restore data on a SQL Server unless both machines use the same sort order. **B,** the sort order of the data will be automatically changed to the default sort order of the new machine, is wrong because the data won't automatically change. **D,** you will be able to restore the data, as sort order has no effect on a restore, is wrong because the different sort orders will have an effect on restoring the data.

6. ☑   **C.** The server is using a binary sort order. When a binary sort order is used, the data is sorted by its ASCII value. For example, capital Z has a lower ASCII value than lowercase a so Zebra would appear in the sort order before apple.

   ☒   **A,** the character set of a foreign language is being used, is wrong because foreign language character sets wouldn't affect the sort order. The sort order is what determines how the data would appear in this manner. **B.,** the Unicode Collation Sequence is set to a certain locale that sorts in this way, is wrong, as the location or language wouldn't affect the sort order in this way. **D,** the server is using a case-insensitive, uppercase preference dictionary order, is wrong, as a case-insensitive, uppercase preference dictionary order would have a capital A followed by a lowercase a, followed by a capital B, and so on.

7. ☑   **C.** Domain account. You can assign services in Windows NT in any of three accounts: LocalSystem, Machine, or Domain. However, of the three, the only one that will allow you to perform activities over a domain network is the domain account. If you are going to perform heterogeneous joins across remote sources, replication, remote procedure calls, SQL mail, or backing up network drives, a Domain account must be used.

☒ **A,** LocalSystem account, and **B,** Machine account, are wrong because the LocalSystem and Machine accounts don't allow you to perform heterogeneous joins across remote sources. The only account you can assign to services that will allow this is the Domain account. **D,** any of the above, is wrong for this same reason. Any of the accounts cannot be used, only the Domain account.

8. ☑ **D.** The "Password never expires" was not checked. If this isn't checked in the NT user account, the password will expire after a period of time. As SQL Mail has been presumably working over the last month, this is most likely the reason for the problem.

   ☒ **A,** the SQL Mail that comes with SQL Server isn't the full version, and it will expire after a one-month period, is wrong because SQL Mail is a full feature that comes with SQL Server, and it has no expiration date determining when it will fail to work. **B,** the wrong type of Windows NT account was assigned to SQL Server services, is also incorrect, as SQL Server services would have been unable to function from the time the account was initially set up. **C,** the "User must change password at next login" was checked, is wrong, as SQL Server services wouldn't have been able to work with this account, since it can't change the password when it first attempts logging in.

9. ☑ **B.** The NET USER command can be used to automate the process of creating large numbers of accounts with the use of a script. This command is followed by a number of parameters to specify attributes of the accounts you create.

   ☒ **A,** User Manager for Domains, is wrong because User Manager for Domains doesn't have a feature for processing scripts to set up user accounts automatically. This must be done through the NET USER command. **C,** the NET GROUP command, is wrong because the NET GROUP command is used to assign the service to groups. This would be used to assign the accounts you create with NET USER to Administrator groups. **D,** SQL Server, is wrong because NT accounts aren't set up through SQL Server.

10. ☑ **D.** Profiler, found under the Management Tools component, is used to trace and record database activity. After selecting Custom setup type, you select this from the Select Components screen.

☒ **A,** SQL Server, under Server Components, is wrong because SQL Server, under Server Components, installs the core SQL Server executables. **B,** Enterprise Manager, under Server Components, is wrong because Enterprise Manager installs Microsoft Management Console and snap-ins for SQL Server administration. It is also wrong because Enterprise Manager is installed through the Management Tools component of Custom setup. **C,** Enterprise Manager, under Management Tools, is wrong because—as mentioned—Enterprise Manager isn't used for tracing and recording database activity.

11. ☑ **C.** If certain settings on this screen aren't set correctly, and if you change them after SQL Server is installed, you will need to rebuild the master database, and you will lose all databases on the server. It is for this reason that you will need to be especially careful when choosing these settings.

☒ **A,** you won't be allowed to change these settings, is wrong because you will be able to change the settings offered on the Character Set/Sort Order/Unicode Collation screen. In doing so, you will have to deal with the repercussions of such changes. **B,** changing these settings will cause the master database to be rebuilt, and you will lose the database currently being worked on, is wrong because all databases on the server will be lost. **D,** you will be able to change the sort order, but not the Unicode collation or character set, is wrong because changing the sort order, Unicode collation, or character set will force the master database to need to be rebuilt, and you will lose all databases on the server.

12. ☑ **A.** The command used to create the setup.iss file containing settings used to perform an unattended setup is "SetupSQL.exe k=rc". Once this command is used, SQL setup will start, allowing you to set the settings to be used in unattended installations.

☒ **B,** use the command SetupSQL.exe –fl followed by the name and path of the initialization file to create, is wrong, as this is the command and argument used to select the initialization file and to start the process of performing an unattended installation. **C,** use the command SetupSQL.exe, is wrong, as this will merely start the SQL Server setup wizard. This won't create the initialization file used to perform unattended installations of SQL Server. **D,** use the existing .ini files for the unattended installation of SQL Server 6.5, is wrong, as the .ini files used for unattended installations of SQL Server 6.5 won't work. You need to create new .iss setup initialization files for the unattended setup of SQL Server 7.0.

13. ☑ **B.** Use the command SetupSQL.exe –fl followed by the name and path of the initialization file to use. For example, if the .iss file containing the settings for the installation is C:\WinNT\setup.iss, then you would enter: SetupSQL.exe –flc:\WinNT\Setup.iss. In entering this, notice that there is no space between the –fl switch and the path.

   ☒ **A,** use the command SetupSQL.exe k=rc, is wrong because SetupSQL.exe k=rc is the command used to create the .iss file that will be used in the unattended setup. **C,** use the SetupSQL.exe command, is wrong because this will start the Setup Wizard to perform a normal installation. **D,** use the existing .ini files for the unattended installation of SQL Server 6.5, is wrong because these files won't work. You need to create new .iss setup initialization files for the unattended setup of SQL Server 7.0.

14. ☑ **B.** Run the SQL Server setup program from the installation disk. Once started, the setup program will detect the older database and ask if you want to run the SQL Server Upgrade Wizard. If you don't have a version 6.x database on your system, then the screen asking this won't appear.

   ☒ **A,** run the SQL Server Upgrade Wizard by starting UPGRADE.EXE on the installation disk, is wrong because there is no UPGRADE.EXE program on the installation disk. **C,** run the SQL Server setup program from the installation disk and select "Upgrade" as the Setup Type, is wrong because there is no "Upgrade" option on the Setup Type screen of the setup wizard. **D,** run the SQL Server setup program from the installation disk and select "Custom" as the Setup Type, is wrong because there is no option for upgrading when you select "Custom" as the Setup Type.

15. ☑ **A, D.** Named pipe and tape are the two methods that can be used to transfer data between servers during an upgrade. Named pipe provides simultaneous import/export. With tape, you must have a Windows NT tape driver installed, or the feature won't be offered.

    ☒ **B,** network, isn't correct because network isn't an actual option or method you can select when transferring the data between servers. **C,** FTP, is also wrong for this reason, as FTP isn't a method that's offered during the upgrade for transferring data.

16. ☑ **A, B.** Named pipes need to be installed and configured, even if the tape method is used to transfer data. In installing named pipes, you configure it to use the default pipe \\pipe\sql\query. You will also need to have a Windows NT tape driver installed, or the tape method won't be offered as an option during the upgrade.

    ☒ **C,** nothing; selecting Tape is the only thing you need to select and configure, is wrong because you will also need to install and configure named pipes. **D,** nothing; tape isn't an option for transferring the data, is also wrong because tape is a method that's offered for transferring the data.

17. ☑ **B.** MSSQL Server is the core service of SQL Server, and it is the only service that is installed that is necessary to the basic operation of SQL Server.

    ☒ **A,** MSDTC, is wrong because MSDTC isn't a necessary component to SQL Server's basic operation. MSDTC is Microsoft Distributed Transaction Coordinator. This service allows clients to receive data from multiple servers in a single transaction. **C,** SQLServer Agent, is wrong because SQLServer Agent is another service that isn't required for the basic operation of the relational database system. SQLServer Agent is used to schedule jobs that need to be performed periodically. **D,** Service Manager, is wrong because Service Manager isn't a service. It is a tool used to start and stop SQL services.

18. ☑ **C.** SQLServer Agent is a tool that allows you to schedule jobs that need to be performed. You can also configure it to respond to on-demand activities raised by SQL Alerter. This means that when an alert goes off in SQL Alerter that requires attention, SQLServer Agent can respond to the alert on your behalf.

☒   **A,** MSDTC, is wrong because MSDTC cannot be configured to respond to activities raised by SQL Alerter. MSDTC is Microsoft Distributed Transaction Coordinator and allows clients to receive data from multiple servers in a single transaction. **B,** MSSQL Server, is wrong because MSSQL Server is the core of the database system. It also can't be configured to respond to SQL Alerter. **D,** Service Manager, is wrong because Service Manager isn't a service. Instead, it is used to start and stop services that are installed for SQL Server.

19. ☑   **A.** The Binn directory—located in the MSSQL7 directory by default—contains the executables that make up the SQL Server 7.0 environment. This includes all of the executables for menu entries that appear on the start menu, as well as others that can be launched through the various GUIs (graphical user interfaces) that appear when these menu items are started.
☒   **B,** Bin, is wrong because there is no Bin directory under the directory containing SQL Server. **C,** Exe, is wrong because there is no Exe directory under the SQL Server directory. **D,** SQL, is wrong because there is no SQL directory residing under the directory containing SQL Server.

20. ☑   **D.** The installation was successful. Error code 0 is the error code that indicates that nothing has gone wrong during the unattended installation. It is the only error code returned during an unattended installation that indicates good news.
☒   **A,** a general error has occurred, is wrong because when a general error occurs, -1 is the error code that's returned. **B,** an invalid option has been selected, is wrong because if an invalid option were used in the script for your unattended installation, then error code –53 would be returned. Finally, if a file didn't exist, error code –5 would be returned. For this reason, **C,** file does not exist, is also wrong.

21. ☑   **B, C, D.** Several files can be used to determine installation problems when installing SQL Server 7.0 on Windows 9x computers. These are SQLstp.log in the Windows directory, Cnfgsvr.out in the MSSQL\Install directory, and files that were left in the MSSQL\Log directory by the installation program. Based on the information in the log files and the files that were left in the MSSQL\Log directory, you will be able to investigate and solve the question of why SQL Server failed to install.

☒ **A,** Application log and Systems log, using EventView, is wrong. The Application log and Systems log can be viewed in EventView to determine a problem when installing SQL Server 7.0. This is available only on Windows NT computers.

22. ☑ **D.** The SQL Server client utilities should be installed on all computers that will access SQL Server 7.0.

☒ **A,** Windows 9x computers, is wrong because you want to install the client utilities on more than just Windows 9x computers. Any computers, whether they be Windows 9x, NT Workstations, or NT Servers, should have these utilities installed if they are going to connect to the SQL Server 7.0 database. For this reason, **B,** Windows NT Workstations, and **C,** Windows NT Servers, are wrong as well.

23. ☑ **D.** The wrong protocol is being used. The question states that NWLink is being used. As users are connecting over the Internet, and the Internet uses only TCP/IP, the wrong protocol is being used. SQL Server is expecting IPX/SPX connectivity, but there is none because a different protocol needs to be in place.

☒ **A,** the network address is wrong, is wrong because a network address is used to connect to a server when NWLink is being used as a protocol. **B,** the IP address is wrong, is wrong because there is no IP address. NWLink doesn't use IP addressing. **C,** the port number is wrong, is also wrong. Although this can prevent connectivity, this isn't the case here, as no port number has been assigned to TCP/IP since it isn't being used.

Configuring SQL Server

1. ☑ **D.** A server that is registered using the Registration Wizard does not display the system databases. SQL Server makes the assumption that if you are using the wizard, you must be fairly new to SQL. Consequently, the system databases are hidden.

☒ **A, B,** and **C** are incorrect because you can register SQL servers in other domains, even though by default only the SQL servers from the same resource domain your client is in are displayed. You can register SQL servers that participate in replication and you can register multiple SQL servers at the same time.

2. ☑ **A.** The only code that will not result in a syntax error is this code segment.
   ☒ **B, C,** and **D** are all incorrect because they result in syntax errors. There are no stored procedures or extended stored procedures named XP_CONFIGURE or SP_RECONFIGURE. Furthermore, the name of the configuration option used to set the minimum range of dynamic memory is min server memory (MB), and the name of that option cannot be abbreviated to *memory*.

3. ☑ **D.** SQL Server allows for an absolute maximum number of user connections equal to 32,767 connections. However, the system resources available and the nature of the applications connecting to the server will determine the true maximum number of connections. The user connections option is a dynamic, self-configuring option. SQL Server will adjust the maximum number of connections within the maximum value, depending on available memory. Most of the time you should not need to change this option. When calculating the amount of memory used for user connections, remember that each connection takes a minimum of 40KB. If the server reaches the maximum number of user connections, the next connection attempt will receive an error and will not be able to connect.
   ☒ **A, B,** and **C** are each incorrect alone because each would exclude the others as correct and all of the choices are correct.

4. ☑ **A.** The SP_PROCESSMAIL stored procedure allows the SQL Server to retrieve and process any queries that have been mailed in since the last time the SP_PROCESSMAIL procedure was run. By combining the XP_FINDNEXTMSG, XP_READMAIL, and XP_DELETEMAIL extended stored procedures, you could accomplish the same thing as using the SP_PROCESSMAIL stored procedure, but it isn't as elegant.

☒ **B** and **D** are incorrect because no such procedures exist. **C** is incorrect because XP_READMAIL alone will not accomplish the goal.

5. ☑ **C.** Connection-level options are not the lowest level of options. Statement-level options, such as query hints, table hints, and join hints, are specified in individual Transact-SQL statements. Connection-level options do override database options.

☒ **A, B,** and **D** are all true statements.

6. ☑ **A.** The best reason to restrict SQL Server to a subset of the processors in a multiprocessor system is to keep SQL Server from overwhelming the system. In order to set which processors SQL Server will use, open SQL Enterprise Manager, right-click on an SQL Server, and select properties. Open the Processors tab and place a check in the box next to each processor you would like SQL Server to use.

☒ **B** is wrong because rarely if ever would you improve the performance of SQL Server by limiting the number of processors for the system. **C** is not a good choice because there are much better methods of simulating loads on systems. Restricting the processors would not allow you to measure the effects of a variety of different load scenarios. **D** is incorrect.

7. ☑ **B.** Full-text indices are repopulated only when scheduled to do so. Unlike other SQL Server indices, the indices are not automatically refreshed when the data is changed. The index is not updated automatically because the update operation of a full-text index is a relatively expensive operation. Therefore, the operation is an asynchronous one.

☒ **A, C, D** are incorrect because full-text indices are both asynchronous, and must be scheduled or initiated by an administrator.

8. ☑ **D.** The full-text index has been created, it just hasn't been populated. This is analogous to querying on a table that has no data or specifying a WHERE clause that does not match any data in a table. The query executes and you get an empty return set.

☒   **A** is wrong because no error message is generated. **B** is incorrect because full-text index populations must be scheduled. **C** is wrong because there is no implicit conversion between operators.

9. ☑   **B.** FREETEXTTABLE can automatically parse the search parameters into words and phrases that can be individually searched for in the destination table.

☒   **A** is not an advantage of FREETEXTTABLE because both commands return a MATCH column. **C** is incorrect because both FREETEXTTABLE and CONTAINSTABLE require the Microsoft search service to be running. **D** is incorrect because FREETEXTTABLE does not search for various tenses of verbs and nouns found in the search parameters.

10. ☑   **C.** Both facilities allow you to test for the existence of a string in a field.

☒   **A** and **B** are incorrect because the LIKE operator does not provide any facilities for ranking, proximity searches, or word variant searches (that is, inflectional forms of words.) The full-text searching facilities within SQL Server provide for these various forms of searches. The one advantage that the LIKE operator has over the full-text search system is that the LIKE operator allows you to search for noise words such as a, an, and. The full-text indexing process filters these words out of the index. **D** is incorrect.

11. ☑   **C.** The proposed solution meets the primary goal, but neither secondary goal. Although FREETEXT does not offer as many options as CONTAINS, it is more useful when the end user and not the developer is defining the search details. You can pass entire phrases to the FREETEXT function and have SQL Server automatically break the phrase into words and smaller phrases.

☒   **A** and **B** are incorrect because both the optional results are asking for syntax that is part of the CONTAINS operator. **D** is incorrect.

12. ☑   **B, D.** One of the advantages of using the rowset variants CONTAINSTABLE and FREETEXTTABLE over the predicate forms CONTAINS and FREETEXT is that you are provided with two additional columns in your result set. These columns are the KEY and RANK columns. KEY is used only to help construct joins and doesn't provide any new uses on its own. RANK on the other hand provides a numerical rating of how well the record matched the search criteria. The RANK field can be sorted and filtered like any other field in the result set.

☒ A and C are incorrect because the predicate forms of the free-text operators do not provide a RANK column.

13. ☑ D. All of the text examples above are equivalent to the phrase Free Text. Capitalization and punctuation do not affect the matching algorithms.

☒ A, B, and C are each equivalent to Free Text, so only D is the correct answer choice.

Monitoring and Tuning SQL Server

1. ☑ B. You can use SQL Server Profiler to monitor query performance and pinpoint poorly performing queries. You could use the Create Trace Wizard and select Find The Worst Performing Queries.

☒ A is incorrect because Performance Monitor will not pinpoint poor query performance, though you can use it to look at overall server performance while running multiple queries. C and D are incorrect because Enterprise Manager & Query Analyzer do not provide any way to monitor performance of queries.

2. ☑ A. Rebuild the clustered index on the SALES table. Scan density indicates the percentage of fragmentation for a table. Sequential IO operations are significantly faster than non-sequential operations. Rebuilding the clustered index will rebuild the table, and also improve query performance.

☒ B, rebuild the clustered index on the database, is incorrect because there is no clustered index on a database, only on a table. C is incorrect because a non-clustered index will not help fragmentation. D is incorrect because contiguous, full-data pages improve read-ahead performance.

3. ☑ **A, B.** Using indexes is the best way of optimizing a query. Determine what the optimal indexes are (start with the WHERE clause), or you can use Index Analyzer, under the Query menu. If an index exists that will increase query performance, but SQL is not using it, you can also use an INDEX_HINT on the query.

☒ **C** is incorrect because you do not necessarily need to create a clustered index. If the query is querying ranges, then a clustered index would be a good solution, but a clustered index does not resolve all table scans. **D** is incorrect because you should avoid table scans when querying larger tables.

4. ☑ **B.** A processor queue length above two per CPU indicates that you need to add more processors or reduce the load on your server. You should also check the settings for SQL to be sure that all processors are being used by SQL. You can check this in Enterprise Manager, in Properties of the SQL Server.

☒ **A** and **C** are incorrect because processor queue length does not reflect memory or disk usage. **D** is incorrect because the optimal value is more than two per CPU.

5. ☑ **A.** You can run the Create Trace Wizard, and use the worst performing queries option to determine the queries that need to be analyzed. You can then analyze the query to determine whether it needs to be rewritten or needs indexes added.

☒ **B** is incorrect because Performance Monitor does not have an option to monitor queries. **C** is incorrect because SP_MONITOR shows all the processes running on the server, and will not pinpoint poorly performing queries. **D**, Set the Query Governor Cost Limit, will limit the amount of time a query can run, but doesn't provide information on which queries are poor performers.

6. ☑ **A.** You can monitor the data files' size and configure Performance Monitor to send an alert when a threshold is reached.

☒ **B**, SP_MONITOR, is incorrect because this displays snapshot statistics of CPU, I/O, or other usage statistics. **C**, SQL Profiler, is incorrect because you cannot monitor file sizes through Profiler and **D**, Query Analyzer, is incorrect because it will not monitor data file sizes.

7. ☑ **D.** SQL Server Agent Monitor monitors the SQL Server Agent service. If the SQL Server Agent terminates unexpectedly, the SQL Server Agent Monitor restarts the service. An extended-stored procedure (XP_SQLAGENT_MONITOR) is started by SQL Server Agent to monitor its availability.
    ☒ **A** is incorrect because you do not need to create any programs to monitor the agent. **B** is incorrect because SQL Server Agent executes jobs. If it is not running, a job is not going to initiate. **C** is incorrect because the startup value indicates if the agent should be automatically started on boot up of the server, not whether it should be automatically restarted.

8. ☑ **B.** Query Analyzer Set statistics I/O ON. This returns scan count, pages read from disk, pages read from cache and number of pages placed in cache by the query.
    ☒ **A** is incorrect because RPC: Completed indicates a remote procedure call completion. **C** is incorrect because it displays the amount of time taken to compile and execute a statement. **D** is incorrect because SQL: BatchCompleted indicates a T-SQL batch has completed, and doesn't indicate disk usage.

9. ☑ **C.** Create Trace Wizard. Select Identify the Cause of a Deadlock and run the trace.
    ☒ **B** is incorrect because Performance Monitor won't help you find the source of deadlocks, but it will help you find the source of bottlenecks. Performance Monitor does have a Number of Deadlocks/sec counter, which will help you identify that there is a deadlocking problem, but not the cause. **A**, Enterprise Manager, does not show deadlock causes, but looking at Current Activity will show you which processes are deadlocked. **D**, SP_MONITOR, shows statistical information about the server.

10. ☑ **A.** DBCC SHOWCONTIG will show you the percentage of fragmentation, or scan density. Creating a clustered index will reorganize the data into contiguous, full-data pages, resulting in better read-ahead performance.

☒ **B** is incorrect because Performance Monitor does not have a counter that monitors SQL table fragmentation. **C** is incorrect because Profiler monitors database activity and not table or database files. **D** is incorrect because SP_MONITOR displays snapshot statistics indicating how busy SQL Server is.

11. ☑ **A, D.** Increasing the amount of memory increases the amount SQL can allocate to locks. SQL will not allocate more than 40 percent of memory available to SQL to the lock pool, and increasing the memory will increase the amount SQL can allocate. You can also increase the Locks configuration option (SP_CONFIGURE).
☒ **B** and **C** are incorrect because adding processors and disks will not help resolve the locking problem.

12. ☑ **A.** Create an alert to notify you when the log is 70-percent full, and run a job to back up the log. You can create an alert in Enterprise Manager to notify operators when a counter falls below or above a specific value, and run a job in response to the alert.
☒ **B** is incorrect because you'd want to monitor the percent of log used, and there is no mention of an alert or of a response. **C** is incorrect because Profiler does not monitor files or file sizes, but events and activity on the server. **D** is incorrect because SP_MONITOR displays statistical information about the server, such as CPU usage and idle time.

13. ☑ **C.** Max server memory. You would need to manually set this to allow enough memory for the MSSearch Service to run. The max server memory setting should allow 1.5 times the physical memory available for the full-text search.
☒ **A** is incorrect because the locks option would change the amount of locks available for the server. **B** is incorrect because the fill factor determines how full data or index pages are. **D** is incorrect because min server memory is the minimum amount of memory SQL will use, and you would want to limit the maximum memory that SQL can use.

14. ☑ **A, C, D.** You would need to manually run UPDATE STATISTICS when a table has been truncated (all the data removed) and refreshed with

new data. When bulk inserting a large number of records, and when an index has changed significantly, it would also require UPDATE STATISTICS to be run.

☒ **B** is incorrect because by default, SQL auto-updates statistics. You do not need to run it on a daily basis.

15. ☑ **D.** Query Analyzer optimizes the query. You can view a text or graphical show plan which shows the steps SQL uses in running the query, and what, if any, indexes are being used. You can also use Index Analysis under the Query menu to run an analysis on that statement.

☒ **A** is incorrect because Performance Monitor does not assist in optimizing queries, but in determining performance and activity on the server. **B** is incorrect because Client Network Utility is used to specify which network libraries the client machine is using. **C** is incorrect because Enterprise Manager does not have an optimization tool.

16. ☑ **C.** Data file size is under the SQL Server databases object and monitors the cumulative size of all the files in a database, including growth. Monitoring this counter could help you determine the optimal size of tempdb. Constant growth can affect performance, so you want to set the initial size to avoid the overhead of frequent expansion.

☒ **A** is incorrect because percent log used monitors the amount of log space that is in use. **B** is incorrect because transaction/sec monitors the number of transactions started for the database per second. **D** is incorrect because Active Transactions monitors the number of active transactions for the database. **A**, **B**, and **D** can give you good information about the load on a database, but would not help you in determining size.

17. ☑ **C.** Upgrading to 7.0 from 4.2 involves first upgrading to SQL 6.5, then upgrading to SQL 7.0. To ensure NULL operations remain the same as SQL 4.2, use a trace flag of 243, DBCC TRACEON (243). Recovering to point of failure in SQL 7.0 entails placing a primary data file on a drive separate from the data drive.

18. ☑ **A.** Lower min server memory. When Exchange and SQL are running on the same server, the min server memory option for SQL should be configured. The default value is not optimal in this case. Since Exchange is the application performing poorly, the min server memory should be lowered.
☒ **B** and **D** are incorrect. When Exchange and SQL are run on the same server, SQL will operate at the min server memory specified. Lowering or increasing the max server memory will not affect either application. **C** is incorrect because increasing the min server memory will increase the amount of memory allocated to SQL, causing Exchange to perform even more poorly.

19. ☑ **A.** Placing the primary data file on the mirrored drive provides point-of-failure recovery. Placing the indexes on a separate disk and controller from the data increases query performance and provides the optimal disk I/O for this scenario.
☒ **B, C,** and **D** are incorrect.

20. ☑ **B.** EXEC sp_fulltext_catalog 'Cat_text', 'start_incremental'.Using incremental population will only retrieve changed rows as long as there is a timestamp column in the table being indexed.
☒ **A** is incorrect because this repopulates the entire catalog, and will definitely not minimize impact. **C** is incorrect because this deletes the existing catalog, re-creates, and re-associates the catalog with the table, but doesn't repopulate it. **D** is incorrect because there is no auto-update statistics option for full-text indexes.

21. ☑ **C.** SP_MONITOR displays system statistics since last executed, indicating how busy a SQL Server is. You can run it manually in Query Analyzer, or you can write a loop in SQL to execute SP_MONITOR periodically.
☒ **A** is incorrect because Profiler monitors database activity. **B** is incorrect because Enterprise Manager allows you to view current activity, such as locks, user activity, and blocked processes. **D,** SP_WHO, displays snapshot information on current users and processes.

22. ☑ **A.** Replay the trace. You can replay the trace you created in order to identify the problem to see if it recurs.

    ☒ **B,** Monitoring the server, will eventually identify the problem if it recurs, but it's much more efficient to replay the trace and see if the problem recurs in the same scenario. **C** and **D** are incorrect because neither SP_WHO nor SP_MONITOR will help you determine whether the error has been resolved.

23. ☑ **B.** SP_SPACEUSED is the fastest way to see the size for a single table.

    ☒ **A** is incorrect because Enterprise Manager is not the quickest way to view a single table, especially if there are 1500 in the database. SP_MONITOR and Performance Monitor do not provide a way to view information about a single table.

Managing Database Files

1. ☑ **A.** The Offline option allows you to take the database offline and copy it to the removable media in order to distribute it. You could set this option through T-SQL in the following way:
   EXEC SP_DBOPTION MYDATABASE, OFFLINE, TRUE

    ☒ **B,** Distribute, is incorrect because there is no Distribute option. **C,** Read Only, is incorrect because it only sets the database to Read Only mode. It does not take the database offline which is what is required for distribution. **D** is incorrect because the Subscribed option allows the database to be subscribed to for replication. Again, the database is not taken offline.

2. ☑ **D.** The script does not achieve the primary goal. The numbers are right, but the default measure of size for the CREATE DATABASE command is megabytes, not kilobytes. This script creates a database that would be allowed to grow to one gigabyte, not one megabyte in size. To correct the script, simply add KB after every number to let the system know that you mean kilobytes.

    ☒ **A, B,** and **C** are incorrect because the primary goal was not achieved.

3. ☑ **D.** The minimum size for a data file is one megabyte, and the minimum size for a log file is 512 kilobytes. Consequently, you will not be able to fit the database on the floppy disk.

☒ **A** and **B** are incorrect because they specify invalid sizes. **C** is incorrect because the system cannot shrink a file below the minimum size requirements for data and log files.

4. ☑ **C.** You may only have one primary data file and that file must have a file extension of .MDF. All other data files must have a file extension of .NDF. All log files on the other hand have a file extension of .LDF.

☒ **A** and **B** are incorrect because the order of the files for the SP_ATTACH_DB command is not important, although by convention, the primary data file is listed, then any non-primary data files, and finally, the log files. **D** is incorrect because .DBF is a file extension associated with D-BASE database files.

5. ☑ **B, C.** A database can be set to grow by an increment measured in megabytes or by a percentage of the total size of the database. So, you would be telling the database to automatically extend the size of the data files by either 4MB at a time, or by five percent of the total size of the database. The preferred method is usually to extend in a fixed increment. If the size of your database fluctuates wildly and you are growing it by percentage, then the actual amount of space being allocated will also fluctuate wildly.

☒ **A** is incorrect because you cannot extend a database in increments measured in kilobytes, and a database must be increased by a minimum of one megabyte at a time. **D** is incorrect because SQL 7.0 introduced the capability to grow data files automatically.

6. ☑ **D.** The owner of the master databases cannot be changed. The owner of the tempdb and model databases cannot be changed, either. This is to ensure that SQL Server service is not accidentally locked out of one of the system databases. However, ownership of user databases can be changed by using the sp_changedbowner system-stored procedure.

☒ **A, B,** and **C** are incorrect because the owner of the system databases must be DBO for SQL Server to function properly. SQL Server will not allow you to change the owner of the system databases.

7. ☑ **C.** The correct command to use is DBCC SHOWCONTIG. The DBCC SHOWCONTIG command displays fragmentation information for the data and indices of the specified table. You should pay the most attention to the scan density value.
☒ **A** is incorrect because SET SHOWPLAN_TEXT ON causes SQL Server to not execute TRANSACT-SQL statements. Instead, SQL Server returns detailed information about how the statements are executed. **B** and **D** are incorrect because they are not valid commands.

8. ☑ **B.** The size of all three of your database files will be roughly the same after the import. This is because SQL Server uses a proportional-fill algorithm and the algorithm is based on free space in the data file. After the third data file is created, it has 100 percent of free space. The server will continue to put proportionally more data in the third data file than the first two data files until all three data files have roughly the same amount of free space.
☒ **A, C,** and **D** are incorrect because they do not reflect the use of the proportional fill algorithm.

9. ☑ **D.** Remember, we were looking for the incorrect statement. Filegroups can be backed up as a unit. Using filegroup backups is a common approach to backing up very large databases that cannot be completely backed up in the allotted backup time. By defining filegroup backups, the backup of the database can be segmented and split over multiple backup periods.
☒ **A, B,** and **C** are all true statements, so they are incorrect answers for this question. Study the differences between the three types of filegroups and be able to define primary, user-defined, and default filegroups.

10. ☑ **A.** The proposed method achieves the primary goal and both secondary goals. By creating a separate filegroup and assigning it as the default, all newly created user objects will be created on the new filegroup instead of the

primary filegroup. By having the user objects in a separate filegroup, you will be able to back them up without backing up the system objects. You will also be able to easily detach the database and move it to another server.

☒   **B, C,** and **D** are incorrect because the solution achieves the primary and both secondary goals.

11. ☑   **A, B.** Either answer would be valid, depending on how many files the database has. **A** would be used for a database with only one file and **B** would be used for a database with multiple files. The TRUE option on the SP_DETATCH_DB command indicates that updating of the database statistics should be skipped. It does not make a difference between the code working or not working.

☒   **C** and **D** are incorrect because they have the parameter names mixed up. This will result in a syntax error when the script is executed.

12. ☑   **C.** The required result is obtained. Transaction logs will not be greater than 5MB. With the appropriate alerts set up, you might even be able to create the new log files before the existing log files are full and the database becomes unusable. However, neither of the secondary goals was achieved. Short of preventing users from making changes to the database, you can't limit the amount of log space that a database requires. In order to clear the log file of unnecessary information, you should set the database option Truncate on Checkpoint on the database options tab in SQL Server Enterprise Manager.

☒   **A, B,** and **D** are incorrect.

13. ☑   **A, B.** Using the Read Only option of the SP_DBOPTION command is particularly useful if you need to script your maintenance procedures and run them unattended during a maintenance window. Keep in mind that there are very few things that can only be done through T-SQL or in SQL Enterprise Manager. On a question like this, you should always look for both ways of accomplishing something.

☒   **C** and **D,** setting the user connections value to zero for the database and pausing the SQL Server service using the control panel services application, will not yield the expected results. They will not result in the database being placed in read only mode and may result in SQL Server becoming unusable.

Managing Security

1. ☑ **C.** The proposed solution achieves your primary and second optional goal. Using mixed mode security allows all clients access to the server. Using roles and views will restrict users from accessing data.
In order to encrypt data transmission, the multiprotocol network library must be used. Multiprotocol will automatically choose an available network protocol, and can encrypt the data sent between client and server.
☒ **A and C** are incorrect because only the first optional goal is achieved. **D** is incorrect because your primary goal is achieved.

2. ☑ **A.** The role has existing users. A role cannot be dropped until all users are dropped.
☒ **B** is incorrect because the syntax used was correct. SP_DROPROLE *rolename* will delete a role if all users are removed first. **C** is incorrect because members of both db_owner and db_securityadmin have permission to drop roles in a database. **D** is incorrect. It is true that fixed server roles cannot be deleted; however, the role in this example is not a fixed server role.

3. ☑ **A.** You must have reference permission on the Customers table in order to create a foreign key in the Orders table. A foreign key is used to enforce relationships between tables, and references another table (or itself) to ensure the value entered in the foreign key column exists in the second table's primary key column
☒ **B,** Reference permission on Orders, is incorrect because the reference permission should be applied to the table that is providing the information for the foreign key in the second table. **C,** Select permissions on Customers, and **D,** Select permission on Orders, are incorrect because select permission is not needed to create a foreign key.

4. ☑ **A, B.** If a user account with permissions to the database already exists for a login, the user account must be dropped first. Then use SP_CHANGEDBOWNER to change the owner to a different login.
☒ **C** is incorrect because SP_ADDUSER is used to add a new user account to a database. **B** is incorrect because SP_CHANGE_USERS_ LOGIN maps a user account to a different login account.

5. ☑ **D.** This is an example of a broken ownership chain. A broken ownership chain happens when an object does not have the same owner as do underlying objects. When User2 tried to use the view, SQL first checked permissions on the view. Then, because the view and the owner of the table are different, SQL Server checks permissions on the table. User2 does not have permissions on the table. If, for instance, the DBO had created the view and then assigned permissions to the view to User2, the view would have worked even though User2 had no permissions to the table. This is because DBO owned both the table and the view and SQL would not need to check permission on the table.
☒ **A** is incorrect because User2 had permissions to the view, granted by User1. **B** is incorrect because User1 created the view, making him the owner of the view. **C** is incorrect because it was stated in the example that User1 had select permission to the accounting table.

6. ☑ **C.** You can create a view that does not show the two columns and grant users access to the view. This will restrict them from viewing the actual table and viewing the confidential columns.
☒ **A and B** are incorrect because though you can use column-level security, a view is the best way to limit access to the columns.

7. ☑ **C.** Since Julie has created an object, her user account was added to the database in the Public role, and her user account cannot be removed. Julie can no longer access the database because she hasn't a login and her user account is orphaned. You can give her NT account access to the server so she will have access to the database. Alternatively, you can change ownership of the object and then remove her user account.

    ☒   **A** is incorrect because the group can be removed. **B** is incorrect because Julie will no longer have access to the server since she doesn't have a login. **D** is incorrect because the group can be removed, whether a login is created for Julie or not. You would create a login for Julie if you still wanted her to have access, or you could transfer ownership of the table she created.

8. ☑   **B.** Create an application role for each group. The application should verify user credentials and call the appropriate role using sp_setapprole.
    ☒   **A** is incorrect because this will not allow two different types of access. **C** is incorrect because it requires more overhead than necessary. **D** is incorrect because it does not allow for different permissions for the two groups, and it has no security.

9. ☑   **B.** The account used for the SQL Server Agent service does not have access to the network share. Add permission for this account to the share and the process will execute correctly.
    ☒   **A** is incorrect because the backup succeeded. If the Agent were not running, the job would not run. **C** is incorrect because the browser service is not required to write to a network drive. **D** is incorrect because you can copy backup files to another server, and the steps work when executing them in Query Analyzer.

10. ☑   **A, D.** Db_datareader allows read access to the entire database. Db_denydatawriter prohibits modifications to data in a database. Applying both roles will enable the assistant to read data, but not change it.
    ☒   **B** is incorrect, because db_datawriter would allow change access and **C** is incorrect because it would deny any read access.

11. ☑   **D.** When removing a user account, you must also remove the login account. Removing the user account does not automatically remove the login. The user can still access the database under the guest account unless the login is removed.
    ☒   **A** and **C** are incorrect, because you would not have been able to delete

the user account if he owned any objects in the database. **B** is incorrect because all memberships in roles are removed when a user account is dropped.

12. ☑ **B, C.** Db_accessadmin allows her to add and modify users and groups. Securityadmin allows her to manage server logins.
☒ **A** is incorrect because the setupadmin role manages linked servers. **D** is incorrect because the processadmin role manages processes running in SQL server.

13. ☑ **A.** The proposed solution meets the primary and both optional goals. Creating two application roles prevents the users from accessing other tables. The custom application is used for all access and modified to check users and set the role (sp_setapprole) based on the user's identity. By using application roles, the employees will not be able to access the database directly.
☒ **B, C,** and **D** are incorrect because all the goals are met.

14. ☑ **A.** Since DENY takes precedence over other permissions, adding the users to a role which is denied access to the table is the best way to restrict their access without changing their other permissions.
☒ **B** is incorrect because removing the users from the Company role would require you to reapply any other permissions they received through that role to the individual users. **C** is incorrect because sp_grantdbaccess creates a user account and **D** removes the login account for a user.

15. ☑ **D.** Once you've created a guest account in the Model database, any database later created will also contain a guest account. Users with valid logins can access a database with a guest account, even if they don't have a user account in that database
☒ **A** is incorrect because logins do not provide access to databases, but to the SQL server itself. **B** is incorrect because users by default do not have permission to create other user accounts. You would have to explicitly give them the ability to create user accounts (by assigning them to the db_accessadmin role, for instance). **C** is incorrect because guest accounts are

not created by default in new databases. The Model database provides a template for new databases and once the Guest account is added to Model, any database created since would have a Guest account.

16. ☑ **D.** Since you are using SQL Server authentication, creating roles and assigning users to the roles is the best way to manage security. Apply the permissions to the roles. For example, role1 would have Select and Update permission and role2 would have Insert and Update permission.
☒ **A** is incorrect because managing security by individual user accounts is inefficient and can be difficult to administer. **B** is incorrect because the server is using SQL authentication, not Mixed Mode, or NT authentication, so users are not connecting using their NT accounts. **C** is incorrect because you would still be applying permissions to individual users, and not to a group of users.

17. ☑ **A, B.** You can change a login password in Enterprise Manager and by using the SP_PASSWORD stored procedure.
☒ **C** is incorrect because you do not need to delete the login, and **D** is incorrect because there is not a password on the user account.

18. ☑ **A, B, C.** Only clients that are logging into NT can use NT logins. Unix and NetWare clients will need to use SQL authentication.
☒ **D** is incorrect because NetWare clients cannot use NT authentication to connect to the server

19. ☑ **D.** To add a user to the database, use the SP_GRANTDBACCESS stored procedure. The SP_GRANTDBACCESS stored procedure is used to add security accounts to a database for a SQL Server login or an NT user or group.
☒ **A** is incorrect because SP_ADD_OPERATOR adds an operator to be notified when alerts and notifications need to be sent. **B** is incorrect because SP_ADDALIAS maps user accounts to login accounts. **C** is incorrect because SP_GRANTLOGIN creates a login account, not a user account.

20. ☑ **D.** None. SQL 7 security model is similar to the Windows NT model. Permissions are cumulative, but a denial of permission takes precedence. John would be denied access to the database because DENY overrides the SELECT, UPDATE, and INSERT permissions.

☒ **A, B,** and **C** are incorrect because the denial of a specific permission takes precedence over other permissions assigned.

21. ☑ **A.** The db_ddladmin role will allow the assistant to add, modify and drop objects in the database.

☒ **B** is incorrect because it would give her more access than needed. **C** is incorrect because you cannot individually assign these permissions; they are implied in specific roles. **D** is incorrect because you'd never give another user your user ID and password.

22. ☑ **D.** In order to delete an account that has granted permission to other users (from the WITH GRANT option) you must first remove the permissions from the other users. Using the REVOKE with CASCADE option will remove access from the accounts that Alan granted rights to. You will then need to drop Alan's user account and login account.

☒ **A** is incorrect because you cannot drop a user account that has given permissions to other accounts (from the WITH GRANT option). You must first revoke the permission on all the accounts, and then drop the original account. **B** is incorrect because revoking the login will not delete the user account. **C** is incorrect because the login was not deleted and Alan could still log in and use the rights assigned the guest account in the database.

23. ☑ **B.** If you do not specify a database when creating a login, the MASTER database will be the default.

☒ **A, C** and **D** are incorrect because MASTER would be assigned as the default. You would have to specify MSDB or PUBS to enable one of them as the default database.

24. ☑ **D.** All of the above. In the SQL 7.0 security model, permissions are cumulative (except the DENY permission, which overrides any other permissions), so the user in this example would have INSERT, UPDATE, and SELECT permission.

25. ☑ **A.** Denying and revoking a login are not the same. DENY will lock Julie out of the SQL database completely, but revoking her login would still allow her access through the Sales group.
☒ **B** is incorrect because revoking Julie's login still allows her access through the Sales group. **C** and **D** are incorrect because you don't need to deny or revoke access to the entire Sales group.

Automating Administrative Tasks

1. ☑ **B.** The correct answer involves the SQLServer Agent service. Alerts are generated by the agent service. If the service is not running, is improperly configured, or does not have a MAPI profile associated with service account, then you won't receive e-mail or pager alerts.
☒ **A**, the MSDTC service is not running, is incorrect because it refers to the Microsoft Distributed Transaction Coordinator. **C**, the MSSQL Service is not running, is incorrect because the SQL Server service is not responsible for alert notifications. **D**, the Windows NT NetLogon Service is not running, is wrong because the Windows NT NetLogon service is the service that manages users logging into a Windows NT system.

2. ☑ **A, C.** E-mail and net send are the options that are available. E-mail would probably be the most reliable method of notification, but net send would probably be the quickest. You should be careful when using net send. An alert that is fired repetitively will result in multiple dialog boxes appearing on an administrator's screen. Each box will have to be closed before the administrator can continue working.
☒ **B**, page, is incorrect because the operators do not have pagers that can receive an alert from the SQL Agent. The agent can send a page only to a pager service that can be accessed through a MAPI interface. Basically, you have to be able to e-mail a message to your pager. There are third-party

pager gateways that integrate with SQL Server and Exchange that will use the TAPI interface to dial a number, but disregard this capability for the certification test. **D**, IRC, is incorrect because the SQL Agent has no native support for Internet Relay Chat.

3. ☑ **B, C, D.** To answer this question, think about the subcategories of the SQL Server Agent. The SQL Server Agent manages operators, alerts, and jobs. Operators define who is notified. Alerts define what conditions warrant an operator being notified. Jobs allow you to automate common administrative tasks, schedule them, and receive notifications of their success or failure.

☒ **A,** administrators, is incorrect because administrators is a group that defines security. The SQL Server Agent does not define who is in the administrators group and what they can do.

4. ☑ **B.** The most likely cause of John's problem is not being configured as an operator on the system that crashed. In order to receive alerts or notifications, an operator must be configured and you must specify the e-mail address, pager address, or network name of the user so that the SQL Agent knows how to send the alert. When setting up alerts, you can then choose an operator and determine how the operator should be notified.

☒ **A,** the e-mail server must have been down because domain administrators receive alerts by default when there is a significant SQL Server error, is incorrect because domain administrators are not notified of anything happening with SQL Server by default. Often the domain administrators and the SQL administrators are the same people, but an operator still must be configured for each domain administrator if you want to notify them individually. **C,** John's account must have been removed from the DBA group, is incorrect for the same reason that **A** is incorrect. Even if you are already a DBA, you still need an operator configured to receive alerts. **D,** John must not be set up as the default operator for the system, is incorrect because there is no such thing as a default operator. There is a fail-safe operator option, but the operator must be configured before that person can be specified as the fail-safe operator.

5. ☑ **B.** The proposed solution does produce the required result and one of the optional results. Your boss will no longer receive any pop-up notifications as a result of error messages coming from your SQL Server. The proposed solution also meets the first optional result. You have provided a way for your boss to receive alerts when sufficiently serious conditions are met. The second option result, however, is not satisfied. Configuration of operators has nothing to do with configuration of the actual alerts. Consequently, you have not affected whether an alert is logged to the Windows NT Event Log.

☒ **A, C,** and **D** are incorrect because **B** is the correct response.

6. ☑ **A.** All SQL-DMO required components are installed for a server or client installation. You may develop applications on either a client or a server.

☒ **B,** you need to install the SQL-DMO package from your SQL Server CD, is incorrect because you have everything you need installed already. **C,** you need to install the SQL-DMO header files from your SQL Server CD, is incorrect because you have everything you need installed already. **D,** Visual Basic provides everything you need to develop tools for SQL Server, is incorrect because Visual Basic does not provide the DLL that you need to develop your tool. You need to get that DLL by installing either SQL Server or the SQL Server client.

7. ☑ **C.** A target server can only have one master server. If you have many target servers you should define your master server on a nonproduction server. Traffic from the target servers will place a significant load on the master server. You might also want to forward events to a single server. If that server was the master server you could centralize all your administration on a single server. Setting up a master server requires creating a master server operator on the master server. The master server operator is the only operator that can receive notifications for multiserver jobs.

☒ **A,** all master servers must be using the same service account, is incorrect because the multiserver architecture does not have to be contained within a single SQL Server domain. **B,** master and target servers must be connected by a high-speed connection, is also incorrect. It's a good idea to have as much bandwidth as possible available between the master and target servers, but a high-speed connection is not a requirement. **D,** a master server can have only one target server, is incorrect because it is backwards.

8. ☑ **C.** All of the job steps prior to and including the backup database step must complete successfully for the job to report successful completion. If any of the steps fails, either the job reports failure immediately or control passes to the restore database step before reporting failure.
   ☒ **A,** all steps must complete successfully for the job to complete successfully, is incorrect because control will not pass to the restore database step if all of the previous steps complete successfully. **B,** the backup database step must complete successfully for the job to complete successfully, is incorrect because more than just the backup database step must complete successfully for the entire job to be a success. **D,** as long as the database is not being restored, the job will report success, is incorrect because restoring the database is part of the job failure routine.

9. ☑ **A.** When a target server contacts the master server, it reads the SYSDOWNLOADLIST table in the MSDB database. Operations assigned to the target server are stored in the SYSDOWNLOADLIST. Common operations include inserting, deleting, and starting jobs.
   ☒ **B,** SYSDOWNLOADLIST table in the MASTER database, **C,** SYSDOWNLOADLIST table in the TEMPDB database, and **D,** SYSDOWNLOADLIST table in the user database that is the target of the job, are incorrect because there is no SYSDOWNLOADLIST table in the MASTER, TEMPDB, or by default in a user database. Remember that almost everything having to do with the SQL Agent, including jobs for single or multiple servers, is stored in the MSDB database.

10. ☑ **A.** The polling interval has a default of one minute. The polling interval controls how often the target server downloads operations. The polling interval also controls how often the target server uploads job outcome statuses. If a job's execution frequency is greater than the polling

interval, it is possible that some job execution outcomes will not be uploaded. You can still view the job history on the target server in order to see all job execution outcomes.

☒ **B,** the server's polling interval is probably set higher than the job's execution frequency, is incorrect because it would not cause the problem you are experiencing. In fact, **B** represents the preferred configuration of the system. **C,** the servers are probably suffering from a lack of bandwidth due to a low-speed connection, could potentially cause the problem that you are having, but it would likely cause a number of other problems first. In any case, it is not the most likely answer. **D,** none of the above, is incorrect because **A** represents a correct answer.

11. ☑ **C.** You should have defected the target server before making the name change, then reenlisted the target server with the new name. You can add and remove target servers from the master server. A target server, however, can be added to only one master server. So, you must remember to remove a target server from one master before you add it to a different one. If you need to change the name of a target server, you should remove it from the master server first, then rename the target server, then add the target server back into the master server.

☒ **A,** you should have changed the target server's name in the MSDB database before changing the name of the system, and **B,** you should have run the sp_update_target system stored procedure before making the name change on the target server, are incorrect because they represent incorrect procedures for changing the name of a target server. Either of these procedures will likely result in additional configuration problems. **D,** there must be some other problem in the system, is incorrect because the master and target servers do not track each other by SID; they use the server name.

12. ☑ **A, B, C, D.** All four options are valid responses. You can also execute a job manually. Scheduling jobs is optional. Only one instance of the job can be run at a time. If you try to start a job manually while it is already running, SQL Server Agent will refuse the request. By default, all jobs are enabled. To temporarily prevent a scheduled job from running, disable the schedule. You

will still be able to execute a disabled job manually. Remember that if you edit the schedule of a job that is disabled, you must enable the job before it will run. Some conditions that result in schedules being automatically disabled include jobs scheduled to run one time, jobs scheduled to run at a specific date and time (and that time has passed), and jobs that are defined to run on a recurring schedule (and the end date has passed.)

Backing Up Databases

1. ☑ **B, C.** Performing regular backups and storing one copy of backups on the premises and a separate copy in an off-site storage facility is the best possible way of safeguarding data from natural disasters. Because this takes more time and money—as two copies of the data must be made—this may not be feasible in some businesses. When this is the case, performing regular backups and storing all backups off site should be done. If servers are damaged, the backups stored off site can be used to restore the data. If the backups stored off site are damaged, then the original data will still be retained on the server.

   ☒ **A,** perform regular backups and store all backups in a location on the premises, is wrong; if you store all backups on the premises where the backups were made, then backups can be destroyed by the same disaster that resulted in the complete loss of servers. If a flood, earthquake, or other events destroyed the premises—or areas where the data is stored—then you would lose all data on the backup media and the servers. **D,** perform backups only when the possibility of a disaster is foreseen; store one copy of backups on the premises and a separate copy in an off-site storage facility, is wrong because it's impossible to predict where and how natural disasters will strike. Even if the weather forecaster predicts a certain kind of weather (and we all know how reliable they are), there is no guarantee how or whether it will affect the premises storing data. In addition, by waiting until the last moment to prepare for such disasters, you put your own life at risk.

2. ☑ **A, B, C, D.** Each of the choices can result in the loss of data in a database. A complete loss of data can occur if one or more hard disks

containing data fail. Invalid entries or modifications by users or applications can result in the data becoming corrupt and the database needing to be replaced. Finally, a complete loss of a server can cause data loss. This may be the result of natural disasters—fire, flood, tornadoes, for example—or such things as theft. If the server is stolen, the data it contains is lost along with it. To deal with the possibility of such occurrences, you should perform regular backups of the data contained on servers. If the data becomes corrupt, the server is lost, or a hard disk fails, you may lose the hardware, but you don't need to lose the data. In the event of data loss, you can use a current backup of data to restore the database.

3. ☑ **B.** When you back up a database, the data and necessary portions of the transaction log are backed up. Only transactions that have occurred since the last backup of the transaction log will be included in the backup. When the database is restored, only the transactions that occurred between the previous and current backup will be restored.

☒ **A,** all transactions that have occurred since the first backup of the database will be restored, is wrong; when the transaction log is backed up, only changes that have occurred in the transaction log since the last backup are backed up. When you restore the transaction log, these changes are subsequently restored. Changes made in previous backups, or changes made since this current backup, will not be restored. **C,** none of the transactions will be restored with data, is also wrong. When you restore a database, you have the options of "Restore database and transaction logs," "Restore filegroups or files," and "Restore backup sets from device(s)." By selecting to "Restore database and transaction logs," you restore both the backed-up data and the transaction logs. There is no specific option to restore only transaction logs. The act of backing up a database copies the data in the database inclusive of any needed portions of the transaction log. For this reason, **D,** backing up a database doesn't copy portions of the transaction log, is also wrong.

4. ☑ **B.** Differential backups are used to back up all changes that have occurred to a database since the time of the last full backup. Because only

changes are backed up, this takes less time and less storage space than a full backup does.

☒ **A**, perform a full backup, is wrong because a full backup backs up the entire database. This takes considerably more time and storage space than a differential backup. Because a full backup is also called a complete backup, **C**, perform a complete backup, is also wrong. There is no such thing as a decremental backup so **D**, perform a decremental backup, is also incorrect.

5. ☑ **C**. When SQL Server reads through the transaction log, all completed transactions are rolled forward. In other words, the completed transactions are reapplied to the database. If there are incomplete transactions, then they are rolled back (that is, they are undone).

☒ **A**, SQL Server will roll forward all of the transactions, is wrong because all transactions won't necessarily be rolled forward. Incomplete transactions are rolled back, ensuring the integrity of data contained within the database. For similar reasons, **B**, SQL Server will roll back all of the transactions, is also incorrect. Again, all transactions aren't necessarily rolled back. In restoring the transaction log from the backup, SQL Server reapplies completed transactions that are recorded in the log to the database. **D**, all completed transactions will be rolled back and all incomplete transactions will be rolled forward, is incorrect because completed transactions are rolled forward, while incomplete transactions are rolled back.

6. ☑ **D**. The proposed solution doesn't product the required result. Because the entire database was destroyed, you must first restore the database with the last full backup. This will restore the entire database. After this, you then restore the last differential backup and all of the transaction log backups that have been created since the last differential database backup was done. This will restore the database to the same condition previous to the failure.

☒ **A**, **B**, and **C** are wrong because the proposed solution doesn't produce the required result. Even though restoring differential backups is faster than restoring a full backup, differential backups contain only changes that were made since the last full backup. Restoring the transaction logs will cause successful transactions to be rolled forward and unsuccessful ones to be rolled back. Despite this, neither of these will restore the entire database. To do this, you need to restore the last full backup and then restore the last differential backup and transaction logs.

7. ☑ **B, C.** When it is imperative that there is little to no downtime, you can use standby servers and cluster servers to keep data available. Standby servers contain identical or nearly identical copies of the data contained on a primary server. When the primary server goes down, the standby server can then be brought online, allowing users to log on and use the replicated data. Cluster servers don't require the user to log on to use another database. If one server goes down in a cluster, the user is unaware of the problem and continues to use the database.

☒ **A,** implement a regimen of regular backups; when the server goes down, restore from the backups, is wrong because restoring backups can take a considerable amount of time if a significant amount of data needs to be restored. As the data is mission critical and there needs to be little to no downtime, this isn't a viable solution. **D,** use mirroring so that data contained on one hard disk on the server is copied onto another hard disk on the server, is also wrong. With disk mirroring, the data on one hard disk is automatically copied to a second hard disk. This ensures that if one disk fails, the second disk will contain an exact duplicate of the data. Although disk mirroring can be implemented through NT Server, both of the hard disks located on the server will be unavailable if the server goes down.

8. ☑ **A.** You will need to synchronize the databases so that the data in each database is identical. During the time the primary server was offline, the standby server's database was being changed. Data was being added, modified, and/or deleted. To ensure that the data in the primary server's database includes these changes, you need to synchronize the primary server's database with the standby server's database.

☒ **B,** you will need to restore a backup of the data in the primary server's database to the standby server's database, is wrong because restoring a backup to the standby server's database would overwrite any changes that have occurred during the time that the primary server was offline. **C,** nothing because the standby server and the primary server are accessed through a virtual server, is wrong because this choice describes a cluster server, not a standby server. **D,** nothing because, on restarting the standby server, the primary server's database will be automatically synchronized with the database on the standby server, is also wrong; the administrator will need to synchronize the databases when the primary server goes back online.

9. ☑ **C.** Standby servers are a way of keeping mission-critical data available, despite the failure of a database or server. When a primary server goes down, or when a database located on that server becomes corrupted or unavailable, then users can log onto the standby server and use the duplicate database located on that server. The data on the primary server can be duplicated on the standby server through backups and transaction logs, or it can be automatically replicated. This ensures that even if the primary server goes down, the data is still available.

☒ **A, B,** and **D** are wrong because the proposed solution produces the required result, but it produces none of the optional desired results. If the server goes down, users will be aware that a problem exists. Users aren't automatically switched over to a standby server. They will need to log onto the standby server to use the database contained on it. Once logged on, they will need to restart any tasks they were performing on the primary server before it went down. In addition, any noncommitted transactions will be permanently lost. They will need to redo any noncommitted transactions upon logging into the standby server.

10. ☑ **A, B, D.** Failover support is a feature of SQL Server 7.0, and it uses clustering to make data available if a single server goes offline. Because failover support is a feature of SQL Server 7.0, you need to have a copy of SQL Server 7.0 running on a Windows NT Server. You also need Microsoft Cluster Server (MSCS) to run on the NT Servers that are used as part of the cluster. SQL Server Failover Support runs on top of MSCS.

☒ **C,** Windows NT Workstation, is wrong because MSCS runs on NT Server, not NT Workstation. It is included with Windows NT Server Enterprise Edition.

11. ☑ **C.** The type of failover support described in the question is Active/Passive. In an Active/Passive setup there are one virtual server, one copy of SQL Server 7.0 on one or more shared drives, and two physical servers. The primary, or active, server controls SQL Server. If this fails, the administrator must change control of SQL Server to the secondary server manually.

☒ **A,** Active, and **B,** Passive, are both wrong because these aren't types of failover support. There are only Active/Passive and Active/Active types of failover support available through SQL Server 7.0. **D,** Active/Active, is wrong because an Active/Active setup has each physical server controlling a virtual server, and it contains two copies of SQL Server. When one server fails, the users are still able to access the SQL Server database through the other server.

12. ☑ **D.** The type of failover support described in the question is Active/Active. In an Active/Active configuration there are two virtual servers, two copies of SQL Server 7.0 on one or more shared drives, and two physical servers. Each of the physical servers controls a SQL Server virtual server. When one physical server fails, users are able to access data controlled on the other physical server.

☒ **A,** Active, and **B,** Passive, are both wrong because these aren't types of failover support. There are only Active/Passive and Active/Active types of failover support available through SQL Server 7.0. **C,** Active/Passive, is wrong because Active/Passive configurations of failover support only use a single virtual server and one copy of SQL Server 7.0.

13. ☑ **A.** Because SQL Server 7.0 failover support runs on top of Microsoft Cluster Server (MSCS), the MSCS Cluster Administrator is used to administer the areas mentioned in this question. MSCS Cluster Administrator is used to control areas of failover support including failover and failback policies, and to move services and resources between servers.

☒ **B,** SQL Server Enterprise Manager, is wrong because it isn't used for administration of such policies and moving services and resources between clustered servers. It is used to manage SQL Server objects from a single location. **C,** SQL Server Profiler, is also wrong, as SQL Server Profiler is used to monitor network traffic. **D**, SQL Server Agent, is also wrong; it is used for scheduling tasks and alerts.

14. ☑ **B.** Regardless of the type of failover support being used, you will need a minimum of two physical servers. When the primary server in the cluster fails, the secondary server takes over. This allows the users to continue doing their work without even realizing a problem has occurred.
☒ **A**, one, is wrong because you can't have a cluster of one server. If a single server went down, you wouldn't have a secondary server to take over. **C**, three, is also wrong, as a minimum of two physical servers are required to make a server cluster and to take advantage of SQL Server 7.0's failover support. **D**, no minimum number of servers, is wrong because a minimum number of servers are required to implement failover support.

15. ☑ **B.** When backing up to a tape device, the tape device needs to be physically connected to the computer running SQL Server. You can't back up to tape devices that are physically connected to other computers running on the network.
☒ **A**, the named pipe used to back up the data hasn't been configured properly, is wrong because a named pipe is used by third-party vendors so that their software can provide backup capabilities for SQL Server databases. **C**, the tape backup device is full, is wrong because you can't use a tape device that's physically connected to another server. If the tape were full on a tape device connected to your computer, you would be prompted to replace the tape with another one. **D**, SQL Server doesn't support tape devices, is also wrong; it does support tape devices as a medium for backing up data.

16. ☑ **B.** Named pipes allow third-party vendors to create devices and applications that connect the software and provide backup capabilities for backing up SQL Server databases. By using named pipes, the third-party device can interact with SQL Server and back up its data.
☒ **A**, disk backup, and **C**, unnamed pipes, are wrong because disk backups and tape backups are methods that are available in SQL Server 7.0. Using SQL Server, you can back up data to each of these kinds of media. **D**,

tape backup, is wrong because SQL Server uses named pipes to allow third-party backup devices and applications to work with SQL Server and back up its databases.

17. ☑ **D.** When the tape becomes full, you'll be prompted to replace the full tape with another one. Upon replacing the tape, you can then continue with backing up the remaining data that didn't fit on the first tape.
☒ **A**, the backup will fail so replace the tape with a blank one, then restart backing up the database, is wrong because the backup won't fail. You will be prompted only to replace the existing tape with another one. By restarting the backup, the same message will appear when the new tape becomes full. **B**, the backup will fail so replace the tape with a blank one, then perform a differential backup of the data, is also wrong because the backup will not fail when the tape becomes full. By performing a differential backup, only changes made to the database since the last full backup will be backed up. You are performing a complete backup so you want to back up the entire database, not merely changes to it. **C**, replace the tape with the existing one that's full; the backup will continue by putting the remaining data over existing data on the tape, is wrong because this will overwrite any existing data on the tape that's become full. This will corrupt the backup so that you won't be able to restore it.

18. ☑ **A, D.** Two programs that can be used to back up a database in SQL Server 7.0: SQL Server Enterprise Manager and the Create Backup Wizard. SQL Server Enterprise Manager has features that allow you to back up databases, while the Create Backup Wizard steps you through the process of backing up data.
☒ **B**, Transact-SQL Enterprise Manager, is incorrect because there is no program called Transact-SQL Enterprise Manager. It was made up for the purpose of this question. **C**, Transact-SQL, is also wrong because Transact-SQL isn't a program. By using Transact-SQL, you can use the "BACKUP DATABASE" statement in a Transact-SQL statement to back up a database. As the question specifically asks for programs you can use to back up a database, this choice is also wrong.

19. ☑ **B.** The syntax for backing up a database is BACKUP DATABASE, followed by the name of the database and the device to which the database is to be backed up. As the database is called Sales and the backup device is Sale_Bak, you would use "BACKUP DATABASE Sales TO Sale_Bak".

☒ **A,** BACKUP Sales TO Sale_Bak, is incorrect because the word DATABASE is missing from the statement. **C,** BACKUP DATABASE Sales TO Sale_Bak WITH RESTART, is incorrect because this statement would be used if you wanted to resume backing up a database that was interrupted. **D,** BACKUP DATABASE Sales TO Sale_Bak WITH RESTORE, is wrong because there is no WITH RESTORE parameter with the BACKUP DATABASE statement.

20. ☑ **C.** The database won't be created, and the backup will continue as normal. While a backup can be performed while the database is online and users are doing various activities, some activities can't be performed. Indexes can't be created, database files can't be created or deleted, the database can't be shrunk, and nonlogged operations can't be performed. If a user attempts to perform any of these operations when the database is being backed up, the operation will fail. The backup will be unaffected by such an attempt, and it will continue as normal.

☒ **A,** the backup will fail and the database will be created, and **B,** the database will be created and the backup will continue as normal, are wrong—a database file can't be created during a full backup of a database. **D,** the database won't be created and the backup will fail, is wrong, as the backup won't fail when someone attempts to create or delete a database file. The user will be prohibited from doing so, but the backup will continue as normal.

21. ☑ **C.** The WITH RESTART parameter is used to restart the backup from the point where it was interrupted. The syntax for backing up a database is using the statement BACKUP DATABASE, followed by the name of the database and the device to which the database is to be backed up. As the database is called Sales and the backup device is Sale_Bak, you would use "BACKUP DATABASE Sales TO Sale_Bak WITH RESTART".

☒ **A**, BACKUP Sales TO Sale_Bak, is incorrect because the WITH RESTART parameter is missing. In addition, the word DATABASE is missing from the statement. As such, this statement would neither restart the backup from where the interruption occurred nor start the backup over from the beginning. **B**, BACKUP DATABASE Sales TO Sale_Bak, is incorrect because this statement would have the backup start over from the beginning, rather than from where the interruption occurred. **D**, BACKUP DATABASE Sales TO Sale_Bak WITH RESTORE, is wrong because there is no WITH RESTORE parameter with the BACKUP DATABASE statement.

22. ☑ **A**. The backup will abort, and the index will be created. Backups can't be performed if a user or users are creating indexes, creating and deleting database files, resizing databases, and performing nonlogged operations. If you attempt to do a backup when such operations are being performed, the backup will abort.

   ☒ **B**, the index will be created and the backup will continue as normal, is wrong because while the index will be created the backup won't continue as normal. **C**, the index won't be created and the backup will continue as normal, and **D**, the index won't be created and the backup will abort, are also wrong. The index will be created. It is the backup that will abort.

23. ☑ **A, C**. You should back up a master database when a user database has been added or deleted or any time server-wide or database configuration options are changed. Other situations where you'd want to back up the master database include when login and security-related operations have been modified, when backup devices are added or removed, or when you've configured the server for distributed queries and remote procedure calls.

   ☒ **B**, any time a user database is backed up, is incorrect, as you need to back up only the master database under the conditions mentioned here. **D**, any time that data is added or changed since the last full backup of a user database, is incorrect because databases can have data being added, deleted, and changed on a regular and frequent basis. This would mean that the master database would constantly need to be backed up.

24. ☑ **A, B, C.** The "Transaction log" option in the Create Backup Wizard will back up a record of all the changes made to the database. When a full or differential backup is performed, the active portion of the transaction log is automatically backed up with the data. The "Database backup" and "Differential database" options will, respectively, perform full and differential backups of data.

☒ **D,** full backup, is wrong because there is no option called Full Backup in the Create Backup Wizard. Selecting the "Database backup" option in the wizard performs a full backup.

25. ☑ **A, C, D.** Three methods can be used to do a differential backup of a database in SQL Server 7.0. They are SQL Server Enterprise Manager, Transact-SQL, and the Create Backup Wizard. SQL Server Enterprise Manager has features that allow you to back up databases, while the Create Backup Wizard steps you through the process of backing up data. By using Transact-SQL, you can use the WITH DIFFERENTIAL parameter in a "BACKUP DATABASE" statement to do a differential backup of a database.

☒ **B,** Transact-SQL Enterprise Manager, is incorrect because there is no program called Transact-SQL Enterprise Manager. It was made up for the purpose of this question.

26. ☑ **D.** The WITH DIFFERENTIAL parameter is used to start a differential backup using Transact-SQL. The syntax for backing up a database is using the statement BACKUP DATABASE, followed by the name of the database and the device to which the database is to be backed up. As the database is called Customer and the backup device is Cust_Bak, you would use "BACKUP DATABASE Customer TO Cust_Bak WITH DIFFERENTIAL".

☒ **A,** DIFFERENTIAL BACKUP Customer TO Cust_Bak, is incorrect because the statement is wrong. The word DATABASE is missing from the statement, and the syntax is wrong. **B,** BACKUP DATABASE Cust_Bak TO Customer WITH DIFFERENTIAL, is incorrect because the order of the database and backup device is mixed up. Customer should appear where Cust_Bak is, and Cust_Bak should appear where Customer is. Finally, **C,**

BACKUP Customer TO Cust_Bak WITH DIFFERENTIAL, is wrong because the word DATABASE is missing from the statement.

27. ☑ **A.** When you perform a file or filegroup backup, one or more files of a database are copied, allowing the database to be backed up into smaller units. Unlike other backups, a file or filegroup backup doesn't back up a portion or the entire transaction log.
☒ **B,** full or complete backup, and **C,** differential backup, are wrong because when you perform a differential backup, or a full or complete backup, the active portion of the transaction log is automatically backed up. **D,** transaction log, is wrong because backing up the transaction logs will obviously back up a transaction log.

28. ☑ **B.** The Database Maintenance Plan Wizard is used to schedule regular backups of databases on a SQL Server. Using this program, you can configure SQL Server to back up a database and transaction log files, compress data files, update index statistics, and verify the integrity of a backed-up database. You can even configure the Database Maintenance Plan Wizard to remove backups after a specific period of time has elapsed.
☒ **A,** SQL Server Enterprise Manager, is wrong because SQL Server Enterprise Manager doesn't have the ability to automate backups. While it is used to back up a database, it can't be used to schedule backups. **C,** Transact-SQL, is also wrong, as Transact-SQL isn't used for scheduling backups. It is, however, used to back up data by entering statements that invoke SQL Server to back up databases. Finally, **D,** The Create Backup Wizard, is wrong because—although the Create Backup Wizard steps you through the process of backing up data—it doesn't have features for scheduling backups.

29. ☑ **A, B.** The Database Maintenance Plan Wizard and the SQL Server Enterprise Manager have options that cause these programs to verify that all files have been written to the backup and that all files are readable. In doing this, the structure of the database isn't checked. When you choose to verify the integrity of a backup on completion, it checks only that files are copied correctly and that they are readable.

☒ **C**, SQL Verify Agent, is wrong because there is no such program as SQL Verify Agent. It doesn't exist and was made up for the purpose of this question. **D**, the Create Backup Wizard, is incorrect because the Create Backup Wizard doesn't provide an option to verify the integrity of a backup.

Methods of Restoring Databases

1. ☑ **B.** The WITH RESTART option allows you to start your restore operation from the point of interruption, so this would be the best option. ☒ **A**, RESTORE DB1 FROM BACKUP1, would restore your backup, but from the beginning. **C**, RESTORE DB1 FROM BACKUP1 WITH UNLOAD, rewinds and unloads the tape; **D**, RESTORE DB1 FROM BACKUP1 WITH REPLACE, overwrites a database that already exists..

2. ☑ **D.** Restore the tables, and recreate the indexes. A table whose indexes are on multiple filegroups must be backed up at the same time its indexes are to recover both the table and indexes. You would need to restore the table, and re-create all indexes.
   ☒ **A** is syntactically correct, but if a table's indexes span multiple filegroups, all filegroups containing the table and its indexes must be backed up together. **B** is the syntax for restoring a full database backup, and **C** is the 6.5 version of RESTORE.

3. ☑ **C, B, A.** In order to bring a standby server online, the active transaction log on the production server needs to be restored to the standby server, so first back up the production server log, then restore the log to the standby server. RESTORE DATABASE WITH RECOVERY will take the standby server out of read-only mode, enabling users to modify the standby database.
   ☒ **D**, none of the above, is incorrect.

4. ☑ **B.** The proposed solution meets the required result and one optional result. Using a standby server would allow you to recover the database in the shortest amount of time. While it is in standby mode, reporting can be run on the standby server. However, the backup time is not minimized, as

you will need to back up the production database and restore the backup to the standby server nightly.

5. ☑ **A, B.** You can copy the data files and use the sp_attach_db command to restore them with a different database name. You can also restore the database from a backup with the REPLACE switch.
   ☒ There is no RENAME switch, so **C**, restore the database with the RENAME switch, is incorrect. **D**, you cannot restore a database with a different name, is incorrect because a database can be restored with a different name, using either Enterprise Manager, or Query Analyzer.

6. ☑ **B.** Restart SQL server using the –m option to run in single-user mode, then restore MASTER.
   ☒ **A**, run REBUILDM.EXE, is.incorrect because running REBUILDM.EXE will rebuild MASTER, but it will also require you to reattach and/or restore all databases. **C**, reinstall SQL Server, is incorrect because reinstalling SQL Server requires much more time than is actually needed. **D**, execute sp_resetstatus, is incorrect because it simply resets the SUSPECT attribute and resolves no corruption issues.

7. ☑ **B.** You can recover to a specific time by using STOPAT < date_time> in the RESTORE statement.
   ☒ **A**, back up the active log, restore the database, and reapply the transaction log with the TIME option, is incorrect because there is no TIME option available in RESTORE. **C**, restore the database, and reapply all transaction log backups, is incorrect because the active log was not backed up first. **D**, you cannot recover to a point in time, is incorrect because you can recover by following the steps in **A**.

8. ☑ **B.** To restore ACCOUNTING, the first step is to back up the active transaction log. You can then restore the last full backup (Wednesday) and restore each log in the order you backed it up. Last, apply the active transaction log backup, using the WITH RECOVERY option.

☒　**A,** restore Wednesday's backup, is incorrect because Wednesday's backup would restore the database to the point it was on Wednesday. **C,** restore Wednesday's backup, then each transaction log backup in the order backed up, is incorrect because the active transaction log was not backed up first. **D,** restore Sunday's backup, restore Wednesday's backup, and restore each transaction log, is incorrect because you do not need to restore the Sunday backup, and you did not back up the active transaction log.

9. ☑　**D.** You use the RECOVERY clause on the last backup you intend to restore.

☒　**A,** the full backup, **B,** the differential backup, and **C,** the transaction log on Friday, 12 p.m., are incorrect because each backup is not the last backup to be restored and should have a NORECOVERY clause. If you were not able to back up the active transaction log, you'd use the recovery clause on the last log you are restoring.

10. ☑　**A.** To bring the production server back online, perform a full backup on the standby server, back up the transaction log, and restore both to the production server, using the RECOVERY clause on the log restore.

☒　**B,** execute RESTORE DATABASE WITH RECOVERY, is incorrect because RESTORE DATABASE WITH RECOVERY is used to bring a standby server online. **C,** back up the log on the standby server and restore to the production server, is incorrect because the database needs to be restored as well to the production server. **D,** rename the production server, is incorrect. The standby server would be renamed when it is brought online, but renaming the production server will not recover the database.

11. ☑　**B.** Restore the secondary filegroup backup and each transaction log backup is correct. Because the secondary filegroup is where the data resides, and because the primary group has not been modified, you would need to restore only the secondary filegroup and apply each transaction log consecutively.

☒　**A,** restore the database backup, the differential backup, and each transaction log backup up until 2 p.m., **C,** restore the database backup, the filegroup backup, and each transaction log backup, and **D,** restore the differential backup and each transaction log backup, are incorrect because you did not back up the active transaction log and the database is not restored to point of failure.

12. ☑ **A.** If the Publisher fails, you can restore the Publisher and resynchronize all publications with the Subscribers.
☒ **B** and **D** are incorrect because the distributor does not need to be restored. **C** is incorrect because the Subscribers should be resynchronized.

13. ☑ **A** is the correct answer.
☒ **B** is incorrect because the last log restore needs the RECOVERY option. **C** is incorrect because the all the logs must be restored, not just the last log, and **D** is incorrect because all the logs must be restored, and the last log restore needs the RECOVERY option.

14. ☑ **C.** Transaction 2 is committed. Any transactions that are committed before the database backup completes will be backed up. The database will be restored to a point where transaction 2 is committed, and Transactions 1 and 3 are rolled back.
☒ **A**, transaction 3 is committed, **B**, transactions 1 and 3 are committed, and **D**, transactions 1, 2, and 3 are committed, are incorrect because transactions 1 and 3 are committed after the database backup has completed. These transactions will be rolled back ("undone") when the database is restored because they had not completed prior to the backup completion.

15. ☑ **B.** A differential backup contains all the changes made since the last full backup, so you'd need to restore the last full backup, the most recent differential backup, and the active transaction log backup.
☒ **A**, restore Wednesday's backup and the active transaction log, is incorrect because the differential backup contains changes since the last full backup, and you cannot restore this backup without the full backup run on Sunday. **C**, restore Sunday's backup, Monday's backup, and Wednesday's backup, is incorrect because you do not need to restore Monday's backup.

Wednesday's backup contains all the changes made since Sunday. **D**, restore Sunday's backup, is incorrect because the differential and the active transaction log were not restored.

16. ☑　**C.** You cannot restore a database once you've removed or added files. You must back up the database after the addition or deletion of files.
　☒　**A**, do nothing and restore as normal, is incorrect because you must restore a backup created after the addition of the file. **B**, add an ALTER DATABASE statement to the restore script, is incorrect because you cannot alter the database in the restore operation. **D**, delete the file in Explorer, is incorrect because you cannot remove the file from SQL by just deleting the file.

17. ☑　**D.** The standby server is set to 6.5 compatibility mode. When upgrading from an earlier version, SQL is automatically set to the earlier version's mode to enable existing applications to run after an upgrade without changes. To restore to the standby server, run sp_dbcmptlevel and set the mode to 70.
　☒　**A**, use the NORECOVERY option, is incorrect because NORECOVERY is used when restoring backups to a production server. **B**, you cannot restore backups to a different server, is incorrect because backups can be restored to a different server. **C**, use the RECOVERY option, is incorrect because RECOVERY is used when restoring the last backup or when bringing a standby server online.

18. ☑　**A.** Restoring the SALES filegroup would be the quickest way to recover the ORDERS table. First the active transaction log should be backed up, then the filegroup should be restored. Then apply the transaction log using a STOPAT option to recover the database to the specified point in time (8:59 a.m. in this scenario).
　☒　**B** is incorrect because the transaction log must be applied to ensure a consistent database. **C** is incorrect for a few reasons. You don't need to restore back to last Friday, and you don't need to restore the Customer filegroup from Tuesday because that file was not affected by the delete. In

addition, the transaction log needs to be reapplied. **D** is incorrect because you cannot roll back a transaction once it has been committed.

19. ☑ **D.** Back up the production database using both tape drives, restore to development using one tape drive. You can use multiple tape devices to back up a database and fewer devices in the restore operation. SQL will prompt for each tape until all tapes have been processed.
    ☒ **A,** back up the production database using one tape drive, and restore to development, is incorrect because you can back up using multiple drives and restore using fewer tape drives. **B,** copy the .MDB files to the development server and use sp_attach_db, is incorrect because Access uses .MDB files, not SQL Server. **C,** use Snapshot replication to copy the data from production to development, is incorrect because you don't need to copy the data more than once; it's much simpler to back up and restore the files.

20. ☑ **B.** It is possible to back up and restore cross-platform. Using this option will enable you to restore the transaction logs to the standby server.
    ☒ **A,** use DTS to move data to the Intel server, **C,** use bcp to move the data to the Intel server, and **D,** copy the database files to the Intel server, are incorrect. You will not be able to apply transaction log backups without first restoring a full database backup.

21. ☑ **A.** To restore this database to a standby server, select "Leave database read-only and able to restore additional transaction logs." This is the same as using the STANDBY option on a RESTORE statement.
    ☒ **B,** select "Leave database operational. No additional transaction logs can be restored," is incorrect because this will enable the database for operation and you will be unable to restore any transaction logs. This is the same as using the RECOVERY option in the RESTORE statement. **C,** select "Leave database nonoperational, but able to restore additional transaction logs," is incorrect because a standby server is left as read-only, not nonoperational. This option is the same as using the NORECOVERY option in the RESTORE statement. **D,** none of the above, is incorrect because A is the correct choice.

22. ☑ C. You can restore up until Wednesday. You cannot restore any log files after a missing log file. All preceding log backups must be applied.
☒ A, Friday, is wrong because no log files after Wednesday can be restored, due to the missing tape. B, Thursday, is wrong because the tape from Thursday is missing. D, Sunday, is wrong because Wednesday's differential backup can be applied.

23. ☑ A. Once you've specified the RECOVERY option, you have to begin the restore process from the beginning to restore any additional backups.
☒ B, continue restoring Friday's log backup, is incorrect because you cannot restore any other backups once the RECOVERY option has been used. C, reapply Thursday's differential backup with the NORECOVERY option, is incorrect because you cannot reapply a backup; you must begin the restore again. D, do nothing and leave the point of restore at Thursday, is incorrect because the database can be restored to Friday, and the restore operation should be started over.

Transferring Data

1. ☑ A. By giving Tom the operator password but not the owner password, he will be able to execute the package, but he will be unable to edit the package. He will also be unable to read it because DTS encrypts the package when a password is applied.
☒ B, give Tom the owner password but not the operator password, is incorrect because if Tom had the owner password, he could make changes to the package. C, in User Manager, assign Tom to the DTSOwner group, but not the DTSOperator group, and D, in User Manager, assign Tom to the DTSOperator group, but not the DTSOwner group, are incorrect because the DTSOwner and DTSOperator groups do not exist.

2. ☑ B, C. Because the source field could store a decimal value like 14.4 but the destination field would have to round this to 14, some precision will be lost. Therefore, you must enable the data type demotion option, which is available under "Custom Transformation flags." You will also have to enable "Allow null conversion."

☒ **A,** "Allow data type promotion," is not needed because the data type is being degraded, not upgraded. Despite its subtitle, **D,** "Default Transformation Flags," enables only null conversions and promotions, so to enable demotions you need to use Customer Transformation Flags.

3. ☑ **D.** Create Task Objects that use DataPump tasks to move the content from one OLEDB object to another, and then create Step Objects to sequence these Task Objects. The Task objects perform the individual data migration steps. (These steps include "Execute SQL," "Data Pump," "Microsoft ActiveX Script," "Execute Process," "Bulk Insert," "Send Mail," "Data Driven Query," and "Transfer SQL Server Objects." The Step objects reference these task objects and control their flow.

☒ **A,** create Connection Objects that use DataPump tasks to move the content from one OLEDB object to another, and then create Task Objects to sequence these Connection Objects, and **B,** create Connection Objects that use DataPump tasks to move the content from one OLEDB object to another, and then create Step Objects to sequence these Connection Objects, incorrectly imply that Connection Objects can control Task or Step objects. (The connection objects define the referenced data sources, but they do not define how that data source should be manipulated.) **C,** create Step Objects that use DataPump tasks to move the content from one OLEDB object to another, and then create Task Objects to sequence these Step Objects, is incorrect because it inverts the relationship between Task objects and Step objects.

4. ☑ **B.** You will see "172-32-1176", "White", "Johnson", "408 496-7223", "10932 Bigger Rd.", "Menlo Park", "CA", 94025, -1. The row delimiters of {CR} and {LF} represent the carriage return and line feed—ASCII characters 13 and 10, respectively. When viewed in a text editor, these characters will not be visible.

☒ **A,** au_id, au_lname, au_fname, phone, address, city, state, zip, contract, and **C,** au_id, au_lname, au_fname, phone, address, city, state, zip, contract {CR}{LF}, are incorrect because the "First row has column names" checkbox is not checked. **D**, "172-32-1176", "White", "Johnson", "408 496-7223", "10932 Bigger Rd.", "Menlo Park", "CA", 94025, -1 {CR}{LF}, incorrectly implies that the Row Delimiter is a text string containing "{CR}{LF}" instead of the ASCII characters for the carriage return and line feed.

5. ☑ **D.** When you use DTS, the content is copied at the intervals you define, and so the external data is not available in real time to SQL Server users. You can schedule the processes to run more frequently if needed, but if you need real-time access to data, you may want to link directly to the needed tables.

☒ Although both of the optional desired results are met by this approach, because the required result is not met, options **A**, **B**, and **C** are all false.

6. ☑ **B.** Create a new format file to map the new fields appropriately. By making modifications to the format file, you can accommodate significant change to the structure of the underlying source data without requiring alterations to other parts of your process. This flexibility allows you to map the input fields to the destination fields as needed. (You can create a format file by using BCP with or without "c" or "n" options. BCP will walk you through the delimiter definitions and field mapping and then export the format file. Then you can point to this format file in subsequent BCP operations using the "f" option.)

☒ **A**, add the DISCOUNT field to your pricing table and import as usual, would fail because your table's columns would be in the wrong order. **C**, creating a batch file to preprocess the source file, could work, but it would be much more difficult than changing the format file. **D**, creating an extra table, would consume additional server resources unnecessarily.

7. ☑ **A.** No records will be loaded. The BCP file will not be imported successfully because there were 16 errors, which is more than the 10-error default threshold. It is possible to change this threshold by using the "-m" parameter. Even if the number of failures is less than the threshold, the entire record is discarded, so it probably would be best to clean the data before importing it.

☒ **B,** all the records will be loaded, but the STARTDATE will be NULL in these 16 records, is wrong because when any field cannot be loaded, the entire record is discarded. **C,** the records with a valid STARTDATE will be imported, and the records with invalid STARTDATES will not be imported, would be true if "-m" was used to set a higher error threshold. Because there is no log file associated with BCP import errors unless the "-e" flag is used, **D,** the records with a valid STARTDATE will be imported, and the records with invalid STARTDATES will be written to a log file, is also incorrect. (Do not confuse the "-e" flag, which outputs the error records, with the "-o" flag, which provides an output log file.)

8. ☑ **C.** Add the "E" flag to the BCP import. Normally, the identity field automatically increments, and the values of the PatientID field for these patients would change, and thus referential integrity would be lost for the foreign tables that depended on these records. The "–E" parameter, however, states that BCP should import the identity fields. By preserving these values, the views should return content again.

☒ None of the other options described would address the issue observed. **A,** add the "k" flag to the BCP import, is incorrect because the "-k" flag states that empty fields should be loaded as NULL instead of loaded with the default. **B,** add the "Usa" parameter to the BCP import, is wrong because "Usa" indicates that the system administrator account should be used to load the records. **D,** add the "F" flag to the BCP import, is incorrect because the "F" flag identifies the first record to be imported from the file.

9. ☑ **C, D.** Delete records that violate table constraints and re-create the indexes for that table. The constraints are not applied as the data is loaded, so if you want to have them apply to the new data, you must do this after importing. If the indexes are not re-created, this could have a very negative effect on performance. (In addition to these steps, you should back up your data after completing a BCP import because the current state is not recoverable from the transaction log.)

☒   **A,** populate default values for columns omitted from the field list, is false because default values will still apply for fields omitted from the column list. All content is automatically populated into the appropriate data type, so **B,** convert imported data to the appropriate data type, is also false. (If a field cannot be converted into the appropriate type, the record is not loaded at all.)

10. ☑   **C.** BCP the file into a global temporary table, and then use two INSERT statements to populate both tables. Unfortunately, you cannot import this content directly into the needed tables. You can, however, migrate this content relatively easily using two INSERT statements. (For example, suppose you had two tables A and B, and A had a foreign key reference into the second table. You could build one query using GROUP BY to populate B. Then you could use a second ungrouped query to populate A.)

☒   **A,** BCP the file directly into the view, is incorrect because you cannot BCP into a view. **B,** BCP the file into a global temporary table, and then loop through record by record to populate tables, could work, but it would be much less efficient than a query-oriented approach. **D,** BCP the file into a global temporary table, and then use INSERT INTO to populate the view, is wrong because you cannot use INSERT on a view that requires writes to multiple tables.

11. ☑   **D.** BCP overwrote any existing text file named "exercise.dat". BCP does not check to see if an existing file of the same name already exists. Therefore, if you use BCP as part of a batch file, you may want to archive these existing exports in your batch file before BCP is executed.

☒   **A,** the "exercise.dat" file can be imported into SQL Server 6.5, is incorrect because a different native format is used in SQL Server 6.5 than in 7.0. **B,** the "exercise.dat" file can be imported into Excel, is wrong because the "n" indicates that the internal format is used, so it could not be imported into Excel. The "T" indicates that BCP used a trusted connection to log in, so **C,** BCP logged in as SA to export the data, is not correct.

12. ☑   **D.** The new record will not be inserted. When a table is created and a column does not have a default value and does not accept nulls, you must specify a value for that field when populating it. If no value is specified, then the INSERT will fail.

☒   Because there will be no new record, options **A, B,** and **C** are all false. (If all of the fields in "Offices" were not defined NOT NULL, then the statement would insert a null value into both LastName and OfficeID.)

13. ☑   **A.** No rows will be added to the table. When you use SELECT as a source for INSERT, if any records cannot be inserted then the entire action is canceled. When we tested the subquery, we observed that the state field was not always populated, so in the output there was a null in the first column. Because the State field cannot support nulls, the entire Insert statement will fail, and no rows are created.

☒   **B,** one row will be added to the table, could be true if there were no GROUP BY clause and if aggregate functions were used in both fields in the Select statement. **C,** three rows will be added to the table, implies that the INSERT INTO statement can be partially successful, which is false. If the StateSales table were defined differently, so that nulls were allowed in the State field, then four rows would have been added to the table (**D**).

14. ☑   **B.** The proposed solution produces the required result and only one of the optional results. Because you are inserting into a view, the DBA can add columns to the table without interrupting your operations. Because the view references the table columns by name, not order, this approach would also be safe even if the DBA rebuilt the base table with the columns in a different order.

☒   As described above, the approach provides the required result and one of the optional results, so **C** and **D** are incorrect. Because the fields are referenced by name, the view would "break" if a field were renamed, so **A,** the proposed solution produces the required result and both of the optional results, is also incorrect.

15. ☑   **B.** You need to include three paramters. When omitting the field list, you must provide a value for every field in the destination table or view.

You do not normally provide a value for identity columns. (This behavior can be changed by using SET IDENTITY_INSERT.)

☒ **A**, 4, would be true if you had to provide a value for the identity field. **C**, 2, would be true if you did not have to populate the UNIQUE IDENTIFIER field. (Unlike IDENTITY fields, fields defined with UNIQUEIDENTIFIER require manual population. If it creates a record through INSERT INTO while omitting the field list, you will need to use the NEWID() function. You may find it easier to include this function as the default value for the field and to specify the field list so you can exclude the EmpUnique field.) **D**, 1, would be true if it were possible to omit Null fields from INSERT INTO when the column list was omitted.

16. ☑ **B.** When you update a query that references multiple tables, you can insert content only if you reference the fields for a single table. Although some of this complexity is concealed from the user when using views, the same principle applies, even if the user is not aware that he or she is attempting to update multiple tables.

☒ It is possible to insert records into the view, so **A**, you cannot insert a new record, regardless of how many tables are referenced in the field list, is wrong. Because you are not allowed to add records to multiple tables with a single INSERT statement, **C**, you can insert a new record but only one of the tables will be updated, and **D**, you can insert a new record and both tables will be updated, are incorrect.

17. ☑ **C.** The query will fail, but it would succeed if the COMPUTE BY clause was removed. You cannot use COMPUTE BY in a SELECT INTO query. (One way to visualize this restriction is that the query has to use the content returned by the query to make a new table. When you use COMPUTE or COMPUTE BY, then you create extraneous rows that do not fit in a table format.) You can create a new table with SELECT INTO and then use COMPUTE or COMPUTE BY on that new table.

☒ Both the WHERE and the HAVING clauses can be used in a SELECT INTO, so option **A**, the query will fail, but it would succeed if the WHERE clause was replaced with a HAVING clause, is false. **B**, the query will fail, but it would succeed if the WHERE clause was removed, incorrectly implies that it is illegal to create a table using a WHERE statement that returns no rows. (In fact, this is a useful technique: You can create a new table based on content from another source, without cluttering the new table with actual content.) **D**, the query will succeed, is wrong because the query will fail.

18. ☑ **D**. 26504. When you use SELECT INTO, both the seed and increment are preserved unless there is a design element in the query that keeps it from being available. (These options include the use of joins, unions, computed columns, or the presence of more than one identity column included in the select clause.) Because the temporary table was created with none of these complexities, these restrictions do not apply.
☒ The other options would only be true if on table creation the seed was lost (**B**, 4), the increment was lost (**C**, 26500), or both were lost (**A**, 1). If you used UNION to combine the sales data from the four cities into one source for your SELECT INTO statement, then **A**, 1, would be true.

19. ☑ **C**. Set "Select Into/ Bulk Copy" to checked. This option needs to be selected to prevent adding to the transaction log. (Of course, you will still use slow BCP if there are indexes in the destination table, so you would want to drop these indexes before proceeding.)
☒ **A**, set "DBO use only" to checked, would restrict your users from accessing the database, which may be appropriate but is not directly related to the fast BCP issue. **B**, set "Read only" to checked, would prohibit the tables from being updated. **D**, set "Truncate log on checkpoint" to unchecked, is used to manage the transaction log during normal operations.

20. ☑ **C**. Select * into ##temporarynames2 from #temporarynames. If you create a temporary table with a single pound sign ("#"), it is a "local temporary table," and other users cannot see this table. By contrast, if you create it with two pound signs ("##"), it is a "global temporary table," and other users can read your content. You cannot convert an existing table from local to global, but you can use your local temporary table as the source for a new global temporary table.

☒   Although you can put a table in "pubs", this does not automatically make it visible, so **A**, select * into #pubs.temporarynames2 from #temporarynames, is incorrect. There is no "with public option" as described in **B**, select * into #temporarynames2 from #temporarynames with public option. The "@" prefix is illegal for a table name, so **D**, select * into @temporarynames2 from #temporarynames, is incorrect.

21. ☑   **A.** The user needs to be in the System Administrators server role to perform BULK INSERT. By contrast, you need only INSERT permissions to perform BCP. This is another advantage of BCP over BULK INSERT— you do not have to grant as many administrative rights to allow users to maintain their tables.
☒   If you grant a user System Administrators role, he does not need any of these other roles to perform BULK INSERT, so **B**, Security Administrators, **C**, Server Administrators, and **D**, Setup Administrators, are all incorrect. In fact, by granting the System Administrators role, you get many of the same permissions that these other roles would provide.

22. ☑   **A.** Maintain a timestamp field in your DB2 tables, and configure HDR to use Snapshot replication to retrieve the changed records. The only kind of replication that HDR supports is Snapshot replication. You can simulate Incremental replication, though, if there is a timestamp field to identify rows that have changed.
☒   If you used the identity field as described in **B**, maintain an identity field in your DB2 tables, and configure HDR to use Snapshot replication to retrieve the new records, you would replicate only the new records, not the records that have changed. **C**, use Incremental replication to copy only the records that have changed since the last update, and **D**, use Incremental replication to copy only the records that have been created since the last update, are invalid because HDR does not support Incremental replication.

23. ☑   **B.** Use the ODBC Driver for DB2. If you use an ODBC link to the mainframe database, the data will be retrieved and provided in real time. (This approach provides data relatively slowly, so you would probably want to use it only when you need small quantities of data.)

☒ **A,** use the ODBC Driver for SNA, is incorrect because there is no ODBC Driver for SNA. If you use HDR Replication, then the data will not be real-time data , so **C,** use HDR Replication for the needed vertical subset, and **D,** use HDR Replication for the needed horizontal subset, are incorrect.

24. ☑ **C.** The proposed solution produces the required result and none of the optional results. All of the content in all of the tables is copied over, so the required result is met. (Although this approach may be inferior to the Transfer Manager in this scenario, it may be best if you are working with different versions of SQL Server that didn't support the use of Transfer Manager.)

    ☒ Because the required result is met, **D** is incorrect. Because neither the constraint nor security rights are preserved, **A** and **B** are both incorrect.

25. ☑ **A.** Use Transfer Manager to move the data and accounts. A major advantage of Transfer Manager is that it can migrate accounts, views, and stored procedures, while DTS can migrate only data. (Transfer Manager is a tool that was a stand-alone application in SQL Server 6.5, but in 7.0 it is integrated with the DTS Import and Export Wizards.)

    ☒ You could create the accounts manually after using Transfer Manager or DTS, but this would take extra steps and be less efficient than **A,** so **B,** use Transfer Manager to move the data, then create the needed accounts manually on the destination server, and **D,** use DTS to move the data, then create the needed accounts manually on the destination server, are incorrect. Because DTS does not support migrating accounts, **C,** use a DTS to move the data and accounts, is wrong.

Replication

1. ☑ **C.** Distributor. On a push subscription, the Distribution Agent runs at the Distributor.

    ☒ **A,** Publisher, **B,** Subscriber, and **D,** Publisher and Distributor, are incorrect because the Distribution Agent runs at the Subscribers only when a pull subscription is created.

2. ☑ **B.** The best option is to implement transactional replication with a pull subscription. The sales force would be Subscribers, and they would pull down incremental changes when they dialed in.

☒ **A**, snapshot, is incorrect because snapshot replication would involve downloading the entire database, which is not a good option for a dial-in connection. **C**, transactional with Immediate Updating Subscribers, and **D**, merge, are wrong because both types of replication are able to make changes to the database, and the sales force does not need to modify the data.

3. ☑ **C.** Publications are the unit of replication available to subscribers. A server may have multiple publications, each containing multiple articles.

☒ **A**, Publisher, is incorrect because a Publisher is the server that makes data available for replication. **B**, Articles, is incorrect because Articles contain data and are grouped under a publication.

4. ☑ **A.** Transactional replication. Changes made at the Publisher are propagated to subscribers within seconds. Because all changes are made at the Publisher, data consistency is high.

☒ **B**, snapshot replication, is incorrect because snapshot replication downloads the entire publication and does not update subscribers within seconds. **C**, merge replication, is incorrect because merge replication allows subscribers to modify data, lowering transactional consistency. **D**, Transactional replication with Immediate Updating Subscribers, is wrong because Immediate Updating Subscribers modifies the data, and in this scenario, the subscribers are read-only.

5. ☑ **C.** Schedule the replication for off-peak hours. Snapshot replication places a share-lock on the tables to be replicated, preventing users from modifying these tables. Scheduling the replication for off-peak hours allows users to make modifications during working hours, and replication can take place with minimal effect.

☒ **A**, schedule update statistics for 8 a.m., is incorrect because it updates the distribution of key values for each index, used to determine which indexes to use in queries. You would use this if a large amount of data changed in a table. B, configure replication to not lock the table, is incorrect because you cannot configure replication to not lock the table. **D,** do not allow users in the database between 9 and 10 a.m., is incorrect because you can schedule replication for a later time that would not impact users, rather than denying them access during working hours.

6. ☑ **C.** Transactional replication with vertical filtering would allow you to publish the PERSONNEL table without the Social Security or Salary columns, allowing the remote site to receive just the information it needed. ☒ **A,** merge replication, is incorrect because merge replication is used for remote sites needing to update the data, and it does not filter those columns. **B,** transactional replication with horizontal filtering on the table, and **D,** snapshot replication with vertical filtering on the table, are incorrect because horizontal filtering is used to filter rows of data, not columns.

7. ☑ **C.** You don't have enough disk space. Snapshot replication creates a snapshot of the data to be published in a folder on the distribution server, which is the same size as the data in the database. It is not compressed, so you would need 25GB of free space on the Distributor to replicate the entire database.
☒ **A,** you can't replicate 25GB of data, is incorrect, as you are not limited to 25GB for replication. **B,** you can't replicate 25GB of data to a server on a different subnet, is incorrect because subnets have no relation to replication.

8. ☑ **B.** The Log Reader Agent executes on the Distributor. The Log Reader Agent reads the Publisher's transaction log, identifies modifications, and copies the transactions to the distributor.
☒ **A,** Publisher, **C,** Subscriber, and **D,** Publisher and Distributor, are incorrect. The Log Reader Agent does not run on the Publisher or Subscriber.

9. ☑ **A.** A Publishing Subscriber would be used when Subscribers are located over a slow link. This shifts the distribution load to the other side of the link. ☒ **B,** Publisher/Distributor in Texas and Subscribers at all other locations, is incorrect because the branch Subscribers are accessed by a slow link, leaving the distribution load on the other side of the link. **C,** Publisher in Texas,

Distributor in New York, and Subscribers at the branches, is incorrect because the Publisher must be connected to the Distributor by high-speed, reliable lines, and the Distributor would be located remotely over a 128K line. **D**, Subscriber in Texas, Publishers at all other locations, is incorrect because Texas is the central database, and it is not subscribing to data, but publishing it to the branches.

10. ☑ **A, B, and C.** When deciding on a replication strategy, consider the degree of data consistency needed, how much autonomy sites need, and how data should be partitioned.
☒ **D**, types of replication, is wrong because the three elements will determine what type of replication you will need to use.

11. ☑ **A.** Transactional replication with Immediate Updating Subscribers allows all sites to modify the database. The changes are not immediately propagated out to other sites, but data consistency is high.
☒ **B**, merge replication, is incorrect because merge replication does not provide as high a level of data consistency as Transactional. **C**, snapshot replication, and **D**, transactional replication, would require all sites except the Publisher be read-only.

12. ☑ **A.** You should implement transactional replication with a corporate Publisher/Distributor and each location as a Subscriber. Because the locations are linked by 128K lines, replicating just the incremental changes is the best way to minimize network traffic and publish the data out to the retail locations. The Publisher and Distributor should be at the corporate office, and each location is a Subscriber.
☒ **B**, transactional replication with a corporate Publisher, and a Distributor and Subscriber at each location, is incorrect because the Distributor should be linked to the Publisher by a high speed line. **C**, snapshot replication with a corporate Publisher/Distributor, and each location as a Subscriber, is incorrect because refreshing the data on the Subscribers would entail a lot of network traffic. **D**, merge replication, is incorrect because the retail locations do not need to update the data.

13. ☑ **A.** When each Subscriber is a local subscription (uses the priority number of the Publisher), the Subscriber who merges with the Publisher first is the winner of the conflict.

☒ **B**, 4.00, and **C**, 4.50, are incorrect because Subscribers B and C were not the first to merge with the Publisher. **D**, 3.83, is an average of the three values, which is incorrect.

14. ☑ **B.** The proposed solution meets the required result and the first optional result. Implementing transactional replication with Immediate Updating Subscribers would allow the highest degree of data consistency while allowing all sites to modify data. The Accounting office would have a read-only database with snapshot replication. The second optional result is not met. Using snapshot replication over a 56K line does not minimize network traffic. A better choice would be transactional replication.

☒ **A** and **C** are incorrect because only the first optional result is met. **D** is incorrect because the required result is met.

15. ☑ **B.** Dallas is the source database, so it must be configured as the Publisher. The Distributor should be linked to the Publisher by a high-speed connection, and it should also be located in Dallas. The server in Japan should be a Publishing Subscriber, acting as a Subscriber to the Dallas office, and a Publisher/Distributor to Okinawa and Taiwan. All other locations should be Subscribers.

☒ **A**, Publisher in Dallas, Distributor in Japan, Subscribers in all other offices, is incorrect because the Distributor should be in Dallas, connected by a high-speed link. **C**, Publisher/Distributor in Dallas, Subscribers in all other offices, is incorrect because the server in Japan should be a Publishing Subscriber, and **D**, Publisher in Japan, Distributor in Dallas, and Subscribers in all other offices, is incorrect because the Publisher should be in Dallas.

16. ☑ **A, C.** To enable a publication for the Internet, you need to set the @enabled_for_internet property of the publication to TRUE, or check the Allow snapshots to be downloaded using FTP on the options tab of the publication's properties screen. You also need to set up the replication directory as an FTP site for Subscribers to pull from.

☒ **B,** install IIS on the Distributor, is incorrect because IIS needs to be installed only on the Distributor if you are allowing pull and anonymous Subscribers. **D,** set up the Publisher inside the firewall and the Distributor outside the firewall, is incorrect because the Publisher and Distributor need to be on the same side of the firewall.

17. ☑ **C.** Because the sales office needs the data at the warehouses, the sales office would be the Subscriber and each warehouse would be a Publisher. Because the sales office is reporting on the data, it will not need to modify the data, making transactional the best type of replication.

☒ **A,** snapshot with warehouses as Subscribers, sales office as Publisher/Distributor, is incorrect because the warehouses need to publish the data, not subscribe to the sales office. The Distributor should be located near the Publisher, not the Subscriber, making **B,** transactional with warehouses as publishers, sales office as Distributor/Subscriber, incorrect. **D,** merge with warehouses as Subscribers, sales office as Publisher, is incorrect because the sales office does not need to modify any data, and it is not the publisher of the data.

18. ☑ **B.** Creating a new distribution database involves starting over. The current publications need to be disabled, and then reenabled as a new Publisher with the new distribution server. All publications, articles and subscribers need to be re-created

☒ **A,** configure the current Publisher to use the distribution database on the new server, **C,** back up the current distribution database and restore to the new server, and **D,** drag and drop the publications to the new distribution database in Enterprise Manager, are all incorrect. There is no other way to change distribution servers, other than re-creating the publishing information.

19. ☑ **B, C.** Set "Allow snapshots to be downloaded using FTP" to checked. This is the same as setting the @enable_for_internet option. This tells the agent to place the initial snapshot files in the MSSQL7\ReplData\ftp

directory. Set "Allow anonymous Subscribers to pull subscriptions" to checked. This allows you to have anonymous subscribers to your publication without maintaining all the information for the Subscribers. This is useful when there is a large number of Subscribers.

☒ **A,** set "Use a Distribution Agent that is independent of other publications from this database" to unchecked, would not allow you to have anonymous subscriptions. Using one Distribution Agent for all publications increases performance at the Distributor, but you must have a separate Distribution Agent if you are using anonymous subscriptions.

20. ☑ **D.** None of the above. Non-SQL Server databases can only be Subscribers.

    ☒ **A,** pull subscription, **B,** both push and pull subscriptions, and **C,** push subscription, are all incorrect. You cannot set up a non-SQL ODBC database as a Publisher, only a Subscriber. (Note that third-party software may give you the ability to set up a non-SQL database as a publisher, but this is not inherent within SQL 7.0.) However, DTS could also be used to move data between the two databases.

21. ☑ **B.** The Replication Monitor is enabled on Distribution servers. You can view scheduled replication and monitor in real time. You can also set up replication alerts.

    ☒ **A,** Publisher, **C,** Subscriber, and **D,** you can install the Replication Monitor on your workstation, are incorrect, as the Replication Monitor is only enabled on a Distributor.

22. ☑ **C.** Merge replication is the best option. Merge replication is useful for sites that need to modify data, yet require autonomy (i.e., sites are disconnected from central database).

    ☒ **A,** transactional, is wrong because transactional would require the stores to be read-only, and not all the sites have permanent connections to Corporate. **B,** snapshot, is wrong because snapshot would require the stores to be read-only. **D,** transactional with Immediate Updating Subscribers, is wrong because not all stores have permanent connections.

23. ☑ **A.** The site with the highest priority wins the conflict (on a scale of 0 to 99.99, with 99.99 being the highest priority), so Site B wins in this case.
☒ **B,** Site C, and **C,** Site D, are incorrect because Site B had the highest priority. **D,** Site A decides the conflict, is incorrect because Site A does not decide the conflict.

24. ☑ **A.** The proposed solution meets the required result and both optional results. Because the sales force already has Access 2000, setting up merge replication with SQL 7 is the simplest and most cost-effective way to implement replication. Whether Access has been installed using the Jet engine or MSDE, replication can be implemented. If Access is using the Jet engine, you need to enable the Jet database as a subscriber. If Access is using MSDE, simply set up merge replication as if the subscriber were a SQL 7 database.
☒ **B** and **C** are incorrect because both optional results are met. **D** is incorrect because the required result is met.

Implementing Replication Scenarios

1. ☑ **C.** Horizontal filtering is the process of selecting a subset of rows from a table based on some criteria. In this example, only the rows pertaining to a particular sales rep in a particular region are replicated.
☒ **A** is incorrect because vertical filtering refers to the practice of limiting which columns are selected for replication. **B** and **D** are incorrect because the terms geographical and zone are not used to describe any type of filtering within SQL Server.

2. ☑ **B.** The replication model that will produce the least amount of demand on the publisher on an ongoing basis is the snapshot replication model. You would replicate the data to the branch offices once a week during a low activity period, such as early in the morning. There would be a significant load on the Publisher during this replication, but once the replication was complete, there would be no load due to replication again until the next snapshot replication.

☒ **A**, **C**, and **D** are incorrect. These replication models require constant involvement from the publisher because they provide models with less latency.

3. ☑ **D.** Distribution is not part of the ACID test for transactions. The D in ACID represents *durability*. Durability insures that once a transaction has been committed, it cannot be reversed. A, for *atomicity*, represents that "all-or-nothing" principle. Either all of the changes are made, or none of the changes are made. C, or *consistency*, requires that a transaction must resolve any inconsistencies it creates during its processing. I, for *isolation*, represents the transaction's ability to isolate itself from other transactions.
☒ **A**, **B**, and **C** are incorrect answers because they are the components of the ACID test for transactions.

4. ☑ **D.** Merge replication does not support guaranteed transactional consistency. Merge replication uses convergence to resolve conflicts between changes made on separate servers. As a result, some transactions that were accepted locally might not be accepted during the merge. This violates the durability requirement of the ACID test.
☒ **A** and **B** are incorrect because they do not identify a major flaw in your plan. You are not providing the basic requirement of your CIO. **C** is incorrect because the major concern is not performance, but data consistency.

5. ☑ **C.** You need a column with the ROWGUIDCOL attribute set. If you do not provide the column when you publish the table, then SQL Server will add a column with this property to the table and call the column ROWGUID. GUID stands for Global Unique Identifier. Even though your ROWGUID column should be unique, this requirement is not enforced. So, if you create the column manually, be sure to add a unique index to the column.
☒ **A** is incorrect because a unique index only provides a unique identifier for a row within a single table. **B** is incorrect because it refers to a clustered index. **D** is incorrect because merge replication does not support timestamp columns. Timestamp values are generated automatically by the local server

and guaranteed to be unique within a specific database only. Therefore, it is impossible for a change to the timestamp value created at one server to be applied to the timestamp column at another server. You must remove the timestamp column from any table you want to publish using merge replication.

6. ☑ **A.** Merge replication has high site autonomy but does not guarantee data consistency.

☒ **B and C** are incorrect. Even though transactional and snapshot replications provide some site autonomy, they do not provide as much autonomy as merge replication. **D** is incorrect because the two-phase commit protocol makes every data change dependent on the capability of every other participating site to successfully and immediately accept the transaction. If one site is unavailable, no work proceeds. The two-phase commit protocol has immediate transactional consistency but a total absence of site autonomy.

7. ☑ **B.** Immediate Updating Subscribers. If you have Configured Immediate Updating Subscribers, updates can be made at the subscribers if the publisher is available to receive the update.

☒ **A** is incorrect. Even though SQL Server is implementing the two-phase commit protocol to provide immediate updating subscribers, the option is Immediate Updating Subscribers, not two-phase commit. **C and D** are incorrect because no such options exist.

8. ☑ **B.** The Snapshot Agent. It is responsible for preparing the schema and the initial data files of published tables. It stores these files on the distribution server and enters synchronization status into the distribution database.

☒ **A** is incorrect because the Merge Agent applies the initial snapshot jobs held in the publication database tables to the subscriber. **C** is incorrect because the Log Reader Agent reads the transaction log on the publisher and moves transactions to the distribution database. **D** is incorrect because the Distribution Agent moves transactions and snapshot jobs held in the distribution database tables to subscribers.

9. ☑ **A.** The Merge Agent. It is responsible for applying the initial snapshot to the subscriber. The agent then merges data changes from the publisher as they become available. The final responsibility of the agent is to reconcile conflicts according to rules you have configured. Alternatively, you can use a custom resolver that you have created.

☒ **B** is incorrect because the Snapshot Agent is responsible for preparing the schema and the initial data files of published tables. **C** is incorrect because the Log Reader Agent reads the transaction log on the publisher and moves transactions to the distribution database. **D** is incorrect because the Distribution Agent moves transactions and snapshot jobs held in the distribution database tables to subscribers.

10. ☑ **B.** A replication method that allows for push subscriptions. When using a push methodology, it is up to the publisher to determine when replication occurs. You could accomplish the same thing with a pull mechanism, but you would have to individually configure all of the subscribers to only request replications during certain periods. This is more work and less reliable than using a push methodology.

☒ **A** is not correct because it does not provide the optimum solution. **C** and **D** are incorrect because they represent specific types of replication. There is a push component to merge replication (the initial snapshot): once the merge and transactional replication are set up and running, the Publisher could be contacted at any time with a replication request.

11. ☑ **C.** With a pull subscription, the Subscriber initiates replication. This works well in environments with large numbers of Subscribers where it is important to propagate transactions as quickly as possible.

☒ **A** is incorrect because the Publisher initiates replication when using push subscriptions. **B** is incorrect because the Distributor is really just a middle man that sits between the Publisher and the Subscribers. **D** is incorrect because the user of a database or database application does not directly initiate replication. The systems in the replication architecture determine how and when replication will occur.

12. ☑ **B, C.** The Replication Monitor is the tool with which you should begin. Using the troubleshooting replication problems with the task history will likely tell you which task failed and the reason for the failure. You could also use the Replication Monitor to view the status of replication agents. Within Replication Monitor, open the server with the Distribution Agent that is serving the subscriber. Next, open the Steps tab and double-click Run Replication Agent option. Copy the string from the command window and paste it into a DOS window preceded with Distrib.exe. Add the Output option. Run this command and examine the output for indications of the problem.

☒ **A** is incorrect because Performance Monitor would probably not be the first tool you would want to use to troubleshoot a replication problem. If, after using Replication Monitor, you determine that you may have a performance problem, then Performance Monitor would be a good tool to use. **D** is incorrect. Even though you access Replication Monitor through SQL Server Enterprise Manager, the more specific answer to this question is Replication Monitor.

13. ☑ **B, C.** Data validation uses row counts and checksums to determine if data at the subscriber has diverged from data at the publisher. However, there are several conditions other than actual data divergence that could cause data validation to fail.

☒ **A** is incorrect because timestamps are not used in replication. **D** is incorrect because the ROWGUID column uniquely identifies a row across all replicated tables. The ROWGUID value will not change, so data divergence is not an issue.

Setting Up Replication

1. ☑ **C.** Configure Publishing and Distribution Wizard. In order to create a replication agent profile, first expand a server group; then expand the distributor. In the Tools menu, point to Replication, and then choose Configure Publishing, Subscribers, and Distribution. Click Agent Profiles. Choose the tab for the type of agent to get a new profile. Choose Copy Selected Profile. Enter the name and optional description of the new profile. Finally, select any parameters you want to change, and then enter the new value.

☒ **A**, Create Distributor Wizard, **B**, Pull Subscription Wizard, and **D**, Create Publication Wizard, are incorrect answers because these wizards do not set values that are considered to be a part of an agent's profile. The Create Distributor Wizard creates a replication distributor. In essence, this wizard creates the distribution database. The Pull Subscription Wizard walks you through the steps of creating a pull subscription to a publication. The Create Publication Wizard walks you through the steps of creating a publication for replication.

2. ☑ **B.** The SQL Server Agent on the subscriber is running as a user in the publications access list for the publication. If the SQL Server Agent is running as a user that is included in the publication access list, the user account of the agent will be used for security purposes and the wizard will not prompt you for a login and password.

☒ **A** is incorrect because if replication were not installed properly, you would not be able to successfully configure a subscriber. **C** is incorrect because the SQL Agent Service, not the SQL Server Service, manages replication. **D** would not be practical. Without any access to the database, the database would not be very useful.

3. ☑ **A.** The stored procedure that you will not need is the SP_SCHEDULE_ PUBLICATION procedure. This stored procedure does not exist.

☒ **B, C,** and **D** are incorrect because all three of these procedures are required to complete the tasks that the Create Publication Wizard would complete for you. The SP_GRANT_PUBLICATION_ACCESS procedure adds a login to the publication's access list. The SP_ADDARTICLE procedure creates an article and adds it to a publication. The SP_ADDPUBLICATION procedure creates a snapshot or transactional publication. As a side-note, creating a publication without using the wizard is fairly complicated and not a recommended procedure.

4. ☑ C. Specify the records you would like to replicate by giving the wizard a WHERE clause. This feature is known as horizontal filtering and is the process of choosing which records are replicated.

   ☒ A is incorrect. Horizontal filtering is supported for SQL Server replication and can be configured through the wizard. B is incorrect because the entire SELECT statement for replication is not specified, only the WHERE clause. D is incorrect because there is no mechanism within the graphical user interface of SQL Enterprise Manager or any of the wizards that allows you to highlight or drag and drop a set of records for replication.

5. ☑ C. The wizard allows you to configure one article per table. For the article, you are asked to specify any horizontal or vertical filters as part of the creation of that article. You can use sp_addfilter or sp_addarticle to add additional filters or articles at a later time.

   ☒ A is incorrect because there is no Add Article Wizard. B is incorrect because one article can be added through the wizard. Any subsequent articles must be added through the stored procedures. C is incorrect because both vertical and horizontal filters can be added when the article is created. Additional filters can be added through the stored procedures.

6. ☑ C. The best configuration for this situation would be a central subscriber. A central subscriber configuration is often referred to as a rollup configuration. Each office has control of their data and can edit it at will. Periodically the data is replicated to the central site where it can be aggregated and used for reporting.

   ☒ A, C, and D would not be good choices because they will all result in potential editing difficulties at the five locations.

7. ☑ C. The biggest disadvantage to supporting anonymous subscriptions is less security. If the data is not sensitive, supporting anonymous subscriptions

provides an easy method of administration, lower overhead, and support for Internet subscribers.

☒ **A, C,** and **D** are incorrect because they are all advantages of setting up anonymous subscribers.

8. ☑ **C.** What determines the number of masters is the number of places where the same data can be edited. Since each site only edits its own data, there is only one master for each publication. If both sites edited both publications, there would be a multimaster configuration.

☒ **A, B,** and **D** are incorrect. The key is to focus on the number of locations where the same data can be edited. Each location represents a master.

9. ☑ **B.** Remote distributor. Site B is functioning as a Remote Distributor because it contains the distribution database and is on a server other than the Publisher. Site A would be the Publisher and site C would be the Subscriber.

☒ **A,** Remote Subscriber, is incorrect because Site C would be the Subscriber. **C,** Publisher, is incorrect because Site A would be the Publisher. **D,** Re-publisher, is incorrect because it is an invalid term for this scenario.

10. ☑ **C.** Neither Site A nor Site C is acting as a Distributor because the distribution database is located on Site B.

☒ **A** is incorrect because Site A is subscribing to data being published from Site C. **B** is incorrect because Site A is publishing data to Site C. **D** is incorrect because Site A contains a database, so it is a database server.

11. ☑ **B.** You do not have a multisubscriber architecture. The only subscriber is the central roll-up server. This is a common configuration when remote sites need a great deal of autonomy.

☒ **A** is incorrect because a single Subscriber is exactly what you have. The roll-up server is the only Subscriber. **C** is incorrect because your Subscriber is central to all of the remote sites. In other words, one remote site does not subscribe to another remote site and republish the data. **D** is not correct because each site is a Publisher. However, do not confuse a multi-publisher architecture with having more than one publisher for the same data. In a multi-publisher architecture, there are multiple publishers, but there is never more than one publisher responsible for a single publication.

12. ☑   **B.** The only solution that provides immediate, guaranteed consistency is the two-phase commit protocol. You must have immediate, guaranteed consistency to be able to take one database offline and bring the other online without losing any transactions and without performing any restores.
☒   **A** and **C** would not be good choices in this situation because both merge and transactional replication provide latent transactional integrity. If inactive, both servers would eventually have exactly the same data. Unfortunately, in the case of an abrupt outage it is entirely likely that the servers would not be consistent and the result would be lost transactions. **D** is incorrect because multi-subscriber is not a type of replication, but a generic description used to identify a replication architecture.

13. ☑   **A.** By definition, the system that contains the master replication database is the Publisher. The Publisher always contains the master replication database.
☒   **B** is incorrect. The distributor is the system that contains the distribution database. It is not uncommon for a server to be both a Publisher and a Distributor. The system could also be a Subscriber, but this is less common. **C** is incorrect because in most replication scenarios the Subscriber maintains a read-only copy of the data, not the master copy. **D** is incorrect because there is no gateway role in SQL Server replication.

Part II

SQL Server 7.0 Designing and Implementing Databases (Exam 70-029)

EXAM TOPICS

Transact-SQL Overview

Creating and Managing Files and Databases

Developing a Logical Data Model

Planning and Creating Indexes

Queries

Summarizing Data

Managing Transactions and Locks

Implementing Views

Implementing Stored Procedures

Implementing Triggers

Working with Distributed and External Data

Design
Questions

Q

&

A

T his section is designed to help you prepare for Exam # 70-029, Designing and Implementing Databases with Microsoft SQL Server 7.0. After completing this exam successfully, you will be one step closer to your MCDBA certification. The following questions mirror the types of questions presented on Microsoft certification tests. Take your time and read each question carefully. Read all the answer choices carefully, as there may be more than one correct answer. Choose all correct answers for each question.

Transact-SQL Overview

1. In your application you have created an SQL cursor. You would like this cursor to represent a snapshot of the data. You don't want the data within the cursor to reflect table updates. What should you do?

   A. Use the INSENSITIVE option of the DECLARE statement.
   B. Omit the INSENSITIVE option of the DECLARE statement.
   C. Use a global variable.
   D. Use a local variable.

2. You are creating a stored procedure that is very complex. One particular calculation is critical and less than intuitive. You would like to leave yourself, as well as any other programmer, some information about the code. Choose the best way to document the calculation.

   A. Put a note in the syscomments table for that stored procedure.
   B. Add a note in the query execution plan.
   C. Add a comment to the stored procedure.
   D. Document the calculation in the project plan.

Note the following rules for PRIMARY KEY constraints:
A table can contain only one PRIMARY KEY constraint.
The PRIMARY KEY must be defined as NOT NULL.
The primary key must be unique—there can be no duplicate primary key values in a table.
Each primary key will generate an index.
In order to modify a PRIMARY KEY constraint in T-SQL, you must first delete it and then recreate it.
Multiple columns can be used to create a primary key.

3. Given the following code example, what would be the next logical step after declaring a cursor?

```
DECLARE my_cursor CURSOR FOR
SELECT my_name FROM my_table
WHERE my_name LIKE "M%"
ORDER BY my_name
```

A. You need to open the cursor using the OPEN statement.

B. You need to fetch all of the data for the cursor using the FETCH statement.

C. You can now start using the cursor.

D. Once you have declared the cursor, there is nothing to do, but destroy it.

4. How would the output of the following code sample appear?

```
FETCH NEXT FROM my_cursor
WHILE @@FETCH_STATUS = 0
BEGIN
    FETCH NEXT FROM my_cursor
END
```

A. `my_name`
```
--------------------------------------
Monet
my_name
--------------------------------------
Montserat
my_name
--------------------------------------
```

B. `my_name`
```
--------------------------------------
Monet
Montserat
```

C. `my_name`
```
Monet
Montserat
```

D. `Monet`
```
Montserat
```

5. You are currently working on a project that requires you to analyze the data for a particular month. It would make your job much easier if you could see dates in a format that would display just the day of the month. The current date format is month, day, four-digit year. How would you change the format of the dates you are looking at without affecting other users of the system?

   A. Use SET DATEFORMAT.
   B. Use CHANGE DATETIME.
   C. Use UPDATE DATEFORMAT.
   D. Use DBCC FORMATDATE.

6. Given the following query, which join(s) would SQL Server choose if both tables had 10 million records each?

```
SELECT table1.name, table2.address
FROM table1 INNER JOIN table2
ON table1.key = table2.key
ORDER BY table1.name
```

A. Nested loop

B. Hash

C. Merge

D. Input

7. Given the following query, you receive many more rows than you should and the data does not look right in the result set. What is the problem with this query?

```
SELECT table1.name, table1.age, table2.address
FROM table1, table2
```

A. You did not include a primary key for each table in the SELECT clause.

B. No join was specified, so a cross join was implied.

C. There is nothing wrong with the query; you don't know your data very well.

D. A foreign key relationship does not exist between the two tables.

8. Given the following query, what is the correct output?

```
SELECT Company, Employee as Name1, Address
FROM hr_db
UNION
SELECT Company, Name2 as Person, Address
FROM old_hr_db
```

A.
Company	Employee	Address
XXXXXXXX	XXXXXXX	XXXXXXX

B.
Company	Name1	Address
XXXXXXXX	XXXXXXX	XXXXXXX

C.
Company	Name2	Address
XXXXXXXX	XXXXXXX	XXXXXXX

D.
Company	Person	Address
XXXXXXXX	XXXXXXX	XXXXXXX

DESIGN QUESTIONS

9. Consider correlated subqueries. Which of the following accurately describes the use and operation of correlated subqueries?

   A. The subquery cannot refer to a field in the parent query.
   B. The subquery can refer to a field in the parent query.
   C. The subquery is evaluated multiple times.
   D. The subquery is evaluated once.

exam
ⓦatch

A foreign key is a column in one table that is linked to a column in another table. Here are some of the rules for FOREIGN KEY constraints:
A FOREIGN KEY constraint can only reference a PRIMARY KEY or a column with the UNIQUE constraint.
There can be a maximum of 253 foreign keys in a table.
A FOREIGN KEY constraint can reference a column in the same table; this is called a self-referencing key.
A FOREIGN KEY constraint is commonly used to join multiple tables; the primary key and foreign key columns are linked.
A FOREIGN KEY constraint ensures referential integrity by not allowing the PRIMARY KEY constraint it is linked with to be deleted. This ensures data integrity. You must first delete the foreign key row in one table and then the primary key row in the other table.

10. Global and local temporary tables are very similar in concept to global and local variables and global and local cursors. However, tables are prefixed differently from variables. How would you define a local and a global table?

   A. One number sign (#) for a global temporary table, and two number signs (##) for a local temporary table
   B. One number sign (#) for a local temporary table, and two number signs (##) for a global temporary table
   C. One dollar sign ($) for a global temporary table, and two dollar signs ($$) for a local temporary table
   D. One dollar sign ($) for a local temporary table, and two dollar signs ($$) for a global temporary table

QUESTIONS AND ANSWERS

How many primary keys can there be in a table?	There can be only one primary key; however, it can be made up of multiple columns.
Can I delete the primary key column in one table before I delete the foreign key in another table?	No! You must delete the foreign key first; then, delete the primary key.
My boss doesn't want to see all of the data in a table, how do I see only a few fields?	A field is a column. To display only a few columns, use the SELECT statement. For example, SELECT part_num, part_price FROM parts.
A consultant set up our database and we have few experienced SQL developers. They created multiple database tables and I need data from both...	The primary and foreign keys link the databases. Use either a SELECT...WHERE or a SELECT...JOIN to match the primary and foreign keys.
My IT manager wants to see a graphical relationship of the tables in our database...	Use the Create Diagram Wizard to accomplish this.
I need to give an across-the-board raise to all of the employees in the current table...	Use the UPDATE statement to modify the pay column.
How can I put comments in my SQL query code?	Use the two symbols /* at beginning of the comment and then reverse them, */, at the end. For example: /* This statement is a comment. */. Note that the double hyphens, --, will also work in lieu of /* and */.
How do I put data into a table?	The INSERT statement is used to insert a new row into a table.
An employee just gave her two-week notice, how can I remove her entry from the employee table?	In order to remove a row, use the DELETE statement.

Creating and Managing Files and Databases

1. You make changes to your production database, OrderEntry. In order to inconvenience as few users as possible, you have decided to make the changes after hours. You have several jobs to run in sequence without interruption. You want to ensure that no users access the database until you complete making the changes to the database. Which option should you set?

   A. EXEC SP_DBOPTION ORDERENTRY, SINGLE USER, TRUE
   B. EXEC SP_DBOPTION ORDERENTRY, READ ONLY, TRUE
   C. EXEC SP_DBOPTION ORDERENTRY, DBO USE ONLY, TRUE
   D. EXEC SP_DBOPTION ORDERENTRY, AUTOCLOSE, TRUE

2. The former database administrator had a policy of not creating a SQL Server database with a size of less than 100 MB. You have discovered a database, PhoneList, which has 90 percent free space after being in use for three years. You want to reduce the database size to a more realistic level. Which statement should you use?

   A. SP_OPTION PHONELIST, AUTOSHRINK, TRUE
   B. ALTER DATABASE PHONELIST MODIFY FILE
      (NAME=phonelist_data, SIZE=15 MB)
   C. DBCC SHRINKDATABASE (PHONELIST, 50)
   D. DBCC SHRINKFILE (PHONELIST_DATA, 15)

3. You are designing a database table that can contain comments with up to 100 characters. You want to ensure that any language can be properly handled. What data type and size should you use?

   A. VARCHAR(100)
   B. VARCHAR(200)
   C. NVARCHAR(100)
   D. NVARCHAR(200)

4. The transaction log on one of your databases is filling up about once a week. You have heard that setting the database option TRUNC LOG ON CHKPT will prevent this by clearing committed transactions each time the checkpoint process occurs. How will this option affect backups?

A. There will be no effect on backups.

B. The transaction log will need to be backed up during the checkpoint process.

C. Full database or differential backups will have to be performed.

D. Transaction logs will have to be backed up at more frequent intervals.

exam
ⓦatch

In earlier versions of SQL Server, it was critical to assign the transaction log to a separate disk device in order to back it up separately. SQL Server 7.0 forces the log onto a separate file by default.

5. You are planning to create SQL scripts from your database in order to document the database schema. You will place the scripts under source control in order to track changes to the database. Which of the following items will be scripted by default using the database scripting tool in the SQL Server Enterprise Manager?

A. Tables

B. User-defined data types

C. Security setting

D. Indexes

6. You are about to process a major conversion of alphanumeric data from a newly acquired subsidiary. You are concerned that logs may fill up during the process. What operations can you use to minimize log use?

A. INSERT INTO ...

B. SELECT INTO ...

C. Bulk copy using the BCP utility

D. Bulk copy using a DTS data pump

DESIGN
QUESTIONS

7. In order to ensure that log files do not fill up disk drives, you have set a maximum size on each log file. You know that if the transaction logs fill up, users of your system will be very unhappy. How can you manually monitor how full the logs are?

A. Use the system stored procedure, SP_HELPDB, to get information on all logs at once.

B. Use the space allocated tab in SQL Server Enterprise Manager for each database.

C. Use DBCC SQLPERF(LOGSPACE) to get information on all logs at once.

D. Use the Windows NT Performance Monitor with the percent log used counter for each database.

8. Your manager has just come back from a conference where he heard that adding a timestamp column to database tables can improve performance of certain operations. He likes the idea of having a column that would give the time each record was modified. What key piece of information should you give your manager to help him decide whether or not to implement timestamp columns?

A. Timestamp columns are modified each time a row is inserted or updated.

B. A timestamp is guaranteed to be unique in a database.

C. Timestamp columns are ideal for use as a primary key.

D. The timestamp cannot be converted to the date-time data type.

---

exam
ⓦatch
SQL Server will return an error (#5123) and fail to create the database if the directory that you attempt to place a file into does not already exist.

---

9. You are trying to understand how SQL Server is executing one of your queries. You are using SQL Server Query Analyzer. The graphical execution plan is shown in the following illustration. What information is the graphical SHOWPLAN giving you about the execution plan?

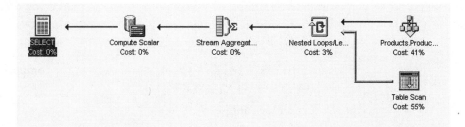

A. The table being joined to the Products table does not have an appropriate index to use for the query.

B. The Products table does not have an appropriate index to use for the table.

C. The query is a GROUP BY query.

D. There are no computed values in the query.

10. You are going to be accessing your SQL Server database from a Visual Basic application. Which method of accessing data are you most likely to use?

A. OLE DB

B. Remote Data Objects (RDO)

C. Data Access Objects (DAO)

D. ActiveX Data Objects (ADO)

11. As usage of your database has grown, performance is deteriorating. You suspect that competition for database resources may be the problem. What is the best tool to identify what bottlenecks are arising?

A. Query Analyzer

B. Profiler

C. Enterprise Manager

D. Performance Monitor

12. You have found that performance is degrading on a stored procedure that builds product summaries from your order detail records. You have run the SQL Server Query Analyzer and noticed that a composite index is no longer being used. Warnings about out-of-date or missing statistics are not

appearing on the graphical execution plan. What should you do to give the query optimizer better information about the composite index?

A. Run the Index Tuning Wizard.

B. Run CREATE STATISTICS for all columns in the composite index.

C. Run UPDATE STATISTICS.

D. Drop the index and re-create it.

Developing a Logical Data Model

1. You have been asked to create a database to assist in the telephone fund-raising efforts of a local charity. Their current donor data is held in a spreadsheet with the following columns:

   Date of Call, Donor Name, Donor Address, Donor City, Donor State, Donor Zip Code, Donor Phone Number, Donation Amount, Donor Called By.

   The new database should support the following goals:

   The donor should be called by the same person that previously contacted him or her.

   The caller should have a complete donation history for the telephone number called.

   Only one call should be made to a telephone number.

   The database should be easy to update if people who formerly lived together no longer do.

   You have decided to create the following tables:

   Caller containing a Caller key and the Caller's Name.

   DonorAddress containing a Donor Address key, Donor Address, Donor City, Donor State, Donor Zip Code, and Donor Phone Number and the Caller key of the last Caller that will be maintained through a trigger on the Call Result table.

   Donor containing a Donor key, Donor Name, and Donor Address key.

   Call Result containing a Caller key, a Donor key, Date of Call, and Donation Amount.

   Which of the objectives were met? (Choose all that apply.)

A. The donor should be called by the same person who previously contacted him or her.

B. The caller should have a complete donation history for the telephone number called.

C. Only one call should be made to a telephone number.

D. The database should be easy to update if people who formerly lived together no longer do.

2. Salesperson identifiers in your database are typically created by using the first seven characters of the salesperson's last name followed by their first initial. To avoid confusion, you want to ensure that the clerk in the sales department won't reuse an identifier if a new salesperson's name is similar enough to an existing one to produce a duplicate identifier. You are aware that, in SQL Server 7, it is preferable to use declarative integrity to enforce this rule. Which method should you use to enforce the business requirement using declarative integrity?

A. Create a stored procedure to check the salesperson identifier column to see if it exists already.

B. Create a UNIQUE constraint to the salesperson identifier column definition in the table.

C. Create an INSERT Trigger that will roll back the transaction if there is a duplicate.

D. Create a subroutine in the application to loop through the database looking for a duplicate before starting the insert transaction.

exam
ⓦatch

The column that has the IDENTITY property can be referenced in a select list by using the IDENTITYCOL keyword. The OBJECTPROPERTY function can be used to determine if a table has an identity column.

3. The shop floor data collection system in your fruit processing plant attaches a six-character grower identifier to batches of fruit being processed if the fruit comes from noncompany farms. For any fruit produced in your own company's orchards, the grower identifier is null. If the grower identifier for a batch of fruit is not in your database's Growers table, you want to be able to have your system move the incoming record to an exception file and create a report to allow the clerks to add the new growers to your database.

How should you define the GrowerID column and any constraints in your Inventory table that receives the data from your shop floor system in order to return an appropriate error to enforce this business rule?

A. Define the GrowerID with the parameter NULL and add a Foreign Key Constraint to the Inventory table referencing the GrowerID column of the Growers table, which is defined as the Primary Key.

B. Define the GrowerID with the parameter NOT NULL and add a Foreign Key Constraint to the Inventory table referencing the GrowerID column of the Growers table, which is defined as a UNIQUE column.

C. Define the GrowerID with the parameter NULL and add a Foreign Key Constraint to the Inventory table referencing the GrowerID column of the Growers table, which is defined as a UNIQUE column.

D. Define the GrowerID with the parameter NOT NULL and add a CHECK constraint to query that the GrowerID is in the GrowerID column of the Growers table, which is defined as a UNIQUE column.

4. Your company needs an application to track the allocation of personnel to projects and the reporting structure for each project. A person can be involved in more than one project either as a manager or as a resource. Because your company believes in a matrix organization, using people where their skills best fit, a person may report to more than one person depending on the project. A person could be a manager of one project, but a resource for another. Projects could have many managers depending on what phase the project is in. What relationships should you have between the Project entity and the Person entity in your logical data model?

A. A many-to-many relationship between Project and Person labeled Project-Managers and a many-to-many relationship between Project and Person labeled Project-Resources.

B. A one-to-many relationship between Project and Person labeled Project-Person and a one-to-many relationship between Person and Person labeled Manager-Resources.

C. A Project-Person entity with a one-to-many relationship between Project and Project-Person labeled Project-Person and a one-to-many relationship between Person and Project-Person labeled Person-Project. The Project-Person table contains a flag to indicate whether the person is a manager or a resource.

D. A many-to-many relationship between Person and Project labeled Person-Project.

5. You have been asked to implement a bill of materials using your company's parts table. Each part in the table may be composed of other parts in the table. The Parts table has a long integer primary named PartID. What Transact-SQL code should you use to add a PartOf column to your database and ensure that that column refers only to other parts in your database?

A.
```
ALTER TABLE Parts
ADD PartOf    INT    NOT NULL
    CONSTRAINT FK_PartOf
    REFERENCES Parts(PartID)
GO
```

B.
```
ALTER TABLE Parts
ADD PartOf    INT    NULL
    CONSTRAINT FK_PartOf
    FOREIGN KEY PartOf
    REFERENCES Parts(PartID)
GO
```

C.
```
ALTER TABLE Parts
ADD PartOf    LONG    NULL
    CONSTRAINT FK_PartOf
    REFERENCES Parts(PartID)
GO
```

D.
```
ALTER TABLE Parts
ADD PartOf    INT    NULL
    CONSTRAINT FK_PartOf
    REFERENCES Parts(PartID)
GO
```

6. Your company has decided to expand its distribution system into Canada. Canadian Postal Codes use a different format than Zip Codes. A sample Canadian postal code is N2H 5Z4. The zip code field in your database can currently accommodate the ZIP+4 format (99999-9999) and validates that the zip code is either in ZIP format (9999) or ZIP+4 format. How will you

have to modify your Address table's Zip column to accommodate Canadian Postal Codes? (Choose two answers.)

A. ```
ALTER TABLE Address
ADD CONSTRAINT CK_CanPostalCode CHECK zip LIKE
'[A-Z][0-9][A-Z] [0-9][A-Z][0-9]'
GO
```

B. ```
ALTER TABLE Address
DROP CONSTRAINT CK_ZipFormat
GO
ALTER TABLE Address
ADD CONSTRAINT CK_ZipFormat CHECK
    (zip LIKE '[A-Z][0-9][A-Z] [0-9][A-Z][0-9]' OR
     zip LIKE '[0-9][0-9][0-9][0-9][0-9]' OR
     zip LIKE
'[0-9][0-9][0-9][0-9][0-9]-[0-9][0-9][0-9][0-9]')
GO
```

C. ```
CREATE RULE Zip_PostalCodeFmt AS
    (@zip LIKE '[A-Z][0-9][A-Z] [0-9][A-Z][0-9]' OR
     @zip LIKE '[0-9][0-9][0-9][0-9][0-9]' OR
     @zip LIKE
'[0-9][0-9][0-9][0-9][0-9]-[0-9][0-9][0-9][0-9]')
GO
sp_bindrule Zip_PostalCodeFmt, 'Address.zip'
GO
```

D. ```
CREATE RULE Zip_PostalCodeFmt AS
    (@zip LIKE '[A-Z][0-9][A-Z] [0-9][A-Z][0-9]' OR
     @zip LIKE '[0-9][0-9][0-9][0-9][0-9]' OR
     @zip LIKE
'[0-9][0-9][0-9][0-9][0-9]-[0-9][0-9][0-9][0-9]')
GO
```

exam
ⓦatch

You cannot place a default on a column with a timestamp data type or on a column with the IDENTITY property specified. In either situation, the system provides the value.

7. Your company's head office has decided to upgrade promised service levels to reduce customer complaints about slow delivery times. The head office is requiring that all foreign subsidiaries comply as well. Currently, if not specified by the client, the default delivery date is 10 days following the date of the order. The default delivery date is to be changed to five days following the date of the order. There is also an existing rule that the promised delivery date cannot be less than seven days from the order date. Orders are always dated the day they are entered. This database has been in use for a long time and uses defaults. How should you implement the change? (Choose all that apply.)

A. Create a DEFAULT constraint of GetDate() – 5 on the PromisedDeliveryDate column.

B. Unbind the current default, drop it, then create a new default using GetDate() + 5. Bind the new default to the PromisedDeliveryDate column.

C. Create a default with the same name as the current one that modifies the default to GetDate() + 5 from GetDate() + 10.

D. Unbind the current default, drop it, then create a new default using GetDate()+5. Bind the new default to the PromisedDeliveryDate column. Unbind the rule restricting the promised delivery date to be greater than or equal to OrderDate + 7.

8. Most of your company's business is local to New York City. All your sales representatives live there. Ninety percent of shipping addresses are within the city. All of your clients' billing addresses are local. In order to make data entry easier, the city and state should be defaulted to New York for addresses in all your tables. What is the best way to implement this requirement?

A. Create a default of "New York". Bind it to the city and state columns of all of your tables using sp_bindefault.

B. Add a DEFAULT constraint of "New York" to each city and state column in your database.

C. Create a stored procedure that will change all blank city and state fields to "New York". Schedule the procedure to run every night using SQLServerAgent.

D. Create an INSERT trigger to change NULL city and state fields to "New York".

9. Your company specializes in providing crop insurance to farms across the United States. Most of the insurance is sold through local brokers. As an incentive to brokers to use your company, the marketing department has instituted a program rewarding brokers by automatically including their logo on all client communication that originates from your company. A brokerage's logo is included on communication if the rolling 12-month total premium collected on business placed by a brokerage exceeds $100,000. Brokers are asked to submit their logos once they achieve $90,000 in annual premiums. About 200 of your 16,000 brokers currently qualify. Since the program was announced two weeks ago, the logo files submitted have varied from 20KB JPEG files to 19MB TIFF files. Your project manager has mandated that the logos must be stored in the database. How can you best implement this requirement?

A. Add a VARCHAR(255) column to the Brokers table containing the path to the appropriate logo image file.

B. Create a user-defined data type called LOGO, which is a nullable IMAGE. Add Logo, a LOGO column to the Broker table.

C. Add two columns to the Brokers table: LogoFormat, a CHAR(4) column to contain the image format, and Logo, an IMAGE column to contain the logo image file. You ensure that IMAGE data is associated with its own filegroup.

D. Add a table to the database called BrokerLogos. The table will have three columns: BrokerID, an INT column containing the BrokerID of the broker that is related to the logo that is the primary key for the table; LogoFormat, a CHAR(4) column to contain the image format; and Logo, an IMAGE column to contain the logo image file. The table is placed in its own filegroup.

10. The logical specification for your system includes the following
Entity-Relationship diagram:

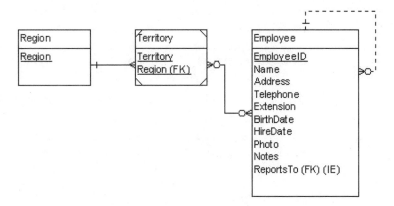

What changes will need to be made to implement this logical design in a
SQL Server 7.0 database? (Choose all that apply.)

A. Add a long integer RegionID to the Region table that will be the
Primary Key and the Foreign Key in the Territory table. Region will
have a UNIQUE constraint.

B. Add a Manager table to implement the ReportsTo relationship.

C. Add a junction table between Territory and Employee to change the
many-to-many relationship to two one-to-many relationships.

D. Define Region as NOT NULL in the Territory table to ensure that at
least one Territory exists for each region.

---

*A table may have more than one combination of columns that could
uniquely identify the rows in a table; each combination is a candidate
key. The database administrator picks one of the candidate keys to be
the primary key.*

---

11. Your company is planning to deploy its new distributed database globally.
The head office of each country will maintain its own copy of the database.
Updates will be consolidated during off-hours to a central site to allow for

worldwide reporting. Which of the following methods is preferred to define the primary keys in your database tables?

A. Use a UNIQUEIDENTIFIER column with a DEFAULT constraint of NEWID().

B. Use a compound primary key using VARCHAR column defaulted to @@SERVERNAME and an IDENTITY column with a seed of 1 and an increment of 1.

C. Use an IDENTITY column with an increment of 1 but assign each country its own seed.

D. Use an IDENTITY column with a seed of 1 and an increment of 1. Merge replication will handle things properly.

12. Current situation: Order entry is complaining about the speed of selecting product information in your order entry system. The product list is so slow to refresh that they have to work overtime to get each day's orders submitted. The extra overtime is costing the company $3,000 per day. Product managers are complaining that their decision support system for new products is taking their whole coffee break to come up and they care about only a few products.

Your company's distribution system handles 15,000 products. The current product table consists of eight columns that are required by the order entry system, 15 columns of additional information about each product including specifications in VARCHAR(1000) columns and printable sales literature in IMAGE columns to support your company's sales force, and eight columns of summary sales statistics that are maintained only for new products to allow product managers to track the products easily in their decision support system. New products are typically tracked for six months. About 100 new products are introduced a year.

Required result: Reduce the time required to select a product in the order entry system.

Optional results: Reduce the time required by the decision support system. Reduce the storage requirements of the product table.

Proposed solution: Vertically partition the product table into three tables. The Product table contains only the information required for order entry. The

ProductSales table contains only the additional sales support information. The ProductStatistics table contains only the summary statistics.
Which of the following results will the proposed solution produce?

A. The proposed solution produces the required result and both of the optional results.

B. The proposed solution produces the required result and only one of the optional results.

C. The proposed solution produces the required result and neither of the optional results.

D. The proposed solution doesn't produce the required result.

13. You have been discussing the requirements of a new pension system with the pension administrator in your human resources department. She told you that government regulations require retaining each plan member's name, date of birth, date of hire, and Social Security Number. The pension plan requires a beneficiary designation, but the beneficiary can be the member's estate. A plan member may elect to join the plan any time following a three-month waiting period. You have used that information to implement business rules in your Member table. Which of the following business rules have been correctly implemented? (Choose all that apply.)

```
A. MemberName    VARCHAR(255)    NULL

B. DateHire      DATETIME        NOT NULL

C. Beneficiary   VARCHAR(255)    NOT NULL
        CONSTRAINT DF_Beneficiary DEFAULT ('ESTATE')

D. DateJoined    DATETIME        NULL
        CONSTRAINT CK_EarliestJoin CHECK DateJoined >=
     DATEADD(month, 3, DateHire)
```

14. You have been asked to start maintaining a database. The previous database administrator took all of the documentation with him when he left. How can you discover all the constraints that are already in place? (Choose all that apply.)

A. Use SQL Server Enterprise Manager to check the table properties.

B. Use SQL Server Enterprise Manager to generate a database diagram.

C. Use SQL Server Enterprise Manager to generate scripts for all the tables, defaults, rules, and user-defined data types and ensure that the "Script PRIMARY Keys, FOREIGN Keys, Defaults and Check Constraints" table scripting option is selected.

D. Use SQL Server Query Analyzer to run the system stored procedure sp_help for each table in the database.

15. You have been asked to import 42 million order-history records from an existing system to the SQL Server database being used by a replacement system. The data has been scrubbed by a conversion application to ensure that it will conform to all validity checks in the new system. What is the safest and quickest way to bring the data into the system?

A. Drop all constraints on the table, import the data, and re-create the constraints using SQL Server Enterprise Manager.

B. Generate a script of the current table definition, drop the constraints, import the data, and run the script to recreate the constraints.

C. Execute the ALTER TABLE statement with the WITH NOCHECK option, then import the data.

D. Execute the ALTER TABLE statement with the NOCHECK CONSTRAINT ALL clause, import the data, then execute the ALTER TABLE statement with the CHECK CONSTRAINT ALL clause.

16. Your company is flattening its organizational structure. Rather than having districts report through regions and divisions, they will now report directly to the president of the company. This will mean that five regional vice presidents and 36 division vice presidents can be eliminated, saving your company $5.3 million in salaries and benefits. The updated Executive Decision Support System has been so successful that the president feels he can manage the 148 district managers personally by knowing which ones need the most attention at a given time.

The OrderHeader table in the database currently has FOREIGN KEY constraints defined to the Region and Division table primary keys and values are required to be entered. How can you deal with this change in business rules?

A. ```
DROP TABLE Region
DROP TABLE District
```

B. ```
ALTER TABLE OrderHeader
    ALTER COLUMN RegionKey    NULL
    ALTER COLUMN DistrictKey NULL
```

C. ```
ALTER TABLE OrderHeader
    ALTER COLUMN RegionKey   INT   NULL
    ALTER COLUMN DistrictKey INT   NULL
```

D. ```
ALTER TABLE OrderHeader
    DROP CONSTRAINT FK_OrderHeader_Region
    DROP CONSTRAINT FK_OrderHeader_District.
```

17. Your company has bought a Canadian company. You have been asked to integrate its product table with your current one. Your current product table has a description column. The Canadian product table has two description columns, one for English and one for French. Your company is considering expanding distribution to Mexico and perhaps Europe. What is the best way for you to modify your database in order to accommodate localization of language?

A. Add new columns to the Product table for each language that can be used.

B. Add a new description table with the product key, a text field describing the language, and the description.

C. Add a new language table that lists the valid languages. Add a new description table with the product key, a foreign key reference to the language table, and a description.

D. You don't need to make any changes to the database. Use a Web-based translation program to translate the descriptions when required.

18. This SQL Server Database Diagram shows a section of the Northwind Traders database:

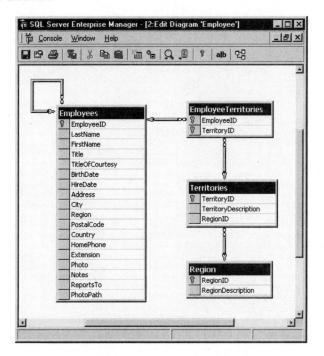

Based on the information given in the diagram, identify the PRIMARY KEY and FOREIGN KEY constraints shown by the database. (Select all that apply.)

A. The Employees primary key is EmployeeID and has a foreign key constraint to EmployeeID in the Employees table.

B. EmployeeTerritories has a compound primary key consisting of EmployeeID and TerritoryID. There are no foreign key constraints.

C. Territories has a primary key of RegionID and a foreign key constraint of TerritoryID.

D. Regions has a primary key of RegionID and no foreign key constraints.

19. Current situation: Your development server has been upgraded to SQL Server 7.0. The production servers are still running SQL Server 6.5. The country of one of your subsidiaries has legislated requirements for all data for operations carried out in that country. Your company will still need to consolidate the subsidiaries' results with those of the parent company. The requirements must be implemented prior to the planned rollout of SQL Server 7.0 to production.

Required result: Production database complies with legislated requirements.

Optional results: Modifications are applicable to future development as well as current system to avoid having to repeat the changes. Replication can be used to merge results into the parent database.

Proposed solution: Add a column to each table with the ROWGUIDCOL property set. Add a UNIQUE constraint to that column. Horizontally partition the database by country and provide the appropriate partition to the subsidiary.

Which of the following results will the proposed solution produce?

A. The proposed solution produces the required result and both of the optional results.

B. The proposed solution produces the required result and only one of the optional results.

C. The proposed solution produces the required result and neither of the optional results.

D. The proposed solution doesn't produce the required result.

20. You work in the IT department of a restaurant chain. The legal drinking age has been raised to 21 years old in your state. As part of the change in legislation, new employees in restaurants that serve alcohol must be at least 21 years old. Existing employees who are under the age of 21 are "grandfathered" so that they can continue working. You have been asked to implement this new business rule in your Human Resources database. You are about to add the following CHECK constraint to the database using SQL Server Enterprise Manager as shown below:

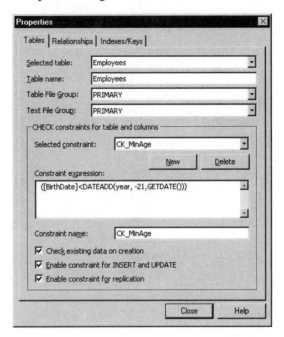

Will the new CHECK constraint meet the requirements of the business rule?

A. Yes, the CHECK constraint will correctly check that new employees are at least 21 when a new employee record is added.

B. No, the CHECK constraint will not be enabled for insert.

C. Yes, the CHECK constraint will check data that is replicated to ensure it meets the requirement.

D. No, the CHECK constraint will check existing data when it is added and report that existing employees do not meet the constraint.

Planning and Creating Indexes

1. You have a large table, and after a period of time, the performance of *INSERTs* seems to decrease significantly, but the performance of *SELECTs*, *UPDATEs*, and *DELETEs* remains relatively unchanged. What is the best way to make the *INSERTs* perform as well as they once did?

   A. Drop and rebuild the clustered index with the original fill factor.

   B. Re-create the clustered index with the *DROP_EXISTING* clause and the original fill factor.

   C. Re-create the nonclustered primary key with the *DROP_EXISTING* clause and the original fill factor.

   D. There's nothing you can do.

2. You have a static table that already has a clustered index, and you would like to add a new index to improve the performance of queries using *State*. You would like to have the most efficient indexes possible on them. Which of the following would be the best choices? (Choose all that apply.)

   A.
   ```
   CREATE NONCLUSTERED INDEX
   idx_Sales_1 ON tblPerson  (State)
      WITH
      FILL FACTOR = 100
   ```

   B.
   ```
   CREATE NONCLUSTERED INDEX
   idx_Sales_1 ON tblPerson  (State)
      WITH
      FILL FACTOR = 50
   ```

   C.
   ```
   CREATE NONCLUSTERED INDEX
   idx_Sales_1 ON tblPerson  (State)
      WITH
      FILL FACTOR = 0
   ```

   D.
   ```
   CREATE NON CLUSTERED INDEX
   idx_Sales_1 ON tblPerson  (State)
   ```

DESIGN QUESTIONS

3. Which index would be best for the following query?

```
SELECT   SalesDate, Sales
FROM     tblSales
WHERE    SalesDate = '10/17/1997'
```

A. A clustered index based on *SalesDate*

B. A nonclustered index based on *SalesDate*

C. A nonclustered index based on *SalesDate* and then *Sales*

D. A clustered index based on *Sales* and then *SalesDate*

4. Which index would be best for the following query?

```
SELECT   SalesDate, Sales
FROM     tblSales
WHERE    SalesDate > '10/17/1997'
AND      SalesDate < '12/5/1999'
```

A. A clustered index based on *SalesDate*

B. A nonclustered index based on *SalesDate*

C. A nonclustered index based on *Sales* and *SalesDate*

D. A clustered index based on *Sales*

5. You create the following index:

```
CREATE CLUSTERED INDEX
idx_Sales_1 ON tblSales   (State)
 WITH
FILL FACTOR = 70
 ON FG_Pubs
```

A month after the table is created, what would be the current fill factor of the table?

A. 70

B. 30

C. 50

D. Unknown

6. You create the following index:

```
CREATE CLUSTERED INDEX
idx_Sales_1 ON tblSales  (State)
WITH
FILL FACTOR = 70
 ON FG_Pubs
```

A month after the table is created, you re-create the index with the following statement:

```
CREATE CLUSTERED INDEX
idx_Sales_1 ON tblSales  (State)
WITH
FILL FACTOR = 30,
DROP_EXISTING
 ON FG_Pubs
```

After this statement is executed, approximately what percentage of space will be full on each page?

A. 70

B. 30

C. 50

D. Unknown

7. You create the following index:

```
CREATE CLUSTERED INDEX
idx_Sales_1 ON tblSales(State)
 WITH
FILL FACTOR = 70
 ON FG_Pubs
```

A month after the table is created, you re-create the index with the following statement:

```
CREATE CLUSTERED INDEX
 idx_Sales_1 ON tblSales  (State)
 WITH
FILL FACTOR = 30 ,
DROP_EXISTING
 ON FG_Pubs
```

After this statement is executed, what will be the approximate percentage of free space on the pages in *tblSales*?

A. 70

B. 30

C. 50

D. Unknown

8. You want to make a clustered index as fast as possible for *SELECT* queries that bring back large ranges of data. What can you do to the index to make the *SELECT* queries as fast as possible?

A. Put the index on a different segment that is managed by a different hard disk controller.

B. Rebuild it daily with a fill factor of 100.

C. Create the index with the *UNIQUE* keyword.

D. All of the above

9. You try to insert some records into table *tblSales*, and SQL Server issues a warning message after the *Inserts* are committed. When you look at the data in the table, you see that some of your *Inserts* were committed and some were not. What is the possible cause?

A. The clustered index on the table was created with *IGNORE_DUP_KEY* option.

B. The clustered index on the table was created with *ALLOW_DUP_ROW* option.

C. The clustered index on the table was created with *IGNORE_DUP_ROW* option.

D. It's impossible; this cannot happen.

10. Given the following statement:

```
CREATE INDEXD idx_Sales_1 ON tblSales  (State)
```

What do you know about *idx_Sales*?

A. It is nonclustered, with a fill factor of 100.

B. It is clustered, with a fill factor of 50.

C. It is nonclustered, with a fill factor of 50.

D. It is clustered, with a fill factor of 100.

---

exam
ⓦatch

While there is a limit of one clustered index per table due to the physical sorting of data, SQL Server allows as many as 249 nonclustered indexes per table.

---

11. You try to create an index on *tblSales* with the following statement:

```
CREATE INDEXD tblSales ON tblSales   (State, Zip, ZipExt,
Address1, Address2, Address3, Address4, City, Person)
WITH PAD_INDEX,
     IGNORE_DUP_KEY
```

Why would this Index fail? (Choose all that apply.)

A. SQL Server allows up to eight columns per index.

B. *IGNORE_DUP_KEY* can only be used on *UNIQUE* indexes.

C. *PAD_INDEX* must be used with the fill factor parameter.

D. The index is the same name as the table.

12. Current situation: You work for a retail store chain that has 50 locations across the Midwest. You instantly log all the data for all the stores over a WAN to the corporate SQL Server into *tblSales*. *tblSales* is a Heap and has no nonclustered indexes on it. The most important reports that are run are the daily sales reports. One shows the total number of sales per store per day. The other shows the total number of sales for the entire chain per day. Required result: Improve the speed of the daily sales reports for each store. Optional desired result: Improve the speed of the daily sales report for the entire chain, and do not slow down the logging of the data.

Proposed solution: Place a clustered index on (StoreNumber), and place a nonclustered index on (SalesDate, Sales).

Which results does the proposed solution produce?

A. The proposed solution produces the required result and produces both of the optional results.

B. The proposed solution produces the required result and produces only one of the optional results.

C. The proposed solution produces the required result but does not produce any of the optional desired results.

D. The proposed solution does not produce the required result.

13. Current situation: You work for a retail store chain that has 50 locations across the Midwest. You instantly log all the data for all the stores over a WAN to the corporate SQL Server into *tblSales*. *tblSales* has a clustered index on *SalesDate*, a nonclustered index on *StoreNumber*, a nonclustered index on *SalesAmount*, a nonclustered index on *Sales,* and a nonclustered index on *SalesItem*. The most important reports that are run are the daily sales reports. One shows the total number of sales per store per day. The other shows the total number of sales for the entire chain per day.

Required result: Improve the speed of the daily sales reports for the each store.

Optional desired result: Improve the speed of the daily sales reports for the entire chain and improve the speed of the logging of the data.

Proposed solution: Drop all the current indexes and replace them with a clustered index on (*StoreNumber*) and a nonclustered index on (*SalesDate, Sales*).

Which results does the proposed solution produce?

A. The proposed solution produces the required result and produces both of the optional results.

B. The proposed solution produces the required result and produces only one of the optional results.

C. The proposed solution produces the required result but does not produce any of the optional desired results.

D. The proposed solution does not produce the required result.

14. Current situation: You work for a retail store chain that has 50 locations across the Midwest. You instantly log all the data for all the stores over a WAN to the corporate SQL Server into *tblSales*. *tblSales* has a clustered index on *SalesDate*, a nonclustered index on *StoreNumber*, a nonclustered index on *SalesAmount*, a nonclustered index on *Sales,* and a nonclustered index on *SalesItem*. The most important reports that are run are the daily sales reports. One shows the total number of sales per store per day. The other shows the total number of sales for the entire chain per day.

Required result: Improve the speed of *INSERTs.*

Optional desired result: Preserve all the constraints and consume as little downtime as possible.

Proposed solution: Create a nightly task to rebuild each index on the database with *DROP_EXISTING* clause setting a fill factor of 70 on the clustered index and 100 on the nonclustered indexes.

Which results does the proposed solution produce?

A. The proposed solution produces the required result and produces both of the optional results.

B. The proposed solution produces the required result and produces only one of the optional results.

C. The proposed solution produces the required result but does not produce any of the optional desired results.

D. The proposed solution does not produce the required result.

15. You create the following table:

```
CREATE TABLE tblTaskD
(TaskID    int NOT NULL,
TaskName   varchar(255) NULL,
TaskOwner  smallint NOT NULL
TaskDate   smalldatetime NULL
CONSTRAINT idx_PK PRIMARY KEY (TaskID)
)
```

Then you create the following indexes:

```
CREATE CLUSTERED INDEX idx_TaskOwner
ON tblTask  (TaskOwner)
CREATE INDEX idx_TaskDate
ON tblTask  (TaskDate)
CREATE NONCLUSTERED INDEX idx_TaskName
ON tblTask  (TaskName)
```

After these statements are executed, how many nonclustered indexes will be on the table?

A. 1

B. 2

C. 3

D. 4

16. You are working on an imaging database designed to contain all the electronic documents within the company. The central entity is *tblDocuments*, which has an *IDENTITY* field *DocumentID* to uniquely identify each document. You execute the following script to enforce integrity and to increase performance:

```
ALTER TABLE tblDocuments ADD CONSTRAINT DocumentID
PRIMARY KEY(DocumentID)

CREATE CLUSTERED INDEX DocumentID
ON tblDocuments (DocumentID)

CREATE INDEX idx_CreateDate
ON tblDocuments (CreateDate)
ON FG_2

CREATE NONCLUSTERED INDEX idx_DocumentType
ON tblDocuments (DocumentType)
```

Errors occur during execution. Why?

A. *idx_CreateDate* cannot be created on another file group because it is a clustered index.

B. Index *DocumentID* is clustered, and a clustered index cannot be placed on a field that is contained in the PRIMARY KEY.

C. The *Primary Key* is named *DocumentID,* and you try to create an index named *DocumentID* that SQL Server will not allow.

D. *idx_CreateDate* will be a clustered index because the *NONCLUSTERED* keyword was not used, and that cannot happen because there is already a clustered index on the table.

17. In SQL Enterprise Manager, you look at tblEmployees, shown in the following illustration:

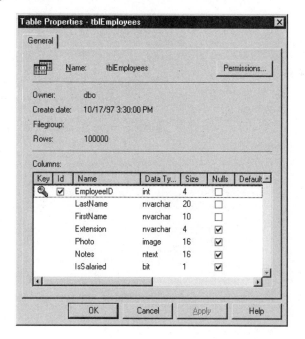

Which of the following indexes could you create? (Choose all that apply.)

A. CREATE CLUSTERED INDEX *idx_LastName* ON tblEmployee (*LastName*)

B. CREATE NON CLUSTERED INDEX *idx_Photo* ON *tblEmployee (Photo)*

C. CREATE UNIQUE INDEX idx_Notes ON tblEmployee (Notes)

D. CREATE UNIQUE INDEX idx_EmployeeID_IsSalaried ON tblPersonType (EmployeeID, IsSalaried) WITH IGNORE_DUP_KEY

18. Current situation: You manage the HR database for a large company. The most important entity in your database *is tblPerson. tblPerson* has seven indexes, and two of them are constraints. Your system incurs a great deal of activity, both for logging data and reporting from it. You have optimized the indexes using the SQL Index Tuning Wizard and, after careful analysis, you believe that you have set the correct fill factor for each index.
Required result: Rebuild the indexes each night to establish the optimal fill factor.
Optional desired results: Preserve all the constraints and ensure that the maintenance on this process is minimal.
Proposed solution: Create a nightly task to run dbcc dbreindex (tblPerson, ", 0) in your database.
Which results does the proposed solution produce?

A. The proposed solution produces the required result and produces both of the optional results.

B. The proposed solution produces the required result and produces only one of the optional results.

C. The proposed solution produces the required result but does not produce any of the optional desired results.

D. The proposed solution does not produce the required result.

19. You are going through each column on a table trying to find out whether you should index the columns and, if so, how to do it. You run the query and get the results shown in the following illustration. After reviewing the information, what conclusion do you reach about indexing this column?

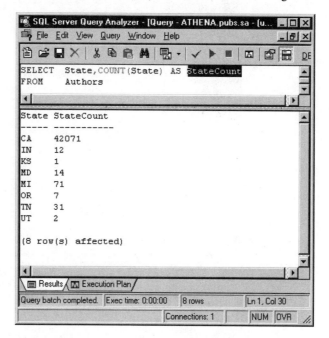

A. It is a good candidate for a clustered index.

B. It is a good candidate for a nonclustered index.

C. It is a good candidate for a nonclustered unique index.

D. You should not index the column.

20. You are going through each column on a table trying to find out whether you should index the columns and, if so, how to do it. You run the query and get the results shown in the following illustration. After reviewing the information, what conclusion do you reach about indexing this column?

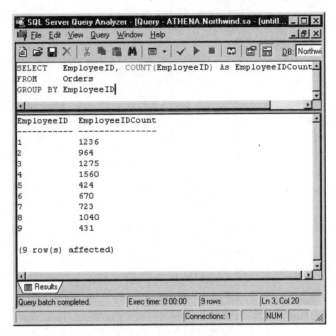

A. It is a good candidate for a clustered index.

B. It is a good candidate for a nonclustered index.

C. It is a good candidate for a nonclustered unique index.

D. You should not index the column.

Queries

1. In order to reconcile the books, Corporate Finance needs to have all the VendorIDs and LineItemAmounts from tblBill where DateReceived is

greater than "4/20/1999." Which of the following queries will give you the correct results? (Choose all that apply.)

A. ```
SELECT *
FROM tblBill
WHERE DateReceived > "4/20/1999"
```

B. ```
SELECT VendorID, LineItemAmount
FROM tblBill
WHERE DateReceived > "4/20/1999"
```

C. ```
SELECT *
FROM tblBill
WHERE DateReceived => "4/20/1999"
```

D. ```
SELECT VendorID, LineItemAmount
FROM tblBill
WHERE DateReceived => "4/20/1999"
```

2. In order to reconcile the books, Corporate Finance needs to have all the VendorIDs and LineItemAmounts from tblBill where DateReceived is greater than "4/20/1999." Which of the following queries will give you the correct results most efficiently?

A. ```
SELECT *
FROM tblBill
WHERE DateReceived > "4/20/1999"
```

B. ```
SELECT VendorID, LineItemAmount
FROM tblBill
WHERE DateReceived > "4/20/1999"
```

C. ```
SELECT *
FROM tblBill
WHERE DateReceived => "4/20/1999"
```

D. ```
SELECT VendorID, LineItemAmount
FROM tblBill
WHERE DateReceived => "4/20/1999"
```

DESIGN QUESTIONS

3. Your company is in the process of converting all its systems from a DOS-based system using nonrelational data storage to an NT-based system that uses SQL Server. The CIO is anxious to show some of the advantages of having the data stored in SQL Server and has asked you to create a report showing all the products that are carried that have not had a sale in the last month. You create the following query:

```
SELECT Name, UPC
FROM tblProducts
WHERE UPC NOT IN ( SELECT UPC
                        FROM tblSales
                        WHERE SalesDate >=
DateAdd(m,-1,getDate()))
AND tblProducts.IsActive = 1
```

The results come back with no products, which you know is incorrect. What is wrong with this query?

A. Some of the UPCs in the query on tblSales are NULL.

B. The second parameter of DateAdd needs to be –1.

C. You cannot use a NOT IN clause with an AND.

D. All of the above

4. You run the "Football Master" Web site that allows people to create, manage, and name their own fantasy football leagues of up to 12 teams. The market leader in providing ad hoc fantasy football over the Internet is the "Devil Dog" Fantasy Football Consortium. It has taken legal action because some of the individual league names that your customers have created have the words "Devil Dog" in them. The "Devil Dog" Fantasy Football Consortium believes that you are unfairly allowing its registered trademark to be used. You need a list of all the leagues in your system that use any variation of "Devil Dog" in their names. How could you find all the leagues that have "Devil Dog" in their names?

A. `SELECT *`
   `FROM tblLeague`
   `HAVING Name LIKE "%Devil Dog%"`

B. `SELECT *`
   `FROM tblLeague`
   `WHERE Name LIKE "%Devil Dog%"`

C. `SELECT *`
   `FROM tblLeague`
   `HAVING Name CONTAINS "%Devil Dog%"`

D. `SELECT *`
   `FROM tblLeague`
   `WHERE Name CONTAINS "%Devil Dog%"`

5. You would like to get a list of all the fantasy football leagues that are using the "Open Draft" rules. Each individual league is stored as a row in tblLeague. Each league has a type that is an attribute of the league, and the details about that type are kept in tblLeagueType. One of the attributes of tblLeagueType is "IsOpenDraft." Which query would give you all the leagues that use "Open Draft" rules?

A. `SELECT LeagueID, Name`
   `FROM tblLeague, tblLeagueType`
   `WHERE IsOpenDraft = 1`

B. `SELECT tblLeague.LeagueID, tblLeague.Name`
   `FROM tblLeague, tblLeagueType`
   `WHERE tblLeague.LeagueTypeID = tblLeagueType.LeagueTypeID`
   `AND tblLeagueType.IsOpenDraft = 1`

C. `SELECT LeagueID, Name`
   `FROM tblLeague, tblLeagueType`
   `WHERE LeagueTypeID = LeagueTypeID`
   `AND tblLeagueType.IsOpenDraft = 1`

D. `SELECT tblLeague.LeagueID, tblLeague.Name`
   `FROM tblLeague, tblLeagueType`
   `WHERE tblLeague.LeagueTypeID = tblLeagueType.LeagueTypeID`

In contrast to an identity field, SQL Server does not automatically maintain the contents of a uniqueidentifier field. (A uniqueidentifier is a globally unique record identifier, and it is useful when merging record sets originally generated at different sources.) If you are using a uniqueidentifier as a primary key, you will need to initialize its value by using the NEWID() function.

---

6. Current situation: You work for a retail store chain that has 50 locations across the Midwest. You instantly log all the data for all the stores over a WAN to the corporate SQL Server into *tblSales*. You are being audited and need to produce all the SalesID, SalesDate, and SalesAmount for a particular product (ProductID =1498) over the last five years.

   Required result: Write a query to get all the sales records for a product over the last five years.

   Optional desired results: Run as fast as possible, and order the results from most recent to least recent.

   Proposed solution:

   ```
   SELECT SalesID, SalesDate, SalesAmount
   FROM Sales
   WHERE DateAdd(year,6, SalesDate)> GetDate()
   AND ProductID = 1498
   ORDER BY SalesDate
   ```

   Which results does the proposed solution produce?

   A. The proposed solution produces the required result and produces both of the optional results.

   B. The proposed solution produces the required result and produces only one of the optional results.

   C. The proposed solution produces the required result but does not produce any of the optional desired results.

   D. The proposed solution does not produce the required result.

7. You need a list of all the ProductIDs from tblProducts with the total quantity that they have ever sold from tblSales, including the products that have never had a sale. Which of the following queries will give you the correct results? (Choose all that apply.)

A. ```
SELECT tblProducts.ProductID,
   IsNull(SUM(tblSales.Quantity),0) AS Quantity
   FROM tblProducts, tblSales
   WHERE tblProducts.ProductID = tblSales.ProductID
   GROUP BY tblProducts.ProductID
```

B. ```
SELECT tblProducts.ProductID,
   IsNull(SUM(tblSales.Quantity),0) AS Quantity
   FROM tblProducts, tblSales
   WHERE tblProducts.ProductID *= tblSales.ProductID
   GROUP BY tblProducts.ProductID
```

C. ```
SELECT tblProducts.ProductID,
   IsNull(SUM(tblSales.Quantity),0) AS Quantity
   FROM tblProducts, tblSales
   WHERE tblProducts.ProductID =* tblSales.ProductID
   GROUP BY tblProducts.ProductID
```

D. ```
SELECT tblProducts.ProductID,
   IsNull(SUM(tblSales.Quantity),0) AS Quantity
   FROM tblProducts LEFT OUTER JOIN  tblSales
   ON tblProducts.ProductID = tblSales.ProductID
   GROUP BY tblProducts.ProductID
```

8. You need to create a report that will show all the sales made in a particular store on "12/5/99." Some of the sales transactions have information about the customer associated with them; others do not. You would like to have the customer zip code displayed wherever possible and, in the cases where there is no customer information available, you would like zip code "99999" to be displayed. Which of the following queries would satisfy this report?

A.
```
SELECT tblSales.*, ISNULL(tblCustomers.ZipCode,"99999")
FROM tblSales  FULL JOIN tblCustomers
ON tblSales.CustomerID = tblCustomers.CustomerID
WHERE SalesDate = "12/5/99"
```

B.
```
SELECT tblSales.*, ISNULL(tblCustomers.ZipCode,"99999")
FROM tblSales, tblCustomers
WHERE  SalesDate = "12/5/99"
AND tblSales.CustomerID = tblCustomers.CustomerID
```

C.
```
SELECT tblSales.*, ISNULL(tblCustomers.ZipCode,"99999")
FROM tblSales  RIGHT JOIN tblCustomers
ON tblSales.CustomerID = tblCustomers.CustomerID
AND SalesDate = "12/5/99"
```

D.
```
SELECT tblSales.*, ISNULL(tblCustomers.ZipCode,"99999")
FROM tblSales LEFT JOIN tblCustomers
ON tblSales.CustomerID = tblCustomers.CustomerID
AND SalesDate = "12/5/99"
```

9. The manager of the northeast region of your company has asked for a report that would show every sales person and, if that sales person has made a sale, all SalesAmounts from each sale made between 1/1/99 and 3/31/99. Which of the following queries will bring up the correct results? (Choose all that apply.)

A.
```
SELECT tSP.Fname + " " + tSp.Lname As SalesPerson,
ts.SalesAmount
FROM tblSalesPerson tSP, tblSales tS
WHERE tS.SalesDate BETWEEN "1/1/99" AND "3/31/99"
```

B.
```
SELECT Fname + " " + Lname As SalesPerson, SalesAmount
FROM tblSalesPerson, tblSales
WHERE SalesDate BETWEEN "1/1/99" AND "3/31/99"
```

C.
```
SELECT tSP.Fname + " " + tSp.Lname As SalesPerson,
ts.SalesAmount
FROM tblSalesPerson tSP, tblSales tS
WHERE SalesDate BETWEEN "1/1/99" AND "3/31/99"
AND tSP.SalesPersonID = ts.SalesPersonID
```

D.
```
SELECT Fname + " " + Lname As SalesPerson, ts.SalesAmount
FROM tblSalesPerson LEFT OUTER JOIN tblSales
ON tSP.SalesPersonID = ts.SalesPersonID
AND SalesDate BETWEEN "1/1/99" AND "3/31/99"
```

10. You are looking for all the books published by authors with the last name "Gorman" and the last name "Erwin." Which of the following queries will produce the correct results? (Choose all that apply.)

A. ```
SELECT *
FROM tblAuthors
WHERE Lname="Erwin"
OR Lname = "Gorman"
```

B. ```
SELECT *
FROM tblAuthors
WHERE Lname ="Erwin"
AND Lname = "Gorman"
```

C. ```
SELECT *
FROM tblAuthors
WHERE Lname = "Erwin"
UNION
SELECT *
FROM tblAuthors
WHERE Lname = "Gorman"
```

D. ```
SELECT *
FROM tblAuthors
WHERE Lname IN ("Erwin","Gorman")
```

11. You need to get all the records from tblProperty. A field in tblProperty is called ExpensableType. Some records have an ExpensableType; others do not. All the defined ExpensableTypes are kept in tblExpensableType. You want a list of all properties, and when they have an expensable type, you want the ExpensableType description listed with the record. What type of join will you have to implement between tblProperty and tblExpensableType?

A. Inner join

B. Outer join

C. Cross join

D. Full join

12. You currently have a table, tblProperty, that has a great number of columns, and you would like to extract all the data for four of the fields into a new table, tblPropertyLite, that you have not created yet. How could you move that data from tblProperty into tblPropertyLite?

A. Perform a SELECT INTO From tblProperty into tblPropertyLite.

B. Write an INSERT statement into tblPropertyLite that had an appropriate SELECT from tblProperty as the execute statement.

C. Write an UPDATE Statement to tblPropertyLite that had an appropriate WHERE clause to join the correct records from tblProperty and tblPropertyLite.

D. All of the above

13. In SQL Enterprise Manager, you look at Employee, as shown here:

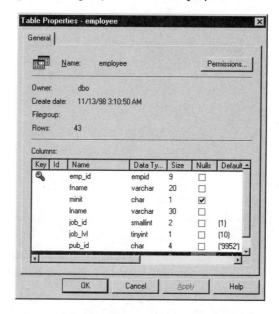

You need to create a table that has the PersonID, Fname concatenated with the Lname, job_id, and job_lvl for all the records that are active. You execute the following statement:

```
SELECT emp_ID, fname + " " + lname As Name, jobid,
job_lvl
INTO tblemployee2
FROM tblPerson
```

What is the data type of field name after this statement is executed?

A. Varchar (20)

B. Varchar (30)

C. Varchar (50)

D. Varchar (51)

14. You have a table, tblPressReleases, and a table, tblAnnouncements. Both of them have a unique ID, followed by a text field and a date. You would like to see all the press releases and announcements, ordered by dates, and then the type of document. Which of the following will get you the correct results?

A.
```
SELECT 'Press Release' AS Type, PressRelease,
PressReleaseDate
FROM tblPressRelease
ORDER BY PressReleaseDate, Type
UNION
SELECT 'Announcement' AS Type, Announcement,
AnnouncementDate
FROM tblAnnouncement
ORDER BY AnnouncementDate, Type
```

B.
```
SELECT 'Press Release' AS Type, PressRelease,
PressReleaseDate
FROM tblPressRelease
ORDER BY PressReleaseDate, Type
UNION
SELECT 'Announcement' AS Type, Announcement,
AnnouncementDate
FROM tblAnnouncement
```

C.
```
SELECT 'Press Release' AS Type, PressRelease,
PressReleaseDate
FROM tblPressRelease
UNION
SELECT 'Announcement' AS Type, Announcement,
AnnouncementDate
FROM tblAnnouncement
ORDER BY AnnouncementDate, Type
```

D.
```
SELECT 'Press Release' as Type, PressRelease,
PressReleaseDate
FROM tblPressRelease
UNION
SELECT 'Announcement' AS Type, Announcement,
AnnouncementDate
FROM tblAnnouncement
ORDER BY AnnouncementDate, Type
```

DESIGN QUESTIONS

15. You sell products to people over the Internet, and you are able to be competitive by constantly updating your prices. The prices you pay for your products are fed into your system by your vendors, and then you go in and update your prices. You now offer too many products to maintain your prices by hand. Which of the following queries would automatically update your software products' prices to be 10 percent more than what you buy them for?

A. ```
UPDATE tblProducts
FROM tblProductType
SET Price = 1.1 * Cost
WHERE tblProducts.ProductType *=
tblProductType.ProductType
AND tblProductType.ProductType = 1
```

B. ```
UPDATE tblProducts
FROM tblProductType
SET Price = 1.1 * Cost
WHERE tblProducts.ProductType =*
tblProductType.ProductType
AND tblProductType.ProductType = 1
```

C. ```
UPDATE tblProducts
FROM tblProductType
SET Price = 1.1 * Cost
WHERE tblProducts.ProductType =
tblProductType.ProductType
AND tblProductType.ProductType = 1
```

D. ```
UPDATE   tblProducts
SET      Price = 1.1 * Cost
```

16. Your company has just completed a merger with your largest competitor, and now you need to create a report that will tell you in which metropolitan areas your company may need more or fewer branches. The current thinking is that fewer than 10 is too few, more than 25 is too many, and in between is perfect.

Required result: A query that tells you which cities have too many, which ones have too few, and which ones have just right the right number of branches.

Optional desired results: Have the results ordered in this manner: too few, perfect, too many, and list the count of the branches in that city.

Proposed solution:

```
SELECT        tblBranch.City, Recommendation =
        CASE
              WHEN COUNT(tblBranch. City) < 10 THEN 'Too Few'
              WHEN COUNT(tblBranch.City)>= 10 AND  COUNT(AUTHORS.CITY)
<=25 THEN 'Perfect'
              WHEN COUNT(tblBranch.City) > 25  THEN 'Too Many'
        END
FROM tblBranch
GROUP BY tblBranch.City
```

Which results does the proposed solution produce?

A. The proposed solution produces the required result and produces both of the optional results.

B. The proposed solution produces the required result and produces only one of the optional results.

C. The proposed solution produces the required result but does not produce any of the optional desired results.

D. The proposed solution does not produce the required result.

QUESTIONS AND ANSWERS

I am building a query that combines an employees table and a sales table. Because the sales data is periodically imported from a remote source, I'm not using foreign keys. Now, when I create an inner join, I am not reporting sales for employees that are not present in the employees table.	When your business processes impede your implementation of referential integrity, you will sometimes get orphan records. However, by using outer joins instead of inner joins, at least you can include these orphan records in your report.
I have two different tables on two different servers in two different cities. The structure of the tables is the same. The reason they are separated is to provide improved performance for views in the cities. I need to generate monthly reports that combine this data. How should I do this?	By using the UNION statement, you can combine these tables in the same columns and present them as a single data source.
I took your advice and used a UNION query, and it worked well for the monthly reports. But now the users want to view these reports in real time. The performance accessing the remote server using UNION queries was unacceptable.	You could select a process to run overnight, using SELECT INTO to create a table based upon the content from both cities. Although updates made during the day would not be immediately available in other cities, the performance of queries accessing this data would be greatly improved.
The queries I am building are nested several levels deep, and they are becoming difficult to understand.	You may want to encapsulate some of the complexity of the query in a view. Views are discussed in Chapter 9.

17. You have a table, tblBooks, which holds all the information about the books that you sell. tblBooks has a field, CategoryID, that has the category that it is in and PublisherID that references the publisher. Each book has a valid CategoryID and PublisherID, and they are foreign keys from tblCategory and tblPublisher, respectively. You would like a title of all books where the author's last name is "Gorman," with the description for publisher and category. Which of the following queries would accomplish this? (Choose all that apply.)

A. ```
SELECT Title, tblc.Description, tblp.Description
FROM tblBooks, tblCategory tblC, tblPublisher tblP
WHERE Lname = "Gorman"
AND tblBooks.CatgegoryID = tblC.CategoryID
AND tblBooks.PublisherID = tblP.PublisherID
```

B. ```
SELECT Title, tblc.Description, tblp.Description
FROM tblBooks, tblCategory tblC, tblPublisher tblP
WHERE Lname = "Gorman"
AND tblBooks.PublisherID = tblPublisher.PublisherID
```

C. ```
SELECT Title, tblCategory.Description,
tblPublisher.Description
FROM tblBooks, tblCategory, tblPublisher
WHERE Lname = "Gorman"
AND tblBooks.CatgegoryID = tblCategory.CategoryID
AND tblBooks.PublisherID = tblPublisher.PublisherID
```

D. ```
SELECT Title, tblCategory.Description,
tblPublisher.Description
FROM tblBooks, tblCategory, tblPublisher
WHERE Lname = "Gorman"
AND tblBooks.CatgegoryID = tblCategory.CategoryID
```

18. In SQL Enterprise Manager, you look at the relationship diagram of database Person:

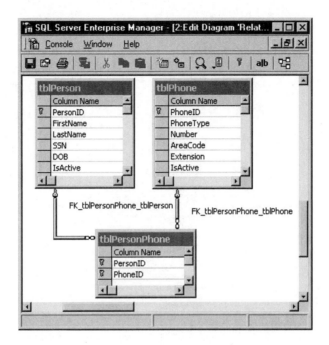

You write the following query:

```
SELECT    *
FROM tblPerson
WHERE tP.PersonID EXISTS (SELECT tPPh.PersonID
                          FROM tblPersonPhone tPPh, tblPhone tPh
                          WHERE tPPh.PhoneID = tPH.PhoneID
                          AND tPH.IsActive = 1
                          GROUP BY PersonID
                          HAVING COUNT(tPPh.PersonID)>1)
```

What does this query return?

A. All the information about the active people that have at least two phone numbers
B. All the information about the people who have at least two active phone numbers
C. All the information about the people who have a phone number
D. All the information about the people and all the phone numbers in a Cartesian product

19. You work for a midsized insurance company, and your database administrator just set up Full Text Search for field LicensingForm in tblLicensingForms, which holds all the state licensing forms. Just to see how it works, you type in the following query:

```
SELECT *
FROM  tblLicensingForms
WHERE CONTAINS(LicensingForm, 'INSURANCE')
```

An error is returned. What is the probable cause of nothing being returned?

A. 'INSURANCE' is all caps, and the search is case sensitive.

B. The SELECT is returning all the fields, some of which are not set up for Full Text Search.

C. 'INSURANCE' is in the noise file that the DBA set up.

D. The search term cannot be contained in single quotes.

20. You need to find all the documents that are in tblDocuments that are about a project called "ARISTOTLE" that are mentioned in close proximity to the word "bug." Which of the following queries would bring back the correct results? (Choose all that apply.)

A.
```
SELECT *
FROM tblDocuments
WHERE CONTAINS(Document, 'bug NEAR ARISTOTLE')
```

B.
```
SELECT *
FROM tblDocuments
WHERE FREETEXT(Document, 'bug NEAR ARISTOTLE')
```

C.
```
SELECT *
FROM tblDocuments
WHERE CONTAINSTABLE(Document, 'bug NEAR ARISTOTLE')
```

D.
```
SELECT *
FROM tblDocuments
WHERE FREETEXTTABLE(Document, 'bug NEAR ARISTOTLE')
```

DESIGN
QUESTIONS

Summarizing Data

1. For the last several years, your department has been calculating equipment depreciation in an Excel spreadsheet. Your users want to be able to reference this historical data from within SQL Server. You notice that there are many "holes" in this spreadsheet data, and none of the fields is populated in every row. You offer to help repair this data, but your users have informed you that they want to see the data in its historical format, "holes" and all. After migrating this data to SQL Server, which of the following techniques would be the best for counting the number of records imported into the table?

   A. SELECT count() FROM depreciation
   B. SELECT count(*) FROM depreciation
   C. SELECT max(count(date), count(authnum), count(requestedby), count(taxschedule)) FROM depreciation
   D. SELECT count(fname) WITHNULL FROM depreciation

2. You have a user who has to perform data migration, so you grant this user permission to create tables. Soon after granting these rights, your user reports that he must not have sufficient privileges because he gets an error whenever he executes the following query:

   ```
   SELECT employee.job_id, Min(employee.hire_date)
   INTO tempjobid
   FROM employee
   GROUP BY employee.job_id
   ```

   What should you advise this user to do differently?

   A. He needs to avoid aggregate functions when using SELECT INTO.
   B. He cannot use the MIN operator on a date field.
   C. He needs to define a title for the aggregated column.
   D. He must use the COMPUTE BY clause when creating a new table.

3. You have developed a report that ranks your regional offices by the number of overdue packages they have outstanding. You receive complaints that

some offices are being unfairly penalized because shipments are counted as overdue even though no destination for those packages has been identified yet. How can you modify your SELECT clause to exclude records with a NULL value in the Destination field?

A. Add "SumP(Destination)" to the Where clause.

B. Add "SumP(Packages, Destination)" to the SELECT clause.

C. Add "Destination is not null" to the Where clause.

D. Add "not null count Destination" to the SELECT clause.

4. Your school uses SQL Server to manage classroom data. Your database administrator has set up a view for you ("ClassData912") that allows you to maintain data for your tenth-grade biology class. You have 20 students, and you have administered one test—"HistT1." The values in the ClassData912 view are as follows:

TeacherID	ClassID	TestID	StudentID	Grade
12345	Bio10	HistT1	837406711	98
12345	Bio10	HistT1	307606759	98
12345	Bio10	HistT1	696186153	95
12345	Bio10	HistT1	934417607	95
12345	Bio10	HistT1	605521981	95
12345	Bio10	HistT1	621575255	95
12345	Bio10	HistT1	780783448	95
12345	Bio10	HistT1	164445992	92
12345	Bio10	HistT1	514289712	92
12345	Bio10	HistT1	129467586	92
12345	Bio10	HistT1	791360930	88
12345	Bio10	HistT1	545904298	85
12345	Bio10	HistT1	116319507	85
12345	Bio10	HistT1	364081667	85

DESIGN QUESTIO

TeacherID	ClassID	TestID	StudentID	Grade
12345	Bio10	HistT1	936254022	85
12345	Bio10	HistT1	640957897	82
12345	Bio10	HistT1	337707832	82
12345	Bio10	HistT1	218817539	83
12345	Bio10	HistT1	797253130	78
12345	Bio10	HistT1	813201018	72

What are the results if you run the following query?

```
Select count(score), count(distinct score), max(score)
max(distinct score) from ClassData
```

A. You receive an error because you cannot use DISTINCT with MAX.
B. You receive an error because you cannot use DISTINCT with COUNT.
C. 20, 20, 98, 98
D. 20, 8, 98, 98

5. You work for an online job-placement service, and you are trying to compare the signing bonuses that employers are offering in different parts of the countries. You want to create a GROUP BY query to report on the bonuses offered by region and by industry. The first two lines of your query are as follows:

```
SELECT Region, Industry, Avg(Bonus) AS AverageBonus
FROM JobsAvailable
```

Which of the following GROUP BY clauses would execute correctly in your query without generating an error?

A. GROUP BY Region, Industry
B. GROUP BY Industry, Region
C. GROUP BY Industry
D. GROUP BY Region

6. You work for an international chain of shoe stores, and you have created a view that exports the sales by branch and uses a batch file to generate text files from this view. Your CFO has been importing the content from this view and pasting each day's data into an Excel spreadsheet. The CFO is complaining that the branches do not line up from day to day in his spreadsheet. After investigating, you find that this occurs because Canadian branches have different holidays than those in the United States. For example, on Boxing Day, the Canadian branches are on holiday and are excluded from your query and hence from his spreadsheet. For all of these branches, there are records present in the source table, but they are being filtered out by a Where clause. Which of the following would best solve the issue?

A. In your query, change "GROUP BY" to "GROUP BY All".

B. Write a stored procedure to pad the export file with the needed extra rows.

C. Create a table with one cent worth of sales for every branch, and UNION this table to your sales table before aggregating. This way, all branches will have "sales," but the branches with one cent will correctly round to zero.

D. Create an outer join on the sales data and a table that includes the branches, and perform the aggregation on this join, so all the branches are present.

7. Situation: You are the CIO for a fast food chain that has been approached with a buyout offer. Your management team is receptive to this offer and wants to provide financial data to this suitor in a flexible format. You have all of your sales data for the last five years in a single view. This view describes the revenue by year, state, and ("breakfast", "lunch", "dinner", and "overnight").

Required results: You must provide the total sales for each combination of year, state, and shift.

Desired optional results: You should be able to perform a CUBE directly on this query to report the total for each year for each state and for each shift. The data should be reported in only two columns.

Proposed solution: Create a formula to concatenate the year, state, and shift, separated by hyphens. Use this formula in the SELECT clause and in the GROUP BY clause, and use the sum(x) function on the sales field.

A. The proposed solution produces the required result and both of the optional results.

B. The proposed solution produces the required result and only one of the optional results.

C. The proposed solution produces the required result and neither of the optional results.

D. The proposed solution doesn't produce the required result.

8. You work for a publishing firm, and you are concerned with the profitability of your college textbook division. You believe that the problem is that your department is being too generous with the authors of psychology books, so you want to calculate the total advances paid for these titles. Which of the following queries would do this?

A. SELECT titles.type, Sum(titles.advance) AS TotalAdvance FROM titles WHERE titles.type="psychology" GROUP BY titles.type

B. SELECT titles.type, Sum(titles.advance) AS TotalAdvance FROM titles GROUP BY titles.type HAVING titles.type="psychology"

C. SELECT titles.type, Sum(titles.advance) AS TotalAdvance FROM titles WHERE titles.type="psychology" GROUP BY titles.type HAVING titles.type="psychology"

D. SELECT titles.type, Sum(titles.advance) AS SumOfadvance FROM titles HAVING titles.type="psychology" GROUP BY titles.type WHERE titles.type="psychology"

9. You are budgeting for the bonuses that will be required for your salespeople at the end of the fiscal year. They receive this bonus only if they have a million dollars in sales for the year. Because you have finished three quarters of the year, you want to find the salespeople who will probably receive this bonus by calculating who has sold more than three-quarters of a million dollars so far this year. Which of the following queries would do this?

A. Select EMPID, Sales Where sales > 750000 GROUP BY EMP_ID.

B. Select EMPID, Sales GROUP BY EMP_ID HAVING sales > 750000.

C. Select EMPID, Sales GROUP BY EMP_ID WHERE sales > 750000.

D. Select EMPID, Sales HAVING sales > 750000 GROUP BY EMP_ID.

10. In your duties as information director for a political party in your county, it is your job to analyze voter registration trends. This year, the county has provided soft copy of this data for a nominal fee, so you have purchased it. You have imported the data into a SQL Server table, and you are preparing to analyze party data. (Only the registered voters who have voted in a primary have a party listed in the Party field; the other voters have null in this field.) You execute the following query:

```
SELECT ALL party, count(party) from registration
GROUP BY party
WITH CUBE, ROLLUP
```

Why does this query fail?

A. You must create two separate lines: "WITH CUBE" and "WITH ROLLUP".

B. You cannot use CUBE in a query that contains nulls.

C. You cannot use ROLLUP in a query that contains nulls.

D. You can't use CUBE and ROLLUP in the same query.

11. Your manager at the auto dealership where you work does not allow you the time to learn how to use all the advanced query options. Create a new table that contains the aggregated output of your monthly sales. None of the fields in your source table have nulls in them. You have created an output table for this purpose using the following definition:

```
CREATE TABLE dbo.AutoSales (
    Dealer int NULL ,
    Promotion varchar (20) NULL ,
    Model varchar (32) NOT NULL ,
    Profit money NULL
)
```

If you are creating an INSERT query to populate this table, which of the following would be legal to use in the GROUP BY clause in this query?

A. GROUP BY Dealer WITH CUBE Promotion, Model

B. GROUP BY Dealer WITH CUBE Promotion

C. GROUP BY Dealer, Promotion, Model

D. GROUP BY Dealer, Promotion, Model WITH CUBE

---

exam
ⓦatch

Before testing, be sure to know the syntax, exceptions, and rules involved in using the aggregate functions. Know the data types of the column values that are allowed for each of the function aggregates. For example, AVG and SUM can only be used against numeric values, whereas COUNT, MAX, and MIN support text values.

---

12. You execute the following query:

```
SELECT titles.type, Sum(titles.advance) AS SumOfadvance
FROM titles
GROUP BY titles.type
WITH cube
```

This yields the following table:

type	SumOfadvance
business	25,125.00
mod_cook	15,000.00
popular_comp	15,000.00
psychology	21,275.00
trad_cook	19,000.00
UNDECIDED	(null)
(null)	95,400.00

What do you get when you add the following line to the end of this query?

```
HAVING titles.type="psychology"
```

A. You get an error because the HAVING clause must be before the CUBE.

B. Psychology	21,275.00
(null)	95,400.00
C. Psychology	21,275.00
D. Psychology	21,275.00
(null)	21,275.00

13. Situation: You have created a view for the marketing department that uses CUBE to summarize the sales from the previous day. Unfortunately, today your network has gone down, but you still have to provide this aggregate data to marketing. You try to copy the content onto a floppy, but the file is about 4 megabytes. The marketing department has mentioned that it is receiving more summary data than it needs, and it only needs rollups of all the columns from right to left.

Required results: Reduce the size of the output file significantly.

Desired optional results: Provide rollups of all the columns from right to left. Be able to reference this new view as a subquery.

Proposed solution: In the view, replace CUBE with rROLLUP.

A. The proposed solution produces the required result and both of the optional results.

B. The proposed solution produces the required result and only one of the optional results.

C. The proposed solution produces the required result and neither of the optional results.

D. The proposed solution doesn't produce the required result.

14. Suppose you have two different queries. One of them contains GROUP BY Zip, Gender, Age WITH CUBE, and the other query contains GROUP BY Zip, Gender, Age WITH ROLLUP. Assuming that the source table is populated with a variety of data, what is the best description of the difference between the results generated by these two queries?

A. The CUBE query will have more rows.

B. The ROLLUP query will have more rows.

C. The CUBE query will have more columns.

D. The ROLLUP query will have more columns.

15. While trying to find out how many publishers there are per state, you create the following query:

```
SELECT State, Count(State) AS Totals
FROM publishers
GROUP BY State
WITH ROLLUP
```

Because some publishers are in foreign countries, some of the records have Nulls in the state field. When this query is executed, how many times does "(null)" appear in the State field?

A. 0

B. 1

C. 2

D. The query generates an error.

QUESTIONS AND ANSWERS

You want to know the total number of rows from a table and aren't very familiar with the columns or column values in the table. What would be the safest way to proceed?	Use COUNT(*). Using COUNT and supplying an explicit column name leaves you open to the possibility that the column you selected contains null values. COUNT ignores null values, and therefore will not return the true row count that you are seeking.
Can I use MIN to return the lowest value, when the values are text?	Yes, MIN returns the lowest value in the collating order.
I am returning values from a column that has duplicates. How do I return just one occurrence of each value?	Use DISTINCT to eliminate your duplicate values.
I am trying to return the top five values from a column. I am not getting any syntax errors, but the values returned are not the highest.	Remember that TOP returns the top number of values or the top percentage of values, based on the current collating order. Make sure that your ORDER BY clause is using DESC to place your records in descending order.

16. Situation: You have installed the SQL Server administrative tools on your manager's PC. Your manager has assigned you to create a report for him that references tables containing daily performance statistics. He wants multiple levels of hierarchy, formatted clearly to emphasize the subtotals. He does not want to use an external reporting tool—he wants to be able to get this content directly from Query Analyzer with all the subtotals. Required results: Provide formatted subtotals, and calculate these subtotals at several levels.

Desired optional results: Allow the query to be used as a subquery. Allow the query to be encapsulated in a view.

Proposed solution: Use COMPUTE BY to provide the subtotals.

A. The proposed solution produces the required result and both of the optional results.

B. The proposed solution produces the required result and only one of the optional results.

C. The proposed solution produces the required result and neither of the optional results.

D. The proposed solution doesn't produce the required result.

17. For each of the stores you manage, you want to know the total sales and the date of the most recent order. You create the following query:

```
SELECT stor_id, ord_num, ord_date, qty
FROM SALES
COMPUTE MAX(ord_date), SUM(qty) BY stor_id, ord_num
```

The query generates an error. You realize this query fails to execute because you omitted the ORDER BY clause. Which of the following ORDER BY clauses would make this query execute?

A. ORDER BY stor_id

B. ORDER BY ord_date

C. ORDER BY ord_num, stor_id

D. ORDER BY stor_id, ord_num

18. You work for a chain of grocery stores, and you have created a view that combines the total sales data for the previous month with the preferred shopper data supplied by your customers, filtering out all shoppers who don't have pets. There are 999 records in this table, and the individual purchases have been SUMmed in the field TotalPurchases. Your manager wants to find the median TotalPurchase for people who have pets. Which of the following would allow you to find this value?

A. Use the MDN function on the TotalPurchases to find the median value.

B. Calculate the average value of the TotalPurchases field using a subquery, and then ORDER BY DESC on the absolute value of the difference between the TotalPurchases and this average.

C. Create one query using TOP to find the top 500 TotalPurchases values sorted in descending order, and then use this as a subquery to pull the lowest TotalPurchases value from these values.

D. Create one query using the RowCount aggregate function to find the top 500 records sorted in descending order by TotalPurchases, and then use this as a subquery to retrieve the lowest TotalPurchases value from these values.

19. You have 200,000 records in your Customers table. Users have created many queries that search on these records to determine their most important accounts, and these queries take up too much time and too many resources. You are encouraging your users to use TOP 10 to improve the performance of these queries. The indexes on the table are as shown in the following illustration:

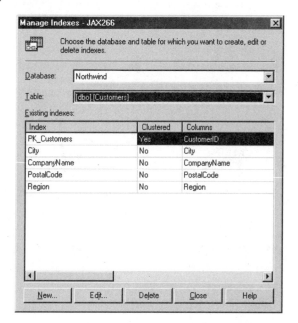

If all of the queries that users created used Order By on a single field, for which of the following sorts would the TOP 10 significantly improve performance?

A. Order By PK_Customers

B. Order By City

C. Order By Region Desc

D. Order By Country

20. You are trying to see which titles had the best sales at your bookstore. You create the following query:

```
SELECT TOP 5 pub_id, title, Sum(ytd_sales) AS TotalSales
FROM titleview
GROUP BY pub_id, title
ORDER BY Sum(ytd_sales) DESC
```

Which is the best description of the content that is returned by this query?

A. The top five publishers, ranked by sales

B. The top five combinations of title and publisher, ranked by sales

C. The top five publishers, ranked by number of books sold

D. The top five titles, ranked by sales

21. You have received a call from the editor of your company newsletter. She wants to list the individuals with the highest sales, and so she has created the following query:

```
Select top 10 empID, sales from sales
```

She does not think the content returned by the query is correct. What is this query actually returning?

A. The first 10 sales records SQL Server finds in the sales table.

B. The top 10 employees with the highest sales, sorted in descending order by sales.

C. The first 10 sales records, sorted in ascending order by emp_id.

D. The top 10 percent of employees, sorted in descending order by their sales.

Managing Transactions and Locks

1. SQL Server is designed to handle large numbers of users accessing the same data at the same time. SQL server is also designed to scale, so that as a business grows, SQL Server can continue to meet the needs of the business. What mechanism does SQL Server use to maintain data consistency with multiple users accessing the same data?

   A. Keys
   B. Switches
   C. Connections
   D. Locks

2. Consider the SQL Server transaction log. The purpose of the log is to capture transactions. If a transaction must be rolled back, the history of that transaction has been captured and can be replayed to facilitate the rollback. If the server crashes, a recent backup and a copy of the transaction log can restore the database to the point at which the system crashed. Which two components of the ACID test does the transaction log address most directly?

   A. Atomicity
   B. Consistency
   C. Isolation
   D. Durability

3. SQL Server maintains a global variable that tracks the number of connections. If you wanted do this, which variable would you use?

   A. @@MAX_CONNECTIONS
   B. @@TRANCOUNT
   C. @@CONNECTIONS
   D. @@IDENTITY

4. In your application you are concerned with performance. You want to avoid locking resources in such a way that will block other user requests. What type of lock should you avoid using?

A. Intent-exclusive locks

B. Exclusive locks

C. Update locks

D. Shared locks

exam
Ⓦatch

Transactions occur within the connections. If a transaction changes modes, the same connection will be used.

5. You have a fairly complicated transaction that you would like to run in parts on two different servers. Unfortunately, you can't seem to get it to work in your current session. What option have you forgotten to set?

A. SET IMPLICIT_TRANSACTIONS ON

B. BEGIN DISTRIBUTED TRANSACTION

C. SET REMOTE_PROC_TRANSACTIONS ON

D. BEGIN TRANSACTION

6. You have written a statement that scans through a table looking for specific values. If the values are found, the associated records will be returned to the user for display. What type of lock will most likely result from your statement?

A. Intent

B. Exclusive

C. Update

D. Shared

7. You are developing an application where performance is much less important than data integrity. You must not allow any opportunity for data to become corrupted or inconsistent. Which locking hint will provide the isolation level that gives you the most safety, at the expense of concurrency?

A. SERIALIZABLE

B. REPEATABLEREAD

C. READUNCOMMITTED

D. READCOMMITTED.

8. Which of the following code examples will not result in an error message?

A.
```
BEGIN TRAN
     UPDATE pubs SET royalty = .05 WHERE  royalty = .03
COMMIT TRAN
```

B.
```
BEGIN TRANSACTION
     UPDATE pubs SET royalty = .05 WHERE  royalty = .03
ROLLBACK TRANSACTION
```

C.
```
BEGIN TRANSACTION
     UPDATE pubs SET royalty = .05 WHERE  royalty = .03
ROLLBACK
```

D.
```
BEGIN TRANSACTION
     UPDATE pubs SET royalty = .05 WHERE  royalty = .03
ROLLBACK WORK
```

---

exam
Ⓦatch
You must run the instcat.sql script against any SQL Server 6.5 servers if you want to run distributed transactions with the linked server options.

---

9. Given the following code example, if the initial number of widgets available is 10, what will be the final inventory count of widgets when the user closes the session?

```
SET IMPLICIT_TRANSACTIONS ON
UPDATE inventory SET available = 5 WHERE product = 'Widget'
BEGIN TRAN
UPDATE inventory SET available = 15 WHERE product = 'Widget'
ROLLBACK
UPDATE inventory SET available = 25 WHERE product = 'Widget'
```

A. 5

B. 10

C. 15

D. 25

---

exam

Watch *Transact-SQL cursors do not support the optimistic with values concurrency option.*

---

10. You are using explicit transactions and need to provide some form of error checking. Given the following code example, how is @@TRAN_COUNT being used to provide error checking?

```
BEGIN TRANSACTION
UPDATE authors SET au_lname = 'White'
WHERE au_lname = 'Grey'
IF @@ROWCOUNT = 1
    COMMIT TRAN
IF @@TRANCOUNT > 0
BEGIN
    PRINT 'A transaction needs to be rolled back'
    ROLLBACK TRAN
END
```

A. @@TRANCOUNT will be greater than zero if only one record is updated.

B. @@TRANCOUNT will be zero if only one record was updated.

C. @@TRANCOUNT will be less than zero if only one record was updated.

D. @@TRANCOUNT will be NULL if only one record was updated.

---

exam

Watch *If an application requests optimistic concurrency with row versioning on a table that does not have a timestamp column, the cursor reverts back to optimistic locking with values.*

QUESTIONS AND ANSWERS

Pseudo Code	Lock Selected
I need to select * from table...	Use Shared locks. They are used for reads.
I need to update a row...	This is a tough one. Should we use Update lock or Exclusive lock? Update lock. Exclusive lock is only for Insert or Delete.
I need to delete a row...	Delete and insert uses Exclusive lock.
I have a lot of transactions and I need to update my row...	Use Intent locks. Intent locks put locks on upper hierarchies, and only those locks are compared instead of comparing all locks in the lower level.

Implementing Views

1. You create the following view of your sales data:

```
CREATE View vewOctoberSales
AS
     SELECT SalesID, SalesAmount, Store, SalesDate
     FROM tblSales
     WHERE SalesDate >= "10/1/2000"
     AND SalesDate < "11/1/2000"
GO
```

Which of the following SQL statements can you commit against this view? (Choose all that apply.)

A. SELECTs

B. INSERTs

C. UPDATEs

D. DELETEs

2. One of the managers in your department is not comfortable dealing with SQL Server, but he is very comfortable dealing with Excel. He needs to examine all the hours worked on each project in your department that are in tblWork since January 1. However, tblWork uses IDs in conjunction with lookup tables to identify the Project and the Employee. You have decided to create a view for him so that he is able to use ODBC to fill his Excel spreadsheet with the correct data in a manner that he can understand. Which of the following will create views that will allow him to see the data he needs in a format he can use? (Choose all that apply.)

A. CREATE VIEW vewWork
```
   AS
       SELECT tW.WorkAmount, tW.WorkType, tP.Description, tWR.Description
       FROM tblWork tW, tblProject tP, tblWorker tWR
       WHERE tW.ProjectID = tp.ProjectID
       AND tW.WorkerID = tWR.WorkerID
       AND WorkDate >= '1/1/2000'
   GO
```

B. CREATE VIEW vewWork WITH ENCRYPTION
```
   AS
       SELECT tW.WorkAmount, tW.WorkType, tP.Description, tWR.Description
       FROM tblWork tW, tblProject tP, tblWorker tWR
       WHERE tW.ProjectID = tp.ProjectID
       AND tW.WorkerID = tWR.WorkerID
       AND WorkDate >= '1/1/2000'
   GO
```

C. CREATE VIEW vewWork WITH ENCRYPTION
```
   AS
       SELECT tW.WorkAmount, tW.WorkType, tP.Description, tWR.Description
       FROM tblWork tW, tblProject tP, tblWorker tWR
       WHERE tW.ProjectID = tp.ProjectID
       AND tW.WorkerID = tWR.WorkerID
       AND WorkDate >= '1/1/2000'
       WITH CHECK OPTION
   GO
```

D. None of the above

---

3. You work at the corporate headquarters of a national grocery store chain. You have decentralized most of the decision making about pricing and replenishment to the actual stores. Your boss believes that if headquarters could provide a view that would show the products with the top 10 quantities in stock, it would be very helpful in letting the stores know which products they need to sell more of. He wants you to write a view to give the people at the stores a list of the 10 products for which the store has the most on hand. Which of the following will do that? (Choose all that apply.)

A. CREATE VIEW vewTOP10inStock
   AS
   ```
        SELECT top 10 ProductName, QuantityPerUnit, UnitsInStock, ProductID
        FROM Products
        ORDER BY UnitsInStock DESC
   ```
   GO

B. CREATE VIEW vewTOP10inStock
   AS
   ```
        SELECT top 10 ProductName, QuantityPerUnit, UnitsInStock,
   ProductID
        FROM Products
   ```
   GO

C. CREATE VIEW vewTOP10inStock
   AS
   ```
        SELECT ProductName, QuantityPerUnit, UnitsInStock, ProductID
        FROM Products
        ORDER BY UnitsInStock DESC
   ```
   GO

D. CREATE VIEW vewTOP10inStock
   AS
   ```
        SET ROWCOUNT 10
        SELECT ProductName, QuantityPerUnit, UnitsInStock, ProductID
        FROM Products
        ORDER BY UnitsInStock DESC
   ```
   GO

4. The new CIO is a big proponent of using views to provide data to the rest of the company and would like you to create views consisting of some of the company's most important queries. Which of the following queries could be made into views? (Choose all that apply.)

A.
```
SELECT SUM(SalesAmount), SalesDate
FROM tblSales
GROUP BY SalesDate
```

B.
```
SELECT SalesAmount, SalesDate
FROM tblSales
COMPUTE SUM(SalesAmount)
```

C.
```
SELECT SalesAmount, SalesDate
FROM tblSales
ORDER BY SalesDate
```

D.
```
SELECT SUM(SalesAmount) AS SumSalesAmount, SalesDate
FROM tblSales
GROUP BY SalesDate
HAVING SUM(SalesAmount)>1000000
```

---

exam
ⓦatch

Most of the answers on Microsoft multiple choice exams are expressed using text. Because of this, there is a bias on the exams towards solutions that can be expressed without using pictures. Even if you find that the visual tools more than meet your needs, for the test you will need to make sure that you are familiar with the SQL-based alternatives to the administrative tools.

---

5. With the following statements you create a view and grant permissions to the appropriate group:

```
CREATE VIEW vewAuthorsPublishers
AS
    SELECT a.lastname, a.firstname, p.name
    FROM pubs..tblPublishers AS p, pubs..tblAuthors AS a
    WHERE a.PublisherID *= p.PublisherID
GO
GRANT EXECUTE ON vewAuthorsPublishers TO domainusers
```

After some members of the domainusers group used this view, you discovered that you needed to change the join in the view from an outer join to inner join. How could you do that and retain the permissions? (Choose as many as apply.)

A. Use DROP VIEW and CREATE VIEW to drop the existing view and to create a new view with the same name and proper join.

B. Use ALTER VIEW to alter the view to have the proper join.

C. Use DROP VIEW and CREATE VIEW to drop the existing view and to create a new view with the same name that has the proper join, and then grant the permissions to the view again.

D. Use ALTER JOIN to alter the view joins from an outer join to an inner join.

6. Current situation: You have just been hired as the database administrator for a midsized telecommunications company. Your database structure is very complex, often requiring many joins for developers to get the information that they desire. Recently, a developer ran a SELECT query without the proper joins between two very large tables that created a Cartesian product that almost took down the server.

Required result: Reduce the number of joins that application developers have to make in order to obtain the information that they need.

Optional desired results: Improve the performance of database access and eliminate any possibility of a Cartesian product happening ever again.

Proposed solution: Remove the developer and user permissions to SELECT from the tables, and then create views that incorporate all the complex joins correctly. Grant SELECT permissions to the views for the users and developers.

Which results does the proposed solution produce?

A. The proposed solution produces the required result and both of the optional results.

B. The proposed solution produces the required result and only one of the optional results.

C. The proposed solution produces the required result but does not produce either of the optional desired results.

D. The proposed solution does not produce the required result.

7. Current situation: All the data in your SQL Server is imported nearly instantaneously from a legacy DOS system. One of the side effects of this is that all text data is fed into the SQL Server in uppercase. Most departments are happy with this and want to keep it this way for regression testing. Other departments, though, do a great deal of reporting and find the uppercase strings difficult to read. They would like certain data to be represented with the first character in uppercase and all of the rest in lowercase.

   Required result: Represent certain data with the first character in uppercase and all of the rest in lowercase.

   Optional desired results: Preserve the data in its current format and let the users be able to update any field on which they can report.

   Proposed solution: Implement views on the table with the data that needs to have the first character in uppercase and all of the rest in lowercase; have the text fields that need to be changed in the select list of the view modified like this:

   ```
   LEFT(FieldName,1)  + LOWER(SUBSTRING(FieldName,2,
   LEN(FieldName)-1)) as FieldName
   ```

   Which result does the proposed solution produce?

   A. The proposed solution produces the required result and both of the optional results.

   B. The proposed solution produces the required result and only one of the optional results.

   C. The proposed solution produces the required result but does not produce either of the optional desired results.

   D. The proposed solution does not produce the required result.

---

exam
ⓦatch

For all objects (not just views), deleting the object and recreating it destroys any user rights that had been applied to that object.

---

8. You create a view in the following batch:

```
Set QUOTED_IDENTIFIER ON
Set ARITHIGNORE ON
CREATE VIEW vewBestEmployees
.  .  .  .  .  .
```

You query the view in a batch like this:

```
Set QUOTED_IDENTIFIER OFF
Set ARITHIGNORE OFF
SELECT * FROM vewBestEmployees
```

What will be the values of QUOTED_IDENTIFIER and ARITHIGNORE for the statements query within the view?

A. QUOTED_IDENTIFIER ON and ARITHIGNORE ON
B. QUOTED_IDENTIFIER OFF and ARITHIGNORE ON
C. QUOTED_IDENTIFIER ON and ARITHIGNORE OFF
D. QUOTED_IDENTIFIER OFF and ARITHIGNORE OFF

9. Current situation: You have three tables that each consist of an ID field that is stored in an integer, a CreateDate field that is stored in a datetime, and a DocumentText field that is stored in a text field. Whenever you perform a search for a document, you do a full-text search on each of the tables and then merge the results.
Required result: Create a way in which you do not have to query each table individually for these full-text searches.
Optional desired results: Improve the performance of the queries and allow the user to update the data through the mechanism that they use to view it.
Proposed solution: Create a view encapsulating the three tables in a UNION query so that they appear to be one table in the partitioned view. Which results does the proposed solution produce?

A. The proposed solution produces the required result and both of the optional results.
B. The proposed solution produces the required result and only one of the optional results.
C. The proposed solution produces the required result but does not produce either of the optional desired results.
D. The proposed solution does not produce the required result.

10. You have just created the following view:

```
CREATE VIEW vewPersonAddress
AS
    SELECT P.PersonID, P.Name, PA.Type, A.Address1, A.City, A.State, A.Zip
    FROM tblPerson P, tblPersonAddress PA, tblAddress A
    WHERE P.PersonID = PA.PersonID
    AND PA.AddressType = "PRIMARY"
    AND PA.AddressID = A.AddressID
GO
```

Which of the following UPDATE statements will you be able to perform on this view? (Choose all that apply.)

A. UPDATE vewPersonAddress
   SET Name = "Will B. Zipf"
   WHERE PersonID =82472

B. UPDATE vewPersonAddress
   SET AddressType = "WORK"
   WHERE PersonID =82472

C. UPDATE vewPersonAddress
   SET Address1 = "5240 Slater Lane"
   WHERE PersonID =82472

D. UPDATE vewPersonAddress
   SET Name = "Will B. Zipf",
   AddressType = "WORK",
   Address1 = "5240 Slater Lane"
   WHERE PersonID =82472

---

exam
ⓌatcH

Sometimes, the same structures used in the demonstration tables (pubs, and now Northwind as well) can show up on the exam. When they do, the table definitions are provided in the question, but if you already have a rough understanding of what the tables do, you may save some time on the exam. Because of this, it is helpful to familiarize yourself with the relationships among the tables in the demonstration databases.

11. You have just created the following view:

```
CREATE VIEW vewPersonAddress
AS
    SELECT P.PersonID, P.Name, PA.Type, A.Address1, A.City, A.State, A.Zip
    FROM tblPerson P, tblPersonAddress PA, tblAddress A
    WHERE P.PersonID = PA.PersonID
    AND PA.AddressType = "PRIMARY"
    AND PA.AddressID = A.AddressID
    WITH CHECK OPTION
GO
```

Which of the following UPDATE statements will you be able to perform on this view? (Choose all that apply.)

A. ```
UPDATE vewPersonAddress
SET Name = "Will B. Zipf"
WHERE PersonID =82472
```

B. ```
UPDATE vewPersonAddress
SET AddressType = "WORK"
WHERE PersonID =82472
```

C. ```
UPDATE vewPersonAddress
SET Address1 = "5240 Slater Lane"
WHERE PersonID =82472
```

D. ```
UPDATE vewPersonAddress
SET Name = "Will B. Zipf",
    AddressType = "WORK"
    Address1 = "5240 Slater Lane"
WHERE PersonID =82472
```

12. You have following view:

```
CREATE VIEW vewTransaction
AS
    SELECT tblTransactionType.TransactionType tblTransaction.Amount,
    tblTransaction.TransactionDate, tblTransaction.IsReconciled
    FROM tblTransaction, tblTransactionType
    WHERE tblTransaction.TransactionType =
tblTransactionType.TransactionType
```

You frequently query this table for transactions on specific dates like this:

```
SELECT *
FROM vewTransaction
WHERE vewTransaction.TransactionDate = "12/5/1999"
```

The performance is horrible. Through the query analyzer you can tell that a table scan is conducted each time that you run a query like this. What can you do to prevent table scans from happening when collecting this information? (Choose all that apply.)

A. You can build an index on the column TransactionDate of the view vewTransaction.

B. You can build an index on the column TransactionDate of the table tblTransaction.

C. You can bypass the view and query the data in the table directly by the TransactionDate field.

D. There is nothing that you can do.

13. You have a table that stores all the employee information, some of which is sensitive, such as salary. It has been dictated to you that some of the information, such as the employee's ID, name, phone number, and address, will be made available to be queried by developers. You do not want the developers to be able to modify any of the data. Which of the following will be able to do that? (Choose the best answer.)

A. Build a view that has the appropriate columns with the WITH READ ONLY OPTION.

B. Build a view that has the appropriate columns with the WITH CHECK OPTION.

C. Build a view that has the appropriate columns and grant only SELECT permissions to the view.

D. Restrict permissions on the table so that it cannot be modified by the developers, and then build a view that has the appropriate columns.

14. You have created the following view:

```
CREATE VIEW vewPrimaryClients
AS
    SELECT ClientName, AccountNumber, CurrentBalance
    FROM tblClient
    WHERE State ='OH'
```

You need to know all of the clients' names and account numbers for clients whose state is OH. Which of the following queries will **not** be able to gather all the needed information? (Choose the best answer.)

A. ```
SELECT *
FROM tblClient
WHERE State ='OH'.
```

B. ```
SELECT *
FROM vewPrimaryClients
WHERE State ='OH'
```

C. ```
SELECT *
FROM vewPrimaryClients
```

D. ```
SELECT ClientName, AccountNumber
FROM vewPrimaryClients
```

QUESTIONS AND ANSWERS

A user wants me to create a view for him, but he requires summary statistics.	Most of the time when views are not permitted, it is still possible to use views to generate most of the intermediate steps. Create a view to aggregate the data you need and then instruct the user to use the COMPUTE statement on that view.
I have created a view that UNIONs two tables: one residing locally, and one on a remote server in Vilnius, Lithuania. I am disappointed by the performance of this view.	You may want to consider replicating or importing some of the remote data locally.
The number of views is constantly growing. I have no idea where they are coming from.	You may have accidentally granted to users the rights not only to create new views, but also to grant the rights to create new views to other users. Both of these rights can be easily revoked.
I thought I removed access rights for a user on a table, but I just found out that this user has been continuing to modify the content in the table anyway.	Confirm that this user does not have rights to any views that have access to this table.
I understand I can't use SELECT INTO in a view, but I still need to distribute the rights to execute this command.	This is a task better suited to stored procedures than to views. Stored procedures are discussed in Chapter 10.

15. You are a literary agent, and your primary responsibility is to represent one author for your firm, Russell Holt. The database administrator, while running SQL trace, noticed that almost all the queries that you run have to do with the set of books that Russell Holt has written, and he has created the following view for you:

```
CREATE VIEW vewRussellsBooks
AS
    SELECT B.BookID, B.Title, B.YearPublished
    FROM tblBooks B, tblAuthors A
    WHERE B.AuthorID = A.AuthorID
    AND A.FirstName = 'Russell'
    AND A.LastName = 'Holt'
```

Which of the following SQL statements use the view correctly? (Choose all that apply.)

A. `SELECT MIN(YearPublished)`
   `FROM vewRussellsBooks`

B. `SELECT tblSales .*`
   `FROM vewRussellsBooks, tblSales`
   `WHERE tblSales.BookID = vewRussellsBooks.BookID`

C. `SELECT Title`
   `FROM vewRussellsBooks`
   `ORDER BY Title ASC`

D. `SELECT YearPublished, Count(YearPublished) AS BookCount`
   `FROM vewRussellsBooks`
   `GROUP BY YearPublished`

16. You have the following view:

```
CREATE VIEW vewTexasDoctors
AS
    Select D.DoctorID, D.Name, D.DoctorType, DT.Description
    FROM tblDoctor D, tblDoctorType DT
    WHERE D.DoctorType = DT.DoctorType
    AND D.State = 'TX'
```

Here are the contents of tblDoctorType:

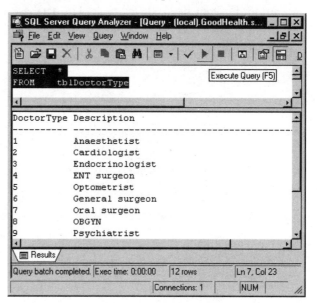

You need to correct your records to show that the Doctor with DoctorID 1492 is a Cardiologist. Which of the following will do that correctly? (Choose the best answer.)

A. `Update vewTexasDoctors`
   `SET Description = 'Cardiologist'`
   `WHERE DoctorID = 1492`

B. `Update vewTexasDoctors`
   `SET DoctorType = 2`
   `WHERE DoctorID = 1492`

C. `Update vewTexasDoctors`
   `SET Description = 'Cardiologist'`
   `WHERE DoctorType = 2`

D. Cannot be done through this view

17. Due to security concerns, you have been asked to evaluate all of your most commonly used queries to determine if you can implement them as views. A junior programmer has asked you to evaluate some of the queries that he uses. In addition to being able to perform SELECTS, he must be able to perform UPDATEs, INSERTs, and DELETEs on these views for them to be a viable option. Which of the following queries could be implemented in their current form as views? (Choose all that apply.)

A. ```
SELECT *
FROM tblProducts
WHERE ProductPrice > (SELECT 2 * AVG(Price) FROM
tblProduct))
```

B. ```
SELECT ProductType, AVG(Price) as AVGPrice,
FROM tblProducts
GROUP BY ProductType
```

C. ```
SELECT SalesID, SalesAmount, SalesDate
FROM tblSales
UNION
SELECT SalesID, SalesAmount, SalesDate
FROM tblSalesArtchive
```

D. None of the above

18. You create the following view:

```
CREATE VIEW vewTestAccounts
AS
    SELECT A.AccountID, A.Balance, A.State, A.Name, A.AccountNumber
    FROM tblAccounts A
    WHERE A.State = 'CA'
    AND A.AccountID > 13572
    AND A.AccountID < 31299
```

Which of the following SQL statements could you execute successfully against this view (assume AccountID is an Identity field)? (Choose all that apply.)

A. ```
DELETE vewTestAccounts
WHERE AccountID =31299
```

B. ```
INSERT vewTestAccounts (Balance, A.State, A.Name,
A.AccountNumber)
VALUES(230000.00, 'TX', 'Hoang Tran', 'D1071CCN')
```

C. ```
UPDATE vewTestAccounts
SET State = 'OH'
WHERE AccountID = 49523
```

D. None of the above

19. Another developer has created a view called vewAllSales. You query it in SQL Server Query Analyzer, as shown here:

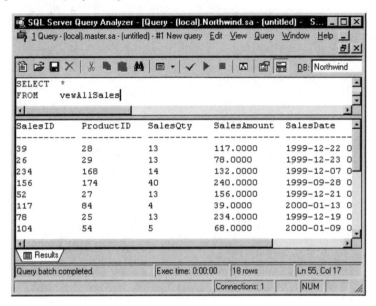

After analyzing the results of your query, what do you know about the view vewAllSales?

A. You can perform INSERT and UPDATE statements.

B. You can bcp the data out of the database.

C. You can delete the records where SalesID =117.

D. SalesID is a unique identity field that is the primary key to vewAllSales.

20. You have created the following view and run it in the SQL Server Query Analyzer:

```
CREATE VIEW vewExpensiveSales
AS
    SELECT SalesID
    FROM tblSales
    WHERE Amount > 2500
```

After you run it, you get the following message:

```
The command(s) completed successfully.
```

Because you created this view successfully, which of the following are true? (Choose all that apply.)

A. tblSales exists.

B. tblSales has a column called SalesID.

C. tblSales has a column called Amount.

D. None of the above

Implementing Stored Procedures

1. You create the following stored procedure:

```
CREATE PROCEDURE My_StoredProcedure
AS
    SELECT *
    FROM    tblSales
GO
```

Which of the following statements will execute it from the query analyzer? (Choose all that apply.)

A. My_StoredProcedure

B. EXEC My_StoredProcedure

C. EXECUTE My_StoredProcedure

D. sp_executesql 'My_StoredProcedure'

2. You create the following stored procedure:

```
CREATE PROCEDURE SL_GetProductByCategoryAndType
    @CategoryID int = 19,
    @TypeID    int
AS
    SELECT *
    FROM    tblSales
    WHERE   CategoryID   =       @CategoryID
    AND     TypeID       =       @TypeID
GO
```

Which of the following statements will return all the items from tblSales where CategoryID =19 and TypeID=71? (Choose all that apply.)

A. SL_GetProductByCategoryAndType @CategoryID=19

B. SL_GetProductByCategoryAndType @TypeID=71

C. SL_GetProductByCategoryAndType @CategoryID=19, @TypeID=71

D. SL_GetProductByCategoryAndType @TypeID=71, @CategoryID=19

3. You have a stored procedure whose parameters are generally similar, but there is one rare instance where it runs with atypical values in the parameter. What could you do to ensure that the stored procedure creates a new appropriate execution plan for the atypical instance? (Choose the best answer.)

   A. Execute it with sp_executesql.
   B. Use the WITH RECOMPILE option when you create the stored procedure.
   C. Execute with EXEC.
   D. Execute the stored procedure with the WITH RECOMPILE.

4. With the following statements you create a stored procedure and grant permissions to the appropriate group:

```
CREATE PROCEDURE PUBS_AuthorsByCity
    @City Varchar(20)
AS
    SELECT au_lname, au_fname
    FROM pubs..authors
    WHERE city = @City
    ORDER BY au_lname, au_fname
GO
GRANT EXECUTE ON PUBS_AuthorsByCity TO public
```

   After some members of the public group used this stored procedure, you discovered that you needed to change the sort order of the results. How could you do that and retain the permissions? (Choose as many as apply.)

   A. Use DROP PROCEDURE and CREATE PROCEDURE to drop the existing stored procedure to create a new stored procedure with the same name that has the right sort order.
   B. Use ALTER PROCEDURE to alter the stored procedure to have the correct sort order.
   C. Use DROP PROCEDURE and CREATE PROCEDURE to drop the existing stored procedure to create a new stored procedure with the same name that has the right sort order and then grant the permissions to the stored procedure again.
   D. Use ALTER ORDER to alter the stored procedure order.

5. You just implemented a series of tables to capture and report on the amount of hours worked for each employee in the company. You are now working on creating the stored procedures with which the developers will interface to the database. You have created the following stored procedure:

```
CREATE PROCEDURE sp_statistics
    @CategoryName VarChar(100)
AS
    SELECT MIN (HoursWorked) AS MINHW , MAX(HoursWorked) AS MAXHW,
AVG(HoursWorked) AS AVGHW
    FROM tblWork, tblCategory
    WHERE tblCategory. Name=@CategoryName
    AND tblCategory.CategoryID =tblWork.CategoryID
```

No error message came up, and you test your stored procedure by executing the following script:

```
DECLARE @CategoryID int
sp_statistics "Human Resources"
```

You receive an empty result set with these column headers: TABLE_QUALIFIER, TABLE_OWNER, TABLE_NAME, NON_UNIQUE, INDEX_QUALIFIER, INDEX_NAME,TYPE, SEQ_IN_INDEX COLUMN_NAME, COLLATION, CARDINALITY, PAGES, and FILTER_CONDITION. What is the most likely cause of this problem? (Choose the best answer.)

A. There is no data in tblWork yet.

B. There is no data in tblCategory yet.

C. A stored procedure named sp_statistics already exists in your database.

D. A stored procedure named sp_statistics already exists in the master database.

6. Currently you have a stored procedure, DS_SalesSummary, that summarizes all the sales of products with CategoryID = 7 (Sporting Goods) for a given day. The application developers have incorporated this stored procedure into a number of sales reports, passing the @SalesDate in by both position and name. Another department head has heard about this and would like to have this information in the sales reports for his department too. Which of the following statements will alter the stored procedure to allow people to summarize the sales for other categories, but still support the reports that currently use DS_ SalesSummary?

A.
```
ALTER PROCEDURE DS_SalesSummary
    @SalesDate smalldatetime,
    @CategoryID int
AS
    SELECT Min(SalesAmount) as SAMin, Max(SalesAmount) SAMax,
AVG(SalesAmount) SAAvg
    FROM tblSales
    WHERE SalesDate = @SalesDate
    AND CategoryID = @CategoryID
```

B.
```
ALTER PROCEDURE DS_SalesSummary
    @SalesDate smalldatetime,
    @CategoryID int = 7
AS
    SELECT Min(SalesAmount) as SAMin, Max(SalesAmount) SAMax,
AVG(SalesAmount) SAAvg
    FROM tblSales
    WHERE SalesDate = @SalesDate
    AND CategoryID = @CategoryID
```

C.
```
ALTER PROCEDURE DS_SalesSummary
    @CategoryID int = 7,
    @SalesDate smalldatetime
AS
    SELECT Min(SalesAmount) as SAMin, Max(SalesAmount) SAMax,
AVG(SalesAmount) SAAvg
    FROM tblSales
    WHERE SalesDate = @SalesDate
    AND CategoryID = @CategoryID
```

D.
```
ALTER PROCEDURE DS_SalesSummary
    @CategoryID int,
    @SalesDate smalldatetime
AS
    SELECT Min(SalesAmount) as SAMin, Max(SalesAmount) SAMax,
AVG(SalesAmount) SAAvg
    FROM tblSales
    WHERE SalesDate = @SalesDate
    AND CategoryID = @CategoryID
```

exam
Ⓦatch

Only members of the sysadmin fixed server role can register and grant permission to access extended procedures.

7. You have a table, tblJobs, that is keyed on an identity field, JobID. You have written a stored procedure that inserts a new job into tblJobs and returns the JobID in an output parameter. You execute the following script to create and test the stored procedure:

```
CREATE PROCEDURE JB_NewJob
    @Description varchar(300),
    @JobID int OUTPUT
AS
    BEGIN
        INSERT tblJobs(Description)
        VALUES(@Description)
    SELECT @JobID = (SELECT MAX(JobID) from tblJobs)
    END
GO
DECLARE @Job_ID int
EXEC JB_NewJob @Job_ID
SELECT @Job_ID
```

You receive the following output:

```
(1 row(s) affected)
-----------
NULL
```

After investigation you see that the record has been inserted. Why is the SELECT @Job_ID statement producing NULL? (Choose the best answer.)

A. There must be a null in the JobID column, and MAX interprets NULL as the greatest value possible.

B. The name of the parameter being passed in, @Job_ID, is different from the parameter in the procedure.

C. You need to specify OUTPUT after @Job_ID in the stored procedure call.

D. None of the above

8. You have just been brought in to replace the current database administrator. All database access is handled through stored procedures, and you would

like to make a good impression quickly. In what ways can you enhance the performance of the existing stored procedures? (Choose all that apply.)

A. Make sure that the datatypes of the parameters being passed to a stored procedure are the same as the ones that are being used.
B. Replace singleton SELECT result set with OUTPUT parameters.
C. Make sure that the datatypes of the parameters used in the queries of the stored procedures are the same as the fields against which they are being compared.
D. Select appropriate recompile options for each stored procedure based on the parameters typically passed to them.

9. You have implemented the stored procedure to use a return code to indicate the status of an insert:

```
CREATE PROCEDURE PS_InsertLicense
    @LicenseNumber varchar(12),
    @State char(2) = 'TX'
AS
    IF @State ='CA'
        RETURN(1)
    IF @State ='NY'
        RETURN(2)
    IF @State ='OH'
        RETURN(3)
    INSERT tblLicense(LicenseNumber, State)
    VALUES(@LicenseNumber, @State)
```

If you execute the following script, what will be the result?

```
DECLARE @Status int
EXECUTE  @Status  = PS_InsertLicense
SELECT @Status
```

A. 0
B. 1
C. 2
D. 3

10. Current situation: You have just been hired as the database administrator for a midsized financial company. The developers in your organization currently have the ability to delete, update, and insert any records to tables to which they have permissions. Recently a developer ran a DELETE query

without a WHERE clause, causing the systems to be unavailable while you restored the data.

Required result: Limit developer and user abilities to insert, update, and delete what is specifically needed for their applications.

Optional desired results: Improve the performance of the database access, and eliminate bottlenecks in the development cycle.

Proposed solution: Remove the developer and user permissions to the table, and replace all needed access to the tables with stored procedures that the database administrator will create. Grant only execute permissions to the stored procedures for the users and developers.

Which results does the proposed solution produce?

A. The proposed solution produces the required result and both of the optional results.

B. The proposed solution produces the required result and only one of the optional results.

C. The proposed solution produces the required result but does not produce either of the optional desired results.

D. The proposed solution does not produce the required result.

11. Under no circumstances should a developer be able to update a record in tblTransaction when the IsReconciled flag is set to 1. You have decided that an error message informing the user that she cannot perform an update to that record should be raised in the stored procedure whenever this is attempted. How could you do this? (Choose all that apply.)

A. Use RAISERROR to pass back an error message that will be stored as a local variable in the stored procedure.

B. Use the sp_addmessage system stored procedure to add the error message with msg_id 122871 to the sysmessages table. Then you can raise it with RAISERROR by passing in the msg_id.

C. Use the sp_addmessage system stored procedure to add an error message with msg_id 122871 to the sysmessages table. Pass back a return code of 122871 anytime this invalid action is encountered.

D. You cannot raise a specific custom error message and instead must invoke one that Microsoft has set up in the syserrors table.

12. Under no circumstances should a developer be able to update a record in tblTransaction when the IsReconciled flag is set to 1. You have decided that you need to raise an error with a specific error message informing the user

that she cannot perform an update to that record with a msg_id of 122871. How could you do this? (Choose all that apply.)

A. With RAISERROR, you can return any msg_id and error message string you want, even if it has not been added to the sysmessages table.

B. Use the sp_addmessage system stored procedure to add an error message with msg_id 122871 to the sysmessages table. Then you can raise it with RAISERROR by passing in the msg_id.

C. Use the sp_addmessage system stored procedure to add an error message with msg_id 122871 to the sysmessages table. Then you can raise it with RAISERROR by passing in the error message.

D. You cannot define a specific msg_id; all msg_id that are raised with RAISERROR will return with a msg_id of 50000.

---

exam
Ⓦatch

If an object within a stored procedure is deleted, when the recompiled stored procedure is run it will return an error. Recompilation does not check for such errors.

---

13. You would like to have a stored procedure return all the authors from the author table and return a return code of 0. Which of the following stored procedures will accomplish this mandate? (Choose the best answer.)

A.
```
CREATE PROCEDURE PUBS_AllAuthors
AS
SELECT *
FROM AUTHORS
```

B.
```
CREATE PROCEDURE PUBS_AllAuthors
AS
SELECT *
FROM AUTHORS
RETURN(0)
```

C.
```
CREATE PROCEDURE PUBS_AllAuthors
AS
RETURN(0)
SELECT *
FROM AUTHORS
```

D. **A and B**

14. Current situation: All the data in your SQL Server is imported nearly instantaneously from a legacy DOS system. One of the side effects of this is that all the people's names and addresses are fed into the database in uppercase. In your applications, this has not proved too difficult because where the data needs to be "propercased," the developers pass the values to a C DLL that has a function to convert a string to propercase. There is no such way of "propercasing" the data in the reporting tool that you use; it merely prints out the data in the manner that it receives it from the stored procedures.

    Required result: Have the output of the reports be propercase in the same manner as the applications.

    Optional desired results: Do not alter the data in the tables, and make no changes to the reports themselves.

    Proposed solution: Create extended stored procedures that will use the propercasing DLL and implement them in the existing stored procedures that are used by the reports to propercase the record sets.

    Which results does the proposed solution produce?

    A. The proposed solution produces the required result and both of the optional results.
    B. The proposed solution produces the required result and only one of the optional results.
    C. The proposed solution produces the required result but does not produce either of the optional desired results.
    D. The proposed solution does not produce the required result.

15. You create the following stored procedure:

```
CREATE PROCEDURE AT_SELECTSalesTransactions
   @SalesDate smalldatetime
   @SalesCount int OUTPUT
AS
   SELECT @SalesCount = (SELECT COUNT(*) FROM tblSales)
   If @SalesCount >250000
      RETURN(1)
   SELECT *
   tblSales
   WHERE SalesDate = @SalesDate
```

How many ways different ways can something calling this application receive output?

A. 1

B. 2

C. 3

D. 4

16. You create a stored procedure in the following batch:

```
Set ANSI_NULLS ON
Set ANSI_PADDINGS ON
CREATE PROCEDURE PUBS_SELECTBestAuthors
. . . . . .
```

You run the stored procedure in a batch like this:

```
Set ANSI_NULLS OFF
Set ANSI_PADDINGS OFF
EXEC PUBS_SELECTBestAuthors
```

What will be the settings of for ANSI_NULLS and ANSI_PADDINGS for the statements in the stored procedure?

A. ANSI_NULLS ON and ANSI_PADDINGS ON

B. ANSI_NULLS OFF and ANSI_PADDINGS ON

C. ANSI_NULLS ON and ANSI_PADDINGS OFF

D. ANSI_NULLS OFF and ANSI_PADDINGS OFF

17. You create a stored procedure in the following batch:

```
Set ARITHABORT ON
CREATE PROCEDURE PUBS_SELECTWorstAuthors
AS
Set ARITHABORT OFF
. . . . . .
```

You run the stored procedure in a batch like this:

```
Set ARITHABORT ON
EXEC PUBS_ SELECTWorstAuthors
```

What will be the settings of for ARITHABORT during the execution of the stored procedure and immediately after the execution of the stored procedure?

A. During execution ARITHABORT ON, and after execution ARITHABORT ON

B. During execution ARITHABORT OFF, and after execution ARITHABORT ON

C. During execution ARITHABORT ON, and after execution ARITHABORT OFF

D. During execution ARITHABORT OFF, and after execution ARITHABORT OFF

18. Current situation: You have a desktop application that is trying to match information from one table to another. One table, tblAccount, holds the account number and the person's first and last name. The other, tblComplaint, holds information that the phone operators type in about a complaint that a customer has made. The first text in tblComplaint is supposed to be the account number, but some operators prefix it with "#" or "# ". In addition, sometimes the operators put the person's name as the first text of the field. Again, because of poor training, there is no consistency. Sometimes it is "last, first"; sometimes it is "last,first"; and other times it is "first, last".

Required result: Attempt to match up the items in tblComplaint with items in tblAccount.

Optional desired results: Use as few trips to the database as possible, and construct a modular solution.

Proposed solution: Create a stored procedure for each case for which rules for matching are clearly defined. Encapsulate them in another stored procedure, CP_MatchComplaints, that will call them in sequence until it exhausts all possibilities or finds a match. CP_MatchComplaints will be called from the desktop application for each item that needs to be matched. Which results does the proposed solution produce?

A. The proposed solution produces the required result and both of the optional results.
B. The proposed solution produces the required result and only one of the optional results.
C. The proposed solution produces the required result but does not produce either of the optional desired results.
D. The proposed solution does not produce the required result.

19. You have just executed the PUBS_SelectAuthors stored procedure as shown next. From the execution and output, what do you know of PUBS_SelectAuthors? (Choose all that apply.)

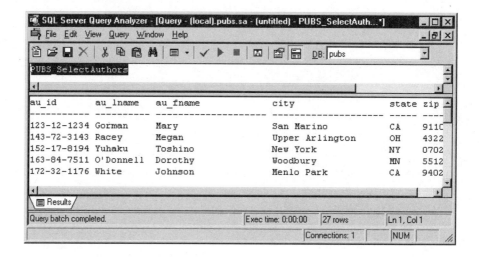

A. You can't give it any parameters.
B. au_lname is a larger field in the database than au_fname.
C. The stored procedure returns 27 rows in these circumstances.
D. The data that is returned lies in the PUBS database.

20. You are having some trouble with a stored procedure, and you look at it through SQL Enterprise Manager:

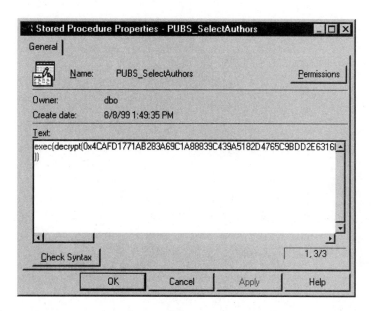

After examining it, what do you know about the stored procedure? (Choose all that apply.)

A. It is encrypted.

B. You can check its syntax.

C. The tables that it depends on exist.

D. It was built using the WITH RECOMPILE option.

Implementing Triggers

1. While implementing a trigger, you determine that there is an error condition that should result in the user receiving an error message. With what statement would you message the user?

A. DISPLAYERR

B. WRITERR

C. RAISERROR

D. SHOWERROR

2. One of the benefits of SQL Server is the ability to nest triggers. How many levels deep can triggers be nested, and what variable would you use to determine which nesting level you are currently at?

   A. 4, @@NEST
   B. 8, @@LEVEL
   C. 16, @@NESTLEVEL
   D. 32, @@PROCLEVEL

3. In many instances the same task can be accomplished by using either a trigger or a constraint. Triggers, however, do have some advantages over constraints. Which of the following would be advantages of using triggers over constraints?

   A. Constraint denial
   B. Complex error handling
   C. Static error messages
   D. Customizable error messages

4. You have a table that requires a great deal of data integrity checking. Over time, performance of this table has been reduced by the number and complexity of the triggers created on this table. After a little review you determine that all of the functionality provided by the triggers can be implemented through constraints. How would you go about removing the triggers from this table.

   A. DELETE TRIGGER
   B. CLEAR TRIGGER
   C. REMOVE TRIGGER
   D. DROP TRIGGER

5. You have noticed a new trigger on a table that you manage. You did not create the trigger, and you are concerned that it may not be valid. Which

stored procedure would you use to determine who owned the trigger and
when it was created?

A. sp_owner

B. sp_helptext

C. sp_depends

D. sp_help

6. SQL Server provides a number of security enhancements. One of these
enhancements is encryption. If you create a trigger using the WITH
ENCRYPTION option, what have you done?

A. Encrypted the options in the trigger

B. Encrypted the trigger in the database where the trigger is defined

C. Encrypted the data for which the trigger was defined

D. Encrypted the entry in the syscomments table that contains the text of
the trigger

DESIGN
QUESTIONS

---

e x a m

ⓦatch

*There are quite a few commands that cannot be executed from a
trigger. You have to know you cannot use the DROP, CREATE,
GRANT, REVOKE, or DISK statements.*

---

7. Current situation: You have an HR table that contains sensitive employee
information including salary and performance data. You would like to
protect this data and be able to track changes to this information.
Required result: You must restrict the viewable columns to only those
columns that do not contain salary and performance data.
Optional result: When a record is inserted or deleted into the HR table, log
the information into another table capturing the date and time as well as the
account name of the person making the change.
Optional result: When salary information is changed, capture the
information about the change as well as the time, date, and account

name of the person making the change and e-mail the information to the HR director.

Proposed solution: Create two views. One view should contain the nonsensitive information, and the other view should contain the sensitive information. Grant appropriate permissions to the views to the appropriate groups in the company. Furthermore, create insert and delete triggers on the views that will capture and log information to another table. On the view with the sensitive information, implement a column update trigger for the salary column that will e-mail change information to the HR director.

A. The proposed solution produces the required result and both of the optional results.

B. The proposed solution produces the required result and only one of the optional results.

C. The proposed solution produces the required result and neither of the optional results.

D. The proposed solution doesn't produce the required result.

8. If you must use variable assignments in the body of your trigger, which option should you set at the beginning of the trigger prior to making the variable assignment?

A. SET NOCOUNT OFF

B. SET NOCOUNT ON

C. SET NOEXEC ON

D. SET NOEXEC OFF

exam
ⓦatch   *If you drop a table, all associated triggers will be dropped as well.*

9. Consider the following code example. If the trigger for the INSERT statement causes a rollback to occur, what is the result?

```
/* Start of Transaction */
BEGIN TRANSACTION
UPDATE employee SET hire_date = '7/1/94' WHERE emp_id =
'VPA30890F'
INSERT employee VALUES ('XYZ12345M', 'New', 'M', 1, 1,
'9952', '6/1/95')
```

A. The update is applied, the insert is applied, and any statements that were part of the trigger are rolled back.
B. The update is applied, the insert is rolled back, and any statements that were part of the trigger are rolled back.
C. The update is rolled back, the insert is rolled back, and any statements that were part of the trigger are rolled back.
D. The update is rolled back, the insert is rolled back, and any statements that were part of the trigger are applied.

10. Current situation: You have a database that has no referential integrity defined. During your last audit, the auditors flagged this as a major problem, so you have been given the task of implementing referential integrity.
Required result: Referential integrity must be enforced.
Optional result: Provide for cascading updates and deletes.
Optional result: Allow values in key columns to match even if the data in those columns is not an exact match (i.e., TX = Texas).
Proposed solution: Implement foreign key constraints.

A. The proposed solution produces the required result and both of the optional results.
B. The proposed solution produces the required result and only one of the optional results.
C. The proposed solution produces the required result and neither of the optional results.
D. The proposed solution doesn't produce the required result.

QUESTIONS AND ANSWERS

I need my updates and deletes to affect other tables...	Use triggers. Unlike the other options to enforce referential integrity, triggers support cascading updates and deletes.
I need to validate data from columns within the same table...	Use constraints. Lower level options such as constraints always perform better than the higher level options such as triggers. Always choose the lower level option unless you gain more with the higher level options.
I need to validate data but it's in a different table...	Use triggers. You cannot use constraints because you cannot compare data in a column in another table.
I just need standard error messages...	Use constraints. Constraints offer minimal error handling and standard error messages.
I need complex error handling...	Use triggers. Triggers are the only referential integrity option that can produce complex error handling.

Working with Distributed and External Data

1. The paradigm that DTS uses provides for information or data to move in one of two different directions. During a move in either direction, the data can be transformed to alter the values of the data or change the format. What are the directions or terms used to define the movement of data?

   A. Import
   B. Create
   C. Export
   D. Delete

2. Transferring data between two SQL Servers that are using different code pages can be problematic. SQL Server provides a couple of methods to make this task much easier. Using the BCP utility, which flags allow you to address this issue?

    A. –w

    B. –N

    C. –6

    D. –C

3. You have a table that contains one year's worth of data. You would like to create a table that contains just June's data. What is the fastest way to create the new table with the subset of data you are interested in?

    A. CREATE TABLE

    B. INSERT

    C. SELECT…INTO

    D. BULK INSERT

4. A legacy HR system resides on an Oracle database, and you need to access employee contact information. Which of the following code examples correctly creates a linked server?

A. `EXEC sp_addlinkedserver 'HRSvr', 'Oracle 8.0',  'MSDAORA', 'ORCLDB'`

B. `EXEC sp_createlinkedserver 'HRSvr', 'Oracle 8.0',  'MSDAORA', 'ORCLDB'`

C. `EXEC sp_makelinkedserver 'HRSvr', 'Oracle 8.0',  'MSDAORA', 'ORCLDB'`

D. `EXEC sp_openlinkedserver 'HRSvr', 'Oracle 8.0',  'MSDAORA', 'ORCLDB'`

---

exam
ⓦatch   *If you are running distributed transactions, the startup type should be set as Automatic.*

---

5. Which of the following code examples correctly executes a query against the linked server created in the previous question? The code example for the linked server is repeated here:

`EXEC sp_addlinkedserver 'HRSvr', 'Oracle 8.0',  'MSDAORA', 'ORCLDB'`

A. `SELECT * FROM REMQUERY(OracleSvr, 'SELECT name, id FROM joe.titles')`

B. `SELECT * FROM OPENQUERY(OracleSvr, 'SELECT name, id FROM joe.titles')`

C. `SELECT * FROM REMOTEQUERY(OracleSvr, 'SELECT name, id FROM joe.titles')`

D. `SELECT * FROM QUERY(OracleSvr, 'SELECT name, id FROM joe.titles')`

6. Which of the following code examples correctly executes a query against the linked server created in Question 4? The code example for the linked server is repeated here:

```
EXEC sp_addlinkedserver 'HRSvr', 'Oracle 8.0',
'MSDAORA', 'ORCLDB'
```

A.
```
SELECT emp.EmloyeeID, ord.OrderID, ord.Discount
FROM SQLServer1.Northwind.dbo.Employees AS emp,
    Orders AS ord
WHERE ord.EmployeeID = emp.EmployeeID
    AND ord.Discount > 0
```

B.
```
SELECT emp.EmloyeeID, ord.OrderID, ord.Discount
FROM SQLServer1.Northwind.dbo.Employees AS emp,
    SchemaX.Orders AS ord
WHERE ord.EmployeeID = emp.EmployeeID
    AND ord.Discount > 0
```

C.
```
SELECT emp.EmloyeeID, ord.OrderID, ord.Discount
FROM SQLServer1.Northwind.dbo.Employees AS emp,
    OracleSvr.Catalog1.SchemaX.Orders AS ord
WHERE ord.EmployeeID = emp.EmployeeID
    AND ord.Discount > 0
```

D.
```
SELECT emp.EmloyeeID, ord.OrderID, ord.Discount
FROM SQLServer1.Northwind.dbo.Employees AS emp,
    Catalog1.SchemaX.Orders AS ord
WHERE ord.EmployeeID = emp.EmployeeID
    AND ord.Discount > 0
```

7. If someone asked you to use the singleton select to assign a value to a variable, what syntax would you use?

A. SELECT INTO
B. SELECT...INTO
C. INSERT...SELECT
D. SELECT

8. There is a server that contains data that you need to query infrequently. You do not want to maintain a linked server configuration. What method could you use to periodically query the server without maintaining a linked server configuration?

A. Define a query using the four-part naming convention of the remote server.
B. Define a query using the OPENQUERY() method.
C. Define a query using the OPENROWSET() method.
D. You must have a linked server definition to be able to query the remote server.

9. Currently a vendor is supplying you with demographic data in the form of large text files. Upon analysis of the data you discover that the vendor is supplying the birthday and age of the contact as a single text field. You really need the age stored separately as an integer. How can DTS help?

A. As part of the import routine you could create a transformation that imported just the age field and converted it to an integer value.
B. As part of the import routine you could create a transformation that imported just the birthday and converted it to a date value.
C. You will not be able get the value you need because an entire field must be imported as a unit during the import routine.
D. You could use DTS to convert the existing field to the values you need, then bcp the data into the table.

10. DTS has a unit of work that defines one or more tasks to be executed in a coordinated sequence. This unit of work can be created manually by using a language that supports OLE Automation, such as Visual Basic, or interactively by using the Data Transformation Services wizards or DTS Designer. What is the name used to identify this unit of work?

A. Task

B. Job

C. Procedure

D. Package

QUESTIONS AND ANSWERS

I want to copy data from an existing table to a new table I haven't created yet ...	Use SELECT INTO. SELECT INTO allows you to create a table based on an existing table.
I need to transfer data from a data file into a table very quickly...	Use BULK INSERT. When speed is at the utmost priority, bulk insert is the only way to go. Please note that you can only retrieve information from the data file. If you want to put data into a flat file, you have to use bcp.
I need to transfer data to and from SQL Server, but I need the database schema too...	Use DTS. DTS is your choice to transfer data AND database schema.
I need to transfer data between SQL Server and a flat file...	Use bcp. Bulk copy is the best option to transfer data when it involves a flat file.
I need to transfer data from an external OLE DB provider...	Use INSERT. INSERT is the best option when you need data from an OLE DB provider.

SQL Server 7.0
Database
Design Answers

Q&A

T he answers to the questions are in boldface, followed by a brief explanation. Some of the explanations detail the logic you should use to choose the correct answer, while others give factual reasons why the answer is correct. If you miss several questions on a similar topic, you should review the corresponding section in the *MCDBA SQL Server 7 Database Administration Study Guide* before taking the test.

Transact-SQL Overview

1. ☑ **A.** The INSENSITIVE option ensures that the data in the cursor does not reflect changes made to data in the table. The option used to create a cursor that makes a temporary copy of the data to be used by the cursor is the INSENSITIVE option. All of the data used by an insensitive cursor comes from a temporary table in tempdb. Consequently, changes made to the real tables are not reflected in an insensitive cursor.

   ☒ **B** is incorrect because omitting the INSENSITIVE option would cause data changes to be reflected in the cursor. **C** and **D** are incorrect because we are dealing with cursors, not variables.

2. ☑ **C.** The most reliable way for you to document a line or set of lines in a stored procedure is to use inline comments. You need to enclose your comments between the /* and */ character combinations. Any text between these characters is not interpreted as executable code. T-SQL is a little different from some languages that only allow comments out to the end of the line. You could have many consecutive lines of comments in a procedure as long as they are all encapsulated between the comment characters.

   ☒ **A** is incorrect because you should not edit the syscomments table directly. **B** is incorrect because you are not able to edit a query execution plan. **D** might be a good idea, but is not the most reliable way to document your code.

3. ☑ **A.** The next logical step after creating a cursor is to open the cursor. The following is the code used to open the cursor:

```
OPEN my_cursor
```

☒   **B** is incorrect because you cannot fetch data from the cursor before you open the cursor. The cursor does not actually contain any data until it has been opened. **C** is incorrect because the cursor must be populated with data before it can be used. **D** is incorrect because the cursor has not been opened yet.

4. ☑   **A.** It is important to remember that unless you take the time to format the output, you may receive a number of characters that you were not expecting. This may make the output unsuitable for some tasks such as creating a temporary table.
☒   **B, C,** and **D** are incorrect because they do not contain the default format that SQL Server uses to return data.

5. ☑   **A.** The SET command is used for session specific settings. Hence, you can format the date any way you need to without affecting other users on the system.
☒   **B, C,** and **D** are not valid SQL commands.

6. ☑   **C.** In all likelihood, SQL Server would choose the merge method of joining these tables. A merge join requires data in the joined columns to be sorted and usually relies on indices for the joined columns. Consequently, a merge join is the most efficient method of joining very large tables. However, it can be very expensive if there is a lot of sorting to be done.
☒   **A** and **B** are not likely choices as both hash and nested loop methods are very efficient when at least one of the tables is not relatively small. A nested loop join works just the way it sounds. You have an outer loop represented by one table and an inner loop represented by another table. Each record in the outer table is checked against every record in the inner table for a match. Then, the outer loop moves to the next record and the entire inner loop is executed again. A hash join uses two inputs. The smaller of the tables is used to create the build input, and the larger of the tables is used to create the probe input. The probe input is probed for the values in the build input in order to join records from the tables. A hashing

algorithm is used for the probe, and requires the probe input to be sorted. **D** is incorrect because there is no such join method.

7. ☑ **B.** No join was specified. As a result, a cross join was implied. This is sometimes referred to as a Cartesian product. Every possible match between the two tables is returned whether the values actually match or not. For example, if each table had 10 records, and the records in each table had a one-to-one relationship, you would expect a result set containing 10 records. If you accidentally create a Cartesian product, you will have a result set of 100 records.
    ☒ **A, C,** and **D** are incorrect because they would not result in a Cartesian product. In fact, these situations would probably result in fewer data being returned instead of more data.

8. ☑ **B.** The heading of the second column would be Name1. Remember that when using the union operator, data is concatenated into one large table. So, there must be the same number of fields. Those fields are titled using the column titles from the first query. You might have been tempted to select Employee, but we used the *as* keyword to rename the column Name1 for display.
    ☒ **A, C,** and **D** are incorrect because columns in a union query are titled by the first query in the union.

9. ☑ **B, C.** A correlated subquery is evaluated multiple times. In fact, it is evaluated once for every record in the result set. Not only can a correlated subquery refer to a field in the parent query, it must refer to a field in the parent query in order to be a correlated subquery.
    ☒ **A** and **D** are incorrect because they are the opposite of the correct responses found in **B** and **C**.

10. ☑ **B.** A local temporary table is prefixed with one number sign and a global temporary table is prefixed with two number signs. Don't get

temporary tables and variables mixed up. Remember that variables use @, instead of #.

  ☒ **A** is incorrect because it is reversed from the way temporary tables are actually named. **C** and **D** are incorrect because the dollar sign ($) is not used to identify any type of temporary table.

Creating and Managing Files and Databases

1. ☑ **C.** Setting database options to DBO USE ONLY ensures that only members of the fixed database role, db_owner, can access OrderEntry while you are performing your modifications.
  ☒ **A,** SINGLE USER, is wrong because a user could access the database while you aren't using the database between steps. **B,** READ ONLY, is wrong because you cannot modify a read-only database. **D,** AUTOCLOSE, is wrong because this closes the database when the last user exits, but the database will automatically reopen when a user tries to use the database again.

2. ☑ **D.** The DBCC SHRINKFILE statement allows you to shrink the file size below the originally created size.
  ☒ **A, B,** and **C** are wrong because AUTOSHRINK, ALTER DATABASE, and DBCC SHRINKDATABASE all restrict the size that a file can be reduced to the original size of the database.

3. ☑ **C.** The NVARCHAR data type uses the UNICODE character set. UNICODE characters take up two bytes each and can accommodate all the symbols needed for business in any language. The size refers to the number of characters allowed, not the amount of space they take.
  ☒ **A,** VARCHAR(100), and **B,** VARCHAR(200), are incorrect because the VARCHAR data type does not accommodate all business languages. **D,** NVARCHAR(200), is incorrect because it would allow up to 200 characters to be entered.

4. ☑ **C.** If the transaction log is truncated on each checkpoint, full or differential database backups are required to ensure that data can be recovered.

   ☒ **A,** there will be no effect on backups, is incorrect because transaction log backups will no longer be of use since committed transactions will be removed from the log. **B** is incorrect because there is no way to trigger a backup during the checkpoint process. **D** is incorrect because increasing the frequency of transaction log backups will not be effective. Committed transactions will still be missing from the backup.

5. ☑ **A, B.** By default, Script All Objects is selected on the general tab of the database scripting tool.

   ☒ **C** is wrong because Security Scripting Options are unchecked by default on the options tab of the database scripting tool. **D** is wrong because Script Indexes is unchecked by default in the Table Scripting Options section on the options tab.

6. ☑ **B, C.** When the SQL Server database option SELECT INTO/BULKCOPY is set to TRUE, only page allocations are logged. This still allows the operation to be rolled back, but not rolled forward. Since each transaction isn't logged, the growth of the log is greatly reduced. It is generally best to drop indexes before and re-create them after bulk copy operations in order to maximize performance.

   ☒ **A** is incorrect since INSERT INTO transactions are logged. **D** is incorrect since the DTS data pump operates at a row level and operations will be logged.

7. ☑ **B, C, D.** The amount of space used in a SQL Server log can be reviewed by selecting each database in SQL Server Enterprise Manager, then selecting the space allocated tab. DBCC SQLPERF(LOGSPACE) is perhaps the easiest way to manually monitor log size since it returns the log size and percentage of log space used for each database on a server. The Windows NT Performance Monitor can be configured to monitor the percentage of log space used by selecting the percent log used counter of the SQL Server databases object for each database that you want to monitor.

☒ **A** is incorrect because the system stored procedure, SP_HELPDB, will not provide information on all logs at once. Running SP_HELPDB with a database name as a parameter will return log size information.

8. ☑ **D.** The timestamp data type is an eight-bit binary field that is incremented every time a row containing a timestamp is inserted or modified. It is simply a sequential number and cannot be converted to a date-time. Since your manager thinks that the timestamp can be converted to the time the record was modified, he should be further informed about timestamps.

☒ **A** and **B** are correct statements about the timestamp columns, but are not relevant to your manager's understanding of what can be done with timestamp columns. **C** is incorrect because timestamp columns are very poor candidates for use as primary keys since they change every time a record is modified.

9. ☑ **A, C.** A table scan is being performed on the table joined to Products. It indicates that the Query Optimizer did not find an appropriate index that would produce a lower cost than scanning the entire table. Stream Aggregate groups sets of columns as required by the GROUP BY clause.

☒ **B** is incorrect because the graphical SHOWPLAN is indicating that an index scan is being performed on the Products table. **D** is incorrect because the execution plan is shown as having a step that computes a value (Compute Scalar).

10. ☑ **D.** ActiveX Data Objects (ADO) is the preferred method of accessing SQL Server databases and other stores from Visual Basic 6.0 and above. It provides a simpler object-encapsulating scheme than OLE DB and ODBC APIs. ADO can be used in other programming environments as well, including Visual C++ and script.

☒ **A** is incorrect because it is inconvenient to use OLE DB directly from Visual Basic. Visual C++ can more easily access the OLE DB API. **B** is incorrect because RDO encapsulates the ODBC API and cannot access the OLE DB API. **C** is wrong because DAO encapsulates the JET API, which is primarily used to interact with Microsoft Access databases.

11. ☑ **B.** SQL Server Profiler is the only tool that will allow you to capture event information and then replay the events in a test environment as they occurred in production. Events can be played either in single step mode to enable examination of the system resources after each event, at the same speed as they originally occurred, or at full speed to stress the system.
☒ **A** is incorrect because Query Analyzer focuses on a single query at a time and does not help analyze the overall performance of the system. **C** is incorrect because Enterprise Manager's current activity section only allows monitoring in real time. Events may happen too quickly for you to fully understand what is occurring. **D** is incorrect because Performance Monitor shows overall system performance, but does not allow you to focus on the actual events that may be causing problems.

12. ☑ **B.** Statistics is automatically created for only the first column of a composite index. The query optimizer may be seeing that the cost of using the composite index may be too high given the distribution of values in the first column. Adding statistics for the other columns in the composite index will allow the query optimizer to more accurately determine whether the index should be used to process the query.
☒ **A** is incorrect because the Index Tuning Wizard will not create new statistics. **C** is incorrect because statistics are up-to-date. Running UPDATE STATISTICS is unlikely to change the query optimizer's strategy based on the distribution of data in the first column of the composite index. **D** is wrong because re-creating the index will just update the statistics for the first column.

Developing a Logical Data Model

1. ☑ **A, B, C.** By denormalizing the Caller Key of the last caller, you have eliminated the necessity to join through the Call Result table (the largest

table) to identify who called a particular donor. Selecting on the Donor Address key of the join between the Donor table and the Call Result table will provide a complete history of donations for the telephone number called. The Donor Address table will allow the list to be limited to a single call to a phone number.

☒   **D,** the database should be easy to update if people who formerly lived together no longer do, is incorrect because having the Donor Address as a fully normalized table could cause a situation where one person's change of address could cause another person's address to be changed inappropriately. In order to easily support household splits, the address and telephone number should be left on the Donor Table. This is an appropriate case for denormalization.

2. ☑   **B.** Create a UNIQUE constraint to the salesperson identifier column definition in the table. SQL Server 7 declarative integrity is implemented by using constraints. A UNIQUE constraint can be declared at either the column level or the table level. Declaring the UNIQUE constraint at the table level allows you to name the constraint and to specify the FILLFACTOR for the associated index.

☒   **A,** create a stored procedure to check the salesperson identifier column, **C,** create an INSERT Trigger that will roll back the transaction if there is a duplicate, and **D,** create a subroutine in the application to loop through the database, are all incorrect. They are examples of enforcing data integrity using procedural methods. Stored procedures and triggers are examples of implementing procedural integrity using SQL Server itself. Creating a subroutine is an example of enforcing integrity outside of SQL Server.

3. ☑   **C.** The GrowerID column must be able to accept NULL as a valid value; therefore the column requires the NULL parameter. The GrowerID column in the Growers table must be defined as a UNIQUE column since a UNIQUE column can contain one record that contains NULL in that column.

☒   **A,** define the GrowerID with the parameter NULL and add a Foreign Key Constraint to the Inventory table referencing the GrowerID column of the Growers table, which is defined as the Primary Key, is incorrect. A column with a Primary Key constraint cannot contain a value of NULL. **B,** define the GrowerID with the parameter NOT NULL and add a Foreign Key Constraint to the Inventory table referencing the GrowerID column of the Growers table, which is defined as a UNIQUE column, is incorrect. The GrowerID column of the inventory must allow NULL as a valid value. The parameter NOT NULL will tell SQL Server to raise an error if NULL is added. **D,** define the GrowerID with the parameter NOT NULL and add a CHECK constraint to query that the GrowerID is in the GrowerID column of the Growers table, which is defined as a UNIQUE column, is incorrect. NULL is not allowed as a valid value, and a CHECK constraint must be a Boolean expression and cannot contain a subquery.

4. ☑ **A.** There are two relationships described that are many-to-many. A person can work on many projects, each of which has many persons. A person can manage many projects, and a project can have many managers. Managers relate to people acting as a resource through the project, not directly.

☒ **B,** a one-to-many relationship between Project and Person labeled Project-Person and a one-to-many relationship between Person and Person labeled Manager-Resources, is incorrect because a person can work on more than one project and a person's manager can change depending on the project. The relationship between Person and Person may be used in a typical hierarchical structure. **C,** a Project-Person entity with a one-to-many relationship between Project and Project-Person labeled Project-Person and a one-to-many relationship between Person and Project-Person labeled Person-Project, is incorrect. We are dealing with the logical data model. Typically a third junction table is introduced when doing the physical design to implement a many-to-many relationship as two one-to-many relationships. **D,** a many-to-many relationship between Person and Project labeled Person-Project, is incorrect because it will not reflect the relationship between managers and resources that is required.

5. ☑ **D.** The column may contain NULL because any parts that cannot be subassemblies of other parts will not have a PartOf to reference. The FOREIGN KEY clause is not required when the foreign key constraint references another column in the same table.

☒   **A** is wrong because NULLs will not be allowed in the column, but there are parts that will not be part of another part. **B** is wrong because the FOREIGN KEY clause is included referring to the same table. **C** is wrong because LONG is the incorrect data type for long integers in Transact-SQL. LONG is the Visual Basic data type for long integers.

6.   ☑   **B, C. B** is the preferred method of validating data in SQL Server 7.0. You need to drop the current formatting CHECK constraint and then add the revised constraint. Because you can't drop and add a constraint in the same step, you need the GO between the lines to ensure that the old constraint is dropped before the new one is added.
If your database was migrated from earlier versions of SQL Server, this type of validity check was performed using rules. The new rule may be created in the database first as long as its name doesn't match the old rule. Use the system stored procedure sp_bindrule to associate the newly created rule with the zip column. Only one rule may be bound to a column at a time; therefore there is no requirement to run sp_unbindrule first. The new rule simply replaces the old association.
Rules are included in SQL Server 7.0 for backward compatibility. CHECK constraints are much more flexible than rules.
☒   **A** is incorrect because it is just adding a second constraint to the zip column. While you are allowed to have more than one CHECK constraint associated with a column, this new one will fail for U. S. zip codes, and the existing CHECK constraint will fail for Canadian postal codes. No data entered for the column will be considered valid. **D** is incorrect because the new rule has not been bound to the zip column.

7.   ☑   **D.** You must drop a default before you recreate it, and it must be unbound from all columns using it prior to being dropped. Once you have created the corrected default, it must be bound to the correct column. Because the new default would violate the existing rule, that rule must be unbound from the column.
☒   **A,** create a DEFAULT constraint of GetDate() – 5 on the PromisedDeliveryDate column. and **B,** unbind the current default, drop it, then create a new default using GetDate() + 5 and bind the new default to the

PromisedDeliveryDate column, are incorrect because the new default would violate the constraint on the earliest a delivery date can be promised. **C,** create a default with the same name as the current one that modifies the default to GetDate() + 5 from GetDate() + 10, is incorrect because you must drop and recreate a default. Running create without dropping the existing default would cause an error. If you created a default with a new name, you would be able to bind the new default without unbinding the previous one because only one default can exist on a column.

8. ☑ **A.** Create a default of "New York". Bind it to the city and state columns of all of your tables using sp_bindefault. When a default value can be used many times, it is preferable to create a default and reuse it on each required column.

☒ **B,** add a DEFAULT constraint of "New York" to each city and state column in your database, is wrong because you would have to make the change to each city and state column in the database and you have a minimum of six of them. **C,** create a stored procedure that will change all blank city and state fields to "New York" and schedule the procedure to run every night using SQLServerAgent, is wrong because running the stored procedure nightly would mean that any addresses used during the day would not contain a valid city and state. **D,** create an INSERT trigger to change NULL city and state fields to "New York", is wrong because a trigger would incur more overhead than a default.

9. ☑ **D.** While logically the logo can be part of the Brokers table, it should be broken out into a separate table with a one-to-one relationship to the Brokers table for performance and usability reasons. If any current reporting queries are written in the form,

```
SELECT * FROM Brokers
```

their performance will immediately suffer as the query attempts to return 19MB TIFF files. Segregating the table into its own filegroup means this potentially large file that changes infrequently can be backed up less frequently than the rest of the database, lowering backup times.

☒ **A,** add a VARCHAR(255) column to the Brokers table containing the path to the appropriate logo image file, is incorrect because you have not been given the option of storing the logos external to the database. Normally this is the preferred method of dealing with images and other large objects. **B,** create a user-defined data type called LOGO, which is a nullable IMAGE, and add Logo, a LOGO column to the Broker table, is incorrect because the IMAGE column could cause severe performance problems with existing queries and doesn't record the format of the image. **C,** add two columns to the Brokers table—LogoFormat and Logo, is incorrect because it could cause severe performance programs. If you could guarantee that no queries selected all columns, this solution could be used.

10. ☑ **A, C.** A long integer RegionID is preferable for performance reasons when joining to another table as required here. A UNIQUE constraint will ensure that no duplicate Region descriptions are entered. Junction tables are required to split many-to-many relationships, which can't be accommodated in a relational database, to one-to-many relationships, which can be accommodated.

☒ **B,** add a Manager table to implement the ReportsTo relationship, is incorrect because a Foreign Key constraint can reference the primary key of its own table. **D,** define Region as NOT NULL in the Territory table to ensure that at least one Territory exists for each region, is incorrect because a NOT NULL constraint in the Territory will not require a Territory exists for each Region.

11. ☑ **A.** The UNIQUEIDENTIFIER contains a Globally Unique Identifier (GUID). The NEWID() function will generate an new GUID. GUIDs use the network card's address and the system time to create an identifier that is unique in space and time. This guarantees that there will be no conflicts between record keys when databases are consolidated. The UNIQUEIDENTIFIER data type was introduced with SQL Server 7.0.

☒ **B,** use a compound primary key using VARCHAR column defaulted to @@SERVERNAME and an IDENTITY column with a seed of 1 and an increment of 1, is incorrect because a compound primary key reduces join performance. Queries that would work on the subsidiary servers because they can safely ignore the server name column will not work on the consolidation server. **C,** use an IDENTITY column with an increment of 1 but assign each country its own seed, is incorrect because eventually one country's number of records could exceed the allowed gap and duplicates would then occur when the data was consolidated. **D,** use an IDENTITY column with a seed of 1 and an increment of 1, is incorrect because merge replication would assume that records with the same key were updates of existing records with that key.

12. ☑ **A.** The proposed solution produces the required result and both of the optional results. Reducing the number of columns in the product table used by the order entry system will reduce the time required to refresh the product table. Removing the sales support information from the table will increase the number of records that can fit on a data page, reducing read operations when the table is scanned. The statistics table will benefit both from removing the sales data and from reducing the number of rows in the table to just those being scanned. Removing the statistics will save the space required for them on over 99 percent of the rows in the table, which will be much more than the additional space required by replicating the primary key to two more tables.
☒ **B, C,** and **D** are incorrect because the proposed solution produces the required result and both of the optional results.

13. ☑ **B, C,** and **D. B** ensures that the date of hire is entered because NULL is not an allowed value. **C** ensures that a beneficiary is designated, defaulting to "ESTATE" if one isn't provided. **D** ensures that the date entered for joining the plan is on or after the waiting period is completed.
☒ **A** is wrong because it will allow nulls and therefore not require a member name.

14. ☑ **C, D.** Generating scripts for all tables, defaults, rules, user-defined data types, primary keys, foreign keys, defaults, and check constraints will

provide you with a script that can reproduce the database. You can read the scripts to get the most up-to-date "documentation" on the database. The system stored procedure sp_help when executed with a table name as a parameter will return a lot of information about the table including what constraints are defined for the table.

☒ **A,** use SQL Server Enterprise Manager to check the table properties, is incorrect because the table properties do not show FOREIGN KEY or CHECK constraints. **B,** use SQL Server Enterprise Manager to generate a database diagram, is incorrect because the database diagram can show everything except CHECK constraints.

15. ☑ **D.** The NOCHECK CONSTRAINT ALL clause will turn off constraint checking for a table until it is enabled using the CHECK CONSTRAINT ALL clause. Because any transactions processed against the database during this time will not be checked against the constraints, you should set the *dbo use only* database option to true prior to doing this type of work. There is no risk that the constraints won't be correctly re-created.

☒ **A,** drop all constraints on the table, import the data, and re-create the constraints using SQL Server Enterprise Manager, is incorrect because manually re-creating the constraints is potentially an error-prone operation. You would also have to ensure that the "Check existing data on creation" option is cleared or the data will be verified when the constraint is added. **B,** generate a script of the current table definition, drop the constraints, import the data, and run the script to re-create the constraints, is safer than **A** but still entails risk because you may miss scripting some of the constraints if you select the wrong options when generating scripts. **C,** execute the ALTER TABLE statement with the WITH NOCHECK option, then import the data, is incorrect because the WITH NOCHECK option applies when adding constraints to existing data, not to adding data to tables with existing constraints.

16. ☑ **C.** The columns can be made nullable, allowing them to be ignored in the order entry application. Any applications providing Region or District keys would still be validated.

☒ **A** is wrong because you cannot drop a table that is referenced by a FOREIGN KEY constraint. **B** is wrong because you must include the data type when changing the nullable constraint. **D** is wrong because some value would still have to be entered in the column because of the NOT NULL parameter implied by values being required.

17. ☑ **C.** The language table will ensure that only the expected languages are added to the description table. As new languages are required, no further database or application changes will be required.

☒ **A,** add new columns to the Product table for each language that can be used, is incorrect because it does not follow normalization rules. As more languages are added, changes will be required to both the database and any application using it. **B,** add a new description table with the product key, a text field describing the language, and the description, is incorrect because there is no constraint on the language description. This leads to the risk that there will be inconsistencies in the field that will lead to errors. **D,** use a Web-based translation program to translate the descriptions when required, is wrong because translation programs can only translate literally and may not give an acceptable result.

18. ☑ **A, D.** SQL Server diagrams clearly show the primary key constraint with the key icon beside the primary key field(s). Foreign key constraints are less clearly shown, but in this case they can be inferred. **A** is correct because the EmployeeID is the primary key and has a self-referencing foreign key constraint. We can't tell from the diagram which column the foreign key constraint is on. **D** is correct because RegionID is the primary key of Regions and there are no foreign key constraints.

☒ **B,** EmployeeTerritories has a compound primary key consisting of EmployeeID and TerritoryID and there are no foreign key constraints, is incorrect because EmployeeTerritories has foreign key constraints to both Employees and Territories. **C,** Territories has a primary key of RegionID and a foreign key constraint of TerritoryID, is incorrect because the foreign key constraint in Territories is RegionID and the primary key is TerritoryKey.

19. ☑ **D.** The proposed solution does not produce the required result. The ROWGUIDCOL property is not compatible with SQL Server 6.5. The script provided to the production database administrator will fail when applied to the production database. In order to be compatible with SQL Server 6.5, defaults, another method of ensuring uniqueness of keys, is required.

    ☒ **B, C,** and **D** are incorrect because the proposed solution does not produce the required result.

20. ☑ **D.** The CHECK constraint will be applied to existing data since the Check existing data on creation is checked. It is also wrong because data will be checked when updated. This business rule would be better implemented as a trigger.

    ☒ **A,** the CHECK constraint will correctly check that new employees are at least 21 when a new employee record is added, and **C,** the CHECK constraint will check data that is replicated to ensure it meets the requirement, are wrong because the CHECK constraint does not meet the requirements of the business rule. **B,** the CHECK constraint will not be enabled for insert, is wrong because the constraint will be enabled for insert.

Planning and Creating Indexes

1. ☑ **B.** You want to rebuild the index with the original fill factor because the pages in the clustered index are likely full and splitting a lot. A page splits when it is full, slowing down the *Insert* because SQL Server must create a new page and move about half of the data to the new page. This decreases the performance of an *INSERT* operation because of the great amount of extra writing needed. Rebuilding the clustered index with a *DROP_EXISTING* clause would greatly enhance the efficiency because SQL Server can take advantage of the existing order of the index.

    ☒ **A,** drop and rebuild the clustered index with the original fill factor, would also improve the speed, but it is not nearly as efficient because all the nonclustered indexes would have to be redone twice. **C,** re-create the nonclustered primary key with the *DROP_EXISTING* clause and the original fill factor, is wrong. The primary key should not affect performance of *Inserts* greatly unless it was a clustered index, which it is not. **D,** there's nothing you can do, is wrong; if B is the solution, then there is obviously something that can be done about it.

2. ☑ **A, C, D.** A fill factor of 100 percent is the fastest to read and should be used on static and semi-static information. This can be generated by specifying a fill factor of 100 or 0, or by not specifying one.

   ☒ **B** is incorrect because a fill factor of 50 means that half of the page is left open for new records, which means that SQL Server will have to do more reading to return the same amount of data.

3. ☑ **C.** A nonclustered index based on *SalesDate* and then *Sales* is correct because it would be a covered index for this query, meaning that all the data the query selects from and uses is contained within the index itself. In this case, both *Sales* and *SalesDate* are within the nonclustered index. The first column in the index corresponds with the field in the *WHERE* clause because that is the field that dominates the layout of the index. In this case, the order needs to be *SalesDate, Sales*.

   ☒ **A,** a clustered index based on *SalesDate*, is incorrect because although a clustered index is very fast, it is not as fast as a covered index. **B,** a nonclustered index based on *SalesDate*, is incorrect because a nonclustered index that is not a covered index is not as fast as one that is. **D,** a clustered index based on *Sales* and then *SalesDate*, is incorrect because the columns are in the wrong order to be useful. The index would be laid out by *Sales* and then *SalesDate* instead of *SalesDate* and then *Sales*.

4. ☑ **A.** A clustered index based on *SalesDate* is correct because clustered indexes excel at bringing back results that are in continuous ranges. In this case, we have a range based on *SalesDate*. If the clustered index is used, all the data access would be sequential because the clustered index controls the layout of the table on the disk.

   ☒ **B,** a nonclustered index based on *SalesDate*, is not as effective because it is a nonclustered index, and they are better used to find specific values. **C,** a nonclustered index based on *Sales* and *SalesDate*, is incorrect because it is a nonclustered index, and the *WHERE* clause uses *SalesDate* but the index has the *Sales* columns first. **D**, a clustered index based on *Sales,* is incorrect because the *WHERE* clause uses *SalesDate* and the index has only the *Sales* field.

5. ☑ **D.** Unknown is correct because the fill factor is not maintained after it is established. Each page will have a different value depending on the number of *Inserts* performed on it. The pages will not have a uniform fill factor after any *Inserts* have been committed.

☒ **A,** 70, is incorrect because there will be no uniform fill factor after any *Inserts,* but 70 is the fill factor initially. **B,** 30, is incorrect because there will be no uniform fill factor after any *Inserts,* but 30 would be the approximate percentage of free space available initially. **C,** 50, is incorrect because there will be no uniform fill factor, although 50 percent would be the approximate fullness of a page after a page split.

6. ☑ **B.** Thirty percent is the correct answer because immediately after an index is rebuilt with a particular fill factor, all the pages will have approximately that much data on them. The fill factor was 30, so after the index was rebuilt, approximately 30 percent of the space on the pages should contain data, and about 70 percent should be empty and ready for data.

☒ **A,** 70, is incorrect because the fill factor determines approximately how much space is used on a page. Seventy percent would be approximately how much free space there would be on each page after the index is rebuilt. **C,** 50, is incorrect because there is a uniform fill factor of 30 percent, although 50 percent would be the approximate fullness of a page after a page split. **D,** unknown, is incorrect because there have been no *Inserts* yet so the fill factor would be uniform and in place.

7. ☑ **A.** Seventy percent is the correct answer. The fill factor tells SQL Server approximately how full each page should be. In this case, it is 30 percent because the fill factor is 30. Because the pages are approximately 30 percent full, about 70 percent of each page should be free space. The fill factor is not maintained after it is created, so each page will have a different value depending on the number of *Inserts* performed on in its page.

☒ **B**, 30, is incorrect because 30 is the approximate percentage of space used on each page, not the percentage of free space. **C**, 50, is incorrect because there is a uniform fill factor of 30 percent, although 50 percent would be the approximate fullness of a page after a page split. **D**, unknown, is incorrect because there have been no *Inserts* yet so the fill factor would be uniform and in place.

8. ☑ **B**. Rebuild it daily with a fill factor of 100 is the correct answer. A fill factor of 100 means that the data pages are completely full, so fewer reads will be needed because there is less space between the pages.
   ☒ **A**, put the index on a different segment that is managed by a different hard disk controller, is incorrect. It is impossible to put the clustered index on a different segment than the data because the clustered index is the layout of the data. **C**, create the index with the *UNIQUE* keyword, is incorrect. Unique values in a clustered index should not improve or detract from the performance because SQL Server is reading large, continuous ranges and is concerned about starting and stopping points for the range. **D**, all of the above, is incorrect because A and C are incorrect.

9. ☑ **A**. The clustered index on the table was created with the *IGNORE_DUP_KEY* option. If you create a *UNIQUE* index with the *IGNORE_DUP_KEY* option, a warning message will be generated when you attempt to insert duplicate data into that index. Without the *IGNORE_DUP_KEY* option, an error message would be generated, and all the records in the batch would not be committed whether they violated the *UNIQUE* constraint or not. The *IGNORE_DUP_KEY* option will allow the commands that do not violate the *UNIQUE* constraint to be committed, while rejecting those that attempt to violate the mandate of the *UNIQUE* constraint.
   ☒ **B**, the clustered index on the table was created with *ALLOW_DUP_ROW* option, is incorrect because *ALLOW_DUP_ROW* was available in SQL Server 6.5 but is not available in SQL Server 7.0. **C**, the clustered index on the table was created with *IGNORE_DUP_ROW*

option, is incorrect because *IGNORE_DUP_ROW* was available in SQL Server 6.5 but is not available in SQL Server 7.0. **D**, it's impossible, is incorrect because this situation can happen.

10. ☑ **A.** It is nonclustered, with a fill factor of 100. By default, SQL Server will assume a fill factor of 100, and the index is nonclustered.
☒ **B,** it is clustered, with a fill factor of 50, is incorrect because the index would not be clustered and would not have a fill factor of 50. **C,** it is nonclustered, with a fill factor of 50, is incorrect because the fill factor would not be 50. **D,** it is clustered, with a fill factor of 100, is incorrect because the index would not be clustered.

11. ☑ **B.** SQL *IGNORE_DUP_KEY* can be used only on *UNIQUE* indexes. If the *IGNORE_DUP_KEY* is used, it will generate a warning message whenever a duplicate value attempts to be inserted.
☒ **A,** SQL Server allows up to eight columns per index, is incorrect because SQL Server allows up to 16 columns per index. **C,** *PAD_INDEX* must be used with the fill factor parameter, is incorrect because you can use *PAD_INDEX* without a fill factor parameter, but it will not do you any good. **D,** the index is the same name as the table, is incorrect because an index can have the same name as the table. An index can have the same name as an index on another table but you cannot have two indexes on the same table with the same name.

12. ☑ **B.** The proposed solution produces the required result but produces only one of the optional desired results. Both reports will now run faster, but placing indexes on a table with no indexes will slow down the logging to some degree because of the extra overhead that indexes create. That minor loss in logging speed, however, is greatly outweighed by the utility that is gained from the indexes with respect to *SELECTs, UPDATEs,* and *DELETEs.*
☒ **A, C,** and **D** are incorrect because they are inaccurate descriptions of the proposed solution.

13. ☑ **A.** The proposed solution produces the required result, and it produces both of the optional desired results. Both reports will now run faster because they have better indexes available to them. *SalesDate* is a bad choice for a clustered index because it is monotonically increasing, meaning that you will always be writing to the last page, providing a high number of page splits. Replacing it with *StoreNumber* will decrease the number of page splits dramatically. Removing the unneeded indexes will also increase speed because they will no longer have to be maintained.

☒ **B, C,** and **D** are incorrect because they are inaccurate descriptions of the proposed solution.

14. ☑ **B.** The proposed solution produces the required result and produces only one of the optional results. Rebuilding the clustered index each night will allow free space to be put on each page so that page splitting will be reduced. You should experiment with the fill factor on this table over time to find the highest one available that will still keep page splitting from becoming a nuisance. All the other queries that use the nonclustered index should benefit from being rebuilt each night. And, a fill factor of 100 ensures a high join density and that each morning the index will be laid out sequentially. After a few *INSERTs*, however, page splitting will occur, and the nonclustered indexes will no longer be sequential.

☒ **A, C,** and **D** are incorrect because they are inaccurate descriptions of the proposed solution.

15. ☑ **C.** Three is the correct answer. *idx_PK, idx_TaskName, idx_TaskDate* are all nonclustered indexes. *idx_PK* is created when the PRIMARY KEY constraint is implemented on the CREATE TABLE statement. Whenever you implement a PRIMARY KEY or UNIQUE CONSTRAINT, you create an index. *idx_TaskDate* does not specify what type of index it is, so it defaults to a nonclustered index. *idx_TaskName* is a nonclustered index because the *CREATE INDEX* statement uses the keyword *NONCLUSTERED*. Likewise, *idx_TaskOwner* is a clustered index because the *CREATE INDEX* statement uses the keyword *CLUSTERED*.

☒ **A,** 1, **B,** 2, and **D,** 4, are incorrect numbers of indexes.

16. ☑ **C.** The *Primary Key* is named *DocumentID,* and you try to create an index named *DocumentID* that SQL Server will not allow, is the correct answer. When the *PRIMARY KEY* constraint *DocumentID* was placed on the table, it automatically generated an index named *DocumentID.* When a second index named *DocumentID* was attempted, an error would have occurred because you cannot have two indexes on the same table with the same name. You could have made the *DocumentID* clustered with the original *Alter* statement by using the *CLUSTERED* keyword like this:

```
ALTER TABLE tblDocuments ADD CONSTRAINT DocumentID PRIMARY KEY CLUSTERED (DocumentID)
```

☒ **A,** *idx_CreateDate* cannot be created on another file group because it is a clustered index, is incorrect because *idx_CreateDate* is nonclustered. The *CLUSTERED* keyword was not used and, as a consequence, it can be placed on a separate file group. If it were a *CLUSTERED* index, then you could not place it on a separate file group. **B,** index *DocumentID* is clustered and a clustered index cannot be placed on a field that is contained in the *PRIMARY KEY,* is incorrect. There are no restrictions about *PRIMARY KEYs* columns being in a *CLUSTERED* index and, as mentioned before, you can even have the *PRIMARY KEY* be the *CLUSTERED* index for a table. **D,** *idx_CreateDate* will be a clustered index because the *NONCLUSTERED* keyword was not used and that cannot happen because there is already a clustered index on the table, is incorrect because SQL Server defaults to a *NONCLUSTERED* index when no index type is specified. If the index does not explicitly mention that it is *CLUSTERED,* then it is not.

17. ☑ **A.** CREATE CLUSTERED INDEX *idx_LastName* ON tblEmployee (*LastName*) is the only one you could create because all the others contain data types that are not allowed as part of an index.
☒ **B,** CREATE NON CLUSTERED INDEX *idx_Photo* ON *tblEmployee (Photo),* **C,** CREATE UNIQUE INDEX idx_Notes ON tblEmployee (Notes), and **D,** CREATE UNIQUE INDEX idx_EmployeeID_IsSalaried ON tblPersonType (EmployeeID, IsSalaried) WITH IGNORE_DUP_KEY, are incorrect because indexes cannot contain image, text, or bit data, respectively.

In addition, an index cannot contain ntext either. All the other standard data types are allowed to be part of indexes in SQL Server.

18. ☑ **A.** The proposed solution produces the required result and both of the optional desired results. You can rebuild any or all of the indexes on a table using DBCC DBREINDEX. It will rebuild them dynamically so that indexes that enforce constraints can be rebuilt while enforcing their constraints. By not specifying a particular index on the table, DBCC DBREINDEX will rebuild all the indexes on the table. Therefore, if you add another index on *tblPerson* one day, it will also get rebuilt automatically, reducing the maintenance. By specifying 0 as the fill factor, DBCC DBREINDEX will enforce the current fill factor on the index, once again reducing your administration of the process. If a number other than 0 is specified as the fill factor, however, all the indexes on the table will be set to that fill factor.

☒ **B, C,** and **D** are incorrect because they are inaccurate descriptions of the proposed solution.

19. ☑ **D.** You should not index the column. The distribution of the data is very poor because almost all the values are "CA," rendering an index next to useless. The following query is a very common and efficient way to determine the distribution of data:

```
SELECT Field, COUNT(Field)
FROM   Table
GROUP BY Field
```

☒ **A,** it is a good candidate for a clustered index, is incorrect because a clustered index would not be useful with this distribution of data. A clustered index would be useful if the values other than "CA" had a better portion of the data. **B,** it is a good candidate for a nonclustered index, is incorrect because a nonclustered index is useful when the data is highly selective; the bulk of the data in the table is not highly selective in terms of the state column because of the poor distribution of data. **C,** it is a good candidate for a nonclustered unique index, is incorrect because you cannot have a unique index on this column because the values in the column are not unique.

20. ☑ **A.** It is a good candidate for a clustered index. The distribution of the data is very good for a clustered index because you have a limited number of values, each with a good proportion of the data.

☒ **B,** it is a good candidate for a nonclustered index, is incorrect because a nonclustered index is useful when the data is highly selective, and the bulk of the data in the table is not highly selective by EmployeeID. **C,** it is a good candidate for a nonclustered unique index, is incorrect because you cannot have a unique index on this column since the values in the columns are not unique. **D,** you should not index the column, is incorrect because you should use an unclustered index.

Queries

1. ☑ **A, B.** They will both gather all the VendorIDs and LineItemAmounts greater than 4/20/1999. Choice A uses "*" in the SELECT clause and, as a consequence, will bring back all the fields for the records. Choice B explicitly enumerates the fields, VendorID and LineItemAmount, that it wants back.

☒ **C** and **D** are incorrect because they will return all the values greater than "4/20/99" and all the values on "4/20/99."

2. ☑ **B.** This will gather all the VendorIDs and LineItemAmounts greater than 4/20/1999, and it will return only the VendorIDs and LineItemAmounts for those records. Returning only what is required will decrease the amount of IO, and by keeping the fields limited, your chances for the query being a covered query is greater. A covered query is a query where all the fields in the SELECT and WHERE clauses are in the same index, called a covered index. A covered index is very efficient because the data pages are never accessed.

☒ **A** is incorrect because it uses "*" in the SELECT clause and, as a consequence, will bring back all the fields for the records, but it does return the correct record set. **C** and **D** are incorrect because they will return all the values greater than "4/20/99" and all the values on "4/20/99."

3. ☑ **A.** Some of the UPCs in the query on tblSales are NULL. If the nested query returns any NULLS, then the outer query will return nothing. To make this query work, you would have to protect against NULLS in the inner query like this:

```
SELECT Name, UPC
FROM tblProducts
WHERE UPC NOT IN ( SELECT UPC
                   FROM tblSales
                   WHERE SalesDate >= DateAdd(m,-1,getDate())
                   AND UPC IS NOT NULL)
AND tblProducts.IsActive =1
```

☒ **B**, the second parameter of DateAdd needs to be –1, is incorrect because if the parameter was 1 instead of -1, it would be comparing SalesDate against a date in the future. In addition, B still would have returned NULL values, which would have eliminated all the records. **C**, you cannot use a NOT IN clause with an AND, is incorrect because you can use the NOT clause in conjunction with IN. **D**, all of the above, is incorrect because one of the options, **A**, is correct.

4. ☑ **B.** Using LIKE in the WHERE clause indicates a pattern search; in conjunction with LIKE, "%" is interpreted as any string of 0 or more characters. So, "Devil Dog%" would be a search for any string that *begins with* "Devil Dog"; "%Devil Dog" would be a search for any string that *ends with* "Devil Dog"; "%Devil Dog%" would be a search for any string that *contains* "Devil Dog."

☒ **A** is incorrect because the HAVING clause is used to set conditions on a GROUP BY clause, so a GROUP BY clause would be needed for it to restrict the records to the correct values. **C** is incorrect because the HAVING clause needs to be used with GROUP BY in order to restrict records and because the CONTAINS predicate is malformed. **D** is incorrect because you would not use the "%" symbol with the CONTAINS predicate. The phrase "Devil Dog" and the field name "Name" need to be specified within the CONTAINS predicate like this:

```
SELECT *
FROM tblLeague
WHERE Name CONTAINS (Name ,"Devil Dog")
```

In order to use CONTAINS, you need to have the column set up for a full-text search.

5. ☑ **B.** This will select all the LeagueIDs and Names for the leagues that use open draft rules. The SELECT clause specifies the right fields, the FROM clause enumerates the correct tables, and the WHERE clause joins the two tables together based on the LeagueTypeID and restricts the results to only those league types that implement "Open Draft" rules.

☒ **A** is incorrect because there is no join between tblLeague and tblLeagueType. **C** is incorrect because it will error out because each table has a field called LeagueTypeID. When LeagueTypeID is referred to in its query, the tablename is not specified. SQL Server doesn't try to guess which table you are referring to and instead will produce an error. **D** is incorrect because the results are never restricted to the leagues that using "Open Draft" rules. **D** will bring back every league of every league type.

6. ☑ **C.** The proposed solution produces the required result, but produces neither of the optional desired results. This query will get you all the sales records for the last five years, but it will not do it as efficiently as possible because in the WHERE clause you manipulate the SalesDate field. Because you are performing an operation on it you will not directly use the index. It would be more efficient to have the GetDate() parameter manipulated like this:

```
SELECT SalesID, SalesDate, SalesAmount
FROM Sales
WHERE SalesDate > DateAdd(year,-6,getdate())
AND ProductID = 1498
ORDER BY SalesDate DESC
```

In addition ORDER BY will automatically sort the items in ascending order if you do not specify descending order. This means that the results would have been ordered by least recent to most recent instead of most recent to least recent.

☒ **A** and **B** are incorrect because the proposed solution produces neither of the optional results. **D** is incorrect because the proposed solution does produce the required result.

7. ☑ **B, D.** They both implement outer joins to bring back the correct records, although **B** implements the legacy syntax of "*=" and "=*" to signify outer joins, and **D** uses the SQL-92 keywords and syntax for outer joins.

☒ **A** is incorrect because it is an inner join, and as a result, will exclude all the products that have no sales from the results. **C** is incorrect because it has the outer join reversed; it takes all the sales whether or not there is a corresponding product, instead of all the products whether or not they have had a sale.

8. ☑ **D.** It will return all sales and, wherever the zip code is available from the customer information, it will return it. Otherwise, it will return "99999." **D** performs a LEFT JOIN between tblSales and tblCustomers, so that it will return every sales record and, where available, the customer information. In addition, it restricts the results to "12/5/99."

☒ **A** is incorrect because a full join will return all records from both tables, whether or not they match. **B** is incorrect due to the fact that it will return only the records from tblSales that have a customer in tblCustomers and exclude any that do not have a customer. **C** is incorrect because it has the join reversed; it should be an outer join where you have all the records from tblSales, as in **D**, not all the records in tblCustomers. **C** would be correct either if the word LEFT was replaced with the word RIGHT or if the tables swapped positions.

9. ☑ **D.** This solution ensures that it has every SalesPerson by performing an outer join between tblSalesPerson and tblSales, and it restricts the Sales records to the correct dates.

☒ **A** is incorrect because tblSalesPerson and tblSales are never joined on any field; the results will be a Cartesian product between tblSalesPerson and all the Sales in tblSales that fall within the date range. **B** is incorrect for the same reasons as **A**. The only difference between the two is that **A** aliases the table to new names and **B** does not. Aliasing tables can make queries easier to write and are mandatory for self joins. **C** is incorrect because it is an inner join and will exclude any sales person who has not made any sales in that time period.

10. ☑   **A, C, D. A** gets the correct answers by using an OR clause in WHERE clause, so that it takes all rows that have an lname of "Erwin" or "Gorman." **C** uses the UNION operator and actually combines the results of two separate queries; one gathers all the authors whose lname is "Gorman" and the other gathers all the authors whose lname is "Erwin." **D** uses IN to grab all the authors whose lname is within the list—in this case, "Erwin" and "Gorman."

　☒   **B** is incorrect because for a row to be returned, when you are using an AND clause it must satisfy all parts of the AND clause for a particular row, and lname cannot be both "Erwin" and "Gorman" at the same time. It will not return any records, including the ones that have an lname of Gorman and Erwin in them.

11. ☑   **B.** Outer join. You need all the rows from tblProperty and the descriptions from tblExpensableType where there is a match. This is what an outer join can produce.

　☒   **A,** inner join, is incorrect because inner joins will return only those records in tblProperty where the ExpensableType has an entry in tblExpensableType, so the records that do not have an ExpensableType will be excluded. **C,** cross join, also known as a Cartesian product, is incorrect because it will return all rows from one table, combined with every row from the other table. If a cross join was attempted between tblProperty and tblExpensableType, every record in tblProperty would be returned with every record in tblExpensableType. If there were 2,000 properties and 20 ExpensableTypes, your query would return 40,000 rows. **D,** full join, is incorrect because it is an invalid term. Full outer join, a correct term for a join, would also not be correct. It would return all rows on both sides.

12. ☑   **A.** A SELECT INTO statement does not return results like an ordinary SELECT statement. Instead, it channels the results into a new table that is specified in the INTO clause. The fields of the new table will have the same data types and nullabilities of the fields from which you have selected.
☒   **B,** write an INSERT statement into tblPropertyLite that had an appropriate SELECT from tblProperty as the execute statement, is incorrect because you cannot insert records into a table that does not exist. **C,** write an UPDATE Statement to tblPropertyLite that had an appropriate WHERE clause to join the correct records from tblProperty and tblPropertyLite, is incorrect because you cannot update records that do not exist in a table that does not exist. **D,** all of the above, is incorrect because **B** and **C** are incorrect.

13. ☑   **D.** Varchar (51). When SELECT INTO is used to create a new table, the fields have the same attributes as they did in the source table. For example, job_id will be a smallint nonnullable field, and job_lvl will be a tinyint nonnullable field in table tblemployee2. In this case, lname was varchar(30), the space character was char(1), and fname was varchar(20). 30+1+20=51.
☒   **A,** varchar (20), is incorrect because it is taking the length of field fname and not combining it with the space and the lname. **B,** varchar (30), is incorrect because it is taking the length of field lname and not combining it with the space and the fname. **C,** varchar (50), is incorrect because it is taking the length of fname and lname, but ignoring the space.

14. ☑   **C.** This solution gets all the entries from both tables and then sorts them correctly, using the UNION operator. UNION combines the results of multiple SELECT statements into one result set. If you need to order the results from a UNION, you need to place an ORDER BY statement at the end of all the SELECT statements. In addition, that ORDER BY statement needs to refer to the field names in the output of the UNION statement.

The field names are taken from the first SELECT in the UNION statement sequence. In this case, the ORDER BY needs to be by PressReleaseDate and then Type because those will be the final names of the fields since those are the names of the fields in the first SELECT.

☒ **A** is incorrect because it tries to order the first set of results and because the second set of results refers to a field name, AnnouncementDate, that is not in the final results. **B** is incorrect because the ORDER BY clause is after the first SELECT, instead of after the last SELECT. **D** is incorrect because the ORDER BY refers to AnnouncementDate instead of PressReleaseDate.

15. ☑ **C.** C would update all records that are for software, by using an inner join.

   A and **B** both use outer joins that will produce erroneous results, and **D** uses no join at all, so all records will be updated, not just the ones that are for software.

16. ☑ **C.** The proposed solution produces the required result but does not produce any of the optional desired results. This query will accurately tell which cities have too few, too many, or just the right amount of branches, but this query will not order the output correctly and does not output the number of branches in each city. An ORDER clause at the end of the SELECT could have ordered the output correctly, and appending COUNT(*) in the SELECT list would have output the number of branches per city.

   ☒ **A** and **B** are incorrect because the proposed solution does not produce any of the optional results. **D** is incorrect because the required result is produced.

17. ☑ **A, C.** Both join tblBooks to tblCategory and tblPublisher on the correct fields and restrict the results to where the author's last name is "Gorman." Because there are three tables being joined, there must be two joins in the WHERE statement (Join tables-1=joins in WHERE clauses). If the key were more complex than a single field, both fields would have to be joined upon in the WHERE clause, but that would still be one join. The difference between A and C is that **A** aliases two of its tables and **C** does not

alias any of its tables. You can alias as many tables as you like in a query as long as the alias name is not the name of another table or alias within the query.

☒ **B** and **D** are incorrect because each of them leaves out one of the joins. **B** omits the join to tblCategory, and **D** omits the join to the tblPublisher. Both will return Cartesian products with the tables with which they did not join.

18. ☑ **B.** This query uses a subquery to get a list of all the PersonIDs that have at least two active phone numbers, and then it gathers all the information about those people from tblPerson.

☒ **A,** all the information about the active people that have at least two phone numbers, is incorrect because the query does not restrict the set to the active people; it just restricts the phone numbers to being active. **C,** all the information about the people who have a phone number, is incorrect because the "HAVING COUNT(tPPh.PersonID)>1)" clause in the subquery will return only those people who have at least two phone numbers. **D,** all the information about the people and all the phone numbers in a Cartesian product, is incorrect because the outer select is not joined with any table; it is instead joined with a list of values, and to have a Cartesian product, you need to have at least two tables joined together.

19. ☑ **C.** If the Full Text Search is using only noise words, SQL Server will throw up an error. Noise files usually contain words like "a," "and," and "the," but they can be modified to include industry-specific words so that searches are more meaningful. An insurance company might add words like "insurance" and "policy" whereas a software company might add "computer" and "software."

☒ **A,** 'INSURANCE' is all caps and the search is case sensitive, is incorrect because all Full Text Searches are case insensitive. **B,** the SELECT is returning all the fields, some of which are not set up for Full Text Search, is incorrect because you can return fields that are not set up for Full Text Searches. **D,** the search term cannot be contained in single quotes, is incorrect because you have to put the search condition in single quotes.

20. ☑ **A.** The CONTAINS predicate lets you search for terms that are close to each other. In addition, it will also allow you to weight your search terms, search for different inflections of terms, and perform pattern matching. CONTAINSTABLE will also let you do these things, but it is written incorrectly to do this in this query. It would need to be written like this:

```
SELECT tblDocuments.*
FROM tblDocuments
        INNER JOIN
        CONTAINSTABLE(Document, 'bug NEAR ARISTOTLE') tDC
        ON tblDocuments.DocumentID= tDC.[KEY]
```

☒ **B** is incorrect because the FREETEXT predicate will not exclude its record set to records that have the word "bug" near the word "Aristotle." **C** is incorrect because, as we mentioned, the query was not written to use the CONTAINSTABLE predicate. The CONTAINSTABLE predicate returns a table, whereas the CONTAINS predicate returns TRUE or FALSE. **D** is incorrect because the FREETEXTTABLE predicate will not exclude its record set to records that have the word "bug" near the word "Aristotle," and because it will return a table and not the TRUE or FALSE that the query is written to expect.

Summarizing Data

1. ☑ **B.** SELECT count(*) FROM depreciation is the best technique. When you use the Count function with a field as a parameter, it excludes records with a null value in that field. By using the "*" parameter instead, SQL Server counts the presence of the record, not the presence of data in the field. Therefore, the presence of null values in any or all of the fields would not keep the record from being counted, and you would get an accurate count of all the records in the table.

☒ **A**, SELECT count() FROM depreciation, is incorrect because the COUNT syntax requires a parameter (either a field or the "*" operator); you cannot omit the parameter as shown in **A**. You can use these operators together with subqueries, but you cannot nest the operators as shown in **C**, SELECT max(count(date), count(authnum), count(requestedby), count(taxschedule)) FROM depreciation, so this answer is also wrong. There is no "WITHNULL" operator, so **D**, SELECT count(fname) WITHNULL FROM depreciation, is incorrect.

2. ☑ **C.** He needs to define a title for the aggregated column. Unless you specify a title for the aggregated column using AS, the result set will be reported with no title for that column. Normally this would not keep the query from executing, but when you use the query to create a new table a column header is required to provide the names of the columns for this newly generated table.

☒ **A**, he needs to avoid aggregate functions when using SELECT INTO, is incorrect because it is legal to use aggregate operators with SELECT INTO; **B**, he cannot use the MIN operator on a date field, is also incorrect because it is legal to use aggregate operators with date fields. **D**, he must use the COMPUTE BY clause when creating a new table, is incorrect because the COMPUTE BY clause must be avoided when creating new tables; this syntax is not permitted.

3. ☑ **C.** Add "Destination is not null" to the Where clause. The behavior of the Sum function is to add the total of all values that appear in the designated field. This aggregation is performed after the Where or Having clause is applied, so to modify the range of records that should be summed, you need to define these restrictions in the Where or Having clauses.

☒ **A**, add "SumP(Destination)" to the Where clause, and **B**, add "SumP(Packages, Destination)" to the SELECT clause, are wrong because there is no SumP function. (SQL Server provides "P" versions of the Std and Var aggregate functions, and the use of these functions can make the query more concise. There is no "P" version of the other aggregate functions. Even if there were a SumP function, the syntax shown in **A** and **B** differs significantly from the syntax used for StdP and VarP.) There is no NULL COUNT option, so **D**, add "not null count Destination" to the SELECT clause, is incorrect.

4. ☑ **D.** The Count operator normally counts the number of records with values present in that column. When you use "distinct" before the field, the function instead counts the number of different values existing in the column. Because the 20 values for the grade column are scattered across only eight different values, 20, 8, 98, 98 is correct.

☒ Although the use of DISTINCT has no effect when used with MAX, it does not generate an error, so **A,** you receive an error because you cannot use DISTINCT with MAX, is wrong. It is legal to use Distinct with count, so **B,** you receive an error because you cannot use DISTINCT with COUNT, is wrong. **C,** 20, 20, 98, 98, would be correct only if the distinct function had no effect when used with Count.

5. ☑ **A, B.** You can use GROUP BY to categorize the aggregated data for multiple fields, as long as these fields are included in the SELECT clause. It is not necessary to present the fields in GROUP BY in the same order as they appeared in the SELECT clause, so both **A,** GROUP BY Region, Industry, and **B,** GROUP BY Industry, Region, are correct.

☒ **C,** GROUP BY Industry, is incorrect because is excludes "region." When you are using aggregated fields and unaggregated fields in the same SELECT statement, all of the unaggregated fields must be included in the GROUP BY clause. Similarly, **D,** GROUP BY Region, is incorrect because it excludes "industry."

6. ☑ **A.** In your query, change "GROUP BY" to "GROUP BY All." When you use "GROUP BY All" your query will include the categories that are present in the source table but with no records that "survive" the Where clause, so the size of the file exported should remain consistent. You may want to work with this user to find other ways of providing this longitudinal data without requiring as many daily steps (for example, using a Pivot Table in Excel.)

☒ **B,** write a stored procedure to pad the export file with the needed extra rows, **C,** create a table with one cent worth of sales for every branch and

UNION this table to your sales table before aggregating, and **D,** create an outer join on the sales data and a table that includes the branches and perform the aggregation on this join, could all return the desired results in a consistent number of rows. All of these options, though, would require more time to develop and more server resources than the use of GROUP BY All.

7. ☑ **B.** The approach described would successfully provide the required result, and the data would be exported in two columns, thereby producing one of the desired results. This approach is not the most flexible, and usually it is better to use GROUP BY on multiple fields instead. Sometimes, though, applications require a single key field. For example, if the query is intended solely for populating an Excel spreadsheet, and if you need to use VLOOKUP in this spreadsheet, then the concatenation may be the best choice.

   ☒ The required results and one of the optional results are met, so **C** and **D** are false. However, you would not be able to use CUBE on this key to provide the combinations required. Therefore, **A** is also wrong.

8. ☑ **A, B, C.** When the GROUP BY clause is used, the HAVING clause is traditionally used to filter the aggregated values. When the data that is being filtered is unaltered by the GROUP BY, it is also possible to use WHERE in these queries to achieve the same effect. In fact, it may sometimes be faster because SQL Server can eliminate records before it has to aggregate them. The use of WHERE and HAVING in **C** is redundant, but it will still return the desired results.

   ☒ **D,** SELECT titles.type, Sum(titles.advance) AS SumOfadvance FROM titles HAVING titles.type="psychology" GROUP BY titles.type WHERE titles.type="psychology", is incorrect because the HAVING clause must be after the GROUP BY clause, and so **D** would generate an error.

9. ☑ **B.** Select EMPID, Sales GROUP BY EMP_ID HAVING sales > 750000 is correct. Your goal is to add up the total sales for the salesperson,

and then filter on this total. When you filter with HAVING, the filtering occurs after the records are aggregated. Therefore, this query would meet your goal.

☒ **A,** Select EMPID, Sales Where sales > 750000 GROUP BY EMP_ID, is incorrect because when you filter with WHERE, the records are filtered before they are aggregated. Therefore, all salesperson records would be excluded unless they had a single sale exceeding three quarters of a million dollars. The other two options are incorrect because the clauses are in the wrong order. **C,** Select EMPID, Sales GROUP BY EMP_ID WHERE sales > 750000, has the WHERE after the GROUP BY, and **D,** Select EMPID, Sales HAVING sales > 750000 GROUP BY EMP_ID, has the HAVING before the GROUP BY.

10. ☑ **D.** CUBE and ROLLUP are both used to provide aggregation, but you cannot use both of them in the same query. The CUBE operator provides a superset of the functionality provided by ROLLUP, so the best approach would probably be to delete the ROLLUP keyword and the preceding comma.

☒ Because CUBE and ROLLUP cannot be used in the same query, **A,** you must create two separate lines: "WITH CUBE" and "WITH ROLLUP" is wrong. There is no restriction about using CUBE or ROLLUP in queries containing nulls, so **B,** you cannot use CUBE in a query that contains nulls, and **C,** you cannot use ROLLUP in a query that contains nulls, are wrong.

11. ☑ **C.** When you use CUBE, nulls will be returned in all of the columns listed in the GROUP BY clause. Because this option doesn't use CUBE, the query will not return nulls, and this option will work.

☒ The WITH CUBE clause does not support parameters, and so **A,** GROUP BY Dealer WITH CUBE Promotion, Model, and **B,** GROUP BY Dealer WITH CUBE Promotion, are incorrect. (The behavior of CUBE is defined by the parameters in the GROUP BY clause.) **D,** GROUP BY Dealer, Promotion, Model WITH CUBE, is wrong because the Model field is defined NOT NULL, and so this field could not accommodate the nulls that the CUBE query would yield.

12. ☑ **D.** Although the HAVING clause is after the CUBE operator, the CUBE adds up the values after the HAVING clause has been applied. Because all the psychology records survive this filter, the subtotal for psychology is the same as the grand total.

☒ **A,** you get an error because the HAVING clause must be before the CUBE, is incorrect because the query executes properly. (If the HAVING clause were before the CUBE, then the query would return an error.) **B,** Psychology 21,275.00 and (null) 95,400.00, incorrectly implies that the HAVING clause applies only to the subtotals, not to the grand total. **C,** Psychology 21,275.00, would be true if you created the CUBE as a subquery and then used HAVING on that subquery.

13. ☑ **A.** The summary data that ROLLUP provides is a subset of the summary data provided by CUBE. While CUBE provides summary data for each combination of all of the fields in the GROUP BY clause, ROLLUP provides only cascading totals from right to left. Because this is all the rollup data that marketing needs, the first optional result is met. Because the number of rows will shrink, the size of the output file would be reduced significantly. Finally, the resulting query could still be used in a subquery. Therefore, **A** is correct.

☒ Because the proposed solution provides the required result, **D** is wrong. Because both of the optional results are met, **B** and **C** are wrong as well.

14. ☑ **A.** The CUBE query will provide aggregates for all of the combinations of Zip, Gender, and Age, while the ROLLUP query will aggregate the values going from left to right. For example, both queries could tell you the grand total for zip code '4107, but only CUBE would give you the grand total for all 27-year-olds. Because of this, there will usually be more rows in a CUBE query than in the corresponding ROLLUP query.

☒ ROLLUP usually returns fewer rows than CUBE, so **B,** the ROLLUP query will have more rows, is incorrect. The number of columns is determined by the SELECT statement, and neither CUBE nor ROLLUP increases this number of columns, so **C,** the CUBE query will have more columns, and **D,** the ROLLUP query will have more columns, are wrong.

15. ☑ **C.** When you roll up a column that contains a null, there are two different meanings for the nulls that appear in the results set: the Null representing the total for fields with a null, and the Null representing the ROLLUP aggregate totals. In this query, the "(null)" that represents a null value in the state field is displayed in the first record returned; another "(null)" representing the ROLLUP aggregate is displayed in the last record returned.

☒ **A,** 0, would be true only if nulls were excluded from the GROUP BY query. **B,** 1, is false because the two instances of Null are not grouped together. Although the results of the query may be confusing, it does not generate an error, so **D,** the query generates an error, is false.

16. ☑ **C.** If a user plans on using Query Analyzer only to use a query (or another interactive tool, like "ISQL/w"), some of the disadvantages of COMPUTE disappear. It is possible to support multiple levels of subtotals using COMPUTE. Because the solution can provide multiple levels of hierarchy, the required result is met. COMPUTE and ROLLUP provide similar subtotals, but ROLLUP provides the data inside the column, while COMPUTE provides the data as semi-formatted subtotals. Alternatively, you may prefer using neither COMPUTE nor ROLLUP, and instead rely on a third-party reporting tool to reference your views and provide the needed subtotaling.

☒ Because the required results are met, **D** is false. However, you cannot use this query in a view or a subquery. Because neither optional result is met, **A** and **B** are also false.

17. ☑ **D.** When you use COMPUTE … BY, you must make sure that the parameters you list after the BY are all present in the ORDER BY clause and that they are listed in the same order. Of the options listed, only **D,** ORDER BY stor_id, ord_num, meets this criterion, and it is therefore the only ORDER BY clause that will make the query work. (Note that this restriction does not apply for the fields between the COMPUTE and the BY.)

☒ **A,** ORDER BY stor_id, and **B,** ORDER BY ord_date, are wrong because columns were present after the COMPUTE … BY that were absent in the

ORDER BY. In **C**, ORDER BY ord_num, stor_id, both fields were present in the ORDER BY, but because the order was different, the query fails.

18. ☑ **C.** Create one query using TOP to find the top 500 TotalPurchases values sorted in descending order, and then use this as a subquery to pull the lowest TotalPurchases value from these values. By using the subquery to discard the top 499 values, and using the parent query to discard the bottom 499, you could retrieve the median. However, if you did not know the number of records in the table before designing the query, you would have to create another subquery to provide this record count.

☒ There is no MDN function, so **A**, use the MDN function on the TotalPurchases to find the median value, is wrong. **B**, calculate the average value of the TotalPurchases field using a subquery, and then ORDER BY DESC on the absolute value of the difference between the TotalPurchases and this average, is incorrect. Although the first record would contain the record closest to the average, unless the data was a perfect bell curve this would not necessarily be the same as the median value. **D**, create one query using the RowCount aggregate function to find the top 500 records sorted in descending order by TotalPurchases, and then use this as a subquery to retrieve the lowest TotalPurchases value from these values, is wrong also. Although you can use RowCount to restrict the number of records associated with a query, it is not a function you can use within a query.

19. ☑ **A, B, C.** Order By PK_Customers, Order By City, and Order By Region Desc would all improve performance. If a field is indexed, then SQL Server does not have to loop through the whole table to find the top 10 values. Although there can be potential time savings from clustered indexes compared to nonclustered indexes, when you are returning 10 records this difference is unlikely to be significant. The performance benefit is realized whether the sort is ascending or descending.

☒ **D**, Order By Country, is wrong because there is no index for the Country field. SQL Server has to sort through all the records before it knows if a field qualifies as one of the top values; therefore adding TOP 10 would not improve performance significantly for queries sorting on this field.

20. ☑ **B.** This query returns the top five combinations of title and publisher, ranked by sales. To help visualize how TOP affects a query, imagine that the rest of the query executes, and then the TOP parameter is applied to the result set. (Due to query optimization, the TOP operator may actually be applied before certain other steps, but the query will still return the content as if the entire query had been processed before the TOP then applied.)

☒ **A,** the top five publishers, ranked by sales, would be correct if "title" were excluded from the GROUP BY. **C,** the top five publishers, ranked by number of books sold, would be correct if "title" were excluded and Count were used instead of Sum. **D,** the top five titles, ranked by sales, would be correct if "pub_id" were omitted from GROUP BY.

21. ☑ **A.** If you omit the ORDER BY clause when using TOP, the records returned are just the first records found by SQL Server, and usually the data will not be in any predictable order. In addition to adding an ORDER BY to the query, the user would also need to aggregate the sales data using Sum and then add a "GROUP BY Emp_ID" clause to get her desired result.

☒ **B,** the top 10 employees with the highest sales, sorted in descending order by sales, would be true if you used Order By Sales Desc and grouped the sales by employee. **C,** the first 10 sales records, sorted in ascending order by emp_id, would be true if you used Order By EmpId Desc. **D,** the top 10 percent of employees, sorted in descending order by their sales, would be true if you used Percent and Order By Sales Desc and grouped the sales by employee.

Managing Transactions and Locks

1. ☑ **D.** Locks provide a way for an SQL statement to work with a subset of data and ensure that the changes that are made in the statement will not interfere with changes made by other statements. Locks are also the primary mechanism for implementing transactions. Transactions allow groups of statements to be treated as one statement. With a transaction, either all of the work is completed successfully, or none is completed successfully.

☒ **A** is incorrect because keys most often refer to columns where a table relates to information in another table. The key columns are often joined. **B** is incorrect because switches most often refer to parameters or options that can be used for a particular command. **C** is incorrect because a connection to SQL Server is the communications pathway that allows a client to communicate with the server.

2. ☑ **B, D.** The transaction log primarily addresses the issues of consistency and durability. The transaction log ensures that data is not left in an inconsistent state by providing a facility to roll back incomplete transactions. This also supports the requirements of atomicity. Durability is a key goal of the transaction log. If a database has to be restored, the transaction log ensures that all successful transactions that occurred between the last backup and the system failure can be applied to the database. This prevents changes to the database from being lost.

☒ **A** is incorrect, but the transaction log does support atomicity. The primary facility for providing atomicity is the transaction itself. All statements that occur within a transaction are treated as a unit of work. **C**, Isolation, is also incorrect because the primary facility for providing isolation is the lock manager.

3. ☑ **B.** The global variable @@TRANCOUNT maintains the count of connections for the current connection. The BEGIN TRANSACTION statement increments @@TRANCOUNT by one. When the ROLLBACK TRANSACTION statement is executed, @@TRANCOUNT decrements to zero. The exception is ROLLBACK TRANSACTION savepoint_name, which does not affect @@TRANCOUNT. Either COMMIT TRANSACTION or COMMIT WORK decrements @@TRANCOUNT by one.

☒ **A** is incorrect because @@MAX_CONNECTIONS returns the maximum number of simultaneous user connections allowed on a SQL Server. **C** is incorrect because @@CONNECTIONS returns the number of connections or attempted connections since SQL Server was last started.

D is incorrect because the @@IDENTITY variable returns the last-inserted identity value.

4. ☑   **B.** You should try and avoid using exclusive locks as most of the other lock types are incompatible with exclusive locks. For example, if two transactions acquire shared-mode locks on a resource and then attempt to update data concurrently, one transaction attempts the lock conversion to an exclusive lock. The shared mode-to-exclusive lock conversion must wait because the exclusive lock for one transaction is not compatible with the shared-mode lock of the other transaction. In this case, a lock wait occurs. The second transaction attempts to acquire an exclusive lock for its update, but, because both transactions are converting to exclusive locks, they are each waiting for the other transaction to release its shared-mode lock. The result is a deadlock. To avoid this potential deadlock problem, update locks are used. Only one transaction can obtain an update lock to a resource at a time. If a transaction modifies a resource, the update lock is converted to an exclusive lock. Otherwise, the lock is converted to a shared-mode lock.
    ☒   **A, C,** and **D** are not the best choices because these types of locks are more compatible with each other than with the exclusive lock.

5. ☑   **C.** The session option that you need to set is the REMOTE_PROC_TRANSACTION option. You would do this by issuing the statement SET REMOTE_PROC_TRANSACTIONS ON. This option specifies that when a local transaction is active, executing a remote, stored procedure starts a Transact-SQL distributed transaction managed by the Microsoft Distributed Transaction Manager (MS DTC).
    ☒   **A** is incorrect because this option turns on implicit transactions. When a connection is in implicit transaction mode and the connection is not currently in a transaction, executing a statement that could result in changes to data results in opening a transaction. The user must then explicitly commit that transaction, or any changes to the data will be rolled back when the user disconnects. **B** is incorrect because the statement specifies the start of a Transact-SQL distributed transaction. It does not enable distributed

transactions. You would still need to issue the SET REMOTE_PROC TRANSACTIONS ON statement before using the BEGIN DISTRIBUTED TRANSACTION statement. **D** is incorrect because the statement does not involve any distributed transaction components.

6. ☑ **D.** Your statement will most likely result in a shared lock on the resource in question. Shared locks allow concurrent transactions to read a resource. When a shared lock exists on a resource, no other transaction can modify that resource. Unless the transaction isolation level is set to repeatable read, shared locks on a resource are released after the data has been read. You can also specify a locking hint to retain the shared locks for the duration of the transaction.

☒ **A, B,** and **C** are incorrect because your statement is a read-only type of statement. An exclusive lock prevents other transactions from modifying or reading data. An intent lock indicates that SQL Server would like to lock a particular resource. Update locks are a special type of lock used to prevent deadlocking. There would be no need for the other lock types.

7. ☑ **A.** The SERIALIZABLE locking hint. The serializable isolation level provides the strongest form of locking. As long as a transaction has not been committed, the data that the transaction is using is locked, and unavailable to other transactions. This results in a high level of safety, but at the expense of performance.

☒ **B, C,** and **D** are incorrect because they do not provide the highest level of safety. However, since they do allow for more concurrency, performance is better for these isolation levels.

8. ☑ **A, B, C, D.** All examples represent valid syntax. Good or bad, SQL Server with Transact-SQL supports a number of equivalent statements according to backward compatibility and programmer preference. A transaction begins with the BEGIN TRANSACTION or BEGIN TRAN statement. The transaction ends with any of the following: COMMIT, COMMIT TRAN, COMMIT

TRANSACTION, ROLLBACK, ROLLBACK TRAN, ROLLBACK TRANSACTION, or ROLLBACK WORK. If a transaction is committed, the changes to the data that were made between the beginning and end of the transaction are permanent. If the transaction is rolled back, the changes are undone and the data is left in the same state as before the transaction was started. The ROLLBACK WORK statement is functionally the same as ROLLBACK TRANSACTION with one major difference; that is, if you have nested transactions and you issue the ROLLBACK WORK statement, changes will be rolled back to the outermost transaction.

9. ☑ **A.** The correct answer is 10 widgets. This is the number of widgets we started with. Not a single one of the updates was committed. The code begins by turning on support for implicit transactions. Then we change widgets to 5. Next, we begin a transaction and update the widgets to 15. We then roll back the transaction leaving the value of widgets at 5. Finally we update the value of widgets one last time to 25. Unfortunately, we forgot to issue a COMMIT statement before we exited the session. Because we were in an implicit transaction from the beginning of the session, both the change to 25 and the change to 5 were rolled back when we exited. That left a final value for widgets of 10.
   ☒ **A, C,** and **D** are incorrect because the changes that would have resulted in these values were rolled back either explicitly or implicitly.

10. ☑ **B.** The author of this code only wants to change the last name of the person if that person is the only Grey in the database. So, a transaction is opened, @@TRANCOUNT is set to one, and the update is performed. The @@ROWCOUNT variable is checked to ensure that only one record was updated. If only one record was updated, then the transaction is committed and @@TRANCOUNT is set to zero. Finally, the @@TRANCOUNT variable is checked. If @@TRANCOUNT is not equal to zero, then the commit was not performed and we need to issue a ROLLBACK.
    ☒ **A, C,** and **D** are incorrect because they do not represent the correct value for @@TRANCOUNT given the code example. @@TRANCOUNT is incremented by one each time a new transaction is started and decremented by

DESIGN
ANSWERS

one each time a transaction completes with either a commit or rollback statement.

Implementing Views

1. ☑ **A, B, C, D.** Any of these statements can be executed against this view. You can always perform a SELECT query against any view, but the degree to which you can perform UPDATEs, INSERTs and DELETEs on a particular view varies with the composition of the view. This view is a simple view because all the data comes from one table and the WITH CHECK option was not used to create it; as a result, you can perform any of these operations on the view just as if it were a table. Had the view been more sophisticated, created from multiple tables, for instance, there would have been restrictions as to the type of INSERTs, UPDATEs, and DELETEs that you could perform.

2. ☑ **A, B, C.** All three of these will perform identically for SELECT statements and provide the correct data for the manager. **A** and **B** are logically the same, and they will perform the same for SELECTs, UPDATEs, and DELETEs. The only difference is that **B** is encrypted. Because **B** is encrypted, you will not be able to use the sp_help stored procedure to look at the source for this view, and the source that makes up this view will appear as gibberish in the syscomments table due to the encryption. **C** is different from **A** and **B** in that it was created with the WITH CHECK OPTION. The WITH CHECK OPTION will restrict the type of UPDATEs and INSERTs that can be done against this view; all the UPDATEs and INSERTs that are performed against this view must be done in such a way that after the operation is complete, the row would still be visible in this view. For example, you could change a WorkDate from "1/7/2000" to "12/28/1999", but you could not change a WorkDate to "12/28/2000."

   ☒ **D,** None of the above, is incorrect because **A, B,** and **C** are correct.

3. ☑   **A** is the correct answer. **A** will create a view that will always have the top 10 UnitsInStock. It does this by using the TOP and ORDER clauses in the SELECT statement that makes up the view. In addition to returning discrete amounts, the TOP clause could be used to limit the view to 10 percent of products that have the most units in stock.

☒   **B** is incorrect; without the ORDER BY clause, the results will return the first 10 records it comes across, not the 10 with the highest units in stock. **C** is incorrect because you cannot have an ORDER BY clause in a view except when it is used with the TOP clause. **D** is incorrect because you cannot use the SET ROWCOUNT statement in a view. If you did, you would get the following error message:

```
Incorrect syntax near the keyword 'SET'.
```

4. ☑   **A** and **D**. The source queries for views can contain GROUP BY clauses and the GROUP BY clause with the HAVING clause as long as they are constructed correctly in the query. Using the GROUP BY clause, however, will make it impossible for you to perform UPDATE, INSERT, and DELETE statements against the view.

☒   **B** is incorrect because the source query of a view cannot contain the COMPUTE or the COMPUTE BY clauses. This makes a great deal of sense because the output for the COMPUTE and the COMPUTE BY clauses is not just a resultset that resembles a table, but instead a format that resembles a report with section breaks. **C** is incorrect because a view cannot contain an ORDER BY clause in its source query unless it is used in conjunction with a TOP clause.

5. ☑   **B** and **C** are the correct choices. ALTER VIEW was added in SQL Server 7 and is the best way of altering an existing view. Using ALTER VIEW will retain any existing permissions and will not affect any dependent stored procedures, views, or triggers. You could drop it and re-create it, as is done in **C**, but then you would have to grant the permissions once again.

☒ **A**, use DROP VIEW and CREATE VIEW to drop the existing view and to create a new view with the same name and proper join, is incorrect because the permissions would not have been explicitly granted, which is needed if you drop and re-create a view. When you dropped the view, all the permissions associated with it were removed. **D**, use ALTER JOIN to alter the view joins from an outer join to an inner join, is incorrect because there is no ALTER JOIN statement in SQL Server, although many new statements like ALTER VIEW and ALTER TRIGGER have been added to SQL Server 7.

6. ☑ **C** is the correct answer. The proposed solution produces the required result but does not produce either of the optional desired results. If you provided a series of views to accommodate all the joins that your developers needed, you would make it easier for them to access data and less likely that they will create a Cartesian product. They still would be able to create Cartesian products by not joining the views correctly. If you absolutely wanted to prevent the possibility of a Cartesian product from ever happening, the best methodology would be to restrict all access to stored procedures. In addition, by implementing views, you are not guaranteeing faster data access. Views can often perform worse than querying against the table directly.
☒ **A**, **B**, and **D** are incorrect because **C** is correct.

7. ☑ **B** is the correct answer. The proposed solution produces the required result and only one of the optional results. A view will let you present another view of the data, so that you can preserve the underlying data. If any of the columns in a view are derived, then the view cannot be updated. The way that this data was formatted, with the first letter uppercased and the successive letters lowercased, made the columns derived columns. You could query against the view, but you would not be able to update or add data directly to the view. If you wanted to add or update data to the view, you would have to update the underlying data on which the view was built.
☒ **A**, **C**, and **D** are incorrect because **B** is correct.

8. ☑ **C**, QUOTED_IDENTIFIER ON and ARITHIGNORE OFF, is the correct answer. When a stored procedure is created or altered, the values of QUOTED_IDENTIFIER and ANSI_NULLS are embedded. The values

that the view was created with will be the values when the view is executed. All the other SET options, such as ARITHIGNORE, are not saved when the view is created. Instead, the values of these SET parameters during the current connection are used.

☒   **A,** QUOTED_IDENTIFIER ON and ARITHIGNORE ON, is incorrect because ARITHIGNORE is not saved. **B,** QUOTED_IDENTIFIER OFF and ARITHIGNORE ON, is incorrect because the view was created with QUOTED_IDENTIFIER ON. **D,** QUOTED_IDENTIFIER OFF and ARITHIGNORE OFF, is incorrect because the view was created with QUOTED_IDENTIFIER ON.

DESIGN ANSWERS

9. ☑   **D** is the correct answer. The proposed solution does not produce the required result. You cannot perform full-text searches on columns in views even if all the underlying columns support full-text searches. Because you cannot issue full-text searches against a view, the view cannot be the solution to this problem.

☒   **A, B,** and **C** are incorrect because **D** is correct.

10. ☑   **A, B,** and **C** are the correct answers. When the columns in a view come from multiple tables, you can update columns from one of the tables only in a single UPDATE statement. **A** updates data only in tblPerson, **B** updates data only in tblPersonAddress, and **C** updates data only in tblAddress.

☒   **D** is incorrect because it attempts to update data in all three tables with one statement.

11. ☑   **A** and **C** are the correct answers. When the columns in a view come from multiple tables, you can update only columns from one of the tables in a single UPDATE statement. **A** updates only data in tblPerson, and **C** updates only data in tblAddress.

☒   **B** is incorrect because it updates only data in tblPersonAddress, but the update it attempts would remove that data from the view. Updates that remove data from a view are not allowed when a view is created or altered with the WITH CHECK OPTION. **D** is incorrect because it attempts to update data in all three tables with one statement, which is not permissible.

12. ☑   **B** is the correct answer. You can build an index on the column TransactionDate of the table tblTransaction. All nonfull-text indexes are available to the query optimizer when referencing a column in a view. If you build an index on a column in a table, that index is available to the views that incorporate that column.

☒   **A**, you can build an index on the column TransactionDate of the view vewTransaction, is incorrect because you cannot build an index on a column in a view. You must build it on the underlying table, as suggested in **B**. **C**, you can bypass the view and query the data in the table directly by the TransactionDate field, is incorrect because querying the table directly will not prevent you from table scanning. A table scan is committed because of the lack of a useful index. Querying the table directly will have the same problem as querying the view. **D**, there is nothing that you can do, is incorrect because **B** is correct.

13. ☑   The correct answer is **C**, build a view that has the appropriate columns and grant only SELECT permissions to the view. Views allow you to restrict the data that a user can see and modify, and users can be granted permissions to views and columns in views just as they can be granted permissions to tables and columns in tables.

☒   **A**, build a view that has the appropriate columns with the WITH READ ONLY OPTION, is incorrect because there is not a WITH READ ONLY OPTION in SQL Server. That is an option in Oracle database systems for views. **B**, build a view that has the appropriate columns with the WITH CHECK OPTION, is incorrect because the WITH CHECK OPTION will not prevent the users from changing the data; it will just prevent them from modifying any data so that the row would fall out of the scope of the view. **D**, restrict permissions on the table so that it cannot be modified by the developers, then build a view that has the appropriate columns, is incorrect because restricting the table will not restrict the view. In systems where views are the primary data access methodology, the tables are usually completely restricted to the database administrator, but views are created so that the users can modify, add, and delete data as needed.

14. ☑ **B** is the correct answer because **B** is an invalid query due to the fact that it is trying to restrict its query by a column, State, that is not in the view. This restriction would not be needed because the query inside the view already restricts the view to rows where State = OH.

☒ **A** is incorrect because you can query the data directly to get information as long as you have permissions to select from a given table. **C** is incorrect because it will provide you with the needed information, the clients' names and account numbers, for all the rows where State =OH. In addition, **C** will also provide you with the additional information of the account balance for each row. **D** is incorrect because it will provide you with exactly the information, the clients' names and account numbers for all the rows where State =OH, that you required.

15. ☑ **A, B, C,** and **D** are all correct. In terms of performing SELECT queries, a view is logically equivalent to a table. Any query that you can perform on a table, you can perform on a view. It is important to note that the restrictions on the queries that make up a view are not in force with how you query the view. For example, **C** uses on ORDER BY clause on the view, which you could not do inside the view. **A** and **D** perform operations that summarize the view, **A** with the Min function and **D** with the GROUP BY clause, that would have been valid within the view. If they were in the view's source query, you would not have been able to perform data modification on the view as you can with the current view. **B** uses the view to perform a join, just as you would with a table. If you had not had a view available, your query would look like this:

```
SELECT S.*
FROM tblBooks B, tblAuthors A, tblSales S
WHERE S.BookID = B.BookID
AND B.AuthorID = A.AuthorID
AND A.FirstName = 'Russell'
AND A.LastName = 'Holt'
```

This query is much more complex and, as such, is more likely to have mistakes and slight variations that would make it less likely that the query optimizer might be able to reuse an existing query plan.

16. ☑ **B** is the correct answer. **B** updates the DoctorType for the row that is identified with the DoctorID of 1492. If the view had been constructed with this query, then **B** would have been wrong:

```
SELECT D.DoctorID, D.Name, DT.DoctorType, DT.Description
FROM tblDoctor D, tblDoctorType DT
WHERE D.DoctorType = DT.DoctorType
AND D.State = 'TX'
```

If this query had been the source, the UPDATE statement would have attempted to change the DoctorType field to 2, so that you would have had two DoctorTypes of 2 in the database (if that was permissible).
☒ **A** is incorrect because it will change the value of the description in tblDoctorType to Cardiologist for the DoctorType of this doctor. That means that all doctors that share this Doctor's DoctorType will now appear to be Cardiologists. **C** would have the same effect as **A** because it would also alter the tblDoctorType instead of tblDoctor. **D** is incorrect because **B** is correct.

17. ☑ **A** is the correct answer. You can have an aggregate function in an updatable view as long as it is in a subquery and is not in the SELECT list. **A** uses a subquery to determine products that have a higher price than twice the average. You could still perform UPDATEs, DELETEs, and INSERTs against this view.
☒ **B** is incorrect because an aggregate function is in the SELECT list, making the AVGPrice column a derived column; a derived column cannot be updated because it is calculated from data in the database and is not actually data in the database. **C** is incorrect because you cannot perform UPDATEs, INSERTs, and DELETEs against a view that is created with the UNION operator. **D**, None of the above, is incorrect because **A** is correct.

18. ☑ **A**, **B**, and **C** are all correct answers. **A** performs a delete on data that is not in the view, which you can do as long as the view has not been created with the WITH CHECK OPTION in force. When this command is executed against the view, deletes will be performed against the base table, but the contents of the view will appear undisturbed. **B** inserts data against the view; depending on the value of the identity field, it may or may not be visible within the view. Either way, it can be executed as long as the WITH CHECK OPTION was not in force. If the view was created with the WITH CHECK OPTION, the AccountID generated would have to be within the valid range for this statement to be executed without an error. **C** performs an UPDATE statement against vewTestAccounts, which would remove the row from the view. As long as the view was not created with the WITH CHECK OPTION in force, this would be a valid statement.

☒   **D**, None of the above, is incorrect because **A**, **B**, and **C** are all correct.

19. ☑ **B** is the correct answer. You can bcp data out from any view in a database to which you have permissions. Because you do not know how the view is constructed, you cannot determine whether you bulk copy data into the database.

☒   **A**, you can perform INSERT and UPDATE statements, is incorrect because you do not know anything about how the view is constructed, and therefore you cannot evaluate whether you can perform INSERTs and UPDATEs. **C**, you can delete the records where SalesID =117, is incorrect because you do not know how the view is constructed, and therefore you cannot determine whether you can perform DELETEs in general or this specific DELETE. **D**, SalesID is a unique identity field that is the primary key to vewAllSales, is incorrect because you do not know anything about the columns of the view except for their names. For instance, SalesID may be a varchar field that happens to have numeric data.

20. ☑ **A**, **B**, and **C** are all correct. Unlike stored procedures, views will evaluate whether the tables and columns that they depend on exist when they are created. If you were able to create vewExpensiveSales, then you know that there is a tblSales in your current database and that it has at least two columns: SalesID and Amount. Stored procedures used to behave in a similar manner, but in SQL Server 7, stored procedures only verify the syntax when they are compiled.

☒   **D**, none of the above, is incorrect because **A**, **B**, and **C** are all correct.

Implementing Stored Procedures

1. ☑ **A, B, C,** and **D.** Any of these statements would execute the stored procedure. If a stored procedure is the first thing in a batch, you can just use the name, as in **A.** If it is not the first statement in a batch, you cannot. You must use EXEC, EXECUTE, or sp_executesql. When any of these three statements is used, the stored procedure is executed as if it is in its own batch. EXEC and EXECUTE have been around quite a while in SQL Server, but sp_executesql was introduced with SQL Server 7. sp_executesql behaves like EXEC and EXECUTE, but it is a stored procedure created to aid the execution of SQL statements by offering parameter substitution.

2. ☑ **B, C,** and **D.** You can assign a default value to a parameter when it is declared in the stored procedure. @CategoryID was assigned a default of 19 when the stored procedure was declared. Anytime a value is not passed to a stored procedure for @CategoryID, 19 will be the value. Since there was no default value set up for @TypeID, it will fail if you attempt to pass the parameters by name and omit it. **B** omits the @CategoryID parameter so the default is assumed. **C** and **D** are inverse of each other, and that is OK because you are passing the parameters by name, so you can pass them in any order, as long as all the required parameters are given values.
☒ **A,** SL_GetProductByCategoryAndType @CategoryID=19, is incorrect because it does not assign a value to the @TypeID parameter.

3. ☑ **D.** Execute the stored procedure with the WITH RECOMPILE. Using the WITH RECOMPILE option when you execute a stored procedure will make sure that SQL Server will not use an existing execution plan or save the one it is using for the stored procedure that is executed. Instead of reusing an existing execution plan, the stored procedure will use a new execution plan that will be thrown away after execution. This helps when the parameters passed to the stored procedure are very different from the typical case because a more appropriate plan will be generated for this special case. This special case's execution plan will be thrown away after execution so other queries will not

be harmed by using this execution plan, which was designed for parameters very different from those of the typical case.

☒ **A,** execute it with sp_executesql, is incorrect because sp_executesql will not force a stored procedure to use a new execution plan each time it runs. Instead, it has a tendency to increase the chances of finding an existing execution plan to reuse. **B,** use the WITH RECOMPILE option when you create the stored procedure, is incorrect because using the WITH RECOMPILE option when you create the stored procedure will force a new execution plan every time, instead of just for this special instance. **C,** execute with EXEC, is incorrect because executing a stored procedure with or without EXEC or EXECUTE will not make a stored procedure create a new execution plan each time it is run.

4. ☑ **B** and **C** are the correct choices. ALTER PROCEDURE was added in SQL Server 7 and is the best way of altering an existing stored procedure. Using ALTER PROCEDURE will retain any existing permissions and retain the startup property, and it will not affect any dependent stored procedures or triggers. You could drop it and recreate it, as is done in **C,** but then you would have to grant the permissions once again.

☒ **A,** use DROP PROCEDURE and CREATE PROCEDURE to drop the existing stored procedure to create a new stored procedure with the same name that has the right sort order, is incorrect. The permissions would not have been explicitly granted, which is needed if you drop and re-create a stored procedure. **D,** use ALTER ORDER to alter the stored procedure order, is incorrect because there is no ALTER ORDER statement in SQL Server even though many new statements like ALTER PROCEDURE and ALTER TRIGGER have been added to SQL Server 7.

5. ☑ **D.** A stored procedure named sp_statistics already exists in the master database. Whenever a stored procedure starts with "sp_", SQL Server will first look for it in the master database so that system stored procedures may be called without using their fully qualified name. If you had called this stored procedure by its fully qualified name, *database*.sp_statistics, it would have executed the one you created. Because of this problem, Microsoft

recommends that you do not prefix the stored procedures you create with "sp_" and instead come up with a different naming convention.

☒ **A,** there is no data in tblWork yet, and **B,** there is no data in tblCategory yet, are wrong because the lack of data would not cause the results to have the wrong column headers. **C,** a stored procedure named sp_statistics already exists in your database, is wrong because you would have received an error when you created your stored procedure if one had already existed with that name in the database in which you are working.

6. ☑ **B** is the correct answer. If you want to support the applications that currently use the stored procedure, then you have to be able to call the procedure with only the @SalesDate parameter and still have it return the results where the CategoryID = 7. **B** does this by making @CategoryID the second parameter and making it default to 7 whenever it is omitted.

☒ **A** is incorrect because the @CategoryID parameter does not have the proper default. The existing reports that call this stored procedure will fail if @CategoryID is not nullable, or they will return incorrect results if it is. **C** is incorrect because @CategoryID has been added as the first parameter; all the existing reports that pass the parameters by position will fail. Reports that pass in parameters by name, however, will succeed. If an organization has standardized on passing parameters to stored procedures only by name, this would be acceptable. **D** is incorrect because it makes @CategoryID the first parameter and because it is not optional.

7. ☑ **C.** You need to specify OUTPUT after @Job_ID in the stored procedure call. Specifying a parameter as an output parameter in a stored procedure gives the parameter the ability to return a value, but only if whatever is executing the stored procedure is requesting it. To request a parameter to return a value in SQL Server, you must have the word OUTPUT listed after the parameter:

```
DECLARE @Job_ID int
EXEC JB_NewJob @Job_ID OUTPUT
SELECT @Job_ID
```

☒ **A,** there must be a null in the JobID column, and MAX interprets NULL as the greatest value possible, is incorrect because MAX ignores all null values when it calculates the maximum value. **B,** the name of the parameter being passed in, @Job_ID, is different from the parameter in the procedure, is incorrect because it is irrelevant whether a parameter had the same name as the parameter to which it is being passed. As long as the stored procedure parameter name and the variable name being passed to it conform with identifier name guidelines, they can be anything. **D,** none of the above, is incorrect because **C** is correct.

8. ☑ **A, B, C, D.** Making sure that the data types of the parameters being passed to a stored procedure are the same as the ones that are being used will improve your performance because a CONVERT will not have to be executed each time the stored procedure is called. Replacing singleton SELECT result sets with OUTPUT parameters particularly improves performance over a network using database access objects such as ADO because a result set is not created if you return only parameters. Making sure that the data types of the parameters used in the queries of the stored procedures are the same as the fields against which they are being compared can increase your performance in the same manner. Like **A,** this approach prevents a CONVERT operation from taking place on either the parameter field or, more importantly, on the database field. This is important to note because, in order to compare fields such as smalldatetime to datetime, a CONVERT operation would have to be implemented on one of the fields. Selecting appropriate recompile options for each stored procedure based on the parameters typically passed to them increases your performance by increasing the opportunity of stored procedures that use fairly consistent values, from execution to execution, of reusing an existing execution plan. It also ensures that stored procedures that are executed with atypical values each time have an appropriate execution plan generated for them.

9. ☑ **A,** 0, is correct. By omitting the @State parameter, @State becomes the default 'TX.' If @State is 'TX', it will perform the insert, and no return code

will be explicitly sent. Because no return code is explicitly sent, the default of 0 is returned.

⊠   **B**, 1, is incorrect because for **B** to have been correct, the state parameter would have had to been explicitly set to 'CA'. **C**, 2, is incorrect because for **C** to have been correct, the state parameter would have had to been explicitly set to 'NY'. **D**, 3, is incorrect because for **D** to have been correct, the state parameter would have had to been explicitly set to 'OH'.

10. ☑   **B.** The proposed solution produces the required result and only one of the optional results. If you restrict the database access to stored procedures, you can prevent accidents like executing a DELETE without a WHERE clause. You can write a stored procedure that would allow a developer to delete only by the key, thus ensuring that only one record is deleted at a time. In addition, if all access is done through stored procedures, the likelihood of reusing execution plans is greater; a database administrator writing the stored procedures should ensure that the queries are written in an optimal manner and configurations. The only problem with this sort of scheme is that relying on a single person to implement and modify all database access is a bottleneck that can potentially cripple development if a great deal of changes and additions are needed.

⊠   **A, C,** and **D** are incorrect because the required and one optional result are produced.

11. ☑   **A** and **B** are correct; you can raise an error with a specific msg_id, but, in order to do so, you must first add it to the sysmessages table with the sp_addmessage system stored procedure. Once it has been added, you can raise the error with the msg_id, and the correct error message will be raised with it. In addition, you can build an ad hoc message within a query and return that information, but if you do so the msg_id will be 50000.

⊠   **C**, use the sp_addmessage system stored procedure to add an error message with msg_id 12287 and pass back a return code of 122871 anytime this invalid action is encountered, is incorrect because setting a return code will not raise an error. You could have some logic in the calling procedure that could interpret the return code and raise an error in the same manner as **A** and **B. D,** you cannot raise a specific custom error message and instead must invoke one that Microsoft has set up in the syserrors table, is incorrect because you can raise a custom error message as outlined in **A** and **B.** In addition, the error messages are stored in the sysmessages table, not in the syserrors table.

12. ☑ **B** is correct; you can raise an error with a specific msg_id, but, in order to do so, you must first add it to the sysmessages table with the sp_addmessage system stored procedure. Once it has been added, you can raise the error with the msg_id, and the correct error message will be raised with it.
☒ **A,** with RAISERROR, you can return any msg_id and error message string you want, is incorrect because you can raise an error by msg_id or by msg_str, not both. In addition, to be able to return the correct error message, the message would need to be added to the sysmessages table. **C,** use the sp_addmessage system stored procedure to add an error message with msg_id 122871 to the sysmessages table, is incorrect because you have to raise an error by msg_id, not by the error message, if you want the appropriate msg_id to be raised with the error. **D,** you cannot define a specific msg_id, is incorrect because you can raise a specific error message as outlined in answer **B.**

13. ☑ **D** is correct. Both **A** and **B** will return 0 and all the authors from the Authors table. **A** does not explicitly set a RETURN CODE, so a RETURN CODE of 0 is implicitly returned. **B** explicitly sets the RETURN CODE to 0, after the SELECT statement has acquired all the information from the Authors table.
☒ **C** is incorrect because it will not return any information from the Authors table. As soon as the RETURN(0) is executed, the stored procedure will exit and return back to the calling procedure.

14. ☑ **A.** The proposed solution produces the required result and both of the optional results. An extended stored procedure allows you to extend SQL Server's abilities using programming languages such as C and C++. Extended stored procedures open up all the things that can be done in these other programming languages, such as adding a login or walking through a file structure, to SQL Server. Extended stored procedures are implemented as DLLs (Dynamic Link Libraries) and, as a consequence, are mapped to the SQL Server's memory space, which makes them pretty fast. By implementing the extended stored procedures in the existing queries, you are able to preserve the names of the parameters of the existing stored procedures. As long as you keep the stored procedure name, the input parameter's names and data types (and in some cases positions), and the result field's names and data types (and in some cases positions) the same, you will not have to modify the existing reports.

15. ☑ **C, 3**, is the correct answer. If you call this procedure, you can receive output from the output parameter, the return code, and the result set from the SELECT statement. Output parameters can return a variety of different data types to whatever invokes them, including nchar, int, and cursors. A return code is always an integer, and a value for the return code is always returned for a stored procedure. If the developer did not explicitly set a value, the stored procedure would implicitly return 0. A result set could be from a SELECT statement or from a SELECT statement in a stored procedure that your stored procedure called.
☒ **A, 1**, and **B, 2**, are wrong because they do not account for all the ways that this stored procedure can return information. **D, 4**, is wrong because this stored procedure does not use the fourth method to return information from a stored procedure: A global cursor that can be referenced outside the stored procedure can be returned as output. This cursor would have to be global in scope in order to be used in this manner.

16. ☑ **C, ANSI_NULLS ON and ANSI_PADDINGS OFF**, is the correct answer. When a stored procedure is created or altered, the values of ANSI_NULLS and QUOTED_IDENTIFIER are embedded, and they will be the values when the stored procedure is executed. All the other SET options, such as ANSI_PADDINGS, are not saved when the stored procedure is executed. Instead, the values of these SET parameters during the current connection are used.
☒ **A, ANSI_NULLS ON and ANSI_PADDINGS ON**, is incorrect because the ANSI_PADDINGS option will be set to OFF; that is its value

when the stored procedure is executed. **B,** ANSI_NULLS OFF and ANSI_PADDINGS ON, is incorrect because the ANSI_NULLS option will be set to ON; that is the value of the parameter when the stored procedure is created. **D,** ANSI_NULLS OFF and ANSI_PADDINGS OFF, is incorrect because the ANSI_PADDINGS option will be set to OFF; this its value when the stored procedure is executed. It is also incorrect because the ANSI_NULLS option will be set to ON, which is the value of the parameter when the stored procedure is created.

17. ☑ **B,** during execution ARITHABORT OFF, and after execution ARITHABORT ON, is the correct answer. The ARITHABORT option is not saved with the execution of a stored procedure, so SQL statements inherit the value of the option from the context of the connection. In addition, if a child stored procedure changes the option value, once that stored procedure is completed, the value will be restored to the original value. In this case, ARITHABORT is ON before the stored procedure is executed, and the stored procedure changes it to OFF with an explicit command. Once the stored procedure completes the value, ON is restored for all successive statements.
    ☒ **A,** during execution ARITHABORT ON, and after execution ARITHABORT ON, is incorrect because ARITHABORT is OFF during the execution of the statements within the stored procedure. After the execution is completed, it will be restored to the value of the context in which the stored procedure was run: ON. **C,** during execution ARITHABORT ON, and after execution ARITHABORT OFF, is incorrect because ARITHABORT is turned OFF explicitly in the stored procedure. It will remain OFF during the execution of the procedure. When the execution is completed, it will be restored to the value of the context in which the stored procedure was run: ON. **D,** during execution ARITHABORT OFF, and after execution ARITHABORT OFF, is incorrect because ARITHABORT is restored back to ON after the execution of the stored procedure. It will be OFF only during the execution of the stored procedure.

18. ☑ **B.** The proposed solution produces the required result and only one of the optional results. This solution will match up as many tblComplaints to tblAccounts as possible and is modular. You make more trips to the

database than needed. If you want to make as few trips as possible, you would create another stored procedure that would open a cursor and then call CP_MatchComplaints for each needed item. You would call this procedure from the desktop application, which would make one trip total, instead of a trip per item. Stored procedures have loops, Boolean logic, and extended stored procedures available to them, allowing them to process data on the server and conserve the costs of communication.

  ☒ A, C, and D are incorrect because answer **B** is correct.

19. ☑ C. The stored procedure returns 27 rows in these circumstances. You can clearly see at the bottom of the screen that 27 rows have been returned.

  ☒ A, you can't give it any parameters, is incorrect. Just because you did not have to pass any stored procedure parameters does not mean that it does not accept parameters. This procedure could have valid default values configured for its parameters, making them optional. But you do not have that information strictly from executing it. **B,** au_lname is a larger field in the database than au_fname, is incorrect because our view of this stored procedure is that of a black box. We can see how to execute it and its results, but we do not know how it got there. In this case, the underlying fields have been presented differently than they are in the database in order to satisfy a business need. **D,** the data that is returned lies in the PUBS database, is incorrect because a stored procedure can gather data from other data sources that are inside and outside of SQL Server. We do not know how this stored procedure works, so we cannot say where the data comes from, and that is a good thing. Today, some of the data may be coming from an Excel spreadsheet, but after a conversion project is finished, it may be coming from SQL Server. As long as the applications rely on the stored procedure that gathers the correct output in the correct format, applications do not need to be concerned with where the data actually is.

20. ☑ A and B are both correct: The procedure is encrypted, and you can check its syntax. This is how an encrypted stored procedure looks in SQL Enterprise Manager. Even though you cannot see its text, SQL Server can decrypt it; as such, if you click the Check Syntax button you can verify if the syntax is correct.

☒ **C,** the tables that it depends on exist, is incorrect because SQL Server uses deferred name resolution, so there is no guarantee that the tables and stored procedures that this stored procedure may depend on do exist. **D,** it was built using the WITH RECOMPILE option, is incorrect because the stored procedure is encrypted, so you cannot read the source. Without looking at the source, you cannot tell if it was compiled with the WITH COMPILE option.

Implementing Triggers

1. ☑ **C.** You would use the RAISERROR command just as you would in a stored procedure. Creating a trigger is very similar to creating a stored procedure. With a few exceptions, creating a trigger and creating a stored procedure are similar processes. Most T-SQL statements work the same way in a trigger as they do in a stored procedure.
   ☒ **A,** DISPLAYERR, **B,** WRITERR, and **D,** SHOWERROR, are incorrect because they are not valid T-SQL statements.

2. ☑ **C.** Triggers can be nested up to 16 levels deep, and the variable you would use to check the current level is @@NESTLEVEL. Each time a stored procedure calls another stored procedure, the nesting level is incremented. When the maximum of 16 is exceeded, the transaction is terminated.
   ☒ **A,** 4, @@NEST, **B,** 4, @@NEST, and **D,** 32, @@PROCLEVEL, are incorrect values and variable names.

3. ☑ **B, D.** Triggers support customizable error messages and complex error handling. These functionalities are not available when creating constraints. SQL Server provides two primary mechanisms for enforcing business rules and data integrity: constraints and triggers. Each has benefits that make them useful in special situations. The primary benefit of triggers is that they can contain complex processing logic that uses Transact-SQL code.

☒ **A**, constraint denial, and **C**, static error messages, are incorrect because constraint denial and static error messages are not generally considered advantages.

4. ☑ **D.** The correct statement to use is the DROP TRIGGER statement. Triggers can be dropped one at a time by using the DROP TRIGGER statement with each of the triggers defined. The DROP TRIGGER statement can also be used to drop all of the triggers on a table in one statement by following the DROP TRIGGER statement with a comma-separated list of triggers.
☒ **A**, DELETE TRIGGER, **B**, CLEAR TRIGGER, and **C**, REMOVE TRIGGER, are incorrect. These statements would result in syntax errors because they are not valid statements.

5. ☑ **D.** The system stored procedure that you would use to find out about the trigger is the sp_help procedure. Issue the sp_help command, and specify the name of the trigger you are interested in. The name of the trigger, the owner, and the date the trigger was created will be returned.
☒ **A**, sp_owner, is incorrect because no such system stored procedure exists. **B**, sp_helptext, is incorrect because sp_helptext prints the text of a rule, a default, or an unencrypted stored procedure, trigger, or view. **B** would be useful for determining what the trigger did, but it would not tell you the owner and creation date of the trigger. **C**, sp_depends, is incorrect because sp_depends displays information about database object dependencies (for example, the views and procedures that depend on a table or view, and the tables and views that are depended on by the view or procedure). **C** would not provide any information on owner or creation date.

6. ☑ **D.** You have encrypted the entry in the syscomments table that contains the text of the trigger. Anytime the WITH ENCRYPTION option is used on any create statement, the result is the text of the procedure or trigger is stored in an encrypted format in the syscomments table. You will still be able to use and modify the trigger; you just won't be able to read the text in the syscomments table.

☒   **A,** encrypted the options in the trigger, **B,** encrypted the trigger in the database where the trigger is defined, and **C,** encrypted the data for which the trigger was defined, are incorrect because they do not properly explain the use of the WITH ENCRYPTION option. Only data in the syscomments table is encrypted.

7. ☑   **C.** The proposed solution meets the required results, but it does not meet either of the optional results. The data has been separated by the views, which was the required result. Unfortunately, you cannot create a trigger on a view. Consequently, neither of the optional results could be met. If you were to create the triggers on the base tables, you could achieve your optional results.

☒   **A** and **B** are incorrect because the proposed solution does not satisfy either of the optional results. **D** is incorrect because the required result was satisfied.

8. ☑   **B.** Setting the NOCOUNT option on eliminates the sending of DONE_IN_PROC messages to the client for each statement in a stored procedure. When using the utilities provided with SQL Server to execute queries, the results prevent the message of the format "nn rows affected" from being displayed at the end of Transact-SQL statements such as SELECT, INSERT, UPDATE, and DELETE.

☒   **A,** SET NOCOUNT OFF, is incorrect because setting NOCOUNT to off will not suppress T-SQL result messages. That means that special processing instructions at the client must be in place to handle the feedback messages. **C,** SET NOEXEC ON, and **D,** SET NOEXEC OFF, are incorrect because the NOEXEC option is an option that causes SQL Server to compile, but not to execute a query.

9. ☑   **C.** If triggers that include ROLLBACK TRANSACTION statements are fired from within a user-defined transaction, the ROLLBACK TRANSACTION statement rolls back the entire transaction. In this example, if the INSERT statement fires a trigger that includes a ROLLBACK TRANSACTION, the UPDATE statement is also rolled back.

☒   **A,** the update is applied, the insert is applied, and any statements that were part of the trigger are rolled back, **B,** the update is applied, the insert is rolled back, and any statements that were part of the trigger are rolled back, and **D,** the update is rolled back, the insert is rolled back, and any statements that were part of the trigger are applied, are incorrect. The correct statements are not rolled back. Always remember that all of a transaction is applied or all of a transaction is rolled back.

10. ☑   **C.** The proposed solution meets the required result, but it does not meet either of the optional results. Foreign key constraints will ensure that tables are related properly and that records with exact key matches can be related. Unfortunately, foreign key constraints do not provide for cascading updates and deletes, or for complex logic that would allow you to define matching conditions other than exact matches. To meet the optional results, you would have had to choose triggers instead of foreign key constraints.
    ☒   **A** and **B** are incorrect because the optional results were not met. **D** is incorrect because the required result was satisfied.

Working with Distributed and External Data

1. ☑   **A, C.** Data can either be imported or exported. This should be evident from the way the DTS wizards are named. There is an Import Wizard and an Export Wizard. If you always think about DTS in terms of importing and exporting, DTS questions will be much easier to answer.
    ☒   **B,** create, and **D,** delete, are incorrect. Even though CREATE and DELETE are valid T-SQL statements, they do not adequately describe the paradigm used by DTS.

2. ☑   **A, B, D.** The –w flag performs the bulk copy operation using Unicode characters. This option should not be used, however, with SQL Server version 6.5 or earlier. The –N flag performs the bulk copy operation using the native (database) data types of the data for noncharacter data and Unicode characters for character data. This option offers a higher-performance alternative to the -w

option, and it is intended for transferring data from one SQL Server to another using a data file. Use this option when you are transferring data that contains ANSI extended characters and when you want to take advantage of the performance of native mode. -N cannot be used with SQL Server 6.5 or earlier. The –C option specifies the code page of the data in the data file. The code page is relevant only if the data contains char, varchar, or text columns with character values greater than 127 or less than 32. The –C option can be used with SQL Server 6.5 and earlier.

☒ **C, –6,** is incorrect because the –6 option performs the bulk copy operation using SQL Server 6.0 or 6.5 data types. Use this option when data files contain values using SQL Server 6.5 formats, such as data files generated by the bcp utility supplied with SQL Server 6.5 and earlier. For example, to bulk copy data formats supported by earlier versions of the bcp utility (but no longer supported by ODBC) into SQL Server, use the –6 parameter.

3. ☑ **C.** The quickest and easiest way for you to create your new table is to use the SELECT…INTO syntax and specify a condition in the WHERE clause that will limit the SELECT statement to June's data. The real time-saving benefit of the SELECT…INTO statement is that the new table will be created automatically for you using the same table format as the existing table.

☒ **A,** CREATE TABLE, and **B,** INSERT, are incorrect because neither of these options will result in a table with data in it. The CREATE TABLE syntax could be used to create the table, and the INSERT statement could be used to populate the table, but those statements could be fairly complex and would require that you know the exact format of the existing table. **D,** BULK INSERT, suffers from some of the same problems. The table must already exist before you try and use the BULK INSERT command.

4. ☑ **A.** You need to create a linked server either through SQL Enterprise Manager or by using the sp_addlinkedserver system stored procedure before attempting to execute distributed queries against that data source.

☒ **B, C,** and **D** are incorrect because they use system stored procedures that do not exist.

5. ☑ **B.** One way of executing a remote query is to use the OPENQUERY() statement. This statement takes two parameters. The first is the name of a linked server that the query should be executed against, and the second is a string that represents the query that should be executed. The main thing to remember about using the OPENQUERY() statement is that the query is actually executed on the linked server, not on the local SQL Server. So, if your data source is not another SQL Server, then you should limit your queries to ANSI SQL as some T-SQL options may not function properly on the remote server. OPENQUERY() often performs better than other methods because the processing occurs where the data is and only the result set is returned.

☒ **A, C,** and **D** are incorrect because the statements used to issue a remote query are not valid statements. They will result in errors. The one to remember is OPENQUERY().

6. ☑ **C.** When executing a distributed query against a linked server, you must include a fully qualified, four-part table name for each data source to query. This four-part name should be in the form linked_server_name.catalog.schema.object_name. The code in this question is an example of running a "SELECT * FROM employees" query against a SQL Server data file and an Oracle data file. The main difference between this code example and the one in the previous question is that all execution occurs on the local SQL Server. That provides more flexibility in how you define the query and what SQL syntax you use. The trade-off, though, is often speed. This type of query will almost certainly generate more round trips to the remote server than the OPENQUERY() method would.

☒ **A, B,** and **D** are incorrect because they do not specify a four-part name for the linked server.

7. ☑ **A.** The SELECT INTO statement retrieves one row of results. The SELECT INTO statement is also known as a singleton SELECT statement. The SELECT INTO statement retrieves one row of results and assigns the values of the items in the select list to the host variables specified in the INTO list. The data type and length of the host variable must be compatible with the value assigned to it.

☒ **B**, SELECT...INTO, is incorrect because this version of the syntax allows you to select a set of rows into a new table. On the test, read carefully when being asked about SELECT syntax. SELECT and UPDATE are probably the two most intricate commands in T-SQL. **C**, INSERT...SELECT, is incorrect because it is a standard form of the INSERT statement. **D**, SELECT, is incorrect because a basic SELECT statement is aimed at retrieving multiple rows from a table, not placing a value into a variable.

8. ☑ **C**. The OPENROWSET() method includes all connection information necessary to access remote data from an OLE DB data source. This method is an alternative to accessing tables in a linked server and is a one-time, ad hoc method of connecting and accessing remote data using OLE DB. The OPENROWSET() function can be referenced in the FROM clause of a query. The OPENROWSET function can also be referenced as the target table of an INSERT, UPDATE, or DELETE statement, subject to the capabilities of the OLE DB provider. Although the query may return multiple result sets, OPENROWSET returns only the first one.

   ☒ **A** and **B** are incorrect because both the four part naming convention and the OPENQUERY() statement require you to provide the name of the linked server where the data can be found. Part of the requirements in this question are that you do not have to maintain a linked server. Only the OPENROWSET() command allows you to access a data source without maintaining a linked server. **D** is incorrect because you do not have to have a linked server defined to use the OPENROWSET() command.

9. ☑ **A** and **B**. Either would satisfy your needs. DTS transformations allow you to pull just the values you need from the source to the destination. As part of an import or export, data can be reformatted or the values can be changed to meet your needs. **A**, create a transformation that imported just the age field and converted it to an integer value, would provide you just the contact's age. **B**, create a transformation that imported just the birthday and converted it to a date value, would provide you with a birthdate in date format from which you could easily calculate the age anytime you needed it.

☒   **C**, you will not be able get the value you need because an entire field must be imported as a unit during the import routine, is incorrect because it is not a true statement. **D**, you could use DTS to convert the existing field to the values you need, then bcp the data into the table, is incorrect because DTS is used to import, transform, and export data. The data would have to be transformed as part of an import and then exported back to the original source in order to change the values at the source.

10. ☑   **D**. A package can be defined using SQL Enterprise Manager or an application using the DTS API. DTS packages include connection objects defining each source and destination OLE DB data source, task objects defining the specific actions that need to be performed, and step objects defining the sequence in which tasks are to be performed. DTS packages can be stored in DTS COM-structured storage files, the SQL Server msdb database, and the Microsoft repository. DTS packages can be executed by using the dtsrun utility, the DTS Designer, the DTS Import and Export Wizards, SQL Server Agent (running a scheduled job), and a COM application that calls the Execute method of the DTS Package object.
☒   **A**, task, is incorrect because task is used to refer to a specific action within a package. For example, importing data from a text file would be a task. **B**, job, is incorrect because job is used to refer to a scheduled piece of work within SQL Server that may or may not involve DTS. **C**, procedure, is incorrect because procedure is a generic term used to refer to a set of things that need to be done in a certain order. Procedure does not have any specific meaning within the context of DTS.

MCDBA
MICROSOFT CERTIFIED DATABASE ADMINISTRATOR

Part III

Practice Exams

Test Yourself: Administration Practice Exam 1 (Exam 70-028)

Q & A

Τhis Test Yourself section will help you measure your readiness to take the Administering Microsoft SQL Server 7.0 exam (#70-028). See if you can complete this test under "exam conditions," before you check any of the answers. Read all the choices carefully, as there may be more than one correct answer.

Administration Practice Exam 1
Test Yourself Questions

1. You are determining the proper size for a transaction log. Which of the following factors will you take into account that will affect the size of the transaction log?

   A. Time required to dump transaction log
   B. Time between transaction log dumps
   C. Size of transaction log entries
   D. Number of transactions

2. You have decided to use the default sort order for a SQL Server database. Which of the following is true?

   A. There will be no uppercase preference.
   B. The sort order will be based on the character's ASCII equivalent.
   C. The sort order will be case sensitive.
   D. There will be an uppercase preference.

3. You have a Publisher, a Distributor, and remote Subscribers with snapshot replication. They are all SQL 7.0 databases. The snapshot data is corrupted and you need to clean it out. Where would you clear the data?

   A. Destination database on the Subscriber
   B. .bcp and .sch files in the snapshot folder on the Distributor
   C. .txt files in the snapshot folder on the Distributor
   D. Distribution database on the Distributor

4. You need to build a server that will support a mission-critical database. You need to maximize the availability of the database and minimize recovery time in the event of a catastrophic failure. The system has a RAID controller and a RAID device that has not been configured yet. You have enough drives to implement whichever form of RAID you choose. Which RAID level do you choose?

A. RAID 0

B. RAID 1

C. RAID 5

D. RAID 10

5. It is November, and you're concerned about the amount of data being entered into a SQL Server database that's running on an NT Server. This computer has a 4GB hard drive, with 1GB of free disk space. On average, users are inputting 150MB of data, but at Christmas this increases by 100MB. As you control your own budget, you can purchase a new hard disk when you need it. How many months will it be until you will run out of hard disk space?

A. One month

B. Four months

C. Six months

D. Seven months

6. You are preparing to upgrade a SQL Server 6.5 database to SQL Server 7.0. Before converting the database to this newer version, which of the following prerequisites will need to be met? (Choose all that apply.)

A. SQL Server 7.0 is running Service Pack 4 or greater.

B. SQL Server 6.5 is running Service Pack 4 or greater.

C. The TempDB is at least 10MB.

D. The TempDB is at least 25MB.

7. Corporate headquarters is located in Atlanta. There are two sites in Orlando and Dallas connected with T1 lines to Atlanta. A SALES database in

Atlanta needs to be available in both Orlando and Dallas. All sites need to be able to modify the data with a high degree of transactional consistency. Which type of replication would you implement?

A. Merge replication

B. Transactional replication with Immediate Updating Subscribers

C. Transactional replication

D. Snapshot replication

8. You have decided that you need to change the default file group for the Sales database from SalesFY99 to SalesFY00. Which of the following T-SQL statements will accomplish your goal?

A.
```
ALTER DATABASE Sales
MODIFY FILEGROUP SalesFY00
DEFAULT
```

B.
```
MODIFY DATABASE Sales
ALTER FILEGROUP SalesFY00
DEFAULT
```

C.
```
ALTER DATABASE Sales
MODIFY FILEGROUP (SalesFY99, SalesFY00)
```

D.
```
MODIFY DATABASE Sales
ALTER FILEGROUP (SalesFY99, SalesFY00)
```

9. You are designing a SQL Server application. In designing the application, you want to reduce network traffic. Which of the following will you use to obtain data from the SQL Server database and to use less bandwidth to acquire information?

A. Queries

B. Stored procedures

C. Paging

D. Broadcast storms

10. You have finished installing SQL Server; upon completion, a number of menu items are added to the Start menu. You want to determine a baseline

of how SQL Server runs before any changes are made to it later. Which of these menu entries will you use?

A. Service Manager
B. Profiler
C. Performance Monitor
D. MSDTC Administrative Console

11. You have branches in Dallas, Atlanta, and New York City. You have decided to implement merge replication among the three sites. What must you do to implement merge replication? (Choose all that apply.)

A. Modify any WRITETEXT and UPDATETEXT operations to include an UPDATE statement.
B. Remove all timestamp columns from tables.
C. Remove any uniqueidentifier columns.
D. Add primary keys to all tables.

12. Creating database files and databases is considerably different in SQL 7.0 compared to SQL 6.5. In SQL 7.0, Microsoft introduced a number of enhancements to improve the way that data was stored on physical disks. Which of the following represent SQL 7.0 enhancements?

A. Mixed extents
B. 8KB data pages
C. Native operating system files support
D. All of the above

13. A primary server running SQL Server fails, but a standby server is online. Users begin to complain that they no longer have access to the SQL Server database they were using. What is most likely the reason for this?

A. The standby server doesn't have a copy of the database.
B. The users need to log onto the standby server to access its database.
C. The standby server is offline.
D. The users need to log back onto the virtual server so that they can then be routed to the database on the standby server.

14. Current situation: Your team is in the process of migrating a SQL Server 6.5 database to version 7.0. The developers are willing to do some modifications to client applications to improve data access performance and enhance application capabilities.

Required result: The ability to use SQL Server 7.0's new data types.

Optional desired result: Reduce the number of layers the client applications must interface with to communicate with the database itself.

Proposed solution: Modify client applications to access the SQL Server databases using the native OLE DB Provider for SQL Server 7.0.

A. The proposed solution produces both the desired result and the optional desired result.

B. The proposed solution produces the desired result but not the optional desired result.

C. The proposed solution produces the optional desired result but not the desired result.

D. The proposed solution produces neither the desired result nor the optional desired result.

15. In order for the SQL Server Agent to notify an operator of an alert, MAPI must be present on the server. MAPI is the Messaging Application Programming Interface that Microsoft uses as a standard for its messaging clients and servers. What can you install on the server to provide the needed API for the SQL Agent?

A. Microsoft Mail

B. Windows Messaging

C. Microsoft Outlook

D. Internet Explorer

16. Immediate, guaranteed consistency is the most stringent form of replication. It requires that all data in all locations reflect the same information at the same time. What does SQL Server support that provides immediate, guaranteed consistency?

A. Snapshot replication

B. Two-phase commit protocol

C. Transactional replication

D. Merge replication

17. You are planning to back up a database, but you find you cannot. Upon checking the Backup Device Properties Window, you find that the tape drive name drop-down list is disabled. It appears grayed out, and nothing happens when you click on it. What does this indicate?

A. The network server that has the tape device attached to it is offline.

B. The local computer that has the tape device attached to it is offline.

C. The tape device physically attached to your computer isn't configured correctly.

D. A tape device isn't physically attached to the computer running SQL Server.

18. A job function once performed by one employee will now be split among three employees. You want to migrate the single-user database into a multiuser database. When you present your recommendation to migrate the data, you want the department head to understand the need for a multiuser database. Which of the following are two key roles of a multiuser database?

A. A multiuser database performs faster than a single-user database because it supports page locks.

B. A multiuser database must ensure that multiple concurrent transactions will produce the same data as if they had been executed in isolation.

C. A multiuser database is much easier to deploy and maintain because there is a central point for data control.

D. A multiuser database must be able to coordinate data modifications in a way that remains consistent with organization-wide policies.

19. You have SQL-DMO installed, and you are beginning to develop an administrative tool in order to streamline some common administrative tasks. What object do you need to create within your application to build your administrative tool?

A. SQLServer

B. SQLServerSession

C. SQLServerConnection

D. SQLServerEvent

20. You have a corporate HR database that has an employee table. The president of the company has asked that an online corporate directory be created to improve communications. All of the contact information for each employee is contained in the employee table. However, this database exists to support HR-related applications and you do not want to adversely affect those applications. The employee table also contains salary and performance-related data that you do not want to make available to the entire company. Which of the following solutions would you consider?

A. Implement replication of the employee table to another server using horizontal filtering to remove the sensitive information.

B. Implement replication of the employee table to another server by implementing record locking to protect the sensitive data.

C. Implement replication of the employee table to another server using vertical filtering to remove the sensitive data.

D. Implement replication of the employee table to another server and implement column locking to protect the sensitive data.

21. You are planning to back up a SQL Server 7.0 database. Which of the following programs can you use to back up this data? (Choose all that apply.)

A. SQL Server Enterprise Manager

B. Transact-SQL Enterprise Manager

C. Transact-SQL

D. The Create Backup Wizard

22. You are in the SQL Server Query Analyzer (QA) configuring database settings. How can you view a list of the server's current configuration from within the QA?

    A. Execute the extend procedure sp_viewconfig.

    B. Choose Settings from the Properties menu.

    C. Execute the stored procedure sp_configure.

    D. Execute the stored procedure sp_viewconfig.

23. You are trying to explain the concept of a job in the context of SQL Server. Your coworker is having a hard time understanding how one job can do multiple things. What is the smallest unit of a job?

    A. The process

    B. The step

    C. The decision point

    D. The response

24. Site autonomy refers to the effect of one site's operations on another. There is complete site autonomy if one site's ability to do its normal work is independent of its connectivity to another site. Which replication option provides the least site autonomy?

    A. Merge

    B. Transactional

    C. Snapshot

    D. Two-phase commit protocol

25. You have installed SQL Server on an NT Server that is acting as a Domain Controller. Which of the following privileges must the SQL Server service account have to properly function?

    A. Local Administrator

    B. Domain Administrator

    C. SQL Server Administrator

    D. All that is required is an average user account, such as a guest account.

26. In previous versions of SQL Server you have encountered limits in data accessibility due to locking contentions. Determining locking escalation thresholds was a tedious and time-consuming task. Why won't this be an issue with SQL Server 7.0?

A. SQL Server 7.0 now uses optimistic locking. It will not lock a record until it is actually updated.

B. SQL Server 7.0 now supports both row-level locks and page-level locks. SQL Server will dynamically determine which locking schematic to use.

C. The Enterprise Manager now has a wizard that helps to determine locking thresholds.

D. Locking contentions have been reduced because SQL Server 7.0 now supports only page-level locks.

27. You need to create a job that will run on multiple servers. You have a number of SQL Servers in your environment. SYSTEM_A is a publishing server, SYSTEM_B is a master server, SYSTEM_C is a target server, and SYSTEM_D is a subscribing server. Where should you create your job?

A. SYSTEM_A

B. SYSTEM_B

C. SYSTEM_C

D. SYSTEM_D

28. You have successfully configured replication. After a few days of operation you begin to see a problem. Transactions do not seem to be moving from the publisher to the distributor even though they are marked for replication. Which agent should you troubleshoot first?

A. Log Reader

B. Snapshot

C. Merge

D. Distribution

29. After setting up a SQL Server you need to set up a user so that she has access to all database objects and is able to perform any task related to databases on the server. To which of the following fixed server roles will this user be added?

A. Sysadmin

B. Serveradmin

C. Securityadmin

D. Diskadmin

30. A user has deleted a record that is referenced in other tables, and you need to replace this record. You are unable to restore from a backup, so you have to use the INSERT statement to add the record manually. How do you populate the Identity column?

A. Use the SET IDENTITY_INSERT statement to turn the option on, then INSERT the needed record value, and then turn the option off again.

B. Use SP_RESETIDENTITY to set the identity value to the needed seed, insert the record, and then turn the option off again.

C. In the INSERT statement, use the IDENTITY flag to force the field to be populated.

D. It is not possible to update this value.

31. You have a development environment that consists of one server currently running SQL Server. Your company has decided that the new HR application should be a Web-based application so that anyone in the company with a Web browser can access their employment information. Unfortunately, the application team did not budget any money to purchase a development Web server so you must now load IIS on the same server as your SQL Server. The SQL Server is not being used excessively, but you're sure that the application developers will be generating a large amount of activity with the IIS server. Your primary goal is that SQL Server and IIS must run on the same server. Secondarily, you wish to reserve as much memory for IIS as possible and allow IIS and SQL Server to dynamically negotiate the amount of memory each product uses in order to get the most efficient use of memory. You propose as a solution using the SQL Server fixed-memory model to assign a block of memory to SQL Server. It must be equal to the minimum amount that you calculated SQL Server would need to run effectively.

A. The proposed solution produces the required result and produces both of the optional results.

B. The proposed solution produces the required result and produces only one of the optional results.

C. The proposed solution produces the required result and produces none of the optional results.

D. The proposed solution doesn't produce the required result.

32. You have a heterogeneous database architecture. You have a number of database products in your environment and you use a number of different database clients to attach to the servers. You have an SQL Server with a database to which almost all of your clients would like to subscribe. Which of the following subscriber types will be able to subscribe to your SQL Server?

A. OLE-DB data source clients

B. ODBC data source clients

C. Other SQL Servers

D. All of the above

33. You have set up SQL Server 7.0 on a Windows NT machine. Once it is installed, which of the following SQL Server services will need to be run as NT services?

A. SQL Server

B. SQL Server Agent

C. SQL Server databases

D. Microsoft Distributed Transaction Controller

34. As a safety precaution, you are making copies of your tables in temporary tables as you prepare for data migration. You have table creation privileges, and so you attempt to execute the following sequence:

```
SELECT * into TEST1 from authors
SELECT * into @test2 from TEST1
```

```
SELECT * into @@test2 from @test2
SELECT * into TEST1 from @@test2
```

What happens?

A. You get an error after executing "SELECT * into TEST1 from authors".

B. You get an error after executing "SELECT * into @@test2 from @test2".

C. You get an error after executing "SELECT * into TEST1 from @@test2".

D. All the queries execute successfully.

35. John has recently configured SQL Mail by setting the MSSQL Service to run using his domain administrator account. He then configured a new operator and specified his e-mail address and pager e-mail address. He also verified that the new operator was enabled seven days a week, 24 hours a day. When he tried to send himself a test message, he received an error. What is the problem?

A. John's domain admin account is locked out and needs to be enabled.

B. John needs to have the MSSQL Service running with the local system account.

C. John did not configure a messaging profile on the server for his domain admin account.

D. John's domain admin account does not have an Exchange mailbox.

36. How would you implement vertical filtering for replication while using the replication wizards?

A. Within the Create Publication Wizard, use the GUI tool to indicate which columns should be replicated.

B. Within the Create Subscription Wizard, use the GUI tool to indicate which columns should be replicated.

C. Within the Create Publication Wizard, define a WHERE clause that will limit the number of columns returned for replication.

D. Within the Subscription Publication Wizard, define a WHERE clause that will limit the number of columns returned for replication.

37. You are responsible for designing your company's plan for upgrading from SQL Server 6.5 to SQL Server 7.0, and you are considering changing your BCP Batch files to Stored Procedures using BULK INSERT. Which of the following are not advantages of BULK INSERT over BCP?

A. You can use BULK INSERT in a stored procedure.
B. You can use BULK INSERT to export data to a text file.
C. You can select your own row and field delimiters with BULK INSERT.
D. You can specify the rows to import with BULK INSERT.

38. You need to increase the performance of an SQL Server. The server is a single processor system with ample memory and a relatively fast disk array. After a little exploring, you determine that none of the resources on the server represents a significant bottleneck. So, you decide to focus on CPU processing optimization. Which of the following options would you set to try to improve the performance of the system?

A. Boost the SQL Server priority on Windows NT.
B. Enable the use of Windows NT fibers.
C. Lower the minimum query plan threshold for considering a query for parallel processing.
D. All of the above

39. You have five regional offices that record sales data in their own local databases. These offices replicate the data to the central office nightly. They also replicate the data to each other for backup purposes. How many publishers are there in this scenario?

A. 0
B. 1
C. 5
D. 25

40. You are planning to install SQL Server on a computer running Windows 95. The computer has 16MB of RAM, an Intel Pentium 133 processor,

CD-ROM, and 190MB of free hard disk space. You want to perform a full install of SQL Server 7.0 on this computer, but you find that you cannot. Why?

A. There isn't enough hard disk space.

B. There isn't enough RAM.

C. SQL Server won't install or run on this operating system.

D. The processor isn't powerful enough.

41. Your transaction log is mirrored, and your primary database file is on a separate disk. You back up your database as follows:
3 a.m. full database backup
8 a.m. log backup
10 a.m. log backup
At 11:30 your primary data drive fails. When is the last point you can restore to?

A. 11:30

B. 10:00

C. 8:00

D. 3:00

42. You are implementing a very large database (VLDB) with a high-end RAID system. The RAID system will be capable of completing more than 32 simultaneous disk transfer requests. What option should you think about changing?

A. Min server memory

B. Max async I/O

C. Disk-queue length

D. SQL cache memory

43. A user belongs to a role that has the Create View permissions. He is unable to create views, and you check access. He also belongs to an NT group that has the Create View permission revoked. His NT user account has been denied access for Create View as well. How can you give him Create View permissions?

A. Grant the user account Create View permission.

B. Grant the group Create View permission.

C. Grant the user account and group Create View permission.

D. Recreate the user account.

44. You are preparing to upgrade SQL Server 6.5 to SQL Server 7.0 on a server that's being used in data replication. Which of the following installation methods will you use?

A. Computer-to-computer

B. Side-by-side

C. Standalone-to-server

D. Network-to-network

45. The Sales Order table is on its own filegroup, Sales_Table. On Mondays and Wednesdays, the Sales filegroup is backed up. Transaction logs are backed up every day at noon. On Friday, the table is corrupted. How do you recover the table?

A. Back up the active transaction log, restore Wednesday's filegroup backup, and restore all transaction log backups since Wednesday.

B. Restore Wednesday's filegroup backup.

C. Restore Monday's and Wednesday's filegroup backup.

D. You cannot restore the table.

46. You are using Performance Monitor to audit performance on your SQL Server. You can't find the SQL Server counters. What is the best way to install them?

A. Reinstall SQL Server.

B. Run setup and select Performance Monitor.

C. Use the ADD function in Performance Monitor.

D. Lodctr.exe c:\mssql7\binn\sqlcrt.ini

47. An employee has left the company. The NT Administrator deletes his NT user account. If the company is not using Integrated Security, what happens to his SQL server login?

A. SQL login exists, but has no permissions.

B. SQL login still exists as is.

C. SQL login is deleted.

D. None of the above

48. You are installing and configuring network libraries on a SQL Server that's running on a Windows 95 computer. Which of the following network libraries will you be able to install and configure on this machine?

A. Named pipes

B. TCP/IP

C. Multiprotocol

D. NWLink

49. You are designing a disaster recovery plan. You have two tape drives on the SQL server.
Required result: Recovery to point of failure in case of media failure.
Optional results: Minimize restore time and minimize backup time.
Proposed solution: Create a database with default filegroups and locate it on an 18GB drive.
Mirror the transaction log.
Complete a full backup every Sunday.
Perform a differential backup every Monday, Wednesday, and Friday.
Perform transaction log backups every day at 12 p.m.
Which of the following results will the proposed solution provide?

A. The proposed solution meets the required result and both optional results.

B. The proposed solution meets the required result and the first optional result.

C. The proposed solution meets the required result and the second optional result.

D. The proposed solution does not meet the required result.

50. You want to run DBCC SHOWCONTIG on a table to determine fragmentation information. You type DBCC SHOWCONTIG (TABLEA) in Query Analyzer, but you get an error stating incorrect parameter. What are you doing wrong?

A. You cannot use Query Analyzer to run this command.

B. You must specify the table ID, not the table name.

C. You do not have access to run DBCC SHOWCONTIG.

D. You cannot run DBCC SHOWCONTIG on a table.

51. You have installed named pipes on a SQL Server running on NT Server. You decide to change a client using a different named pipe name to use the default pipe name that the newly installed SQL Server uses. What is the default pipe name that you will enter?

A. \\.\pipe\sql\query

B. //./pipe/sql/query

C. There is no default pipe name.

D. A random alphanumeric entry that's different for each installation

52. A user needs permission to read data in the HR database. No other databases should be available to him and he should not be able to change any data. To what database role should you assign him?

A. Db_datareader

B. Db_ddladmin

C. Db_owner

D. Db_accessadmin

53. You are restoring a database in Enterprise Manager. All the backups are listed in the Restore Database dialog box. Where are the backup history files kept?

A. Master database

B. System tables in the production database

C. Model database

D. Msdb database

54. You receive an error 7303 while running a distributed query, the text of the message is "could not initialize the data source object of the OLE DB provider." How can you resolve this?

   A. Check OLE DB driver settings.

   B. Check user name and password.

   C. Verify the MS DTC service is running.

   D. Check linked-server parameters.

55. You have a Windows 95 workstation on a NetWare network with data encryption. What network library should be enabled on the SQL Server?

   A. Multiprotocol

   B. TCP/IP

   C. Named Pipes

   D. None of the above

Administration Practice Exam 1
Test Yourself Answers

1. ☑ **B, C, and D.** The time between transaction log dumps, the size of entries in the log, and the number of transactions will all affect the size of a transaction log. The longer the time between transaction log dumps, the greater the size. This happens because the log has more time to grow before it is dumped. The number of transactions accumulated over the time between dumps and the number of transactions appearing in the log will increase the size of the log.
   ☒ **A**, time required to dump transaction log, is wrong because the time won't affect the size of the log file. The size of the log will, however, affect how long it takes to dump it.

2. ☑ **A.** There will be no uppercase preference. The default sort order for a SQL Server database is case-insensitive dictionary order. Because the case isn't specified, and because there is no preference between uppercase and lowercase, the database may sort data as A, a or b, B.
   ☒ **B**, the sort order will be based on the character's ASCII equivalent, is wrong because the binary sort order is the sort order based on the ASCII equivalent. C, the sort order will be case sensitive, is also wrong, as the default sort order is case insensitive. Finally, D, there will be an uppercase preference, is wrong because there is no uppercase preference with the default sort order.

3. ☑ **B.** The .bcp and .sch files represent a table at a single point in time. These are stored in the Distribution database server, in a subfolder of the working directory, C:\MSSQL7\REPLDATA. The data is stored as native SQL bulk copy files.
   ☒ **A**, destination database on the Subscriber, is incorrect, as the snapshot data is not stored on the destination database. C, .txt files in the snapshot folder on the Distributor, is incorrect because .txt files are used for heterogeneous replication. D, distribution database on the Distributor, is incorrect because the data is not stored in the distribution database.

4. ☑ **C.** In the real world, you would probably choose **D**, RAID 10. Unfortunately, this is one of those cases where a Microsoft certification test diverges from reality. Because Windows NT only supports RAID 5 within the operating system, the certification test does not acknowledge the existence of other levels of RAID that rely strictly on hardware. Consequently, RAID 5 is the highest level of RAID available to you (on the test) even if they list RAID 10. By the way, since we were only interested in minimizing recovery time and nothing was mentioned about optimizing read or write operations you can eliminate the performance considerations for the various levels of RAID.

☒ **A** is incorrect because RAID 0 (striping) does not provide any fault tolerance. **B** is incorrect because RAID 1 (mirroring) will not provide us with the superior combination of fault tolerance and performance that we achieve with RAID 5 (striping with parity). **D** is incorrect (as far as the test is concerned) because RAID 10 is not an option that Windows NT supports through software.

5. ☑ **C.** As you have 1GB of free disk space, and 150MB is being used monthly—with an additional 100MB for one of these months—there will be zero hard disk space in six months. In six months of normal usage, 900MB would be used. As one of these months uses an additional 100MB, the disk space will be used up in this time.

☒ **A,** One month, is wrong because if you were calculating from the beginning of November, only 150MB is used (leaving 850MB free). If you calculated from the end of November (beginning of December) 250MB would be used, leaving 750MB free. **B,** Four months, is wrong because only 750MB would be used over the next four months. **D,** Seven months, is wrong because in seven months, users would have used up all the free disk space a month earlier.

6. ☑ **B, C.** In running the Upgrade Wizard, SQL Server 6.5 needs to be running Service Pack 4 or higher, and TempDB needs be at least 10MB. If these requirements aren't met, the upgrade will not succeed.

☒ **A,** SQL Server 7.0 is running Service Pack 4 or greater, is wrong because SQL Server 7.0 hasn't been run yet. You are preparing to install it, and you will use the Upgrade Wizard to upgrade the database. It is also wrong because there is no Service Pack 4 for SQL Server 7.0. **D**, the TempDB is at least 25MB, is wrong because the TempDB will need to be at least 10MB. This is used for temporary files created during the upgrade. During the upgrade, a new disk device is created using 25MB, and the TempDB is altered to a size of 25MB. Before the upgrade, though, TempDB needs to be only 10MB.

7. ☑ **B.** Because the sites are networked with a high-speed line, and because all need to be able to modify the data, transactional replication with Immediate Updating Subscribers is the best option.
☒ **A**, merge replication, is incorrect because merge replication does not provide high transactional consistency. **C**, transactional replication, and **D**, snapshot replication, are incorrect because transactional and snapshot replications do not allow all sites to modify the data.

8. ☑ **A.** To change the default filegroup from SalesFY99 to SalesFY00, you would first state which database you needed to alter. Then you would state that you were changing the default filegroup using the MODIFY FILEGROUP statement. The ALTER DATABASE statement is used to add or remove files and filegroups from the database. ALTER DATABASE can also modify the attributes of files and filegroups. The MODIFY FILEGROUP clause specifies which filegroup is to be modified.
☒ **B, C**, and **D** are all incorrect because they would result in syntax errors.

9. ☑ **B.** Stored procedures transmit only the stored procedure name and necessary parameters across the network. This lowers network traffic as less information is being passed.
☒ **A**, queries is wrong because queries pass more information than stored procedures. **C**, paging, is wrong because paging occurs when a computer uses disk space for virtual memory and writes and reads data to the disk rather than to RAM. **D**, broadcast storms, is wrong because broadcast storms bog down a network with continuous broadcastings of messages.

10. ☑ **C.** Performance Monitor gives you a SQL Server specific view of system performance. Using this tool once SQL Server is installed, you can determine how it is running when first installed, then use Performance Monitor to see how it has changed over time.

   ☒ **A**, Service Manager, is wrong because Service Manager is used to start and stop SQL services. **B**, Profiler, is wrong because Profiler is used to collect extended information about SQL Server. This includes such elements as login attempts, server connects and disconnects, and so forth. **D**, MSDTC Administrative Console, is wrong because MSDTC is used to configure, administer, and monitor the Distributed Transaction Coordinator.

11. ☑ **A, B.** Merge replication will support text and image columns only if they are modified by an UPDATE statement. Any WRITETEXT and UPDATETEXT operations should be modified to include an UPDATE statement. Merge replication does not support timestamp columns, and they must be removed from any table you intend to replicate.

   ☒ **C**, remove any uniqueidentifier columns, is incorrect. If there is a uniqueidentifier column in a table, SQL will use it as the row identifier for that table. If none exist, SQL will add a rowguid column to the table, and use that as the row identifier. **D**, add primary keys, is incorrect because SQL uses either uniqueidentifier or rowguid as the row identifier for that table.

12. ☑ **D.** Among the enhancements in SQL 7.0 are mixed extents, 8KB data pages, and native operating system file support. Mixed extents are data extents that are shared by up to eight objects. Previously, objects could not share data space, which led to a less than efficient allocation of space. When the table or index grows to the point that it has eight pages, it is switched to uniform extents. 8KB data pages also help provide more efficient use of space, and the capability to store larger record formats. Native operating system file support replaced database devices and made managing data storage much simpler.

   ☒ **A, B, C** are incorrect because there are multiple enhancements listed.

13. ☑ **B.** When a primary server goes offline and a standby server is online, the users of a SQL Server database on the primary server aren't automatically switched over to the database on the secondary server. The users must log onto the standby server to use its database because the standby server is a different physical server. Until they log onto the standby server and restart the tasks they were performing on the primary server, they won't be able to continue with their work.

☒ Standby servers are used when a primary server goes offline. They contain identical copies of databases that are available on the primary server. This allows users to access a duplicate database, and it is for this reason that **A,** the standby server doesn't have a copy of the database, is incorrect. **C,** the standby server is offline, is also wrong, as the question states that the standby server is, in fact, online. Finally, **D,** the users need to log back onto the virtual server so that they can then be routed to the database on the standby server, is incorrect because standby servers don't use virtual servers. A virtual server is used in clustering, and it automatically switches the user to a different physical server when a server in the cluster goes down.

14. ☑ **A.** The proposed solution produces both the desired result and the optional desired result. Client applications need to be modified to use the native OLE DB Provider for SQL Server 7.0. This driver supports the new data types and features that have been added to SQL Server 7.0. Using the native provider also reduces the number of layers your application must use in order to communicate with the SQL Server database.

☒ **B, C,** and **D** are wrong because using the native OLE DB provider for SQL Server will allow the use of the new data types, and it will reduce the number of layers between the client application and SQL Server.

15. ☑ **A, B, C.** Microsoft Mail, Windows Messaging, and Microsoft Outlook will all provide the needed API for the SQL Agent. Windows Messaging and Microsoft Outlook are probably the most popular options. Windows Messaging is included with all Microsoft operating systems and can be installed and configured through the control panel. Outlook is Microsoft's universal in-box client. Microsoft Mail will also provide the needed API, but it is an antiquated system that relies on store-and-forward post offices. Consequently, Microsoft Mail is not heavily used.

☒ **D,** Internet Explorer, is incorrect. MAPI is not an integral part of the Internet Explorer Web browser. This can be a little confusing because you often install Outlook Express as part of the IE install. Outlook Express does contain the MAPI API, but Outlook Express is a separate application from Internet Explorer.

16. ☑ **B.** The two-phase commit process is the only way to achieve immediate, guaranteed consistency. In the two-phase commit process, each site must simultaneously commit every change, or no site can commit the change. Such a solution is obviously not feasible for large numbers of sites because of realities, such as network outages.

☒ **A, C,** and **D** are incorrect because snapshot replication, merge replication, and transactional replication all represent various forms of latent, guaranteed consistency. Each site will eventually have the same data, but there may be a time lag.

17. ☑ **C, D.** If the tape drive name drop-down list on the Backup Device Properties Window is disabled, it means that there is no tape device attached to that computer or that the tape device hasn't been properly configured.

☒ **A,** the network server that has the tape device attached to it is offline, is wrong because you can use only tape devices that are physically attached to your computer. You can't use tape devices that are attached to other computers on the network. **B,** the local computer that has the tape device attached to it is offline, is also wrong. If the local computer were offline, you wouldn't be able to view the Backup Device Properties Window. The local computer is the computer being used that has a tape device attached to it. If this is offline, it means that it's shut off, meaning that nothing is accessible.

18. ☑ **B, D.** A multiuser database must ensure that multiple concurrent transactions will produce the same data as if they had been executed in isolation, and a multiuser database must be able to coordinate data modifications in a way that remains consistent with organization-wide policies.

☒ **A,** a multiuser database performs faster than a single-user database because it supports page locks. is incorrect because multiuser databases are not inherently faster than single-user databases. **C,** a multiuser database is much easier to deploy and maintain because there is a central point for data control, is also incorrect because multiuser databases are not easy to deploy. Correct deployment of multiuser databases takes time and careful planning.

19. ☑ **A.** A SQLServer object must be created within your application in order to access any other SQL-DMO objects, properties, or methods. All other objects with the exception of the SQLServer collection are subordinated to the SQLServer object. You can create a SQLServer object for every server that you need to communicate with.
    ☒ **B,** SQLServerSession, **C,** SQLServerConnection, and **D,** SQLServerEvent, are incorrect answers because they specify nonexisting SQL-DMO objects.

20. ☑ **C.** You want to replicate the information to another server in order to protect the performance of the HR server, and you want to implement vertical filtering to remove the columns from the table that contain sensitive information.
    ☒ **A, B,** and **D** are incorrect because neither horizontal filtering nor record locking will provide the necessary security. Horizontal filtering is the process in which rows are replicated. Record locking ensures that two users do not try and change the same record at the same time.

21. ☑ **A, D.** Two programs can be used to backup a database in SQL Server 7.0: SQL Server Enterprise Manager and the Create Backup Wizard. SQL Server Enterprise Manager has features that allow you to back up databases, while the Create Backup Wizard steps you through the process of backing up data.
    ☒ **B,** Transact-SQL Enterprise Manager, is incorrect because there is no program called Transact-SQL Enterprise Manager. It was made up for the purpose of this question. **C,** Transact-SQL, is also wrong because Transact-SQL isn't a program. By using Transact-SQL, you can use the "BACKUP DATABASE" statement in a Transact-SQL statement to back

up a database. As the question specifically asks for programs you can use to back up a database, this choice is also wrong.

22. ☑   **C.** Execute the stored procedure sp_configure. The stored procedure sp_configure will display the server's current configuration. sp_configure can also be used to change server settings using the syntax *sp_configure option, value;* where option is the setting you want to change and value represents the new value being assigned. Changes made with sp_configure will not take effect until the server has restarted unless sp_configure is used in conjunction with *Reconfigure* or *Reconfigure With Override.*
    ☒   **A,** execute the extend procedure sp_viewconfig, and **D,** execute the stored procedure sp_viewconfig, are incorrect because there are no such extended stored procedures. **B,** choose Settings from the Properties menu, is incorrect because there is no such menu in the Query Analyzer.

23. ☑   **B.** A job step is an action that the job takes on a database or a server. Every job must have at least one job step. Job steps can be operating system commands, Transact-SQL statements, Microsoft ActiveX scripts, or replication tasks.
    ☒   **A,** the process, **C,** the decision point, and **D,** the response, are incorrect because they refer to things that are not part of the job hierarchy. Jobs do have a mechanism for controlling logic flow, but this mechanism is not referred to as a decision point. It is referred to as flow control.

24. ☑   **D.** Two-phase commit protocol. The two-phase commit protocol requires that every participating site be able to commit the transaction before any site is allowed to commit the transaction. If one site is unavailable, the transaction cannot be committed and no changes to the data can be made. On the other hand, sites participating in merge replication work independently. Merge replication sites don't even need to have a permanent connection with each other. Merge replication has high site autonomy but does not guarantee data consistency. The two-phase commit protocol has immediate transactional consistency, but no site autonomy.
    ☒   **A, B,** and **C** are incorrect because they provide some site autonomy.

25. ☑ **B.** A SQL Server running on an NT Server that is a Domain Controller would require a service account with the privileges of a Domain Administrator.

☒ **A,** Local Administrator, is wrong. While a SQL Server on a normal NT Server would require only the privileges of a local administrator, one residing on a Domain Controller would need a Domain Administrator's privileges. Without this level of access, the service account wouldn't be able to function properly. **C,** SQL Server Administrator, and **D,** an average user account such as a guest account, are also wrong. A SQL Server on a computer acting as a Domain Controller would require a Domain Administrator account. The lower access and privileges of a guest account or that afforded to a SQL Server Administrator wouldn't be enough for the service account to perform its tasks.

26. ☑ **B.** SQL Server 7.0 supports row-level locking, which is the default locking mode. SQL Server 7.0 will dynamically scale from row-level to page or table locking when it determines that row-level locks are impeding the overall performance of the server.

☒ **A,** SQL Server 7.0 now uses optimistic locking, is incorrect because optimistic locking does not exist for SQL Server; that is a locking schematic supported by Microsoft Access. **C,** the Enterprise Manager now has a wizard that helps to determine locking thresholds, is incorrect because no such wizard exists. **D,** locking contentions have been reduced because SQL Server 7.0 now supports only page-level locks, is incorrect because SQL Server 7.0 supports more than just page-level locks. It is page-level locks that are more prone to producing locking contention.

27. ☑ **B.** The system that you should create your job on is SYSTEM_B because it is a master server. You can define a Windows NT server running SQLServerAgent to be the master server. You can enlist other servers running SQLServerAgent to be target servers. Each target server reports to only one master server, which is recommended to be running Windows NT Server. The target server must be running on Windows NT.

☒ **A,** SYSTEM_A, and **D,** SYSTEM_D, are incorrect because they refer to replication architecture. **C,** SYSTEM_C, is incorrect because you don't create jobs on the target servers; you create them on the master server.

28. ☑ **A.** The correct answer is the Log Reader Agent. The Log Reader Agent reads the transaction log on the publisher and moves transactions to the distribution database. Remember that there is one Log Reader Agent for each database that is using transactional replication so it is possible for one database replication to work properly while another database replication on the same publisher fails.

☒ **B** and **C** are incorrect because the Snapshot Agent prepares snapshot files containing schema and data of published tables, stores the files in the snapshot folder on the distributor, and records synchronization jobs in the publication database. The Merge Agent applies the initial snapshot jobs held in the publication database tables to the subscriber. **D** is incorrect because the Distribution Agent moves transactions and snapshot jobs held in the distribution database tables to subscribers.

29. ☑ **A.** When a user is added to the fixed server role of Sysadmin, she has full access to all database objects and can perform any task.

☒ Each of the other choices is wrong because it doesn't have the level of power attributed to the Sysadmin role. **B**, Serveradmin, is wrong because users added to the role of Serveradmin have the ability to shut down a server and set all server-related options. **C**, Securityadmin, is wrong because Securityadmin has the power to set login and CREATE DATABASE permissions. **D**, Diskadmin, is also wrong because the Diskadmin role has full access to disk files. Although each of the roles listed as choices has considerable power, except for Sysadmin, none has full access to database objects or can perform any task.

30. ☑ **A.** Use the SET IDENTITY_INSERT statement to turn the option on, then INSERT the needed record value, and then turn the option off again. Normally, the INSERT statement does not update identity columns. If you use the SET IDENTITY_INSERT statement, however, you can UPDATE content in these columns. If you do this, you want to make sure you turn the option off as soon are you are done, so you do not have a negative effect on other queries.

☒ There is no "sp_resetidentity" stored procedure, so **B**, use sp_resetidentity to set the identity value to the needed seed, insert the record, and then turn the option off again, is incorrect. There is no

IDENTITY flag available for the INSERT statement, so **C**, in the INSERT statement, use the IDENTITY flag to force the field to be populated, is also wrong. It is possible to update the value using IDENTITY_INSERT, so **D**, it is not possible to update this value, is incorrect.

31. ☑ **B.** By using the fixed memory model, you are restricting SQL Server to a fixed amount of memory. All of the rest of the memory is available to the Windows NT operating system and the IIS. Both IIS and SQL Server will run on the one server, so the required result has been achieved. Since you assigned to SQL Server the minimum amount of memory that it would need and left all the rest of the memory available to the OS and IIS, the first secondary goal was met. Unfortunately, the fixed-memory model is the opposite of the dynamic memory model, which is what meeting the second goal requires. Therefore, you did not satisfy the second optional requirement.
☒ **A, C,** and **D** are incorrect because option B is the only correct answer.

32. ☑ **D.** Almost any client can subscribe to a SQL Server publication if the client uses one of the common data sources such as OLE-DB or ODBC and the client has an application that will allow it to participate in replication.
☒ **A, B,** and **C** are incorrect because there are multiple correct answers. Be wary of test questions that sound like they came straight out of the Microsoft marketing machine. When questions concern features and benefits, they are often answered *All of the above.*

33. ☑ **A, B, D.** SQL Server, SQL Server Agent, and Microsoft Distributed Transaction Controller (MS DTC) are SQL Server services that need to be run under Windows NT as Windows NT Services. They run as NT services by running under a Windows NT account.
☒ **C,** SQL Server databases, is wrong because SQL Server databases aren't run as services.

34. ☑ **C.** You get an error after executing "SELECT * into TEST1 from @@test2". You cannot create tables that have the same name as a table that already exists, whether these tables are permanent, global temporary, or local temporary. Because you created the TEST1 table in the first line, the fourth line generates an error.

☒ **A,** you get an error after executing "SELECT * into TEST1 from authors," would be true only if you did not have table creation privileges. The table names "mytable", "@mytable", and "@@mytable" are all considered different names, so SQL Server does not generate the error implied by **B,** you get an error after executing "SELECT * into @@test2 from @test2". The fourth line fails, so **D,** all the queries execute successfully, is incorrect.

35. ☑ **C.** In all likelihood, John has forgotten to configure a messaging profile for his domain admin account. Opening the control panel and using the Mail control panel application to create the profile can accomplish this. John will have to be logged on using his domain admin account in order to create this profile.

☒ **A** is incorrect. It represents the common problem of using a user account to run the MSSQL Service. If the user account is locked out or disabled, then SQL Server will fail to start. If this were truly the problem, John would not even be able to open the server, let alone send a test message. **B** is incorrect because the MSSQL Service needs to be running as a domain account, not as the local system account. **D** is incorrect because SQL Mail is MAPI compliant. Many companies that use SQL Server also use Exchange Server, but Exchange Server is not a requirement.

36. ☑ **A.** The correct procedure would be to use the Create Publication Wizard to select which columns should be replicated. Vertical and horizontal filtering are implemented in different ways within the replication wizard. WHERE clauses are used for horizontal and selecting columns using the GUI is used for vertical.

☒ **B** and **D** are incorrect because filtering is not defined by the subscriber. Filtering is a function of the publisher, so it must be configured using the Publication Wizard. **C** is incorrect because WHERE clauses limit which rows are returned (horizontal) rather than which columns (vertical) are replicated.

37. ☑ **B.** You cannot use BULK INSERT to export data to a text file. Although BULK INSERT supports most of the functionality of BCP, one major restriction is that it cannot be used to export text files.

☒ **A,** you can use BULK INSERT in a stored procedure, is available for BULK INSERT but not for BCP. **C,** you can select your own row and field delimiters with BULK INSERT, (row and field) and **D,** you can specify the rows to import with BULK INSERT, are both supported by BCP and BULK INSERT.

38. ☑ **A, B.** Boosting the priority of the SQL Server processes within Windows NT will allow the SQL Server to use the processor more often. As long as SQL Server and Windows NT are not competing for the same processing cycles, this should increase the performance of SQL Server. Enabling Windows NT fibers should reduce the number of context switches between user mode and kernel mode. Context switches are basically overhead and should be minimized to improve performance. **C** is incorrect because this is a single processor system. Regardless of what the threshold is, without two processors there is no parallel processing. **D** is incorrect.

39. ☑ **B.** Microsoft SQL Server replication only allows one publisher for a set of data.

☒ **A, C,** and **D** are incorrect because they would violate a basic design requirement of any replication strategy. There can and must be only one publisher for a set of data. All systems could be publishers of different data sets. However, if all systems were also subscribers to all systems that were publishers that could result in lot of network traffic.

40. ☑ **B.** There isn't enough RAM. SQL Server 7.0 requires a minimum of 32MB of RAM. If there isn't enough RAM, SQL Server won't install or run properly.

☒ **A,** there isn't enough hard disk space, is wrong because a full install of SQL Server 7.0 requires a minimum of 190MB of free hard disk space. **C,** SQL Server won't install or run on this operating system, is wrong because SQL Server 7.0 can be installed on computers running Windows 9x operating systems. **D**, the processor isn't powerful enough, is wrong because you can install SQL Server 7.0 on a computer with an Intel Pentium 133 processor.

41. ☑ **B.** You can restore to your last log dump at 10:00. You cannot restore to point of failure (**A**, 11:30) because you lost your primary data file. It is only possible to back up the currently active transaction log if both the primary data file and the transaction log files are accessible. The primary file contains system tables and objects, and it points to the rest of the files in the database, and the active log cannot be backed up without it.
☒ **C**, 8:00, and **D**, 3:00, are both incorrect. You can restore to 8 a.m. or 3 a.m.; however, you can recover to a later point in time. **A**, 11:30, is incorrect because you cannot restore to point of failure without the primary data file.

42. ☑ **B.** Max async I/O defaults to 32, which is adequate for most disk subsystems. However, for a higher-end RAID system capable of high disk I/O transfer rates, this value may be insufficient. Be aware that setting this too high will degrade performance. You can set this option using SP_CONFIGURE MAX ASYNC IO *value*.
☒ **A** is incorrect because min server memory does not handle disk I/O, but establishes a minimum amount of memory available to SQL Server. **C**, disk-queue length, is incorrect because this is a Performance Monitor counter that is monitored to determine if the disk subsystem is a bottleneck. **D**, SQL cache memory, is a Performance Monitor counter that monitors the total amount of dynamic memory the server uses for dynamic SQL cache.

43. ☑ **A.** Since the user was explicitly denied permission to create a view, granting permission would only need to be applied to the individual user account.
☒ **B** is incorrect because the user account has been denied the CREATE VIEW permission and granting permission to the group would not override the DENY. **C** is incorrect because the revoke on the group is not the reason the user cannot create a view. **D** is incorrect because the user account needs to be granted the Create View permission; it doesn't need to be re-created.

44. ☑ **B.** Side-by-side upgrades are the only method supported for servers that are involved in data replication. If a server is being used in data replication, you will need to do a side-by-side upgrade.

☒ **A,** computer-to-computer, is wrong because if a server is being used in data replication, you can't perform a computer-to-computer installation. **C,** standalone-to-server, and **D,** network-to-network, are wrong because there are no installation methods called "standalone-to-server" and "network-to-network." These terms were made up for the purpose of this question.

45. ☑ **A.** You always back up the active transaction log first, then restore the most recent full backup. Then restore all transaction log backups since Wednesday.

☒ **B,** restore Wednesday's filegroup backup, and **C,** restore Monday's and Wednesday's filegroup backup, are incorrect because you must restore all log backups when restoring a filegroup to bring the database to a consistent state. **D,** you cannot restore the table, is incorrect because you can restore the table, as shown in **A.**

46. ☑ **D.** To reload Performance Monitor counters for SQL, use lodctr.exe.

☒ **A** is incorrect because reinstalling SQL is not the best way to install the counters. **B** is incorrect because there is no option to install Performance Monitor in SQL setup. **C** is incorrect because there is no ADD function in Performance Monitor.

47. ☑ **B.** The SQL login is not deleted when an NT account is deleted. You must manually remove the login.

☒ **A** is incorrect because the login still retains any roles and permissions assigned to it until it is removed or the permissions are revoked. **C** is incorrect because the login is not deleted. **D** is incorrect because the SQL login still exists.

48. ☑ **A.** Named pipes. If you are installing on a Windows 95 computer, named pipes won't be supported because the server portion of the Named Pipes API isn't supported in Windows 95.

☒ **B,** TCP/IP, is wrong because Windows 95 computers support the use of the TCP/IP protocol. **C,** Multiprotocol, is wrong because you can install the Multiprotocol network library on Windows 95 computers. Upon selecting this, a compatible client/server communication library is automatically chosen, based on the computer to which it is installing. Therefore, named pipes won't be used. **D**, NWLink, is a network protocol that is primarily used for communicating on Novell NetWare networks. Windows 95 supports this protocol, so the network library for it can be installed and configured.

49. ☑ **D.** The proposed solution does not meet the required result. When installing SQL with default filegroups and file locations, only a primary data file will be created, and recovery to point of failure is not possible. The primary data file is needed to back up the active transaction log. To be able to recover to point of failure, a primary data file should be created on the mirrored drive, and a secondary data file should be created and marked default.

50. ☑ **B.** You must use the table ID, not table name in DBCC SHOWCONTIG. To determine the object ID of a table, use the OBJECT_ID function. For example,

```
USE MASTER
select OBJECT_ID ('DB1.dbo.TABLEA')
```

will return the object ID (117575457) which you can then use to run DBCC SHOWCONTIG (DBCC SHOWCONTIG (117575457))
☒ **A** is incorrect because Query Analyzer is where you would run this command. **C**, You do not have access to run DBCC SHOWCONTIG, is incorrect because you are receiving an incorrect parameter statement, meaning the parameter, or table name, is not correct for that DBCC statement. **D** is incorrect because DBCC SHOWCONTIG can be run on a table. It can also be run on an index.

51. ☑ **A.** The default pipe name used by SQL Server 7.0 is \\.\pipe\sql\query. If the pipe name on the server and client don't match, they won't be able to communicate.
☒ **B**, //./pipe/sql/query, is wrong because it uses forward slashes instead of backslashes in the name. **C**, there is no default pipe name, is wrong because the default pipe name that SQL uses is \\.\pipe\sql\query. **D**, a random alphanumeric entry that's different for each installation, is wrong because

the default pipe name isn't a random entry. It is the same on each installation of SQL Server.

52. ☑ **A.** Db_datareader can view all tables in the database, but cannot change the data in any way.

☒ **B** is incorrect because db_ddladmin has permissions to add, change, and drop objects in the database. **C** is incorrect because db_owner has full access to the database and can modify data. **D** is incorrect because Db_accessadmin is used to add or remove users in a database.

53. ☑ **D.** The backup history tables are stored in the msdb database, as well as the restore history tables.

☒ **A,** master database, is incorrect because Master stores login accounts and the location of the primary data files for all user databases. **B,** system tables in the production database, is incorrect because systems tables in user databases store database system information such as index information and filegroup information. **C,** model database, is incorrect because the model database is the template database for all new databases created.

54. ☑ **A, B, C, D.** If the data source cannot be initialized, check to see if the username and password for the remote server are correct, and verify the parameters in the linked-server configuration. Check to be sure the MS DTC service is running, and finally, reinstall the OLE DB driver.

55. ☑ **A.** Using multiprotocol allows you to enable encryption of the data sent between the client and server. It also allows automatic selection of the network protocol used to connect to SQL Server. The client can have IPX, TCP/IP, and Named Pipes installed, and the Multiprotocol network library will choose the first available.

☒ **B** and **C** are incorrect because TCP/IP and Named Pipes network libraries do not support data encryption.

MICROSOFT CERTIFIED DATABASE ADMINISTRATOR

Test Yourself: Administration Practice Exam 2 (Exam 70-028)

Q & A

T his Test Yourself section will help you measure your readiness to take the Administering Microsoft SQL Server 7.0 exam (#70-28). See if you can complete this test under "exam conditions," before you check any of the answers. Read all the choices carefully, as there may be more than one correct answer.

Administration Practice Exam 2 Test Yourself Questions

1. You are doing capacity planning for SQL Server 7.0 databases that will be used on your network. In doing so, you need the number of bytes of data that is available on each data page to perform some calculations. Which of the following figures will you use for showing the number of bytes available on a page for storing data?

   A. 2016
   B. 2048
   C. 8060
   D. 8192

2. You are trying to restore a tape acquired from the Japanese office of your organization. Your office uses a U.S. character set, while the other office uses one for that native tongue. Each time you attempt restoring the data, an error occurs. Why?

   A. One of the servers is using a binary sort order.
   B. Both servers are using the same nonbinary sort order.
   C. Two different code pages are used on each server.
   D. Both servers are using the same code pages.

3. You have a database that needs to be reattached to a server. The database is a rather large database that consists of four data files and four log files. Which command would you use to reattach the database to the server?

A. SP_DB_ATTACH

B. SP_ATTACH_SINGLE_FILE_DB

C. SP_ATTACH_DB

D. SP_ATTACH_MULTI_FILE_DB

4. A file called MYDATA.NDF is a member of the DataMine file group. When you attempt to make the file a member of the MineData group, you find you cannot. Why?

A. A file can be a member of only one file group.

B. DataMine hasn't been correctly configured to allow the file to be a member of multiple groups.

C. MineData hasn't been correctly configured to allow files in other groups to be a part of it.

D. The file groups need to be on different physical hard disks before this will work.

5. You have used a script to automate the creation of accounts that will be used for SQL Servers and SQL services. These accounts have yet to be assigned to groups, so SQL Servers and services don't have the ability to access resources it requires. How will you assign all of the accounts you've created to groups at once?

A. User Manager for Domains

B. The NET USER command

C. The NET GROUP command

D. SQL Server

6. Current situation: The corporate headquarters is in New York, and there are two remote sites, in California and Texas, connected by 56KB. California and Texas need to access pricing data located in a SQL database in New York, which is updated daily.
Required result: California and Texas must be able to access the pricing data.
Optional results: Minimize access response time. Be able to update the data.

Proposed solution: Set up a SQL server in California and Texas, and implement transactional replication. What does the proposed solution do?

A. The proposed solution meets the required result and both optional results.

B. The proposed solution meets the required result and the first optional result.

C. The proposed solution meets the required result and the second optional result.

D. The proposed solution does not meet the required result.

7. You are reconfiguring a database when you discover that there is a data file in use by the database that you would like to eliminate. The data file contains tables that are still in use in the database. You'd like to get rid of the data file. What should you do?

A. DBCC SHRINKFILE, using the TRUNCATEONLY option

B. DBCC SHRINKFILE, using the NOTRUNCATE option

C. DBCC SHRINKFILE, using the FILEEMPTY option

D. DBCC SHRINKFILE, using the EMPTYFILE option

8. You are planning the physical hardware to be used for a computer running SQL Server 7.0. What is the minimum amount of RAM required for SQL Server 7.0 to be installed?

A. 16MB

B. 32MB

C. 48MB

D. 64MB

9. You are upgrading a SQL Server 6.5 database to SQL Server 7.0. The server participates in replication, and you must configure how this upgrade will be

performed. Which of the following will you need to configure in setting how the upgrade will be done? (Choose all that apply.)

A. Computer-to-computer upgrade must be done, as the server participates in replication.

B. Side-by-side upgrade must be done, as the server participates in replication.

C. Both computers must be in the same domain.

D. Both computers must have the same name.

10. Your sales force uses laptops. They want to be able to enter orders and access product and pricing information locally. What type of replication should you use?

A. Snapshot

B. Transactional

C. Transactional with Immediate Updating Subscribers

D. Merge

11. Your company has recently been purchased by another company. Your new managers feel that the database names should reflect the name of the new company. They have asked you to rename the database. What stored procedure can you use to accomplish this task?

A. sp_dbrename

B. sp_db_rename

C. sp_rename_db

D. sp_renamedb

12. You are planning to restore the last backup that was made of a database. You are concerned about data errors that may have existed when the

database was last backed up. There are several backups on hand. What will happen when you restore the most current backup of the database?

A. The database will be restored to the same condition it was in after it had been backed up.

B. The database will be restored to the same condition it was in when it was backed up.

C. The database will be restored to the same condition it was in when it was initially created.

D. The database will be restored to a condition previous to that when the errors occurred.

13. You are preparing to install SQL Server client utilities on computers in your department. Which of the following will you need to include when installing these utilities?

A. ODBC drivers

B. Network library support for all libraries

C. Administrative console

D. Query Analyzer

14. You need to replicate a SQL 7 database to a SQL 6.5 server. What must you do to ensure successful replication? (Choose all that apply.)

A. Ensure that no table names are longer than 30 characters.

B. Ensure that there are no unique identifier columns.

C. Run REPL70.EXE on the SQL 7 server.

D. Execute **sp_addpublisher70** at the SQL 6.5 server.

15. You have a database that is set to grow automatically. This database increases in size over a financial quarter. At the end of the quarter, financial statements are produced, the data is archived to tape, and the database tables are truncated to prepare for the next quarter. You've noticed that the amount of space allocated to the database does not change. There are other

databases on the server that would benefit from additional space, if it were available. Choose the best option for reducing the size of the database after the tables have been truncated?

A. Manually use the DBCC SHRINKDATABSE or DBCC SHRINKFILE statements.
B. Automatically shrink periodically using the sp_dboption system-stored procedure.
C. Automatically shrink periodically by configuring settings on the database property page of SQL Server Enterprise Manager.
D. All of the above

16. Current situation: A SQL Server database is being used for 911 calls. This database is used for storing mission-critical data. Any downtime is critical, and data needs to always be available.
Required result: Develop a solution that will have data available 24 hours a day, 7 days a week. If a server goes down, the data will still be available.

Optional desired result: If the server goes down, users won't be aware that a problem exists; no data is lost when the server goes down.
Proposed solution: Implement a cluster server.

A. The proposed solution produces the required result and produces both of the optional results.
B. The proposed solution produces the required result and produces only one of the optional results.
C. The proposed solution produces the required result and produces neither of the optional results.
D. The proposed solution doesn't produce the required result.

17. You have successfully migrated a Microsoft Access database to SQL Server 7.0. A team of developers and database administrators has been assigned to manage the database and build new front-end applications for the data. The team needs only the SQL Server utilities that manage SQL Server databases and the ability to perform ad hoc queries. Everyone is concerned about the resources needed to install SQL Server on their laptops. What can you do to

provide the functionality needed, yet install the minimum amount of software needed?

A. Install only the SQL Server Client software on each laptop. The Client software contains the utilities needed to manage the SQL databases as well as create ad hoc queries.

B. Install the Enterprise version of SQL Server on the developers' desktops. The Enterprise edition contains only the utilities needed for enterprise-level development.

C. Install the Desktop edition of SQL Server on each laptop. The Desktop edition contains only the tools needed to connect remotely to SQL Server.

D. Install the Desktop edition of SQL Server on each laptop. After installation, configure SQL Server to consume the fewest resources by restricting database sizes, the number of concurrent connections, and memory used for each connection.

18. You are creating a job to import a large amount of data for analysis. This is a one-time occurrence, but you want to schedule the job to run after midnight so that it does not affect performance of the system. Which option should you use when scheduling the job?

A. When the job succeeds

B. Automatically delete job

C. When the job fails

D. Whenever the job completes

19. You have a client and a server that are both running SQL Server 7.0. You are writing an application that resides primarily on the client. You would like to build into your application a form of replication. Data consistency is of the utmost importance. Reducing the load on your server by running as few components on the server as possible is also a consideration. Which of the following solutions is not implemented on the server side of an application, and so is the best choice for your application?

A. Open Data Services

B. Snapshot replication

C. Two-phase commit protocol

D. Transactional replication

20. You are preparing to back up the master database of a SQL Server. What type of backup must you perform?

A. Differential

B. Full

C. Cluster

D. Transaction log

21. Current Situation: For all front-end applications that are built to use information from the customer's database, certain sets of data will always be acquired. The steps for acquiring much of this data require complex queries. Desired result: You want the data acquired in a consistent manner, and you want it to be simple enough that even the least senior member of the development team will be able to correctly retrieve the data.
Optional desired result: You want the data retrieval to be as efficient as possible.
Proposed solution: Create stored procedures that produce the data sets that are consistently needed and are complicated to acquire. What will be the result of the proposed solution?

A. The proposed solution produces the desired result but not the optional desired result.

B. The proposed solution produces the optional desired result but not the desired result.

C. The proposed solution will satisfy both the desired and optional desired results.

D. The proposed solution produces neither the desired result nor the optional desired result.

22. The Make Master Server Wizard assists you in creating your multiserver environment. Which of the following tasks will the wizard perform for you?

    A. Check the security settings for the SQL Server Agent
    B. Check that all servers are running SQL Server version 7.0
    C. Create a master server operator
    D. Start the SQL Server Agent service

23. There are a number of tables created to support merge replication. One of these tables contains one row for each row modified in the current database since it was published. The other table contains information on deleted rows and allows deletions to be propagated to other subscribers. These tables are:

    A. merge_tombstone
    B. merge_contents
    C. msmerge_contents
    D. msmerge_tombstone

24. You are running SQL Server on a Windows 98 computer. You are determining which login authentication mode you will use with SQL Server on this computer.

    A. Windows NT authentication mode
    B. Mixed authentication
    C. Windows User authentication
    D. Windows 98 authentication

25. You need to pause both MSSQLServer and SQLServerAgent services on your server. How can you accomplish this task?

    A. Use the Enterprise Manager to pause both services.
    B. Use the Services applet located in the Windows Control Panel. Locate each service and use the pause button to temporarily pause services.
    C. Use the Query Analyzer to pause MSSQLServer, which will automatically pause SQLServerAgent.
    D. Use the SQL Server Service Manager applet to pause both services.

26. SQL Server has the ability to generate and log a great number of system-defined events and user-defined events. These events are logged in the Windows NT Application Log. By default, which of the following alerts are logged?

A. Severity 19 or higher sysmessages errors

B. Any RAISERROR statement invoked by using the WITH LOG syntax

C. Any application logged by using xp_logevent

D. All of the above

27. You have SQL Servers and other heterogeneous databases that need to be integrated for replication. Which of the following technologies will help you accomplish this task?

A. ODS

B. ODBC

C. SQL-DMO

D. DB-Library

28. After assessing security models, you have decided to use the integrated security model. Which of the following requirements must be met to implement this security model?

A. Named pipes must be installed.

B. Windows 9x client computers must be used.

C. Multiprotocols must be installed.

D. RAS must be used.

29. A user needs to be able to add and remove users from a database. To what role should they be assigned?

A. Db_securityadmin

B. Db_accessadmin

C. Securityadmin

D. Processadmin

30. Your office has been hit hard by viruses, and so your SEs have shut down your WAN for a few days. You still need to process sales information, so your offices are burning CDs and overnighting them to each other. You have received a CD of data from a branch office that is still on SQL Server 6.5, but you are having trouble loading the BCP file on your SQL Server 7.0. Which of the following options could solve the problem?

A. Ask the other office to export the file using the "-c" flag.

B. Import your file using the "–L" flag.

C. Ask the other office to export the file using the "–7" flag.

D. Import your file using the "-6" flag.

31. You need to register a new remote SQL server from within a T-SQL script. You have a number of options and you remember from your SQL Server training that Microsoft prefers you to use one particular method. Which method does Microsoft suggest that you use?

A. The SQL Server registration wizard

B. The SP_ADDLINKEDSERVER command

C. The SP_REGISTERSERVER command

D. The SP_ADDSERVER command

32. You are about to use one of the subscription wizards to set up a subscription. Using a wizard has many advantages, as it automates many of the requisite tasks done in order to set up a subscription. Which of the following things is not true when selecting your destination database using a subscription wizard?

A. SQL Server will create the schema if necessary.

B. The destination database must already exist.

C. The destination database can have a different name than the source.

D. The destination database can have the same name as the source database.

33. A user has become a member of a fixed database role on a database called dat_cust. When this user attempts using a database that is completely new, what will happen?

    A. The user will be able to access the database because this role works at the server level.

    B. The user will be able to access the database because this role applies to all databases on a single server.

    C. The user won't be able to access the database because this role works at the database level.

    D. The user won't be able to access the database because only user-defined and fixed server roles work at the server level.

34. You have created a stored procedure to perform monthly data maintenance. You are using the INSERT statement with a nested SELECT statement. After execution of the Insert statement, the value for @@ROWCOUNT is zero. What can you infer from this?

    A. There are no records in the destination table.

    B. The query added no records to the table.

    C. The query was part of a transaction and was not committed.

    D. The query generated an error.

35. Which of the following statements are true about the SQL Mail client?

    A. SQL Mail is a proprietary client that can only access a Microsoft exchange server or Microsoft mail post office.

    B. The SQL Mail client will not function properly if the MSSQL Server service account is not a local system account.

    C. As long as a mail service is compatible with the MAPI standard, it will work with the SQL Mail client.

    D. The SQL Mail client can be used to alert administrators to the completion of jobs or potential problems with the server.

36. You would like to implement a two-phase commit relationship between a publisher and a subscriber, but you can't find the two-phase commit option anywhere in the Create Publication Wizard. What should you do?

  A. Nothing. Two-phase commit is the default behavior for publications created by the Create Publication Wizard.

  B. Nothing. You cannot implement a two-phase commit relationship through the wizard.

  C. Configure the wizard to support Internet subscribers.

  D. Configure the wizard to support updateable subscriptions.

37. You have decided to control the type of access that users can have to a database through components of an n-tier application. When performing the actions to control access through roles, you find the roles to be disabled. What will you do?

  A. Standard roles are disabled by default and must be activated by the sp_setaddrole system procedure.

  B. Standard roles are disabled by default and must be activated by the sp_addlinkedsrvlogin system procedure.

  C. Application roles are disabled by default and must be activated by the sp_setaddrole system procedure.

  D. Application roles are disabled by default and must be activated by the sp_addlinkedsrvlogin system procedure.

38. You need to add several hundred thousand records of data to a table, but you do not want these operations to be logged. Which of the following strategies could you use?

  A. BCP

  B. Bulk Insert

  C. Select Into

  D. Insert

39. Assume a typical SQL Server install and default ANSI database and connection options. If the following code segment is executed in Query Analyzer, what will the results be?

```
SELECT databaseproperty('model','isansinulldefault') as ANSINullsDefault,
databaseproperty('model','isansinullsenabled') as ANSINullsEnabled
```

A.
```
ANSINullsDefault ANSINullsEnabled
---------------- ----------------
0                0
(1 row(s) affected)
```

B.
```
ANSINullsDefault ANSINullsEnabled
---------------- ----------------
0                1
(1 row(s) affected)
```

C.
```
ANSINullsDefault ANSINullsEnabled
---------------- ----------------
1                0
 (1 row(s) affected)
```

D.
```
ANSINullsDefault ANSINullsEnabled
---------------- ----------------
1                1
(1 row(s) affected)
```

40. Current situation: You have an environment that consists of Windows NT Servers running SQL Server, Windows NT Workstation clients, and Windows 95/98 clients. All SQL Servers are SQL 7.0 and all workstations are running Office 2000. You would like to build a replication architecture that will allow any system to publish to any other system.
Required result: All systems must be able to publish and subscribe to each other.
Optional result 1: All clients should be configured the same way in order to reduce support costs.
Optional result 2: All clients must have almost immediate updates in order to ensure that they have the most current data.

Proposed solution: Implement transactional replication between the SQL Servers and the clients and configure enough distributors to ensure that response time is within acceptable limits.

Which of the preceding results will the proposed solution produce?

A. The proposed solution produces the required result and produces both of the optional results.

B. The proposed solution produces the required result and produces only one of the optional results.

C. The proposed solution produces the required result and produces none of the optional results.

D. The proposed solution doesn't produce the required result.

41. A user attempts to access a database without a valid account. The SQL Server database has only SA and DBO accounts. What will occur?

A. The user will be refused any access.

B. The user will default to a guest account.

C. The user will default to the SA account.

D. The user will default to the DBO account.

42. You have to combine content in an Oracle table with content in SQL Server tables. You have to reference the Oracle table only occasionally, and speed is not critical, but the data must be real-time. Of the following, what is the best option?

A. Schedule DTS to copy the needed content.

B. Create a stored procedure on the Oracle server, and schedule it to export text files to a common directory. Then schedule batch files to import the file using BCP.

C. Create remote pass-through stored procedures that Oracle can execute, and create SQL Server queries that reference these stored procedures.

D. Create a linked server connecting to the Oracle Server, and create distributed queries that reference the Oracle tables directly through these links.

43. Which of the following objects must be changed or configured in order to completely configure the full-text search service?

A. Server

B. Database

C. Full-text catalog

D. Table

E. Column

F. All of the above

44. Which server will determine whether or not an anonymous subscription will be accepted?

A. Internet Information Server

B. Subscriber

C. Distributor

D. Publisher

45. You don't want NT administrators accessing your SQL servers. How can you deny access?

A. Delete the NT Administrators group on the local machine.

B. Reinstall SQL.

C. Rename the NT Administrators Group.

D. Remove the NT Administrators group from the sysadmin role.

46. You have an NT Server 3.51 computer on your network running SQL Server 6.5. What will you need to do before upgrading to SQL Server 7.0?

A. Uninstall the previous version of SQL Server.

B. Upgrade the NT Server computer's operating system.

C. Upgrade NT Server using the Upgrade Wizard in SQL Server.

D. Install Service Pack 3 on the NT Server.

47. A disk failure has occurred on your SQL server, and the MASTER database has been corrupted. You have no backup of MASTER. What is the best way to recover?

A. Reinstall SQL server and sp_attach_db to recover your databases.

B. Reinstall SQL server, recreate all databases, and reload data.

C. Shut down SQL services, run the REBUILDM.EXE utility, and use sp_attach_db.

D. Start SQL in single-user mode, and run the REBUILDM.EXE utility.

48. You are implementing a SQL Server database. You are concerned with performance on one table in particular, which has one million rows. You know most of the queries accessing this table are based on ranges of data in Field A, and will return a large amount of data. You also know that Field A does not change often. How can you optimize this table?

A. Add multiple nonclustered indexes.

B. Use DBCC CHECKTABLE.

C. Add a clustered index on the field that will be queried most.

D. Use DBCC UPDATEUSAGE.

49. You are planning to migrate data from delimited text files into a SQL Server 7.0 database. The person who will actually do the migration is unfamiliar with SQL Server 7.0 tools, but he knows the tools included in SQL Server 6.5. Which of the following would you tell him to use to import the data?

A. Bulk Copy Program

B. Data Transformation Services

C. Data Migrator

D. NT Explorer

50. You have a SQL 6.5 database. You want to move the database to a new server and upgrade it to SQL 7.0 at the same time. Required result: Move the 6.5 database to the new server. Optional results: Upgrade the database to SQL 7.0. Minimize downtime.
Proposed solution: Back up the 6.5 database and restore it to the 7.0 server.

A. The proposed solution meets the required result and all optional results.
B. The proposed solution meets the required result and the first optional result.
C. The proposed solution meets the required result and the second optional result.
D. The proposed solution does not meet the required result.

51. Your users are creating ad-hoc queries. The queries are taking too long and impacting system performance. How can you prevent this?

A. Query Governor Cost Limit.
B. Create an alert in Performance Monitor to kill long-running queries.
C. Use SP_MONITOR to monitor queries, and use KILL to kill the query process.
D. Use SP_WHO to monitor queries, and use KILL to kill the query process.

52. By default, SQL Server creates a number of server roles. Which of these roles would you use if you wanted a user to have full rights to the system?

A. Database creator
B. Security administrator
C. System administrator
D. Server administrator

53. The Publisher's database is backed up every Monday, Wednesday, and Friday. You are using Merge replication. The Publisher fails on Thursday. What is the best way to recover?

A. Restore the Wednesday backup, recreate all publications and subscription.

B. Restore the Wednesday backup and synchronize all Subscribers.

C. Restore the Wednesday backup, and restore all Subscribers' most recent backups.

D. Restore the Wednesday backup.

54. You want to monitor ad-hoc queries that are created by a particular user. What can you use to monitor this?

A. Query Analyzer

B. Enterprise Manager

C. Profiler

D. Performance Monitor

55. You need to set up SQL Server security access for two applications. The applications are named Accounting and HR. Two types of users exist in the Accounting application, those who can modify data and those who can only query on existing data. There is only one type of user in the HR application, those who can both modify and query on existing data. What should you do to set up security access to the table?

A. Create one application role for both applications.

B. Create one application role for HR and two application roles for Accounting.

C. Create an application role for each application.

D. None of the above

Administration Practice Exam 2
Test Yourself Answers

1. ☑ **C.** The number of bytes available on a page for storing data is 8060. Each page is 8KB less the 32 bytes of overhead. While 8KB is actually 8192 bytes, when you subtract the overhead, you actually have 8060 bytes available for data use.

   ☒ **A,** 2016, and **B,** 2048, are wrong because SQL Server 7.0 uses 8KB pages. This is different from older versions, which used 2KB pages. This meant that each page was 2048 bytes, but—minus the 32 bytes of overhead—only had 2016 bytes available for storing data. **D,** 8192, is wrong because this is the number of bytes in a page with the overhead. Due to the overhead, you need to subtract 32 bytes from the 8192 to get the number of bytes available for storing data.

2. ☑ **C.** Two different code pages are used on each server. You can restore data on a SQL Server only when both servers are using identical character sets. If the character sets (i.e., code pages) don't match, then an error will result.

   ☒ **A,** one of the servers is using a binary sort order, is wrong because if both machines were using a binary sort order, then it wouldn't matter that differing character sets were being used. The exception to using different code pages occurs when a binary sort order is being used. **B,** both servers are using the same nonbinary sort order, is wrong because if both servers are using the same sort order, then an error won't occur. Data can't be restored if SQL Servers are using different sort orders. **D,** both servers are using the same code pages, is wrong because if both servers were using the same code pages (i.e., character sets) a problem wouldn't exist.

3. ☑ **C.** The system-stored procedure sp_attach_db allows for attaching databases consisting of multiple files. Up to 16 files can be attached with the SP_ATTACH_DB command.

   ☒ **B,** SP_ATTACH_SINGLE_FILE_DB, is incorrect even though it is a valid system-stored procedure. Here is a common example of using this command:

EXEC SP_ATTACH_DB @DBNAME = N'MYDB',
@FILENAME1 = N'C:\MSSQL7\DATA\MYDB.MDF',
@FILENAME2 = N'C:\MSSQL7\DATA\MYDB_LOG.LDF'
SP_ATTACH_SINGLE_FILE_DB is used to attach databases that have only
one data file.
A, SP_DB_ATTACH, and **D**, SP_ATTACH_MULTI_FILE_DB, are
incorrect because no such system-stored procedures exist.

4. ☑ **A.** One of the rules of dealing with files and file groups is that a file can
be a member of only one file group at a time. As such, the MYDATA.NDF
file can be a member of either DataMine or MineData. It can't be a
member of both groups at once.
☒ **B**, DataMine hasn't been correctly configured to allow the file to be a
member of multiple groups, and **C**, MineData hasn't been correctly
configured to allow files in other groups to be a part of it, are both wrong.
There are no configurations for allowing a file to be a member of more than
one file group. A file can be a member of only one group. **D**, the file groups
need to be on different physical hard disks before this will work, is wrong
because it doesn't matter where the files or file groups are physically located.
Regardless of where they are, you can have a file as a member of just a single
file group.

5. ☑ **A.** User Manager for Domains. By using the multiple select feature in
User Manager for Domains, you can select all of the accounts and set them
at once.
☒ **B**, the NET USER command, is wrong because it is used to create
accounts. It doesn't, however, enable you to add these accounts to groups in
Windows NT. **C**, the NET GROUP command, is wrong as well. Although
the NET GROUP command is used to add users to Windows NT groups,
it allows you to add only one user at a time. **D**, SQL Server, is wrong
because NT accounts aren't added to groups through SQL Server.

6. ☑ **B.** The proposed solution meets the required result and the first
optional result. Transactional replication would allow California and Texas
to have a read-only copy of the pricing data locally, reducing response time.

☒   A and C are incorrect because transactional replication does not allow California and Texas to update the data without immediate-updating subscribers option. D is incorrect because transactional replication does give California and Texas the ability to access the pricing data.

7. ☑   **D.** When you use the EMPTYFILE option, SQL Server migrates all data from the specified file to other files in the same file group. SQL Server no longer allows data to be placed on the file. This option allows the file to be dropped using the ALTER DATABASE statement.
☒   **A** is incorrect because the TRUNCATEONLY option causes any unused space in the files to be released to the operating system and shrinks the file to the last allocated extent, reducing the file size without moving any data. No attempt is made to relocate rows to unallocated pages. **B** is incorrect because the NOTRUNCATE option causes the freed file space to be retained in the files. **C** specifies a nonexistent option.

8. ☑   **B.** SQL Server 7.0 requires a minimum of 32MB of RAM to be installed and to run properly. To improve performance, 64MB or higher is recommended.
☒   **A,** 16MB, is wrong because you can't install and run SQL Server 7.0 on a computer with less than 32MB of RAM. **C,** 48MB, is also wrong, as this number exceeds the minimum requirement, as asked for in the question. **D,** 64MB, is wrong because although 64MB is recommended, it isn't the minimum amount.

9. ☑   **B, D.** If a server participates in replication, you must perform a side-by-side upgrade. In doing so, the source and destination names of the servers must match. This means that the server exporting the data and the one importing data must have identical names. If these elements aren't set and configured, then the upgrade will fail.
☒   **A,** computer-to-computer upgrade must be done, as the server participates in replication, is wrong because when a server is participating in replication, a side-by-side upgrade needs to be performed. **C,** both computers must be in the same domain, is wrong because both computers

don't need to be in the same domain when a side-by-side upgrade is done. This is the case only when a computer-to-computer upgrade is performed.

10. ☑ **D.** You should use merge replication. The sales force is using laptops, and they are not always connected to the network, so they need a degree of autonomy. They also need to modify the data without dialing in to the network. Merge replication will allow them to enter orders on their laptops and merge the data back into the database when they dial in.
☒ **A,** snapshot, is incorrect as snapshot replication would allow read-only data on the laptops. **B,** transactional, is incorrect because transactional replication would require all changes to be made at the Publisher, allowing only read-only data on the laptops. **C,** transactional with Immediate Updating Subscribers, is incorrect because the laptops are not always connected to the network to allow immediate updates to the publisher.

11. ☑ **D.** The command that you would use is:
```
EXEC sp_renamedb 'CompanyX_Sales', 'CompanyY_Sales'
```
Only members of the fixed server role sysadmin can execute the SP_RENAMEDB command and the database must be placed in single-user mode before it can be renamed.
☒ **A, B,** and **C** are not correct because they are not valid system stored procedures.

12. ☑ **B.** When you restore a database from a backup, the database is returned to the same condition it was in when it was backed up. This means that all data that existed in the database at the time it was backed up will be restored to the database. It also means that any errors that existed in the data will be restored. When the database is restored, it will revert to the same state as when it was initially backed up.
☒ **A,** the database will be restored to the same condition it was in after it had been backed up, is wrong because databases are restored to the condition they were in when the backup was made. Any changes made after the database was backed up won't appear when the database is restored.

C, the database will be restored to the same condition it was in when it was initially created, is also wrong; the database will not be restored to the state it was in when it was first created. It will restore the data that appeared in the database when it was backed up. D, the database will be restored to a condition previous to that when the errors occurred, is also wrong; any errors that appeared in the data when it was backed up will be restored. If you are concerned about restoring the database to a state previous to these errors, you would need to use an older backup. Of course, in doing so, you would lose any changes that occurred after the date that the backup was made.

13. ☑ A, B. When installing client utilities, you will need to install network library support for all libraries and a version of the SQL Server ODBC drivers. If these aren't present, users won't be able to properly use SQL Server 7.0.

☒ C, administrative console, is wrong because the administrative console is optional. You don't need to include it when installing client utilities on computers that will access SQL Server. D, Query Analyzer, is wrong because this isn't a component of client connectivity. Query Analyzer is a Management Tool that can be installed through SQL Server's setup program.

14. ☑ A, B, D. When replicating to a SQL 6.5 server, table names cannot be longer than 30 characters, and you cannot replicate unique identifier columns. Sp_addpublisher70 registers the SQL Server 7.0 Publisher at the SQL Server 6.5 Subscriber

☒ C, run Repl70.exe on the SQL 7 server, is incorrect because Repl70.exe needs to be executed at the SQL 6.5 subscriber. It is located in the MSSQL7\Install directory.

15. ☑ A. Given that the database only grows over time, periodically shrinking the database will not recover any free space. It will only monopolize system resources to try and shrink a database that can't be shrunk. Consequently, shrinking manually after the tables have been truncated is the best approach.

☒ B and C are not good choices in this situation because there is not an excessive amount of free space allocated to the database at any time. This is common in databases that grow slowly and constantly over time. **D** is incorrect because you would be using significant system resources to shrink a database that does not have an excessive amount of free space.

16. ☑ **A.** Implementing a cluster server will allow users to access mission-critical data, even if a server goes down. When a server goes down, the users are automatically switched over to another server in the cluster, so that they aren't even aware that a problem existed. Because they are accessing the same database through another server in the cluster, no data is lost.
☒ **B, C,** and **D** are wrong because the proposed solution produces the required result and both optional desired results.

17. ☑ **A.** Install only the SQL Server Client software on each laptop. The Client software contains the utilities needed to manage the SQL databases as well as create ad-hoc queries. Using this solution the developers will have the tools they need to assist them in application development, without unnecessarily consuming resources.
☒ **B,** install the Enterprise version of SQL Server on the developers' desktops, is incorrect because the Enterprise edition of SQL Server installs more components onto a desktop than the client software needed. **C,** install the Desktop edition of SQL Server on each laptop, is also incorrect because the Desktop edition would, like the other editions of SQL Server, install more software than is needed. **D,** install the Desktop edition of SQL Server on each laptop, is incorrect because restricting the sizes of new databases, the number of concurrent connections, or memory used for each is not the issue. The developers don't need to host SQL Server database applications on their desktops, merely connect to existing ones.

18. ☑ **B.** You want to automatically delete the job after it has run. That will ensure that the job is run only once. This is a common practice for one-off imports or exports. Some administrators will script the entire job in a stored procedure, then schedule the stored procedure, setting the job to be deleted after it is run. That way, the job runs only once, but you still have the stored procedure in case you need to run the job again in the future or if you need some documentation of the job.

☒ **A,** when the job succeeds, **C,** when the job fails, and **D,** whenever the job completes, are incorrect because they represent conditions that are used to specify when an operator is notified or when an event is written to the event log. These options do not affect the scheduling of jobs, only notification.

19. ☑ **C.** The best choice is the two-phase commit protocol. This option is implemented as part of the client side application. The protocol requires that data be updated in all locations or that the update be cancelled.
☒ **A, B,** and **D** are incorrect because all of these forms of replication are implemented through the server.

20. ☑ **B.** You can perform only full database backups of SQL Server 7.0 system databases. You can't do differential backups on system databases. You can perform a full backup of the master database using SQL Server Enterprise Manager, Transact-SQL, and the Create Backup Wizard.
☒ **A,** differential, and **D,** transaction log, are wrong because you are unable to perform differential or transaction log backups on a master database. The only type of backup you can do is a full backup. **C,** cluster, is also wrong because there is no such backup type as a cluster backup.

21. ☑ **C.** The proposed solution will satisfy both the desired and optional desired results. Creating stored procedures will allow developers to execute the stored procedures in order to acquire their data. In this way, those data sets will be acquired in a consistent and uniform manner. In addition, having developers execute stored procedures or views is typically more efficient than including embedded Transact SQL in a front-end application.
☒ **A, B,** and **D** are incorrect because stored procedures will produce both the results outlined.

22. ☑ **A, B, C, D.** The wizard will complete all of these tasks for you in addition to enlisting one or more servers as targets of the MSX and defining a job that includes selecting one or more target servers.
There are no incorrect answers for this question. All tasks are performed by the SQL MSX Wizard.

23. ☑ **C, D.** The msmerge_contents and msmerge_tombstone tables use the rowguid to track all inserts, updates, and deletions made to the table since it was published. The msmerge_tombstone table holds information about deleted rows and helps in the propagation of deletions to subscribers. The msmerge_contents table contains the rows that have changed since the publication was created.
☒ **A** and **B** are incorrect because they are not the proper names for the tables created for merge replication.

24. ☑ **B.** Mixed authentication mode is the only type of authentication that can be used on a Windows 98 computer. With this security mode, if NT authentication isn't available, then SQL Server authentication is used.
☒ **A,** Windows NT authentication mode, is wrong because, as its name implies, Windows NT authentication is available only for SQL Servers running on Windows NT computers. If SQL Server isn't running on an NT Server or NT Workstation, then this authentication mode can't be used. **C,** Windows User authentication, and **D,** Windows 98 authentication, are wrong because there are only two types of login authentication modes: Windows NT authentication and Mixed. Mixed bases access on NT authentication and—if this isn't available—uses SQL Server for authentication. There are no such things as Windows 98 or Windows User authentication modes.

25. ☑ **A, B, D.** Use the Services applet located in the Windows Control Panel. Locate each service and use the pause button to temporarily pause services. The SQL Server Service Manager applet can be used to pause both services. You can also use the Enterprise Manager to start, pause, and stop either of those services by right-clicking the service in the Enterprise Manager.
☒ **C,** use the Query Analyzer to pause MSSQLServer, which will automatically pause SQLServerAgent, is incorrect because the Query Analyzer can't be used to pause a server, and pausing the server will not automatically pause SQLServerAgent.

26. ☑ **D.** All of the answers are correct. Sp_altermessage is used to designate specific error messages as "always logged" and to log error messages with a severity lower than 19. The RAISERROR WITH LOG syntax is the recommended way to write to the Windows NT application log.

27. ☑ **C.** SQL Distributed Management Objects (SQL-DMO) provides the objects necessary for other platforms to participate as publishers. Through SQL-DMO, a developer can integrate heterogeneous data sources with SQL Server replication. To accomplish this, the developer first creates an SQL-DMO program written in Microsoft Visual Basic, C, or C++. Second, the developer must write a program using the Replication Distributor Interface. This program must be written in C or C++. The first program defines the publication, articles, and subscriptions. The second program stores the replication transactions in the distribution database on the distributor.
☒ **A** is incorrect because Open Data Services are server APIs provided with SQL Server which allows them to function as a gateway between clients and other database platforms. **B** and **D** are incorrect because ODBC and DB-Library are used by clients to communicate with SQL Server.

28. ☑ **A, C.** Named Pipes and multiprotocols need to be installed for the integrated security model to be implemented. If these aren't in place, the integrated security model can't be used.
☒ **B,** Windows 9x client computers must be used, is wrong because you're not limited to using Windows 95 or Windows 98 computers as clients when the integrated security model is used. **D,** RAS must be used, is also wrong, as implementing RAS on the network isn't a requirement of the integrated security model.

29. ☑ **B.** DB_accessadmin role can add and remove users for a database.
☒ **A** is incorrect because db_securityadmin manages permissions, roles, and object ownerships. **C,** Securityadmin, is incorrect because this role

manages logins and create database permissions. **D** is incorrect because processadmin manages processes in SQL server.

30. ☑ **A, D.** The other office may be exporting its content using the "native" SQL format. Unfortunately, this native format changed between SQL Server 6.5 and 7.0, so by default you would not be able to import its content. This could be solved either by having SQL Server 6.5 export the file as text (using the "-c" flag), or by having SQL Server 7.0 import it using the Version 6.5 internal format (using the "-6" flag). You may be able to tell if the file was exported in native format by opening it with a text editor.
☒ **B**, import your file using the "−L" flag, is incorrect because the "-L" flag is used to determine the last row to bulk copy, not to specify the format of the BCP file. **C**, ask the other office to export the file using the "−7" flag, is incorrect because the native format is the SQL 7.0 standard unless you specify otherwise and there is no "-7" flag.

31. ☑ **B.** The SP_ADDLINKEDSERVER command is Microsoft's preferred method of registering remote SQL servers within scripts or from a command line interface like Query Analyzer.
☒ **A, C,** and **D** are incorrect answers. The registration wizard is designed for novice administrators and cannot be used within a script. You can still register a remote server using the SP_ADDSERVER command, but that command is only available for backward compatibility and may be removed in future versions of SQL Server. There is no such command as SP_REGISTERSERVER.

32. ☑ **B.** The destination database must already exist. The subscription wizards provide the option of creating a new database to be used as the destination database.
☒ **A** is incorrect because SQL Server will create the database and schema if needed. **C** and **D** are incorrect because the destination database can and,

indeed, often is named the same as the source database, but it can have another name, as well.

33. ☑ C. When a user has become a member of a fixed database role, the user will be able to access only that particular database. This is because the fixed database role works at the database level.

☒ A, the user will be able to access the database because this role works at the server level, is wrong. The fixed database role works at the database level, not at the server level. As such, the user won't be able to access the database. B, the user will be able to access the database because this role applies to all databases on a single server, is wrong because the user won't be able to access the database. In addition, each role applies to a specific database; it doesn't apply to every database on a server. D, the user won't be able to access the database because only user-defined and fixed server roles work at the server level, is wrong. User-defined database roles work at the database level, and fixed server roles work at the server level.

34. ☑ B. The query added no records to the table. The @@ROWCOUNT describes how many records were affected by the last action. Zero is a valid number—it may be that the underlying query returned no records.

☒ A, there are no records in the destination table, is incorrect because it is possible that there are existing records in the destination table, just no new records added by the operation. Even if the action were part of a transaction, the results of the statement would still be "visible" within the transaction, so C, the query was part of a transaction and was not committed, is false. Because you cannot assume the query returned an error (D), you should use @@ERROR instead of @@ROWCOUNT for error testing.

35. ☑ C, D. SQL Mail is a MAPI compatible service, so the client can use any MAPI mail provider. Using SQL Mail to alert administrators of errors and developers or end users of the completion of jobs is a common practice.

☒ **A** and **B** are incorrect because SQL Mail complies with the MAPI standard. For the SQL Mail service to function properly, the MSSQL Server account should be a Windows NT domain account.

36. ☑ **D.** The correct action is to configure the wizard to support updateable subscriptions. This setting will establish a two-phase commit relationship between the two servers.

☒ **A** is incorrect because the default replication configuration specifies that all replication occurs from the publisher to the subscriber, with all updates being done on the publisher. **B** is incorrect because you can implement a two-phase commit relationship through the wizard. The immediately updating subscriber option is integrated seamlessly into both snapshot and transactional replication. These are optional properties of publications and subscriptions and can be enabled using SQL Server Enterprise Manager, or programmatically by using stored procedures or SQL-DMO. **C** is incorrect because it refers to a publication setting that enables replication to Internet subscribers. It has nothing to do with the two-phase commit behavior.

37. ☑ **C.** Application roles are disabled by default and must be activated by the sp_setaddrole system procedure.

☒ **A**, standard roles are disabled by default and must be activated by the sp_setaddrole system procedure, and **B**, standard roles are disabled by default and must be activated by the sp_addlinkedsrvlogin system procedure, are wrong because application roles, not standard roles, are used to control access in an n-tier application. **B** and **D**, application roles are disabled by default and must be activated by the sp_addlinkedsrvlogin system procedure, are also wrong because the sp_addlinkedsvrlogin procedure isn't used to activate application roles.

38. ☑ **A, C.** BCP and Select Into can be executed either as logged or as unlogged operations, depending on how you have set the "SELECT INTO / bulkcopy option." Of course, because the current state of the data is now unrecoverable, you probably want to back up the database soon.

☒ Both **B,** Bulk Insert, and **D,** Insert, are always logged operations, so they are not valid strategies for your purposes.

39. ☑ **A.** By default, the ANSI null default option is set to false, or NOT NULL, and the ANSI nulls option is also set to false. When ANSI null default is set to true, all user-defined data types or columns that are not explicitly defined as NOT NULL during a CREATE TABLE or ALTER TABLE statement default to allowing null values. Columns that are defined with constraints follow constraint rules regardless of this setting. When ANSI nulls is true, all comparisons to a null value evaluate to NULL, or unknown. When ANSI nulls is false, comparisons of non-Unicode values to a null value evaluate to TRUE if both values are NULL.

☒ **B, C,** and **D** are incorrect.

40. ☑ **D.** The proposed solution does not produce the required result. Transactional replication is only supported on Windows NT Publishers. Snapshot and merge replication are supported on all platforms.

☒ **A, B,** and **C** are incorrect because the required result has not been met. The Windows 95/98 systems will not be able to act as publishers.

41. ☑ **A.** The user will be refused any access. Because the user doesn't have a valid account for the database, and because no guest account exists for this database, the user doesn't have any access or permissions to use the database. As such, the user won't be allowed access.

☒ **B,** the user will default to a guest account, is wrong because the question states that a guest account doesn't exist for this database. **C,** the user will default to the SA account, and **D,** the user will default to the DBO account, are wrong because the SA (System Administrator) and DBO (Database Owner) accounts are high-level accounts. SQL Server wouldn't default to these accounts because doing so would give any user without a valid account considerable access and would be a security threat.

42. ☑ **D.** Create a linked server connecting to the Oracle Server, and create distributed queries that reference the Oracle tables directly through these links. When you use a linked table, the foreign content can be queried directly within SQL Server statements. If the data needs to be referenced only occasionally, the advantages of real-time data would outweigh the performance implications of these links.

☒ If you used **A**, DTS, or **B**, scheduled batch, the data would not be up to date. **C**, remote pass-through stored procedures, are still supported in 7.0, and they are available for backward compatibility, but they are less flexible than the server links available in 7.0.

43. ☑ **F.** The server must have the service installed. The database must be configured to enable the use of the full-text search service. A full-text catalog must be created to facilitate the service. A table must be registered and activated to support full-text queries. A column must be added to a registered active table to perform full-text queries against the table.

☒ **A, B, C, D,** and **E** are incorrect because there is a better answer.

44. ☑ **D.** The publisher determines whether or not an anonymous subscription will be accepted. If the anonymous subscription option was set when the publication was created, the publisher will allow an anonymous connection from a subscriber. The subscriber will make an anonymous connection to the publisher if the subscriber is not in the subscriber list and if anonymous subscribers are allowed.

☒ **A** is incorrect because the Internet Information Server is not involved in replication unless Internet subscribers are involved. **B** and **C** are incorrect because these servers do not determine whether or not an anonymous subscriber can access a publication.

45. ☑ **D.** The NT Administrators group has access to SQL server by default, due to being assigned to the sysadmin role. To prohibit access, just remove the NT Administrators group from the sysadmin role.

☒ **A** is incorrect because you cannot delete the Administrators group. **B** is incorrect because reinstalling SQL will not remove the Administrators group from the sysadmin role. **C** is incorrect because SQL is unaware of the name change. SQL will query the domain controller for the name and still allow access.

46. ☑ **B.** Upgrade the NT Server computer's operating system. SQL Server 7.0 can be installed only on version 4.0 or higher of Windows NT. Previous versions of Windows NT will need to be upgraded before SQL Server 7.0 is installed.

☒ **A**, uninstall the previous version of SQL Server, is wrong because you can upgrade SQL Server 6.5 to SQL Server 7.0 using the Upgrade Wizard in SQL Server. **C**, upgrade NT Server using the Upgrade Wizard in SQL Server, is wrong because you can't upgrade NT Server to a higher version using the Upgrade Wizard in SQL Server. The Upgrade Wizard is used to upgrade previous versions of SQL Server to version 7.0. **D**, install Service Pack 3 on the NT Server, is wrong because installing a Service Pack on NT Server 3.51 won't change the fact that SQL Server 7.0 needs to be installed on versions of Windows NT that are equal to or greater than version 4.0.

47. ☑ **C.** If MASTER needs to be rebuilt you will need to shut down all SQL services, and run REBUILDM.EXE, found in the MSSQL7\BIN directory. To reattach your database files and log files, run sp_attach_db for each database.

☒ **A,** reinstall SQL server and sp_attach_db to recover your databases, and **B,** reinstall SQL server, recreate all databases, and reload data, will recover your databases; however, both options are time-consuming and not necessarily the best way to recover. SQL should not be running at all when recovering MASTER, making **D,** start SQL in single-user mode, and run the REBUILDM.EXE utility, incorrect.

48. ☑ **C.** Adding a clustered index is the best way to optimize queries using ranges to select data. Clustered indexes are useful when the columns' indexes do not change often, are accessed sequentially, and return large result sets when queried.
☒ **A** is incorrect because adding nonclustered indexes is best suited for returning exact matches and returning small result sets. **B** is incorrect because DBCC CHECKTABLE is used to check the integrity of the pages associated with the table (data, index, image pages). **C** is incorrect because DBCC UPDATEUSAGE updates the sysindexes table, which is used by the sp_spaceused procedure to report space used.

49. ☑ **A.** Bulk Copy Program is a command-line tool that can be used to load data from standard delimited text files into SQL Server databases. This tool has been part of previous versions of SQL Server, and it is included with SQL Server 7.0.
☒ **B,** Data Transformation Services, is wrong because Data Transformation Services is new to SQL Server 7.0 and hasn't been included in previous versions. **C,** Data Migrator, is wrong because there is no such tool called Data Migrator in SQL Server 7.0. **D,** NT Explorer, is wrong because although NT Explorer could move the files on the hard disk, it can't move the data into other databases.

50. ☑ **D.** The proposed solution does not meet the required result. You cannot restore 6.5 backups to a 7.0 server. You must use the upgrade wizard to upgrade the database. You can move a database from a SQL 7 server to

another SQL 7.0 server using sp_attach_db or by restoring backups, but a 6.5 database cannot be moved to a SQL 7.0 server.

51. ☑ **A.** You can use the query governor cost limit option to limit the amount of time queries run. You can set this option in the properties of the SQL Server or you can use SP_CONFIGURE to change the value, which applies server wide.

☒ **B** is incorrect. Performance Monitor does not monitor specific queries and cannot pinpoint a query that is exceeding a time limit. **C** is incorrect because SP_MONITOR displays snapshot statistics that do not indicate query processes nor process ID. **D** is incorrect because SP_WHO does not indicate how long a process has been running.

52. ☑ **C.** The only server role created by default in SQL Server 7.0 that has full access is system administrator. Users assigned to this role have full access on the system.

☒ **A**, database creator, is wrong because database creators have the ability to alter, create, extend, and rename a database. They don't have full access, however. **B**, security administrator, is wrong because security administrators also don't have full access. They can add and drop logins, read the audit log, and grant the ability to create a database. **D**, server administrator, is wrong because there is no default server role called server administrator.

53. ☑ **B.** When using Merge replication and the Publisher fails, restoring the Publisher and synchronizing Subscribers is the best way to recover.

☒ **A**, restore the Wednesday backup and recreate all publications and subscriptions, is incorrect because you do not need to recreate the entire topology and reinitialize. **C**, restore the Wednesday backup and all Subscribers' most recent backups, is incorrect because there would be no way to ensure all backups were performed when the database was consistent across all databases. **D**, restore the Wednesday backup, is incorrect because changes would not be applied to the Publisher.

54. ☑ **C.** You can use Profiler and Monitor RPC Completed and SQL Batch Completed to monitor the queries performed. To view just the queries created by one user, filter by NT username or SQL username.

    ☒ **A, B** and **D** are incorrect since none of these utilities enables you to monitor queries generated by a specific user.

55. ☑ **B.** An application role would need to be created for each type of access needed and the application would need to verify user credentials, and use sp_setapprole based on the type of access the user needed.

    ☒ **A** is incorrect because one application role would allow everyone the same rights in both applications, allowing users to access or change data that they should not. C is incorrect because HR requires two types of access; so two roles are required for HR.

MCDBA

MICROSOFT CERTIFIED DATABASE ADMINISTRATOR

Test Yourself: Database Design Practice Exam 1 (Exam 70-029)

Q & A

T his Test Yourself section will help you measure your readiness to take the Designing and Implementing Databases with Microsoft SQL Server 7.0 exam (#70-29). See if you can complete this test under "exam conditions," before you check any of the answers. Read all the choices carefully, as there may be more than one correct answer.

Database Design Practice Exam I
Test Yourself Questions

1. You create the following indexes on a table:

```
CREATE CLUSTERED INDEX idx_Subject ON tblBooks(Subject)
CREATE NONCLUSTERED INDEX idx_Author ON tblBooks(Author)
CREATE NONCLUSTERED INDEX idx_SubjectAuthor ON
tblBooks(Subject ,Author)
```

Which index would be used for the following query?

```
SELECT Author
FROM    tblBooks
WHERE   Subject LIKE "%FICTION"
```

A. idx_Subject
B. idx_Author
C. idx_SubjectAuthor
D. None of the above

2. You are concerned about the employee turnover rate at your company, so you are taking a look at the employees with the lowest compensation. The nine records in the Jobs table contain the following values in the "min_lvl" field: 10, 20, 30, 40, 50, 60, 70, 80, and 90. You want to create a report for the jobs with the lowest min_lvl, and so you write the following query:

```
SELECT TOP 50 PERCENT jobs.* FROM jobs ORDER BY jobs.min_lvl
```

How many records does this query return?

A. One

B. Four

C. Five

D. Nine

3. Which of the following is not a true statement about triggers?

A. The CREATE TRIGGER statement must be the first statement in the batch.

B. Permission to create triggers defaults to the table owner, who cannot transfer it to other users.

C. Triggers are database objects, and their names must follow the rules for identifiers.

D. You can create a trigger only in the current database; as such a trigger cannot reference objects outside of the current database.

4. A new accounting system has been implemented. You want to drop the SQL Server database that was used by the old accounting system. What reasons could prevent you from dropping the database?

A. DTS Packages depends on it.

B. The database is publishing tables to other databases as part of SQL Server replication.

C. Tables are linked to an access database used for ad hoc queries left open.

D. A maintenance plan is in place for the database.

5. You have decided to build a clustered index *idx_PropertyType* on column *PropertyType* on table *tblProperty*. What attributes of *idx_PropertyType* might have made it a good choice to be a clustered index?

A. *PropertyType* is used to sort data with *GROUP BY* and *ORDER BY* in many queries.

B. Often *PropertyType* pulls back ranges of data.

C. *PropertyType* is a nonvolatile column.

D. All of the above

6. You create the following view of your sales data:

```
CREATE View vewOctoberSalesSummary
AS
SELECT SUM(SalesAmount) as TotalSales, AVG(SalesAmount) AS AVGSales,
MAX(SalesAmount) as MaxSales, MIN(SalesAmount) AS MinSales
FROM tblSales
WHERE SalesDate >= "10/1/2000"
AND SalesDate < "11/1/2000"
GO
```

Which of the following SQL statements can you commit against this view? (Choose all that apply.)

A. SELECTs

B. INSERTs

C. UPDATEs

D. DELETEs

7. There are two special tables related to triggers. These tables make it possible for triggers to be able to insert, update, or delete data, and for the programmer to check the status or receive information about the state of the trigger and what actions the trigger took. What are these tables? (Choose two.)

A. Temp

B. Inserted

C. Updated

D. Deleted

8. You are creating a new database with the following statement:

```
CREATE DATABASE Account
ON
    PRIMARY ( NAME=Account_data,
    FILENAME='c:\mssql7\data\account.mdf',
    SIZE=20MB,
    MAXSIZE=200MB,
    FILEGROWTH=10MB)
```

How big will the transaction log file be?

A. A transaction log will not be created since it is not specified by the CREATE DATABASE statement.
B. 512KB
C. 1MB
D. 5MB

9. You are evaluating your indexes and trying to figure out which ones are useful and which ones you may want to eliminate. Your primary query on *tblPerson* is the following:

```
SELECT    *
FROM      tblPerson
WHERE     BirthDate   >=    '10/17/97'
AND PersonID   >=    12599
```

Which indexes will be used in this query?

A. *idx_Birthdate*, a nonclustered index based on *Birthdate*
B. *idx_PersonID*, a nonclustered index based on *PersonID*
C. *idx_Lastname*, a clustered index based on *Lastname*
D. A and B

10. Another developer has created a view called vewMonthlyFinancials that summarizes the company's financials on a monthly basis. You select all the values from it, and it appears that it has the right type of data you need. The values in the columns are somewhat different from the values you had expected. Which of the following commands would allow you to look at the source query of a view to help determine if the view is producing the correct data?

A. sp_help vewMonthlyFinancials
B. sp_helptext vewMonthlyFinancials
C. sp_helpuser vewMonthlyFinancials
D. sp_helprole vewMonthlyFinancials

11. You have a stored procedure whose parameters wildly fluctuate between executions and optimally would use very different execution plans almost every time it executes. What could you do to ensure that the stored procedure will create a new appropriate execution plan for each execution? (Choose the best answer.)

A. Execute it with sp_executesql.
B. Use the WITH RECOMPILE option when you create the stored procedure.
C. Execute with EXEC.
D. Execute the stored procedure with the WITH RECOMPILE.

12. You want to create an index on column *PersonType* on *tblPersonType*. The table already exists, has no indexes, and has the following distribution of data: (NULL, NULL,1, 3, 7, 11, 13, 17, 29). Which of the following indexes could be created?

A. CREATE CLUSTERED INDEX *idx_PersonType* ON tblPersonType (*PersonType*)
B. CREATE NONCLUSTERED INDEX *idx_PersonType* ON *tblPersonType (PersonType)*
C. CREATE UNIQUE INDEX idx_PersonType ON tblPersonType (PersonType)
D. CREATE UNIQUE INDEX idx_PersonType ON tblPersonType (PersonType) WITH IGNORE_DUP_KEY

13. Current situation: Your company has written a Human Resources and Payroll program with a great deal of the business logic implemented in views. Required result: Prevent outsiders from using SQL Enterprise Manager to see the source queries that make up your views.
Optional desired results: Prevent outsiders from seeing the source queries to your views by querying syscomments and allow your application to use your views in the same fashion as they do today.

Proposed solution: Create all your views with the WITH ENCRYPTION option.

Which results does the proposed solution produce?

A. The proposed solution produces the required result and both of the optional results.

B. The proposed solution produces the required result and only one of the optional results.

C. The proposed solution produces the required result but does not produce either of the optional desired results.

D. The proposed solution does not produce the required result.

14. You are getting an error when you execute the following statement:

```
PUBS_GetAuthorsByState 'OH'
```

Which of the following commands would allow you to look at the text of the stored procedure to help you figure out the problem? (Choose the best answer.)

A. sp_help PUBS_GetAuthorsByState

B. sp_helptext PUBS_GetAuthorsByState

C. sp_help PUBS_GetAuthorsByState 'OH'

D. sp_helptext PUBS_GetAuthorsByState 'OH'

15. You have decided to build a nonclustered index *idx_AcqusitionDatePropertyID* on column *AcquisitionDate, PropertyID* on table *tblProperty*. What attributes of *idx_AcqusitionDatePropertyID* might have made it a good choice to be a nonclustered index?

A. There is high selectivity on the *AcqusitionDate, PropertyID* combination.

B. Some covered queries are using the *AcquisitionDate, PropertyID* combination.

C. *AcquisitionDate, PropertyID* is a foreign key to the *tblAcqusition*.

D. All of the above

16. You are evaluating the benefits of views in SQL Server so that you can make decisions about how to best use them in your applications. Which of the following can a view do for you?

A. Make visible only certain columns from a table.

B. Make visible only certain rows from a table.

C. Present two tables as a single table.

D. Be precompiled for better performance.

17. Current situation: Your company has written an incredibly efficient computer-assisted ordering application entirely through stored procedures.
Required result: Prevent outsiders from using SQL Enterprise Manager to see the source code of your stored procedures.
Optional desired results: Prevent outsiders from seeing the source code to your stored procedures by querying syscomments, and allow your employees to view the stored procedure's source code on an as-needed basis.
Proposed solution: Create all your stored procedures with the WITH ENCRYPTION option.
Which results does the proposed solution produce?

A. The proposed solution produces the required result and both of the optional results.

B. The proposed solution produces the required result and only one of the optional results.

C. The proposed solution produces the required result but does not produce either of the optional desired results.

D. The proposed solution does not produce the required result.

18. You run the "Football Master" Web site that allows people to create, manage, and name their own fantasy football leagues of up to 12 teams. The market leader in providing ad hoc fantasy football over the Internet is the "Devil Dog" Fantasy Football Consortium. It has taken legal action because some of the individual league names that your customers have created have the words "Devil Dog" in them. The "Devil Dog" Fantasy Football Consortium believes that you are unfairly allowing its registered trademark to be used. You have notified all the users and ordered them to change their names. Some of them have not complied with the edict to change their names as of this time. In order to avoid a bitter legal action, you need to modify the names of all the leagues in your system that use any variation of "Devil Dog" in their names to "Name not allowed." How could you change all the league names that currently have "Devil Dog" in their names?

A. ```
   UPDATE tblLeague
   SET Name = 'Name not allowed'
   HAVING Name LIKE "%Devil Dog%"
   ```

B. ```
   UPDATE *
   FROM tblLeague
   SET Name = 'Name not allowed'
   WHERE Name LIKE "%Devil Dog%"
   ```

C. ```
   UPDATE Name
   FROM tblLeague
   SET Name = 'Name not allowed'
   HAVING Name CONTAINS "%Devil Dog%"
   ```

D. ```
   UPDATE tblLeague
   SET Name = 'Name not allowed'
   WHERE Name LIKE "%Devil Dog%"
   ```

19. The Marketing department has asked for access to specific client information that you track in the SQL Server table tblClient. They need to have access to only a few of tblClient's many columns: ClientID, ClientName, Zip, and Age. You create a view for them of tblClient like this:

```
CREATE VIEW vewMarketingClients
AS
SELECT ClientID, ClientName, Zip, Age
FROM tblClient
WITH CHECK OPTION
```

You grant them full permissions to the view and e-mail them to tell them the name of the view. Shortly after, you receive a response claiming that they cannot perform INSERT statements into the view, but they can perform UPDATEs. What is the most likely reason that they cannot perform INSERTs into vewMarketingClients?

A. They tried to insert data that fell outside the scope of the view. With the WITH CHECK OPTION in force, that would not be allowed.

B. Some of the other fields on tblClient that are not in the view do not have a default value and are not nullable.

C. The lack of an aggregate function in the SELECT list makes this view nonupdatable.

D. The zip column in the view is a derived column.

20. Which of the following statements will return the correct au_id from PUBS_BestAuthor?

A. PUBS_BestAuthor

B. PUBS_BestAuthor @auid

C. PUBS_BestAuthor @auid OUTPUT

D. PUBS_BestAuthor @au_id = 7 OUTPUT

21. You have been asked to ensure that when a new region is created for your sales division in your database's Regions table the new region always has an active sales manager from your database's Managers table. What type of data integrity have you been asked to provide?

A. User-defined integrity

B. Entity integrity

C. Referential integrity

D. Domain integrity

22. You are trying to define the change control management procedures for database objects in your company, and you were hoping to use the ALTER PROCEDURE statement to modify the existing stored procedures. Which of the following things could you **not** do with ALTER PROCEDURE?

A. Alter the sort order of query results.

B. Change the number of parameters that the stored procedure expects.

C. Make an encrypted stored procedure unencrypted.

D. Change the name of the stored procedure.

23. You currently have a table, tblProperty, that has a great number of columns, and you would like to extract all the data for four of the fields into an empty table you have created called tblPropertyLite. How could you move that data from tblProperty into tblPropertyLite?

A. Perform a SELECT INTO from tblProperty into tblPropertyLite.
B. Write an INSERT statement into tblPropertyLite that had an appropriate SELECT expression from tblProperty.
C. Write an UPDATE statement to tblPropertyLite that had an appropriate WHERE clause to join the correct records from tblProperty and tblPropertyLite.
D. All of the above

24. Current situation: The price list for your company's products is being maintained in a spreadsheet. The price list is to be moved to your order entry database so that prices can be automatically looked up by the system instead of being looked up on a price sheet printed from the spreadsheet by the order entry clerk.

Required result: Current price for each product must be available in multiple currencies. The prices in different currencies vary according to market conditions.

Optional results: A price history should be retained. A simple, single field reference to the price used should be available to the OrderDetail table.

Proposed solution: You create the following table:

```
CREATE TABLE PriceList
    (DateEffective        datetime       NOT NULL
     Currency             char(3)        NOT NULL
     ProductID            int            NOT NULL
     Price                money          NOT NULL
     CONSTRAINT           PK_PriceList PRIMARY KEY CLUSTERED
                          (DateEffective, Currency,
    ProductID))
```

Which of the following results will the proposed solution produce?

A. The proposed solution produces the required result and both of the optional results.

B. The proposed solution produces the required result and only one of the optional results.

C. The proposed solution produces the required result and neither of the optional results.

D. The proposed solution doesn't produce the required result.

25. Data Transformation Services (DTS) provides the functionality to import, export, and transform data between SQL Server and any OLE DB, ODBC, or text file format. DTS is capable of transferring which of the following objects?

A. Data

B. Stored procedure

C. Trigger

D. All of the above

26. After a transaction has been reconciled for six months, you no longer need it. What query could you run to purge the old data from tblTransaction most efficiently?

A.
```
DELETE *
FROM tblTransaction
WHERE ReconciledDate < DateAdd(month, -6, GetDate())
```

B.
```
DELETE tblTransaction
WHERE DateAdd(month, -6, ReconciledDate ) < GetDate()
```

C.
```
DELETE tblTransaction
WHERE ReconciledDate < DateAdd(month, -6, GetDate())
```

D.
```
DELETE *
FROM tblTransaction
WHERE DateAdd(month, -6, ReconciledDate ) < GetDate()
```

27. Your company's order processing system has eight statuses an order can have during its lifetime: opened, completed, picked, shipped, invoiced, collected, returned, and cancelled. You have decided to track the statuses in your database by using Boolean flags. Which datatype is best for implementing this type of flag in a SQL Server 7.0 table?

A. BOOLEAN because this datatype was specifically designed to hold true/false data

B. BIT because up to eight flags can be held in a single byte of your table

C. CHAR(1) because you can use 0/1, Y/N, or T/F to signify completion of a stage

D. INT because long integer is the standard register size in a 32-bit processing system; therefore it will be loaded into memory faster

28. Consider the DTS architecture. After you have defined a copy operation it must be validated according to the transformation flags that you specified on the advanced tab. Which component of the DTS architecture is responsible for this validation?

A. DTS Import Wizard

B. DTS Export Wizard

C. Data Pump

D. Data Packager

29. Your audit department is insisting that they should be able to find out who created a record and when, and who last modified a record and when. The additional fields must be maintained automatically by the database in order to avoid updates to the fields from unauthorized sources. Each user has been assigned his or her own SQL Server login. All access to the database is through views and stored procedures. Only the database administrator has access to the data directly through the tables. The database login is separate from the NT login in order to allow supervisors to submit overrides from any user's workstation. What steps should you take to implement this audit requirement when adding CreatedBy, DateCreated, ModifiedBy, and DateModified to each table in your database?

A. Add DEFAULT constraints of GETDATE() to DateCreated and DateModified.
B. Add DEFAULT constraints of SYSTEM_USER to CreatedBy and ModifiedBy.
C. Add a CHECK constraint of GETDATE() to DateModified.
D. Add a CHECK constraint of SYSTEM_USER to ModifiedBy.

30. Current Situation: Your company has a great deal of information that has been accumulated over the years in your SQL server in text fields. You have written many routines that allow users to search them with LIKE pattern matching, but they are often frustrated with how linguistic nuances radically change their results, how the results are not in any particular order, and how certain words specific to your industry have a tendency to bring back a great deal of wrong results.
Required Result: Find a way to search the existing data that takes into account linguistic nuances.
Optional Desired Results: Be able to order results by score, and the searches must query up-to-date data.
Proposed Solution: Redo all the tables so that the tables that need to be searched have a single-column primary key, and then implement full-text searches with Microsoft Search Service with an appropriate noise file for the your company.
Which results does the proposed solution produce?

A. The proposed solution produces the required result and produces both of the optional results.
B. The proposed solution produces the required result and produces only one of the optional results.
C. The proposed solution produces the required result but does not produce any of the optional desired results.
D. The proposed solution does not produce the required result.

31. You are developing a distributed application and have coded procedures for both the inventory and sales databases. These databases are on separate servers. You want to keep the sales procedures on the sales database server and the inventory procedures on the inventory server. Your application will need to use combinations of these procedures. What SQL Server facility would you choose to implement your design?

A. Remote stored procedures

B. Distributed queries

C. Remote queries

D. Distributed stored procedures

32. You are running out of hard disk space on your SQL Server, but you do not have the budget to upgrade your server. You notice that there is a table "OLDSALES" with 10 million records in it. After investigation, you find out that this table was a remnant of previous data migration, and it has not been needed for more than a year. You want to delete the content in this table but not its design. You execute the following query:

```
DELETE FROM HR.OLDSALES
```

You want to confirm that the records have been deleted. If there are no records in the table, which of the following would be returned when you execute 'select Max(Salary) from hr.oldsales'?

A. "0"
   "(1 row(s) affected)"

B. "(null)"
   "(1 row(s) affected)"

C. "(null)"
   "(0 row(s) affected)"

D. You will get an error because you need to specify a "*" when using DELETE

33. You have been asked to modify constraints on a SQL Server 7.0 database. Which constraints can be modified in the database diagram without using an additional dialog?

    A. NULL constraints

    B. PRIMARY KEY constraints

    C. UNIQUE constraints

    D. FOREIGN KEY constraints

    E. CHECK constraints

    F. DEFAULT constraints

34. When using the bcp command line utility or the BULK INSERT T-SQL command, you often provide a format file. What issues does a format file help you address?

    A. Cases where the data file contains more or fewer columns than the table or view

    B. Cases where the columns are in a different order

    C. Cases where the column delimiters vary

    D. Cases where there are other changes in the format of the data

35. You are planning your annual SEC filings, and you need to group overdue Accounts Receivable so that you can estimate the allowance for uncollectables. You are using a formula to calculate the number of months overdue. Which of the following approaches would be the simplest way to successfully accomplish this?

    A. Create a view that includes this formula in the SELECT clause, and then create a query that references this view, using GROUP BY on your computed column.

    B. Create a subquery that includes this formula in the SELECT clause, and then in the parent query use GROUP BY on this computed column.

    C. Create a query including this formula in the GROUP BY clause and the SELECT clause.

    D. Create a query including this formula in the GROUP BY clause but not in the SELECT clause.

36. While writing the code for a trigger, you realize that there is an error condition that should result in no changes to the database. If the error condition occurs, you want to halt processing and undo any modifications that have been made. What option will accomplish this?

A. END TRANSACTION

B. ROLLBACK TRANSACTION

C. CLOSE TRANSACTION

D. HALT TRANSACTION

37. The dtsrun utility allows you to retrieve, execute, delete, and overwrite a package created using Data Transformation Services. The DTS package can be stored in the SQL Server msdb database, a COM-structured storage file, or the Microsoft Repository. Which of the following commands correctly executes a DTS package stored in the msdb database?

A. `dtsrun /Ffilename /Npackage_name /Mpackage_password`

B. `dtsrun /Sserver_name /Uuser_nName /Ppassword`
   `/Npackage_name /Mpackage-password`

C. `dtsrun /Sserver_name /Uuser_nName /RRepository_nName`
   `/Ppassword /Npackage_name /Mpackage-password`

D. `dtsrun /Npackage_name`

38. You are trying to learn more about the guests who visit your hotel to determine where you should target your advertising. You execute the following query:

```
SELECT state, Count(state) AS CountGuests
FROM guests
GROUP BY state
```

Five records are returned. How many records will be returned when you run the following query?

```
SELECT state, Count(state) AS CountGuests
FROM guests
GROUP BY state
WITH ROLLUP
```

A. 36

B. 6

C. 5

D. 0

39. Recently your boss has returned from a security briefing where SQL Server was discussed. One of the things that your boss is concerned about is SQL Server's ability to nest triggers. He's afraid that a malicious programmer could crash the server with a string of cascading triggers. He wants to make sure that triggers can't be nested. Which command should you issue?

A. sp_configure 'nested triggers', 0

B. sp_configure 'nested triggers', 1

C. sp_configure 'cascaded triggers', 0

D. sp_configure 'cascaded triggers', 1

40. You want to ensure that NULL handling in your database complies with the ANSI SQL-92 specification. What database options do you have to set to ensure this behavior?

A. SET ANSI_NULLS ON

B. SET ANSI_NULL_DFLT_ON

C. SET ANSI_NULLS OFF

D. SET ANSI_NULL_DFLT_OFF

41. You have created a CUBE query that categorizes your workers by the building in which they are working. Some of your users are complaining about this query because some employees work at home and have a Null for the building field. Your users cannot distinguish between the Nulls representing the rollups and the Nulls representing nulls in the source table. What function could you add at the beginning of your query to clarify the results?

A. Add "Filternulls(Building)" to the SELECT clause.

B. Add "CubedID(Building)" to the ORDER BY clause.

C. Add "Grouping (Building)" to the SELECT clause.

D. Add "Cube(Building) is false" to the WHERE clause.

42. You receive an error message while trying to create a trigger. You suspect that you may be using a SQL statement that is not allowed in a trigger. Which of the following statements will result in an error message if used in the body of a trigger?

A. CREATE TRIGGER

B. UPDATE

C. DENY

D. GRANT

43. Your insurance company has just completed a five-year audit. Five years of history can now be archived. The original size of the database history was 30MB. It is currently 170MB. The space used is 20MB after archiving history. You run the command DBCC SHRINKDATABASE (history, 25) What will be the size of the database after running the command?

A. 20.0MB

B. 26.6MB

C. 30.0MB

D. 127.5MB

44. The clerks entering orders into your order-entry database are complaining that performance badly degrades during the week following month end. The accounting department is running many access queries against the order-entry history tables to create their month-end reports. They complain that the queries run faster in the evening, but they don't want to pay overtime. The entire database currently resides on one of four drives on your SQL Server. Backups on your single backup tape drive have been getting longer. The SQL Server does not have a RAID controller. The president of your company has stated that getting orders in is the most important function. He also doesn't want to spend any more on hardware at the moment. Your primary goal is to improve performance of order-entry application. Secondarily, you would like to improve performance of the accounting department queries and improve backup performance. Your plan is to create a new filegroup on a second drive and move the history tables to the new file group. What is the result of your plan?

A. The plan achieves the primary goal and both of the secondary goals.
B. The plan achieves the primary goal and only one of the secondary goals.
C. The plan achieves the primary goal and neither of the secondary goals.
D. The plan does not achieve the primary goal.

45. You are reviewing the fragmentation of key files in your database. The output of DBCC SHOWCONTIG for the loan history file shows the following:

```
DBCC SHOWCONTIG scanning 'loanhist' table...
Table: 'loanhist' (245575913); index ID: 1, database ID:
7
TABLE level scan performed.
- Pages Scanned...............................: 453
- Extents Scanned.............................: 57
- Extent Switches.............................: 56
- Avg. Pages per Extent.......................: 7.9
- Scan Density [Best Count:Actual Count].......: 100.00%
[57:57]
- Logical Scan Fragmentation .................: 0.00%
- Extent Scan Fragmentation ..................: 1.75%
- Avg. Bytes Free per Page....................: 58.7
- Avg. Page Density (full)....................: 99.28%
DBCC execution completed. If DBCC printed error messages,
contact your system administrator.
```

What does this tell you about the database table?

A. The table is designed for best performance in a reporting environment and has minimal fragmentation.
B. The table is designed for best performance in a transaction processing environment and has minimal fragmentation.
C. The table is designed for best performance in a reporting environment and has a high level of fragmentation.
D. The table is designed for best performance in a transaction processing environment and has a high level of fragmentation.

Database Design Practice Exam I
Test Yourself Answers

1. ☑   **D.** None of the above. The query optimizer would like to use an index on the *Subject* column, but because you are doing an "ends with" with the *LIKE*, it cannot use it. It would be more efficient to do a *table scan* in this case than an *index scan* because in a *table scan*, SQL Server will read all the data sequentially.

   ☒   **A,** idx_Subject, is not used because you are doing an "ends with." **B,** idx_Author, is not used because it is not on the right field. **C,** idx_SubjectAuthor, is not used because you are doing an "ends with."

2. ☑   **C.** Five. Normally, the number after the TOP refers to the number of records to return, but if you include "Percent" after this number, it refers to the proportion of records that should be returned instead. When the percentage specified does not divide evenly into the record set, the records round up. In this case, 50 percent of nine records is 4.5, which rounds to 5.0.

   ☒   **A,** One, would be correct if the data was aggregated after it was queried. **B,** Four, would be correct if the percentage calculation rounded down instead of up. If you selected TOP 50 instead of TOP 50 percent, all nine records would be returned, yielding **D,** Nine, is incorrect because it is the number of records you started with in the Jobs table, and the 50 percent in the query would return 4.5, rounded to 5.

3. ☑   **D.** It is true that you can create triggers only in the current database, but triggers can reference objects outside of the current database. This is one of the advantages to using triggers. Integrity with other databases can be maintained in this way.

   ☒   **A,** the CREATE TRIGGER statement must be the first statement in the batch, **B,** permission to create triggers defaults to the table owner, who cannot transfer it to other users, and **C,** triggers are database objects, and their names must follow the rules for identifiers, are incorrect answers because they are true statements. If you are creating a trigger through a utility such as SQL Query Analyzer, then the CREATE TRIGGER statement must be the first statement in the batch of statements. Only the table owner has permission to create and drop triggers, and that permission cannot be transferred. If you are using database roles, you should remember that there are two roles that will allow users to create and drop triggers. Those roles are the db_owner and db_ddladmin roles. Finally, triggers are database objects and are subject to all naming restrictions that apply to other database objects.

4. ☑ **B, C.** A database cannot be dropped if the database is open for reading or writing. A database that is publishing to other databases cannot be dropped.
☒ **A** is incorrect because DTS Packages are independent of databases. **D** is incorrect because existence of a maintenance plan will not prevent the database from being dropped.

5. ☑ **D.** All of the above is the correct answer. A clustered index determines the physical order of the table. As a consequence, a clustered index is very efficient when retrieving sequential values. Any operation that uses any kind of sorting benefits from a clustered index because it can take advantage of the data already being sorted. Nonvolatile columns are good for clustered indexes because each time a column is updated, the entire row may have to physically move.

6. ☑ **A.** All the columns in this view are derived columns, and if any of the columns are derived, you cannot perform queries that modify data such as UPDATEs, INSERTs, and DELETEs. A derived column in a view is any column that is not an actual data element that exists in a table; any column that is modified in any way to be represented differently is a derived column and will prevent data modification to that view. Any field that is calculated from multiple fields is a derived field.
☒ **B**, INSERTs, **C**, UPDATEs, and **D**, DELETEs, are incorrect because you cannot perform UPDATEs, INSERTs, and DELETEs on views where any of the columns are derived. TotalSales, AVGSales, MaxSales, and

MinSales are all derived columns because they do not exist in the database, but instead are calculated from data in the database.

7. ☑ **B, D.** Two special tables are used in trigger statements: the deleted table and the inserted table. You can use these temporary tables to test the effects of certain data modifications and to set conditions for trigger actions. You cannot alter the data in the trigger test tables directly, but you can use the tables in SELECT statements to determine whether the trigger was fired by an INSERT, UPDATE, or DELETE statement. The deleted table stores copies of the affected rows during DELETE and UPDATE statements. During the execution of a DELETE or UPDATE statement, rows are deleted from the trigger table and transferred to the deleted table. The inserted table stores copies of the affected rows during INSERT and UPDATE statements. During an INSERT or UPDATE transaction, new rows are added simultaneously to both the inserted table and the trigger table. The rows in the inserted table are copies of the new rows in the trigger table. An UPDATE transaction is like a delete followed by an insert; the old rows are copied to the deleted table first, and then the new rows are copied to the trigger table and to the inserted table.
☒ **A,** temp, and **C,** updated, are incorrect because no such tables exist. The only two tables used by triggers are the inserted and deleted tables.

8. ☑ **D.** 5MB. The default size of the transaction log file is 25 percent of the total of all files created. In this case only a primary file was created so the size is 25 percent of 20MB, or 5MB.
☒ **A,** A transaction log will not be created since it is not specified by the CREATE DATABASE statement, is wrong because SQL Server requires that a transaction log be created. **B,** 512KB, is wrong because 512KB is the minimum size of a transaction log file. **C,** 1MB, is wrong because 1MB is the default size of secondary data or the log file, if it is not specified by a SIZE option.

9. ☑ **D.** SQL Server 7.0 introduced multiindex processing, allowing several indexes to be used in one query. SQL Server will use *idx_Birthdate* to gather all IDs of the rows with birth dates after 10/17/97, and it will use the *idx_PersonID* to gather all the rows with *PersonID*s that are greater than or equal to 12599. Server 7.0 will then use index intersection on the two sets of IDs to get the correct results for this query.

☒ C, *idx_Lastname*, a clustered index based on *Lastname*, is incorrect because *idx_LastName* offers nothing to help with this search, and it may be a good candidate to be eliminated.

10. ☑ B, sp_helptext vewMonthlyFinancials, is correct. sp_helptext is a system stored procedure that will allow a user to see the text that makes up an unencrypted view. sp_helptext takes one parameter, a string representing the object name, and issues a return code (0 for success, 1 for failure). In addition, sp_helptext will allow a user to view the text from other database objects such as triggers, stored procedures, rules, and defaults.

☒ A, sp_help vewMonthlyFinancials, is incorrect because the sp_help system stored procedure will show the owner, create date, and column information about the view. sp_help is most commonly used to gather information about tables and views. C, sp_helpuser vewMonthlyFinancials, is incorrect because sp_helpuser is used to return information about a user or role in the database, not about a view. D, sp_helprole vewMonthlyFinancials, is incorrect because sp_helprole returns information about a role within the current database and does not have anything to do with views.

11. ☑ B. Using the WITH RECOMPILE option when you create a stored procedure will make sure that SQL Server will not use an existing execution plan or save the one it is using every time it executes the stored procedure. Instead, it creates a new execution plan for the stored procedure to execute and throws it away after execution. This will help when the parameters passed to the stored procedure are very different from each other, and it will preserve the existing execution plans that other queries may use.

☒ D, execute the stored procedure with the WITH RECOMPILE, is incorrect because using the WITH RECOMPILE option when you run the stored procedure will only prevent an execution plan from being used for that execution. **A**, execute it with sp_executesql, is incorrect because sp_executesql will not force a stored procedure to use a new execution plan each time it runs, and instead it has a tendency to increase the chances of finding an existing execution plan to reuse. **C**, execute with EXEC, is incorrect because executing a stored procedure with or without EXEC or EXECUTE will not make a stored procedure create a new execution plan each time it is run.

12. **A, B.** You could create CREATE CLUSTERED INDEX *idx_PersonType* ON tblPersonType (*PersonType*), or you could create CREATE NONCLUSTERED INDEX *idx_PersonType* ON *tblPersonType (PersonType)*. You can always add a simple index on a column as long as you have fewer than 250 indexes on the table already.

   ☒   **C**, CREATE UNIQUE INDEX idx_PersonType ON tblPersonType (PersonType), and **D**, CREATE UNIQUE INDEX idx_PersonType ON tblPersonType (PersonType) WITH IGNORE_DUP_KEY, are incorrect because you cannot make the index unique if duplicate values exist, and that includes NULLs. *IGNORE_DUP_KEY* is used to reject only the items that violate the uniqueness of index when batch *INSERTs* are used; it would not have helped in this circumstance.

13. ☑   **A.** The proposed solution produces the required result and both of the optional results. Using the WITH ENCRYPTION option will encrypt your views so that no one will be able to read their source either in SQL Enterprise Manager or by querying the syscomments table. The WITH ENCRYPTION option will allow the view to be used by queries, stored procedures, and other views as they would be if they were not encrypted. The WITH ENCRYPTION option encrypts the source query in the syscomments table so that only the SQL Server itself knows what makes up the query for the view.

   ☒   **B, C**, and **D** are incorrect because **A** is correct.

14. ☑   **B.** Sp_helptext is a system stored procedure that will allow a user to see the text that makes up an unencrypted stored procedure. Sp_helptext takes

one parameter, a string representing the object name, and issues a return code (0 for success, 1 for failure). In addition, sp_helptext will allow a user to view the text from other database objects such as triggers, views, rules, and defaults. ☒ **A,** sp_help PUBS_GetAuthorsByState, is incorrect because the sp_help system stored procedure will show the owner, the create date, and information about the parameters of the stored procedure. Sp_help is most commonly used to gather information about a table.
C, sp_help PUBS_GetAuthorsByState 'OH', is incorrect for the same reasons **A** is incorrect: When you pass a stored procedure to sp_help, you do not include any of the parameters, and doing so will cause an error. **D,** sp_helptext PUBS_GetAuthorsByState 'OH', is incorrect because sp_helptext takes only one parameter, the object name. If you include the parameters which are passed to the stored procedure that is the sp_helptext parameter, it will cause errors.

15. ☑ **D.** All of the above. A nonclustered index excels at finding specific values. A covered index is a special kind of nonclustered index that has all the fields in the *WHERE* and *SELECT* clauses in the index. This is extremely fast because SQL Server will never have to follow the pointers to the actual data; all the values being retrieved are already in the index. Foreign keys are often used in joins, and by having a nonclustered index on a foreign key, joins with a table on that foreign key will be greatly accelerated.

16. ☑ **A, B,** and **C.** A view can limit which columns are shown from a table. If you had a table with 50 columns across but only 10 of those columns need to be viewed by the Finance department, you could create a view of that table that made visible only those 10 columns. In addition, a view can limit which rows are visible. If one department in your company was concerned only with records of a certain type, you could build a view for them that was limited to the data that they needed to see. A view can also combine tables in a join and make them look as if they are from a single unified source of data. Database administrators like to normalize databases as much as possible, making maintenance easier. Normalizing the database, however, makes the data less intuitive to end users. With views, you can

allow the data to reside in a normalized manner but present it to the users in an easier-to-understand, denormalized way.

☒   **D**, be precompiled for better performance, is incorrect because views are no longer precompiled in SQL Server 7.

17. ☑   **B.** The proposed solution produces the required result and one of the optional desired results. Using the encrypt option will encrypt your stored procedures so that no one will be able to read their source in either SQL Enterprise Manager or by querying the syscomments table. This is not selective; no users will be able to read the source for those stored procedures, whether they are your competitors or your employees.

☒   **A**, **C**, and **D** are incorrect.

18. ☑   **D.** An UPDATE is very much like a SELECT, except that instead of returning records, it modifies them. Because of this, it is often recommended to write your UPDATE statement as SELECT statements first because you can then verify that you are bringing up the correct records to modify. Only choice **D** brings up the correct set of records. In addition, UPDATEs cannot be used with GROUP BY and HAVING clauses.

☒   **A** is incorrect because the HAVING clause needs to be used with a GROUP BY clause and because the HAVING clause cannot be used in UPDATES statements. **B** is incorrect because "*" is not a proper parameter after the UPDATE clause. Immediately following the UPDATE keyword needs to be the name of the table on which the updates will be performed. **C** is incorrect because the name of the field (in this case "Name") follows the UPDATE keyword, instead of the table.

19. ☑   **B** is the correct answer. The columns in the source tables that are not represented in the view must be nullable or have defaults for you to perform INSERT statements against the view. When you attempt to insert against the view, you cannot specify other fields that may be needed in the base tables. In order to have a view that you can perform INSERT statements against, all nonnullable fields in the base tables must be in the view.

☒   **A**, they tried to insert data that fell outside the scope of the view, is incorrect because there is no WHERE clause in the view's source query by which to restrict new entries. The WITH CHECK OPTION in this view will veto no INSERTs because there is no criteria by which to judge them. **C**, the lack of an aggregate function in the SELECT list makes this view nonupdatable, is incorrect because the lack of an aggregate function in SELECT list allows you to insert rows through a view, not prevent them. **D**, the zip column in the view is a derived column, is incorrect because the zip field is not derived. In addition, if it were a derived column, UPDATEs would not be able to be performed.

20. ☑   **C.** PUBS_BestAuthor @auid OUTPUT is correct. In order to retrieve output parameters from a stored procedure, you must mark it for output by having the OUTPUT keyword follow the parameter.

☒   **A**, PUBS_BestAuthor, is incorrect because you must pass in a variable to the stored procedure in order to retrieve the value. Because no variable is provided, the following error message will be generated:

```
Server: Msg 201, Level 16, State 1, Procedure PUBS_BestAuthor, Line 0
Procedure 'PUBS_BestAuthor' expects parameter '@au_id', which was not supplied.
```

B, PUBS_BestAuthor @auid, is incorrect because the variable that is being passed in is not marked for output. If you check it after the stored procedure is executed, the value will be NULL. **D**, PUBS_BestAuthor @au_id = 7 OUTPUT, is incorrect because you cannot pass a constant in as the output parameter; it must be a variable. You could have passed it in by name like this:

EXEC PUBS_BestAuthor @au_id = @auid OUTPUT

21. ☑   **C.** Referential integrity ensures that the relationship between the primary key in a referenced table and the foreign key in the referencing table is maintained. Because you have been asked to ensure that the manager defined for the region is a valid manager in the Manager table, this is an example of referential integrity.

☒   **A**, user-defined integrity, is incorrect because this can correctly be classified as referential integrity. **B**, entity integrity (also know as table integrity), refers to the fact that each row of a table must have a unique identifier or primary key. **D**, domain integrity (also know as column integrity), refers to the constraints on a value in a column either by data type, format, or range.

22. ☑   **D.** You cannot change the name of a stored procedure with the ALTER PROCEDURE statement.

☒   **A,** alter the sort order of query results, is incorrect because you can change the sort order of the query results using ALTER PROCEDURE. In fact, you can change the query altogether from a SELECT to an INSERT or UPDATE. The SQL statements inside a stored procedure can be changed from anything to anything using ALTER PROCEDURE. **B,** change the number of parameters that the stored procedure expects, is incorrect because you can change the number and type of the parameters that the stored procedure expects and needs, just as you can change the statements inside the stored procedure. This may not be wise to do, though, because if you alter the number and type of parameters, then you must update all the statements and applications that depend on this stored procedure to work with the new organization of the parameters. **C,** make an encrypted stored procedure unencrypted, is incorrect because you can toggle change an unencrypted stored procedure to an encrypted one and vice versa; in addition, you can change the RECOMPILE and FOR REPLICATION options with the ALTER PROCEDURE statements.

23. ☑   **B.** The correct way to fill tblPropertyLite would be to use an INSERT statement that had an appropriate SELECT expression from tblProperty. An INSERT statement to accomplish this would look like this:

```
INSERT tblPropertyLite
(Field1, Field2, Field3, Field4)
(SELECT Field1, Field2, Field3, Field4
FROM tblProperty)
```

☒   **A,** perform a SELECT INTO from tblProperty into tblPropertyLite, is incorrect because the table already exists. If you try to do a SELECT INTO into a table that already exists, you will get an error because the statement will not be able to create the table. A SELECT INTO query to accomplish this would look like this:

```
SELECT Field1, Field2, Field3, Field4
INTO tblPropertyLite
FROM tblProperty
```

You can select the data into either a permanent table or a temp table, and you can reference it and manipulate it like any other table in the database. **C**, write an UPDATE statement to tblPropertyLite that had an appropriate WHERE clause to join the correct records from tblProperty and tblPropertyLite, is incorrect because an UPDATE statement will modify existing data, not insert new data. **D**, all of the above, is incorrect because **A** and **C** are incorrect.

24. ☑ **B.** The proposed solution produces the required result and only one of the optional results. Prices can be recorded in multiple currencies. A date history is retained using the effective date. The compound primary key does not provide a simple single field reference for the OrderDetail record.
☒ **A**, the proposed solution produces the required result and both of the optional results, is wrong; while the proposed solution produces the required result, it doesn't produce both of the optional results.. In order to produce the optional result of allowing a single, simple reference for the OrderDetail table, the PRIMARY KEY constraint should be on an IDENTITY field and the current PRIMARY KEY constraint changed to a UNIQUE constraint. **C**, the proposed solution produces the required result and neither of the optional results, is incorrect because the proposed solution does produce the required result and one of the optional results. **D**, the proposed solution doesn't produce the required result, is wrong because the required result is met. The table allows prices to be recorded in multiple currencies.

25. ☑ **D.** Data Transformation Services is capable of transferring complete database objects between source and destination SQL Server 7.0 data sources. The Transfer SQL Server Objects task can be used to transfer all of the metadata and data for some or all of the objects in one SQL Server 7.0 database to another SQL Server 7.0 database. For example, the Transfer SQL Server Objects task can be used to move a table with all of its associated index,

constraint, rule, default, and trigger definitions and the existing rows in the table. The Transfer SQL Server Objects task also can be used to transfer the definitions of objects such as views and stored procedures.

☒ **A, B,** and **C** are incorrect because **D** includes them all.

26. ☑ **C.** This query deletes all the records that have been reconciled for at least six months the most efficiently. A DELETE statement first must find the records it is going to DELETE, so what makes a SELECT more efficient will make a DELETE more efficient.

☒ **B** is incorrect because it is less efficient than C due to the fact that you modify ReconciledDate instead of modifying the GetDate(), although **B** would commit the correct deletes. **A** and **D** are incorrect because there is a syntax error by using the "*." A DELETE operates on an entire row, so specifying the fields with a "*" will cause an error.

27. ☑ **B.** BIT is the most compact method of storing this type of data. The only drawback to the BIT datatype is that it cannot be indexed.

☒ **A,** BOOLEAN, is wrong because BOOLEAN is a Visual Basic datatype that is not available in SQL Server. **C,** CHAR(1), is wrong because allowing multiple methods of designating whether the step was complete would be confusing to handle in selection queries. **D,** INT, is wrong because INT columns would consume 32 bytes of your record size and have a much larger range than required.

28. ☑ **C.** The DTS Data Pump checks to see if the copy can be done using the options that you selected. SQL Server provides a multithreaded OLE DB service provider known as the DTS Data Pump. The DTS Data Pump provides the infrastructure to import, export, and transform data between heterogeneous OLE DB data sources. OLE DB is used because it provides access to the broadest possible range of relational and nonrelational data stores. The DTS Data Pump is a high-speed in-process COM server that moves and transforms OLE DB row sets from a source to a destination.

☒ **A,** DTS Import Wizard, and **B,** DTS Export Wizard, are incorrect because the wizards are not part of the DTS architecture. They are applications that help a user define a DTS Package using the architecture. **D,** Data Packager, is incorrect because there is no such component in the DTS architecture.

29. ☑ **A, B.** Default constraints of GET_DATE() and SYSTEM_USER will ensure that the four fields are set correctly when a record is inserted. There is no appropriate constraint to automatically set the ModifiedBy and DateModified when a record is modified. This requirement would have to be implemented with an update trigger. It could also be implemented as part of your update stored procedure. Because this is an audit requirement, a trigger would be preferable because it would fire even if someone was able to obtain dba privileges and modify tables directly.

☒ **C,** add a CHECK constraint of GETDATE() to DateModified, and **D,** add a CHECK constraint of SYSTEM_USER to ModifiedBy, are wrong because a CHECK constraint can only raise an error. CHECK constraints will not modify the data to make it comply to the constraint.

30. ☑ **B.** The proposed solution produces the required result and produces only one of the optional results. Microsoft Full Text Search will open powerful avenues of searching char, varchar, nchar, nvarchar, and text fields that will let you search through the results accounting for noise, linguistic variation, and proximity. In addition, it will let you score the results of a search and assign different weights to different words, but the full-text indexes are not kept up-to-date automatically. They will need to be periodically repopulated in order to be useful.

☒ **A** and **C** are incorrect because the proposed solution produces one of the optional results. **D** is incorrect because the required result is produced.

31. ☑ **B.** You should use distributed queries. Remote stored procedures are a legacy feature of SQL Server. Their functionality in Transact-SQL is limited to executing a stored procedure on a remote SQL Server installation. The distributed queries introduced in SQL Server 7.0 support this ability along with the ability to access tables on linked, heterogeneous OLE DB data sources directly from local Transact-SQL statements. Instead of using a remote stored procedure call on SQL Server 7.0, use distributed queries and an EXECUTE statement to execute a stored procedure on a remote server.

☒ **A,** remote stored procedures, is incorrect because it is not the preferred method of implementing the functionality you need. **C,** remote queries, and **D,** distributed stored procedures, are incorrect because they are not the correct terms for identifying the two methods.

32. ☑ **B.** There are no records in the table, so there is, of course, no highest value in the salary field. When used in this context, however, the MAX function will always return a scalar value, even if that value is a null. The "rows affected" line refers to the result set, not the source data. Therefore, a row is "affected" even though there is no content in the table.

☒ **A,** "0" and "(1 row(s) affected)", is incorrect because the absence of a value for a numeric field is a null, not a zero. **C,** "(null)" and "(0 row(s) affected)", is wrong because this null counts as a record, so "zero records" are not returned. **D,** you will get an error because you need to specify a "*" when using DELETE, is incorrect because the "*" is not required in SQL Server, but it is required when using Delete in Access or in DAO.

33. ☑ **A, B, D, F.** Null constraints, PRIMARY KEY constraints, and DEFAULT constraints can all be added directly in the database. NULL and DEFAULT constraints can be modified by selecting the Column Properties view of tables in the diagram. The PRIMARY KEY is set by selecting the row(s) to be in the primary key and pressing the Set primary key toolbar button. **D,** FOREIGN KEY constraints, is correct because, although you can drag one field to another to establish a FOREIGN KEY constraint, a Create Relationship dialog will be presented with additional options.

☒ **C,** UNIQUE constraints, and **E,** CHECK constraints, are wrong because UNIQUE and CHECK constraints must be set through the Table Properties dialog box.

34. ☑ **A, B, C,** and **D.** All answers are correct. Format files are usually created by using the bcp utility and modified with a text editor as needed. A format file describes the contents of the data file so that you do not have to answer questions in interactive mode. The file contains stored responses created using the bcp utility on the same table or view.

35. ☑ **C.** Create a query including this formula in the GROUP BY clause and the SELECT clause. Although GROUP BY is frequently performed on a field in the source table, it is also possible to use GROUP BY on a formula calculated on a field. To do this the calculation must also exist in the SELECT clause.

    ☒ **A,** create a view that includes this formula in the SELECT clause, and then create a query that references this view, using GROUP BY on your computed column, and **B,** create a subquery that includes this formula in the SELECT clause, and then in the parent query use GROUP BY on this computed column, both require extra steps and so are not the simplest approaches **D,** create a query including this formula in the GROUP BY clause but not in the SELECT clause, would fail because you need to include this formula in both the SELECT clause and the GROUP BY clause.

36. ☑ **B.** The correct option to use is ROLLBACK TRANSACTION. As in any other situation, when you need to leave the database in the state it was in before making modifications, you can issue a ROLLBACK TRANSACTION statement to undo the current transaction.
    ☒ **A,** END TRANSACTION, **C,** CLOSE TRANSACTION, and **D,** HALT TRANSACTION, are incorrect because they are not valid Transact-SQL statements.

37. ☑ **B.** To execute a DTS package stored in the msdb database of a SQL Server you must provide the name of the server, a valid SQL Server login with permissions to execute the package, the correct password associated with the SQL Server login, the name of the package, and the password on the package if one has been set.
    ☒ **A** is incorrect because it is an example of how to execute a DTS package from a COM-structured storage file. **C** is an example of how to execute a DTS package from the Microsoft Repository. **D** will result in a syntax error because you have not specified enough options to run a DTS package from any location.

38. ☑ **B.** Six records are returned. When you add WITH ROLLUP to the end of a query that has only one field in the GROUP BY, there will be only one record added to the query, and this record will contain the sum of all the other records. (In fact, even though WITH CUBE normally returns more records than WITH ROLLUP, when there is only one column in the GROUP BY clause, the number of records returned is the same for both functions.)

☒   **A,** 36, would be the answer if adding WITH ROLLUP squared the number of records returned. **C,** 5, might be the answer if no record was added by WITH ROLLUP, or if it added it on a separate line like COMPUTE. **D,** 0, might be true if the query returned no content.

39. ☑   **A.** The correct answer is to issue the command in **A.** By default support for nested triggers is enabled. To disable support for nested triggers, you need to set the server option called "nested triggers" to 0.
☒   **B,** sp_configure 'nested triggers', 1, is incorrect because this command enables support for nested triggers. **C,** sp_configure 'cascaded triggers', 0, and **D,** sp_configure 'cascaded triggers', 1, are incorrect because there is no server option called "cascaded triggers."

40. ☑   **A, B.** SET ANSI_NULLS ON ensures that the way NULLs are treated in comparisons conforms to the ANSI SQL-92 standard by ensuring that a comparison of anything to NULL returns FALSE, including NULL itself, whether the comparison is equal or not equal. SET ANSI_NULL_DFLT_ON ensures that the default nullibility state of a column is set to allow NULLs.
☒   **C** is incorrect because SET ANSI_NULLS OFF allows comparisons of NULL=NULL to be true. **D** is incorrect because SET ANSI_NULL_DFLT_OFF will set the default nullibility state of a column to NOT NULL.

41. ☑   **C.** When using CUBE, it can be difficult to distinguish between Nulls used as a category from the source data, and Nulls used for rows added by the CUBE field. When you add the "Grouping" function to the select list, it returns a "1" for the records that are added by rollup for that field. Therefore, if a Null is on the same line as a "0", your user knows that it is an aggregated category; if it is on the same line as a "1", it is the CUBE total. (This same approach also applies for ROLLUP.)
☒   The other three functions listed—"Filternulls" (**A**), "CubeID" (**B**), and "Cube(x) is false" (**D**)—are all fictional, so all of these answers are wrong.

42. ☑   **A,** CREATE TRIGGER, **C,** DENY, and **D,** GRANT, are all correct answers. Certain types of SQL statements are not allowed in the body of a trigger. For example, you cannot grant or deny permissions to objects within a trigger, so the GRANT and DENY statements are not allowed. You are also not allowed to create new database objects within a trigger, so pretty much any statement starting with CREATE is off limits.

☒   **B,** UPDATE, is the only wrong answer. You are allowed to issue an UPDATE statement within the body of a trigger.

43. ☑   **C.** 30.0MB. The DBCC SHRINKDATABASE cannot shrink the database below the original size of the database, even if that means that the 25 percent free-space target will not be achieved.

☒   **A,** 20.0MB, is wrong because the statement requested at least 25 percent free space remains. **B,** 26.6MB, is not correct because, even though this size gives 25 percent free space, it is below the original size of the database. **D,** 127.5MB, is wrong because the parameter, 25, requires a target percentage of free space remaining, not the percentage the database is to shrink.

44. ☑   **B.** Moving the history tables to their own filegroup on another drive will increase the performance of both the order-entry application and the accounting department queries. However, backup performance will not be increased without reducing that backup frequency of the history filegroup or adding new backup devices.

☒   **A, C,** and **D** are incorrect because the plan meets the primary and one secondary goal.

45. ☑   **A.** The average page density is high at 99.28 percent. This reduces the number of pages that need to be read when doing reporting at the expense of poorer transaction processing performance. The fragmentation in the table is minimal because the scan density is 100 percent and the logical and extant scan fragmentation percentages are near zero.

☒   **B** is incorrect because the table will have best performance in a reporting environment. A lower page density is preferable in a transaction processing environment because having free space on each page will allow more records to be added without causing pages to split. **C** and **D** are wrong because fragmentation is minimal.

Test Yourself:
Database Design
Practice Exam 2
(Exam 70-029)

Q&A

This Test Yourself section will help you measure your readiness to take the Designing and Implementing Databases with Microsoft SQL Server 7.0 exam (#70-029). See if you can complete this test under "exam conditions," before you check any of the answers. Read all the choices carefully, as there may be more than one correct answer.

Database Design Practice Exam 2 Test Yourself Questions

1. You need to create a nonclustered index on the following three fields: Subject, Author, and Publisher. The Subject column has a moderate degree of selectivity, the Author column has a high degree of selectivity, and the Publisher column has a low degree of selectivity. What would be the best order for the columns in the index to be in?

   A. Subject, Author, Publisher
   B. Publisher, Author, Subject
   C. Author, Subject, Publisher
   D. Publisher, Subject, Author

2. You are creating a query using COMPUTE to provide subtotals of your sales at two levels—per salesperson and for the whole organization. The first two lines of your query are as follows:

   ```
   SELECT empid, sales From sales
   ORDER BY empid
   ```

   Which of the following queries would provide the desired rollups?

   A. COMPUTE Sum(sales) BY EmpID, Sum(Sales)
   B. COMPUTE Sum(sales) BY EmpID
      COMPUTE Sum(sales)
   C. COMPUTE Sum(sales), Sum(sales) BY EmpID
   D. COMPUTE Sum(sales)
      COMPUTE Sum(sales) BY EmpID

3. You are the only owner of a table that many people work with. You are constantly receiving requests to create, drop, or update triggers on the table. You decide that it would be much easier if others had the ability to do these tasks. Who is allowed to work with the triggers on your table?

A. DBA

B. Database owner

C. Database owner and anyone to whom the owner has granted permission

D. NT Network Administrators

4. A trainee programmer has brought you a Transact-SQL batch he has been preparing because he can't understand why it doesn't work. What is wrong with the following batch?

```
USE Northwind
GO -- This procedure is on the Northwind Traders sample database

CREATE TABLE Sales_Summary
     (ProductID    INT      NOT NULL,
      Number       INT      NOT NULL,
      Cost         MONEY    NOT NULL)

INSERT Sales_Summary
    SELECT    ProductID,
              Sum(Quantity),
              Sum(Quantity * UnitPrice * (1-Discount))
    FROM      [Order Details]
    GROUP BY ProductID

SELECT * FROM Sales_Summary

DROP TABLE Sales_Summary     GO  --Drop the table to clean up
```

A. A GO statement is required between creating the table and inserting the data.

B. A GO statement is required between inserting data into the table and selecting data from the table.

C. A GO statement is required between selecting data from the table and dropping the table.

D. The GO statement following the DROP statement must appear on a separate line.

5. You want to make a nonclustered index as fast as possible for *SELECT* queries that find a specific value. What can you do to the index to make the *SELECT* queries as fast as possible?

A. Put the index on a different segment that is managed by a different hard disk controller.

B. Rebuild it daily with a fill factor of 100.

C. Create the index with the *UNIQUE* keyword.

D. All of the above

6. You create a query to report the real estate agents who have sold the most houses for the month. You receive complaints that although the 10 records returned by your query are not in error, your report excludes agents who should also be on the list. Which of the following is least likely to begin your existing query?

A. Select top 10 matching...

B. Select all top 10...

C. Select top 10 percent...

D. Select top 10 with ties...

7. Which of the following statements about triggers is not a true statement?

A. A table can have multiple triggers of a given type provided they have different names.

B. A table can have multiple triggers with the same name as long as they are of different types.

C. Each trigger can apply to only one table.

D. A single trigger can apply to all three user actions (UPDATE, INSERT, and DELETE).

8. You are developing an application that will allow limited ad hoc access to your database. You would like to obtain a list of tables for which the current user has permissions. You don't want the user to know about tables for which he doesn't have permissions. What is the best method of obtaining this list of tables?

A. Run SP_HELP and select objects with a type of user table.

B. Run a query against the system table, sysobjects, selecting all objects with an xtype of U.

C. Run a query against the INFORMATION_SCHEMA.TABLES view.

D. Run SP_HELP_CATEGORY with a category parameter of Table.

9. In order to distribute the processing load, your primary SQL Server replicates all the data in *tblSales* to a second reporting database. The second database has several more indexes on it to provide better performance for the users. When you look at the size of the table the primary SQL Server's copy of *tblSales*, however, you see that it is much larger than the one in the reporting database. What is the probable reason for this?

A. The fill factor on *tblSales* in the primary SQL Server is 100 and on the reporting SQL Server is 50.

B. The fill factor on *tblSales* in the primary SQL Server is 50 and on the reporting SQL Server is 100.

C. *PAD_INDEX* was used on the primary SQL Server but not used on the reporting SQL Server.

D. *PAD_INDEX* was not used on the primary SQL Server but was used on the reporting SQL Server.

10. Due to security concerns, you have been asked to evaluate all of your most commonly used queries to determine if you can implement them as views. Which of the following queries could be implemented in their current form as views? (Choose all that apply.)

A. `SELECT @@CONNECTIONS as Connections, GetDate() AS CurrentDate`

B. ```
SELECT Type, Amount, TransactionDate
FROM tbl1999Transactions
UNION
SELECT Type, Amount, TransactionDate
FROM tbl2000Transactions
```

C. ```
SELECT 71 as SalesType, SalesAmount, SalesDate
FROM tblSales
WHERE SalesDate > "8/3/90"
```

D. ```
SELECT SUM(SalesAmount), SalesDate
FROM tblSales
GROUP BY SalesDate
HAVING SUM(SalesAmount)>1000000
```

**11.** You have a very large table with a delete trigger. You would like to delete all of the records in the table, but you do not want to wait for the delete trigger to fire for every record. How can you delete the data without the trigger firing?

A. Drop the table and recreate it.
B. Truncate the table.
C. Drop the trigger and recreate it after the delete.
D. All of the above

**12.** After lengthy analysis, you decide to drop index idx_MAP on tblWorld with the following statement:

```
DROP INDEX tblWorld.idx_MAP
```

An error occurs, and the index is not dropped. Why would the index not be dropped?
```

A. idx_MAP is a clustered index.

B. The index was created to implement either a *PRIMARY KEY* or *UNIQUE* constraint.

C. A query is accessing the index, making it impossible to drop.

D. The index contains the column that is the *ROWGUIDCOL* for the table.

13. You are trying to define the change control management procedures for database objects in your company. You would like to use the ALTER VIEW statement as the standard way to modify the existing views. Which of the following could you **not** do with the ALTER VIEW statement?

A. Add criteria enforcement with CHECK OPTION.

B. Change the number of columns in the view.

C. Make an unencrypted view encrypted.

D. Change the name of the view.

14. You have decided to implement stored procedures for some common SQL statements that you use. These SQL statements' results and actions are often dictated by parameters that come in a variety of different datatypes. Which of the following datatypes can you use for input parameters?

A. Text

B. Image

C. Cursor

D. nvarchar

15. You have a large table and each night, with *DELETEs*, you purge a great deal of data that is no longer needed. What can you do to counteract any adverse effects from these *DELETEs*?

A. Run *UPDATE STATISTICS* after the *DELETEs*.

B. Rebuild all the indexes after the *DELETEs* with *DBCC REINDEX*.

C. Rebuild all the indexes after the *DELETEs* with *DROP_EXISTING*.

D. All of the above

16. Your sales data is kept in a series of tables that share an identical structure and are grouped by month. The December sales data is kept in a table called tblDecember1999, and the January sales data is kept in a table called tblJanuary2000. You have created a view of all the sales data in the following manner:

```
CREATE VIEW vewSalesData
AS
SELECT * FROM tblDecember1997
UNION
......... .
UNION
SELECT * FROM tblJanuary2000
```

What are the limitations of using a view like this? (Choose all that apply.)

A. You cannot perform UPDATEs and INSERTs through the view.

B. The data must be on the same server.

C. Searches will have to scan each table serially.

D. Searches will not be able to use the indexes on the table.

17. You have a stored procedure that is called by another stored procedure, and you would like to have the parent stored procedure be able to understand whether the child stored procedure executed as it thought it was supposed to. How can the child stored procedure pass information to the parent stored procedure? (Choose all that apply.)

A. Output parameters

B. Return codes

C. Status parameters

D. rv_sendmsg

18. In order to reconcile the books, Corporate Finance needs to have all the VendorIDs, LineItemAmounts from tblBill where DateReceived is greater than "4/20/1999," and all the descriptions of the vendors stored in tblVendor along with the appropriate VendorID. Which of the following queries will give you the correct results? (Choose all that apply.)

A. SELECT *
   FROM tblBill, tblVendor
   WHERE DateReceived > "4/20/1999"

B. SELECT VendorID, LineItemAmount, Description
   WHERE DateReceived > "4/20/1999"
   AND tblVendor.VendorID = tblBill.VendorID

C. SELECT *
   FROM tblBill, tblVendor
   WHERE DateReceived > "4/20/1999"
   AND tblVendor.VendorID = tblBill.VendorID

D. SELECT tblVendor.VendorID, tblBill.LineItemAmount, tblVendor.Description
   FROM tblBill
   WHERE DateReceived > "4/20/1999"
   AND tblVendor.VendorID = tblBill.VendorID

19. Views are great security mechanisms, and you want to implement them in your database. What are some of the limitations of using views as the primary interface to the data in your database?

A. Views cannot take advantage of full-text indexes.

B. You cannot bcp data out of the database from a view.

C. ODBC connections cannot be used in conjunction with views.

D. All of the above

20. The database administrator has just created a global temporary stored procedure, ##PUBS_SelectAuthor, for you. You have executed it a few times in the PUBS database, and it seems to be getting the results that you want, so you decide to look at the source for it with sp_helptext. You get the following error message:

Server: Msg 15009, Level 16, State 1, Procedure sp_helptext, Line 52
The object '##PUBS_SelectAuthor' does not exist in database 'pubs'.

Why can't SQL Server find the procedure?

A. You cannot run sp_helptext on a temporary stored procedure.

B. ##PUBS_SelectAuthor was created with the encryption option.

C. ##PUBS_SelectAuthor resides in tempdb.

D. ##PUBS_SelectAuthor was created with the recompile option.

21. Current Situation: You capture a great deal of information about your company's clients, including their address, phone number, and sales history, through a VIP program where you offer them discounts.
Required Result: Send out a customer satisfaction questionnaire to 10% of the participants in the VIP program.
Optional Desired Results: Ensure that if another customer satisfaction questionnaire is done the same VIP members are not solicited again, and do not alter the structure of any existing database tables.
Proposed Solution: Select the participants from the VIP table using the TOP 10 PERCENT clause in the SELECT, and use the SELECT INTO syntax to move all the VIP_Ids (the primary key) into a table that can be referenced in the future.
Which results does the proposed solution produce?

A. The proposed solution produces the required result and produces both of the optional results.

B. The proposed solution produces the required result and produces only one of the optional results.

C. The proposed solution produces the required result but does not produce any of the optional desired results.

D. The proposed solution does not produce the required result.

22. Your company did not have a formal IS department, but instead had developers assigned to each department. As a consequence, there were no uniform naming schemes for database objects. Recently, it has been decided that your company would be best served to pull all the developers from the disparate departments into an official IS department. A uniform database scheme has been decided on, and all the views that you administer now must be prefixed with "vw_". Which of the following will allow you to rename the existing views?

A. Use sp_rename to rename the views.

B. DROP the views and recreate them with the CREATE VIEW.

C. Use ALTER VIEW to change the name.

D. Use sp_depends to rename the views.

23. You have decided to implement stored procedures for some common SQL statements that you use. These SQL statements' results are often singleton record sets that would be best replaced with output parameters. Which of the following datatypes can you use for output parameters?

A. Text

B. Image

C. Cursor

D. nvarchar

24. You are thinking about adding a new office supplier for your organization. As part of your analysis, you would like to generate a list of all your branches with all the new suppliers' offices that are in the same city. Which of the following would do that? (Choose all that apply.)

A.
```
SELECT tblBranch.Name, IsNull(tblNewSupplier.Address,"NONE")
FROM tblBranch RIGHT JOIN tblNewSupplier
ON tblBranch.City = tblNewSupplier.City
```

B.
```
SELECT tblBranch.Name, IsNull(tblNewSupplier.Address,"NONE")
FROM tblBranch LEFT JOIN tblNewSupplier
ON tblBranch.City = tblNewSupplier.City
```

C.
```
SELECT tblBranch.Name, IsNull(tblNewSupplier.Address,"NONE")
FROM tblNewSupplier RIGHT JOIN tblBranch
ON tblBranch.City = tblNewSupplier.City
```

D.
```
SELECT tblBranch.Name, IsNull(tblNewSupplier.Address,"NONE")
FROM tblNewSupplier LEFT JOIN tblBranch
ON tblBranch.City = tblNewSupplier.City
```

25. The business analyst has decided that if no sales representative has been indicated on an order, the sale should be credited to a default sales representative record in your database called "Cash Sale." The SalesRepID for "Cash Sale" is 9999. There are no other columns in the database that require this default. What is the best way to implement this requirement for SQL Server 7.0?

   A. Create a default called default_salesrep of 9999 and bind it to the SalesRepID column of the OrderHeader table.

   B. Define the SalesRepID column in the OrderHeader table as NOT NULL and inform the user interface programmer that she has to set the SalesRepID to 9999 before passing it to the database if it is left blank.

   C. Add a DEFAULT Constraint to the SalesRepID column in the OrderHeader table with a constant of 9999.

   D. Add an INSERT and UPDATE trigger that will change SalesRepID in the OrderHeader table to 9999 if it is NULL.

26. You have just created a temporary stored procedure in the query analyzer. After you are satisfied with it, you open a new query analyzer window in the same database and attempt to run it. You get the following error message:

```
Server: Msg 2812, Level 16, State 62, Line 1
Could not find stored procedure '#My_StoredProcedure'.
```

Why can't SQL Server find the procedure?

   A. You did not grant yourself permissions to the stored procedure.

   B. Local temporary stored procedures are not accessible outside of the connection that created them.

   C. Global temporary stored procedures are not accessible outside of the connection that created them.

   D. All temporary stored procedures can be accessed only in the batch that created them, and when that batch is completed, they are dropped.

27. A subquery is a query nested in a SELECT, INSERT, UPDATE, or DELETE statement, and it can appear anywhere an expression can appear.

A correlated subquery is a special type of subquery. Which of the following is true about correlated subqueries?

A. They cannot be resolved independently of the main query.
B. The subquery is executed repeatedly, once for each row that might be selected by the outer query.
C. They depend on the outer query for their values.
D. All of the above

28. Your company is implementing territories for its sales representatives because of complaints about representatives poaching sales from other representatives' existing clients. The Territory table consists of a long integer identifier that serves as the primary key and a variable character column for the description. You want to ensure that descriptions are not duplicated in the table. What type of constraint should you implement to enforce this business rule?

A. A DEFAULT constraint that will add a serial number if a duplicate is added
B. A UNIQUE constraint that will reject a duplicate entry
C. A CHECK constraint that will reject a duplicate entry
D. A NULL constraint that will change a duplicate entry to NULL

29. You have an 800MB text file that contains raw data. You are able to import this data only during a scheduled maintenance window, so the data needs to be imported into SQL Server as quickly as possible. Which method would you choose to import the data?

A. Bulk Copy Program
B. SQL Enterprise Manager
C. SQL DTS
D. BULK INSERT

30. You have just merged with another company that has hired a lot of your employees in the past. You have imported their employee tables into your database, and you have notice that they store the employees SSN without the dashes and you store it with the dashes. You would like to make a list of all their employees, with a "*" next to the name if they used to be one of your employees.

A. ```
SELECT tblEmployee.Name
FROM tblACMEEmployee RIGHT JOIN tblEmployee
ON tblEmployee.SSN = LEFT(tblACMEEmployee.SSN,3) + '-' +
SUBSTRING(tblACMEEmployee.SSN,4,2) + RIGHT(tblACMEEmployee.SSN,4)
```

B. ```
SELECT tblEmployee.Name
FROM tblEmployee LEFT JOIN tblACMEEmployee
ON tblEmployee.SSN = LEFT(tblACMEEmployee.SSN,3) + '-' +
SUBSTRING(tblACMEEmployee.SSN,4,2) + RIGHT(tblACMEEmployee.SSN,4)
```

C. ```
SELECT tblEmployee.Name
FROM tblACMEEmployee RIGHT JOIN tblEmployee
ON LEFT(tblEmployee.SSN,3) + SUBSTRING(tblACMEEmployee.SSN,5,2) +
RIGHT(tblACMEEmployee.SSN,4) = tblACMEEmployee.SSN
```

D. ```
SELECT tblEmployee.Name
FROM tblEmployee LEFT JOIN tblACMEEmployee
ON LEFT(tblEmployee.SSN,3) + SUBSTRING(tblACMEEmployee.SSN,5,2) +
RIGHT(tblACMEEmployee.SSN,4) = tblACMEEmployee.SSN
```

31. Constraint checking can be turned off when modifying a table's constraints in order to improve performance by skipping the step of ensuring that current data passes the constraint. Which of the following statements are true about turning off constraint checking when adding or modifying constraints? (Choose all that apply.)

A. Constraint checking can be disabled when adding a UNIQUE constraint.

B. Constraint checking can be disabled when adding or modifying a FOREIGN KEY constraint.

C. Constraint checking can be disabled when adding or modifying a CHECK constraint.

D. Constraint checking must be reenabled by using the CHECK CONSTRAINT clause of the ALTER TABLE command.

32. The BCP utility offers an interactive mode that will prompt you for information concerning the fields of data you are working with. In interactive mode, what pieces of information will the utility ask you for?

A. Field length

B. File size

C. File storage type

D. File location

33. All your documents are stored in tblDocuments. You have configured tblDocuments for Full Text Search. You would like the search to bring back documents that match the meaning of what the user is looking for, but not necessarily the exact wording. Which predicate would allow you to do these fuzzy searches? (Choose all that apply.)

A. CONTAINS

B. CONTAINSTABLE

C. FREETEXT

D. FREETEXTTABLE

34. Your company has purchased a new accounting package that uses SQL Server 7.0 as its database. The accounting database will be installed on the same SQL Server as your application's database. Your manager would like you to take advantage of the new database by using the accounting database's chart of accounts to validate accounting transactions generated from your application. Is it possible to implement this as a constraint and why?

A. Yes. You can link the chart of accounts to your database and create a FOREIGN KEY constraint to the linked table.

B. Yes. You can create a FOREIGN KEY constraint by providing the fully qualified, four-part name of the chart of accounts table.

C. No. The database is residing on the same server so it isn't foreign, so you can't use a FOREIGN KEY constraint.

D. No. FOREIGN KEY constraints can refer only to tables in the same database.

35. One of the greatest enhancements of SQL Server 7.0 is support for linked servers. There are many advantages of SQL linked servers over previous methods of distribution like ODS gateways and remote stored procedures. Which of the following is not an advantage of linked servers?

A. Common access point for heterogeneous data sources

B. Distributed queries against heterogeneous data sources

C. Common interface to heterogeneous data sources

D. Integrated security with the Windows NT operating system

36. You work for a small chain of hardware stores, and you have created a table called Inventory that provides the number of parts in stock for all the items you sell. The information is stored in the field "QTY", which is an Int field. You have eight records in this table, and in the QTY field the eight values are as follows: 5, 5, 5, 5, 10, 10, 10, and NULL. What is the result of the following query?

```
SELECT avg(qty) from Inventory
```

A. 6

B. 6.25

C. 7 (true)

D. 7.142857

37. You have decided to use Social Security Number as a UNIQUE constraint for your employee table to ensure that duplicate employees are not entered. What type of data integrity have you been asked to provide?

A. User-defined integrity

B. Entity integrity

C. Referential integrity

D. Domain integrity

38. Recently you have created a number of Data Transformation Services (DTS) packages. These packages are fairly complex, and you do not want to lose them. A backup is in order. Which of the following databases should you backup?

A. master

B. model

C. msdb

D. tempdb

39. You work for an HMO, and you are checking up on licensing requirements for out-of-town doctors. Because all doctors who became doctors this decade received the needed training in medical school, you create the following query to see how many doctors you have to research:

```
SELECT DoctorID, count(DoctorID) AS TotalDoctors
FROM HealthCareProviders
WHERE GradDate < '1/1/90'
ORDER BY city, state
GROUP BY state, city HAVING city <> 'Cleveland'
```

Unfortunately, when you try to run this query, you get an error. Why doesn't this query work?

A. You included a clause in HAVING that is not in GROUP BY.

B. You need to put the ORDER BY clause after the HAVING clause.

C. You need to change the single quotes used to delimit the date to pound signs.

D. You cannot have the ORDER BY sort in a different order than the two different GROUP BY fields.

40. There are a number of conditions that determine how long it takes for a trigger to execute. Which of the following conditions is likely to have the most impact on the execution time of a trigger?

A. The location of the trigger

B. The location of the target table

C. The length of the trigger

D. The type of trigger

41. Data Transformation Services (DTS) is one of the most powerful new tools in SQL 7.0. A company may gain many benefits by using DTS. Which of the following would be valid uses of DTS?

    A. Build data warehouses and data marts in Microsoft SQL Server by importing and transferring data from multiple heterogeneous sources on a regularly scheduled basis.
    B. Create custom transformation objects that can be integrated into third-party products.
    C. Access applications using third-party OLE DB providers. This allows applications for which an OLE DB provider exists to be used as sources and destinations of data.
    D. All of the above

42. One of your users wants you to create a CUBE query to provide total sales. He wants you to provide the most dimensions of data you can. If you are providing totals for only one column (sales), what is the maximum number of fields you can include in your SELECT clause?

    A. 12
    B. 11
    C. 10
    D. 9

43. You are creating an UPDATE trigger. You can specify that the trigger should fire when which of the following objects is updated?

    A. Row
    B. Column
    C. Table
    D. Database

44. Addresses will appear frequently in a series of new databases. You would like to have a consistent method of dealing with zip codes that can be reused.

Your primary goal is consistent data definition for zip codes. Secondarily, you want the definition to be reusable across databases and also would like definition constrained to only five digits, followed by a dash and four more digits. You decide to create a user-defined data type as follows:

```
USE model
GO
EXEC sp_ADDTYPE zipcode, 'varchar(10)', 'NOT NULL'
```

What is the result of your plan?

A. The plan achieves all your goals.

B. The plan achieves your primary and one secondary goal.

C. The plan achieves your primary, but neither secondary, goal.

D. The plan doesn't achieve the primary goal.

45. The transaction log is integral to meeting the requirement that a relational database management system be able to recover all data to a known point of consistency in the event of a failure. What is the order of events in the log process?

A. Data pages are loaded into memory. The modification is written to the data page, the modification is written to the log. The data page is written back to disk. The log is marked with a checkpoint that the modification was committed.

B. Data pages are loaded into memory. The modification is recorded in the log. The modification is made to the data page in memory. The transaction is marked as committed in the log. The checkpoint process writes the committed transaction to disk.

C. The modification is written to the log. The data page is loaded into memory. The log is marked as being committed. The modification is written to disk. The log is marked with a checkpoint to confirm that the data was written.

D. Data is written to the log. Data is written to disk. The log is marked that the data has been committed to disk.

Database Design Practice Exam 2 Test Yourself Answers

1. ☑ **C. Author, Subject, Publisher.** You should always order the columns in a nonclustered index from the most exclusive to the least exclusive because this will help SQL Server find the correct data faster.

   ☒ **B,** Publisher, Author, Subject, is incorrect because it starts with the least selective field, Publishers. **D,** Publisher, Subject, Author, is incorrect because it also starts with the least selective field. **A,** Subject, Author, Publisher, is incorrect because it starts with the Subject column, which has only a moderate degree of selectivity.

2. ☑ **B.** One advantage of COMPUTE over ROLLUP is that you can have more precision over which columns are rolled up. While ROLLUP simply provides these totals for all the columns listed in the GROUP BY clause, you can include or exclude levels by adding as many COMPUTE statements as you need. These clauses, however, must be in ascending order of hierarchy, as shown in **B.**

   ☒ When you put multiple parameters on the same COMPUTE line, they report at the same level of hierarchy, so **A,** COMPUTE Sum(sales) BY EmpID, Sum(Sales), and **C,** COMPUTE Sum(sales), Sum(sales) BY EmpID, are wrong. **D,** COMPUTE Sum(sales) and COMPUTE Sum(sales) BY EmpID, is wrong because the highest level of hierarchy should be last.

3. ☑ **B.** Only the database owner has permission to create and drop triggers on a table. The only way that you can allow your coworkers to make changes to the triggers on a table is to make them database owners.

   ☒ **A,** DBA, is incorrect because DBA is not a role in SQL Server; it is a generic term used to refer to someone who administers a database server. **C,** database owner and anyone to whom the owner has granted permission, is incorrect because there is no trigger permission that can be granted or revoked. **D,** NT Network Administrators, is incorrect because the NT

Administrators group does not have any permissions within SQL Server by default.

4. ☑ **D.** The GO statement cannot appear on the same line as other Transact-SQL statements. Comments can appear on the same line as the GO statement.
☒ **A** and **C** are incorrect because SQL Server 7.0 implements deferred name resolution so that DDL statements and other statement that refer to the same objects can appear in the same batch. These additional GO statements are required in a SQL Server 6.5 database. **B** is incorrect because a GO statement is not required between DML statements in a batch.

5. ☑ **D.** All of the above is correct. If you put the index on a different segment than the data, you can read from both disks at the same time. A fill factor of 100 will make all the data pages full, so fewer disk reads have to be committed to scan the entire index. If all the values in the index are unique, SQL Server should be able to pinpoint the exact value faster.

6. ☑ **D.** When you use TOP, you instruct SQL Server to truncate the result set after the designated number of records. If you have multiple records that have the same value for that bottom slot, some of the records will be excluded. The WITH TIES syntax will include records that had the same values as the lowest qualifying record. (This means that you will not be able to predict the number of records the query will return.)
☒ There is no "matching" predicate, so **A,** Select top 10 matching..., is wrong. Using the "All" alters the behavior of GROUP BY, not Top, so **B,** Select all top 10..., is wrong. The ties issue applies whether you use it for number of records or percent, so **C,** Select top 10 percent..., is wrong.

7. ☑ **B.** A table can have multiple triggers with the same name as long as they are of different types. Every trigger must have a unique name. Triggers cannot have the same name even if they are of different types. If you create a new trigger in SQL Enterprise Manager with the same name as an existing

trigger, the existing trigger will be replaced with the new trigger. If you are using T-SQL, you will need to drop the trigger before creating a new trigger with the same name.

☒ **A**, a table can have multiple triggers of a given type provided they have different names, **C**, each trigger can apply to only one table, and **D**, a single trigger can apply to all three user actions, are incorrect because they are true statements about triggers.

8. ☑ **C.** INFORMATION_SCHEMA.TABLES is a view conforming to the ANSI SQL standard for information schema. It will return the same information, even if future versions of SQL Server change the underlying system tables.

☒ **A** is incorrect because SP_HELP returns multiple record sets and requires a second query to extract the table names. **B** is incorrect because the system tables may change in a future version of SQL Server, breaking the application. **D** is incorrect because SP_HELP_CATEGORY gives information about jobs, alerts, and operators, not about database objects.

9. ☑ **B.** The fill factor on *tblSales* in the primary SQL Server is 50 and on the reporting SQL Server is 100. A lower fill factor on a clustered index will cause the table to take up a great deal more space because the clustered index controls the layout of the data on a SQL Server table.

☒ **A**, the fill factor on *tblSales* in the primary SQL Server is 100 and on the reporting SQL Server is 50, is incorrect because the primary SQL Server has the higher fill factor, which would make it smaller, not larger, than the reporting database. **C**, *PAD_INDEX* was used on the primary SQL Server but not used on the reporting SQL Server, and **D**, *PAD_INDEX* was not used on the primary SQL Server but was used on the reporting SQL Server, are both incorrect. A different PAD_INDEX value should not cause a huge discrepancy in the size of a table relative to the fill factor.

10. ☑ **A, B,** and **C** are all correct. **A** is a view consisting of a system variable and SQL function; both are valid in views. This view would not be able to be updated because none of the columns' source is a field in a table. For a column in a view to be updateable, it must be from a table and unaltered by

the view. **B** is a view created from partitioned data. You implement these types of views using the UNION keyword to join tables that have similar columns. You could not perform UPDATEs, INSERTs, or DELETEs on views that are constructed like the one in **B**. **C** is a straightforward view, but with a constant in the SELECT list. This is acceptable as long as the constant has been given a column name. In this case, the column has been given the name "SalesType", and the SalesType column will always have the value of 71.

☒ **D** is incorrect because there is no column name for SUM(SalesAmount) column. All fields in a view's select list must have a unique column name.

11. ☑ **D**. All of the above options would accomplish your goal. Dropping the table or the trigger and recreating them will work, but probably are not the ideal solution because permissions will have to be reset. Truncating the table is the preferred method. Truncation is a very fast operation; it does not require permissions to be reapplied, and delete triggers do not fire when a table is truncated.

12. ☑ **B**. An index was created to implement either a *PRIMARY KEY* or *UNIQUE* constraint and can be dropped only with an *ALTER TABLE* statement. The *ALTER TABLE* must be used so that the constraint would be dropped before the index.

☒ **A**, idx_MAP is a clustered index, is incorrect because you can drop a clustered index that is not on a constraint, just as you would drop any other index. **C**, a query is accessing the index, making it impossible to drop, is incorrect because the *DROP INDEX* would not fail; it would just wait until the query had finished. **D**, the index contains the column that is the *ROWGUIDCOL* for the table, is wrong because whether or not a column in the index is the *ROWGUIDCOL* will not affect your ability to drop it with a *DROP* statement.

13. ☑ **D**. You cannot change the name of a view with the ALTER VIEW statement. In order to change the name of a view, you must drop it and recreate it, or use the sp_rename stored procedure.

☒ **A,** add criteria enforcement with CHECK OPTION, is incorrect because you *can* alter, add, or remove the CHECK OPTION from a view. If you do not specify CHECK OPTION in the ALTER VIEW statement of a view that already has CHECK OPTION, CHECK OPTION will not be in force after the view is altered. **B,** change the number of columns in the view, is incorrect because you *can* change the number and type of the columns in a view with the ALTER VIEW statement. In fact, you can change the underlying query entirely. This may not be wise to do, however, because other stored procedures, views, and triggers may be depending on the existing columns of your view. **C,** make an unencrypted view encrypted, is incorrect because you *can* change an unencrypted view to an encrypted one and vice versa.

14. ☑ **A, B,** and **D.** Text, image, and nvarchar can all be used as datatypes for input parameters, but the text datatype cannot be used for variables that are output parameters.

☒ **C,** cursor, is incorrect because a cursor can be the datatype of an output parameter, but it cannot be used as an input parameter. If the output parameter is a cursor, the VARYING keyword must be used with it.

15. ☑ **D.** All of the above. The *DELETES* would make the index statistics out of date. SQL Server uses those statistics to determine which indexes to use in the queries, so if they are wrong, SQL Server may use the wrong indexes. If you updated the statistics for each of the indexes, SQL Server would have up-to-date statistics available to help it make decisions. If you rebuild the indexes, the statistics are updated for each index; in addition, the indexes would be defragmented, and their original fill factors could be reestablished. This would use more resources and may not be as practical in some environments, but rebuilding would provide more value than just updating statistics.

16. ☑ **A.** You cannot perform UPDATEs, INSERTs, or DELETEs to a partitioned view; you can only query it.

☒ **B,** the data must be on the same server, is incorrect because the data sources can be in different databases or even on different servers. This allows you to unify data that is kept in disparate locations. **C**, searches will have to scan each table serially, is incorrect because the main advantage of organizing your data into partitioned views is that the SQL Server can look at each needed underlying data source at the same time and run the necessary queries in parallel. **D**, searches will not be able to use the indexes on the table, is incorrect because queries that use views can use all the nonfull-text indexes on the data sources when they are queried. Full-text indexes and full-text searches cannot be performed through a view.

17. ☑   **A**, output parameters, and **B**, return codes, are correct. Both methods will allow a stored procedure that has been called by another stored procedure to pass information back to the calling procedure. Return codes are generally used to communicate this type of information. Return codes are already built into all stored procedures and are strongly typed; all stored procedures will issue a return code of 0 unless the stored procedure explicitly returns a different value, and a return code is always an int. An output parameter can be a number of different datatypes, which gives it a great deal of flexibility.

☒   **C**, status parameters, is incorrect because there is nothing called a status parameter; stored procedures have only input parameters and output parameters. **D**, srv_sendmsg, is incorrect because srv_sendmsg is an API call that allows communication from the server to the client, not from one stored procedure to another.

18. ☑   **C, D.** These will both gather all the VendorIDs and LineItemAmounts greater than 4/20/1999, and they both will return the correct description associated with the VendorID from tblVendor. C will return all fields from both tables; D will just return the VendorID, LineItemAmount, and Description. D takes the VendorID from tblVendor, not tblBill, which is correct because the where clause specified that the VendorIDs on the two tables had to be equal.

☒   **A** is incorrect because it does not join the tblBill to tblVendor on VendorID. Because they do not join, the results will be a Cartesian product between the bills that have been received after 4/22/99 and the Vendor descriptions. **B** is incorrect because both tables have a Vendor ID and you did not specify which one in the SELECT clause. If tblVendor.VendorID or tblBill.VendorID had been substituted in the SELECT clause, B would have been correct.

19. ☑ **A.** You cannot issue a full-text query against a view and, as a consequence, views do not take advantage of full-text indexes. If you need to perform full-text searches, then implementing views of your data is not an option.

☒ **B,** you cannot bcp data out of the database from a view, is incorrect because you can bulk copy data out of a view with bcp and, in some circumstances, you can bulk copy data into a view. **C,** ODBC connections cannot be used in conjunction with views, is incorrect because ODBC can be used in conjunction with a view in a manner very similar to using ODBC with a table. **D,** all of the above, is incorrect because both **B** and **C** are incorrect.

20. ☑ **C.** ##PUBS_SelectAuthor resides in tempdb. All temporary stored procedures reside in tempdb, and all of them can be run from any database context. If you want to see the source for the stored procedure, you have to run the sp_helptext stored procedure in tempdb.

☒ **A,** you cannot run sp_helptext on a temporary stored procedure, is incorrect because you can run sp_helptext on a temporary stored procedure; you just have to do it in tempdb. **B,** ##PUBS_SelectAuthor was created with the encryption option, is incorrect because if you had created the temporary stored procedure with encryption, you would have been provided with this message:

```
The object comments have been encrypted.
```

D, ##PUBS_SelectAuthor was created with the recompile option, is incorrect because the recompile option has nothing to do with whether a stored procedures source can be read. The recompile option dictates whether a stored procedure can use existing execution plans.

You create the following stored procedure:

```
CREATE PROCEDURE PUBS_BestAuthor
@au_id id OUTPUT
AS
SELECT @au_id = au_id
    FROM    Authors
WHERE TotalSales = (SELECT MAX(TotalSales) FROM Authors)

GO
```

21. ☑ **A.** The proposed solution produces the required result and both of the optional desired results. The TOP clause will allow you to grab either a percentage or an absolute number of records. By placing the records in a new table, you can join against it in the future and prevent duplicates from ever being sent out without modifying existing tables.

☒ **B and C** are incorrect because the proposed solution produces both of the optional results. **D** is incorrect because the proposed solution does produce the required result.

22. ☑ **A, B.** You can use the system stored procedure, sp_rename, to change the name of a database object such as table, column, stored procedure, or view. Using sp_rename will not force the dependent database objects to be recompiled. You will need to clear the procedure cache to ensure that all dependent objects are recompiled. Dropping and recreating the view in effect will rename the view and force all the dependent database objects to be recompiled the next time that they are executed.

☒ **C,** use ALTER VIEW to change the name, is incorrect because you cannot change the name of view with the ALTER VIEW statement. **D,** use sp_depends to rename the views, is incorrect because sp_depends cannot change the name of a view, but it can tell you what database objects depend on your view and what your view depends on.

23. ☑ **C and D.** Cursors, nvarchar, and any datatypes except text and image can be used as output parameters. If the output parameter is a cursor, the VARYING keyword must be used with it.

☒ **A**, text, and **B**, image, are incorrect because text and image parameters cannot be used as output parameters.

24. ☑ **B, C.** Both will work and are equivalent to each to other. **B** is written using a LEFT JOIN, whereas **C** flips the tables and is written as a RIGHT JOIN. A right or left outer join can always be flipped to be the other. tblBranch is the table from which we have to include all members, so if it is on the right, it needs to be a RIGHT OUTER JOIN. If it is on the left, it needs to be a LEFT OUTER JOIN.
☒ **A** and **D** are incorrect because the tables are on the wrong side for this outer join.

25. ☑ **C.** The preferred method of implementing a default in SQL Server 7.0 is by using a DEFAULT constraint. DEFAULT constraints may be bound directly to a column without having to execute a system stored procedure. They also have a lower processing overhead than defaults.
☒ **A**, create a default called default_salesrep of 9999 and bind it to the SalesRepID column of the OrderHeader table, **B**, define the SalesRepID column in the OrderHeader table as NOT NULL and have the user interface programmer set the SalesRepID to 9999 before passing it to the database, and **D**, add an INSERT and UPDATE trigger that will change SalesRepID in the OrderHeader table to 9999 if it is NULL, would all meet the requirement. **A** is incorrect because you have only one column that requires the default; therefore you don't need to incur the overhead of creating a default. **B** is incorrect because the database is not protected in case a new process is used to access your database. For instance, if your company decided to create an e-commerce Web site, the sales rep might not be set correctly. **D** is incorrect because a trigger would impose unnecessary overhead, slowing the transaction.

26. ☑ **B.** Local temporary stored procedures can be seen and used only within the connection that created them. Once the connection is terminated, so is the temporary stored procedure.

☒   **A,** you did not grant yourself permissions to the store procedure, is incorrect because the creator of a stored procedure implicitly has permissions to it and, even if you do not have permissions to it, you would still be able to see it. **C,** global temporary stored procedures are not accessible outside of the connection that created them, is incorrect because a global stored procedure is able to be seen and run outside its own connection. **D,** all temporary stored procedures can be accessed only in the batch that created them, and when that batch is completed, they are dropped, is incorrect because a local temporary stored procedure's lifetime is terminated when the connection that created it is terminated, not when the batch that creates it is finished.

27. ☑   **D.** All of the above are true. A correlated subquery is a special type of subquery that depends on the outer query for its values. An easy way of recognizing a correlated subquery is to look at the tables that the subquery references. If it uses any table that is not in its WHERE clause and is in the outer expression, it is a correlated subquery. Because of this it is dependent on the parent expression. An ordinary subquery can be executed by itself, but a correlated subquery can be executed only in the context of a parent query. An ordinary subquery is executed once and then the value is substituted into the outer query, but a correlated subquery must be executed repeatedly, once for each row that might be selected by the parent query.

28. ☑   **B.** A UNIQUE constraint will ensure that duplicate descriptions cannot be added to the descriptions column.
☒   **A,** a DEFAULT constraint that will add a serial number if a duplicate is added, is wrong because DEFAULT constraints must use constants or niladic functions. **C,** a CHECK constraint that will reject a duplicate entry, is wrong because CHECK constraints cannot check for duplicates. **D,** a NULL constraint that will change a duplicate entry to NULL, is wrong because a NULL constraint will allow NULLs in the database but will not change a value to NULL.

29. ☑ **A, D.** The BULK INSERT command is very similar to the BCP (Bulk Copy Program) utility. BCP is a little more cumbersome to work with because it is a command-line utility, but it may be slightly faster than BULK INSERT in some cases. You have the option of using the BULK INSERT command within a T-SQL transaction, allowing you to roll back all inserted rows if the BULK INSERT fails in any way. For the absolute fastest import possible, remember to turn logging off. With logging turned off, each insert is not written to the transaction log, which greatly reduces the amount of time needed to import the data.

    ☒ **B**, SQL Enterprise Manager, and **C**, SQL DTS, are incorrect in this case because we are interested in raw throughput. We're trying to insert as many rows as possible as fast as possible. These options are much easier to work with, but they are not as fast.

30. ☑ **A, B, C, D.** This query required either a left or right outer join, but it did not require one over the other; that was strictly your preference in implementing. It also required that you manipulate the field on which you will join. This is not the most efficient thing to do generally, but in this case it was required. Once again you could have manipulated either side to make a match. You had the choice of removing dashes from one or adding them to the other. Either way you had to use the basic string parsing functions in SQL: LEFT, RIGHT, and SUBSTRING. Note: LEFT was not available in SQL Server 6.5.

31. ☑ **B, C.** Constraint checking can be turned off when adding or modifying FOREIGN KEY and CHECK constraints only. Typically, you would turn off constraint checking for large tables whose existing data is known to comply or will not be updated. The WITH NOCHECK option of the ALTER TABLE command is used to specify that the new constraint is not to be evaluated against existing data when it is added. The constraint will be applied if any column in the record is modified.

    ☒ **A**, constraint checking can be disabled when adding a UNIQUE constraint, is wrong because data is always checked when PRIMARY KEY or UNIQUE constraints are added. **D**, constraint checking must be reenabled by using the CHECK CONSTRAINT clause of the ALTER TABLE command, is wrong because constraint checking is enabled immediately after a constraint is added or modified.

32. ☑ **A, C.** The utility will ask for field length and file storage type. If data is being copied between Microsoft SQL Server and other programs, such as another database program, the default data type formats (native, character, or Unicode) may not be compatible with the data structures expected by the other programs. Therefore, the BCP utility allows more detailed information regarding the structure of the data file to be specified. If the –n, –c, –w, or –N parameters are not specified, the BCP utility will prompt for further information. You will be prompted interactively for each column of data being copied. BCP prompts for file storage type, prefix length, field length, and field terminator.
☒ **B,** file size, and **D,** file location, are incorrect answers because BCP does not prompt for them.

33. ☑ **A, B, C, D.** All of them are capable of doing fuzzy searches, but the CONTAINS and CONTAINSTABLE will also let you do precise searches. CONTAINSTABLE and FREETEXTTABLE return tables that can be joined with other tables in a query, but FREETEXT and CONTAINS merely return TRUE or FALSE. This makes CONTAINS and FREETEXT easier to work with, but less powerful than their counterparts. The FREETEXT and FREETEXTTABLE predicates allow SQL Server to search the column based on how it parses the input. This is very useful for most searches because SQL Server will take any string and interpret how to search it, instead of having a programmer first parse the input and create an appropriate CONTAINS or CONTAINSTABLE predicate.

34. ☑ **D.** FOREIGN KEY constraints must refer to tables within the same database. In order to enforce referential integrity to another database, you would be required to use triggers.
☒ **A,** you can link the chart of accounts to your database and create a FOREIGN KEY constraint to the linked table, is wrong because linked

tables occur when you link to another server. The accounting database is on the same server. **B,** you can create a FOREIGN KEY constraint by providing the fully qualified, four-part name of the chart of accounts table, is wrong because you cannot use a fully qualified table name in the FOREIGN KEY constraint clause. **C,** the database is residing on the same server so it isn't foreign, is wrong because "foreign" in the context of FOREIGN KEY constraints is with respect to a primary key in a given database. It has nothing to do with the server on which the database resides.

35. ☑ **D.** Integrated security is a benefit of SQL Server itself, not an advantage of linked servers. When considering data security in a distributed environment, you may or may not be able to implement a centralized security scheme. It all depends on the security methods provided by the individual data sources. Data can be secured at the application level only (in which case you could have integrated Windows NT security), but a truly well-implemented security scheme secures data at the lowest possible level that does not interfere with legitimate data access.

 ☒ **A,** common access point for heterogeneous data sources, **B,** distributed queries against heterogeneous data sources, and **C,** common interface to heterogeneous data sources, are incorrect because they are advantages of linked servers.

36. ☑ **C.** There are eight records in the table, and the sum of the values is 50. Although we normally think of an "Average" as the sum of the entries divided by the number of those entries, in SQL Server the Avg function does not include Nulls when counting the number of records. Therefore, the sum is divided by seven, not by eight. The results are displayed in the same format as the parent column, so the actual average of 7.142857 (50/7) is displayed as 7.

 ☒ The answer would be **D,** 7.142857, if the value was not converted to the format of its parent column. It would be **B,** 6.25, if the null records were counted and the total was divided by 8; it would be **A,** 6, if the total was divided by 8 and then truncated.

37. ☑ **B.** Entity integrity (also known as table integrity) refers to the fact that each row of a table must have a unique identifier or primary key and that items in a row must relate to the primary key only. You are ensuring that a Social Security Number relates to only one primary key.

☒ **A,** user-defined integrity, is incorrect because this can correctly be classified as referential integrity. **C,** referential integrity, ensures that the relationship between the primary key in a referenced table and the foreign key in the referencing table is maintained. **D,** domain integrity (also known as column integrity), refers to the constraints on a value in a column either by data type, format, or range.

38. ☑ **C.** Do not forget to back up the msdb database whenever you make changes to the configuration of DTS packages or jobs. The msdb database is one of the most important databases on the system. SQL Server won't start without a good version of the master database, but the msdb database holds the majority of the work you will do as a developer.

☒ **A,** master, is incorrect even though it is a good idea to get regular copies of your master database. The master database contains information about the databases and locations of data files on the SQL Server. DTS packages are not stored in the master database, so in this situation you want to focus on the msdb database. **B,** model, and **D,** tempdb, are incorrect because they do not hold DTS information. The model database holds a template that is used for the creation of any new databases, and tempdb is used for temporary storage.

39. ☑ **B.** You need to put the ORDER BY clause after the HAVING clause. When you have ORDER BY and HAVING in the same query, the GROUP BY must precede the ORDER BY. Here is one phrase to help you remember: SQL Server tries to optimize performance, and it is faster to filter and then sort, rather than sort and then filter. (This is a phrase to help you remember only—not necessarily the way the query plan actually executes.)

☒ **A,** you included a clause in HAVING that is not in GROUP BY, is wrong because it is legal to have fields in the HAVING clause that are not in the GROUP BY clause. **C,** you need to change the single quotes used to delimit the date to pound signs, is incorrect because although pound signs are used in Access or DAO to delimit dates, single quotes are used in SQL Server. It is not necessary to have the ORDER BY parameters listed in the same order as they are in the GROUP BY clause, so **D**, you cannot have the ORDER BY sort in a different order than the two different GROUP BY fields, is wrong.

40. ☑   **B.** The location of the target table is likely to have the largest impact on the processing time of the trigger. Triggers are stored with the target table. If the target table is slow to access either because of its location on the disk or because the target table is located on another server, then the execution of the trigger (from the application's standpoint) will be slow. There are some other things you should take into consideration. For example, if the detail table is large and is not indexed by the fields that the parent trigger is deleting with then it will be a very slow, inefficient trigger.
☒   **A**, the location of the trigger, is not the best answer because triggers are stored with the target table, so the location of the trigger is really the location of the target table. **C**, the length of the trigger, is incorrect because the number of lines of code is somewhat irrelevant to the processing time of the trigger. **D**, the type of trigger, is incorrect because regardless of the type of trigger, the trigger is still acting against the target table, so access time to the target table will be the limiting factor.

41. ☑   **D.** All are valid uses of DTS. If you think this question sounded like a marketing question, you're right. Certification tests are peppered with Microsoft marketing questions. Microsoft wants to make sure that its certified professionals know the features and benefits of the products for which they are certified. Whenever you see a marketing question like this look for the "All of the above" option and give it close consideration. If you can't identify at least one option that is absolutely wrong, then a good bet would be to go with the all-inclusive option.
☒   **A, B,** and **C** are incorrect because all options are valid uses of DTS.

42. ☑   **B.** The maximum number of columns that can be aggregated in a CUBE query is 10. Therefore, when you add one field to account for the Sum(Sales) field, 11 is correct. (Because the number of records grows unwieldy as you add columns to a CUBE query, it is unlikely that you

would create a CUBE query of this size.)

☒ C, 10, would be correct if the threshold of 10 applied to the total number of columns, not to the GROUP BY columns. A, 12, and D, 9, are wrong because they are not the threshold number of columns.

43. ☑ B, C. Column and table correctly identify the objects for which you can define an update trigger. If you define the update trigger for the table, then an update to any column of any row in the table will fire the trigger. If you define the update trigger on a specific column, then only updates to that column for any row in the table will fire the trigger.

☒ A, row, and D, database, are incorrect because you cannot define any type of trigger for a specific row or for an entire database.

44. ☑ B. The plan achieves your primary goal and one secondary. The user-defined data type as defined will give a consistent format for zip codes in databases. By adding it to the model database, the zip code user-defined data type will automatically be included in any subsequently created database. Since a rule constraining the format has not been bound to the user-defined data type, the secondary goal of defining the format has not been achieved.

☒ A, C, and D are incorrect because the proposed solution achieves the primary and one secondary goal.

45. ☑ B. SQL Server uses a write-ahead log to ensure database consistency. If a failure occurs, all committed transactions can be rolled ahead and written to the database, and any uncommitted transactions will be rolled back from the log.

☒ A, C, and D are incorrect because SQL Server's transaction log does not operate as described. Any of these methods could give rise to inconsistency of data in the event of a failure.

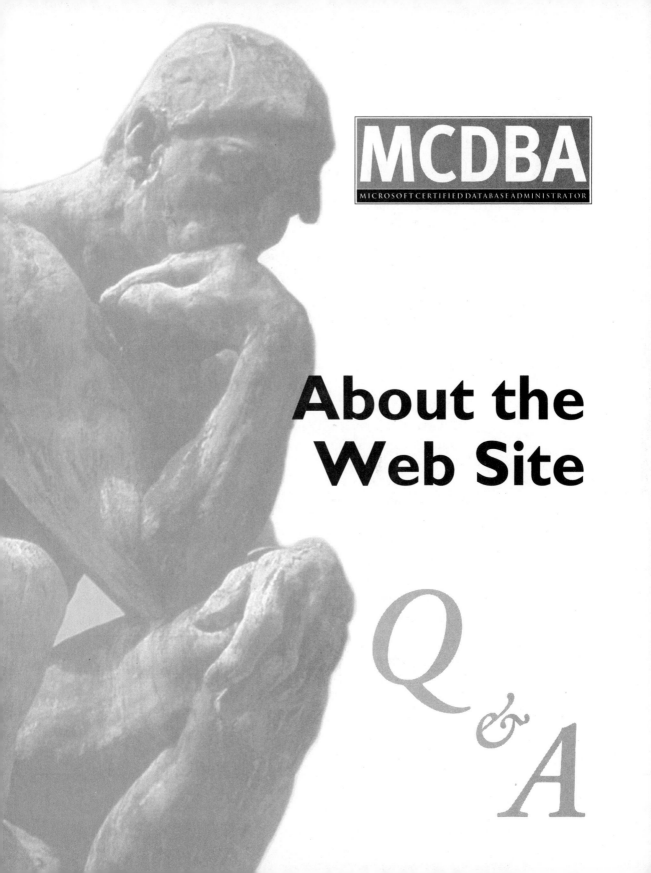

About the
Web Site

Q & A

Access Global Knowledge

As you know by now, Global Knowledge is the largest independent IT training company in the world. Just by purchasing this book, you have also secured a free subscription to the Global Knowledge Web site and its many resources. You can find it at http://access.globalknowledge.com.

You can log on directly at the Global Knowledge site, and you will be e-mailed a new, secure password immediately upon registering.

What You'll Find There. . .

The wealth of useful information at the Global Knowledge site falls into three categories:

Skills Gap Analysis

Global Knowledge offers several ways for you to analyze your networking skills and discover where they may be lacking. Using Global Knowledge's trademarked Competence Key Tool, you can do a skills gap analysis and get recommendations for where you may need to do some more studying. (Sorry, it just might not end with this book!)

Networking

You'll also gain valuable access to another asset: people. At the Access Global site, you'll find threaded discussions, as well as live discussions. Talk to other MCSD candidates, get advice from folks who have already taken the exams, and get access to instructors and MCTs.

Product Offerings

Of course, Global Knowledge also offers its products here, and you may find some valuable items for purchase—CBTs, books, or courses. Browse freely and see if there's something that could help you take that next step in career enhancement.

ACID test   A transaction must have the ability to pass four primary tests: atomicity, consistency, isolation, and durability.

aggregate functions   Return summary values, such as averages and sums, from values in a particular column. The returned values represent a single value for each set of rows to which an aggregate function was applied. The aggregate functions are: AVG, COUNT, COUNT(*), MAX, MIN, SUM, STDEV, STDEVP, VAR, and VARP.

alerts   Created using SQL Server Enterprise Manager, these are broadcasts to administrators of potential problems using benchmarks or parameters set by the administrator. SQL Server has two types of alerts: SQL Server Event Alert and SQL Server Performance Alert.

Alpha server   A generation of processors developed and marketed by Digital/Compaq Computer Corporation.

American National Standards Institute (ANSI)   An American organization of business and industry groups that develops communication and trade standards for the United States. These standards are coordinated with corresponding international standards. SQL Server is based on an ANSI-92 standard.

American Standard Code for Information Interchange (ASCII)   A character set built into every PC consisting of 96 uppercase and lowercase letters and 32 control characters. Note that ASCII does not include any formatting information such as font variances, bold face, or italics.

AppleTalk   The protocol designed for communicating with Macintosh computers. It is one of the protocols supported by SQL Server.

application database roles   Allows administrators to protect a database with a password. These types of roles do not contain any members (a user is associated with an application role only), and application roles are by default inactive. They require a password to be activated.

application programming interfaces (API)   The set of routines in an application that are available to be used by programmers when they are designing an application interface. OLE DB, ODBC, and DB-Library are examples of APIs.

article   A grouping of data to be replicated. This may consist of an entire table, a subset of the columns of a table (via a vertical filter), or a subset of the rows of a table (via a horizontal filter).

atomicity   Part of the ACID test, this "all or nothing test" stipulates that a transaction must complete its run fully or be discontinued and completely rolled back and suspended by its process.

base data type   A system-supplied data type. User-defined data types are made from base data types. Examples of base data types include: char, varchar, binary, and varbinary.

base table   The table on which a view is based. A view can have more than one base table.

batch   A group of SQL statements submitted and executed together.

binary sort order   The simplest of sort methods, it uses ASCII values to distinguish characters based on a preset group of parameters.

Binn   The nerve center of the SQL Server directory (MSSQL7), it contains the executable files that run all SQL Server services, protocols, objects, data requests, and options.

Boolean search   A search method that allows the user to employ the use of Boolean operators: and, not, and or. Boolean operators are powerful search methods supported on most popular search engines such as AltaVista and InfoSeek. Microsoft SQL Server 7.0 also supports Boolean operators in its full-text search feature.

bulk copy program (bcp)   A command line utility that allows external sources the ability to paste information into SQL Server. In previous versions of SQL Server, this was the only method to migrate data from earlier versions of SQL Server and from Sybase databases and text files. The ability to use this utility still exists in Microsoft SQL Server 7.0. *See also* **Data Transformation Services.**

cache   A buffer that holds data during an input/output (I/O) transfer between a disk and the random access memory (RAM).

candidate key   A unique identifier for a row in a table. It can be made up of one or more columns. A table can have more than one candidate key, but every table must have at least one. If a table has only one candidate key, that key becomes the primary key.

cascading delete   Deletes all of the database rows or columns that are related.

cascading update   An update that updates all of the database rows or columns that are related.

character set   The collection of letters, numbers, and special characters that will define the values used in the char, varchar, and text character-based data types.

CHECK constraints   Acceptable data values for a column. A column can have multiple CHECK constraints and you can apply CHECK constraints to many columns.

client   (1) A workstation accessing the resources in a client/server model. *See also* **client/server model.** (2) A program that runs on a computer, such as Microsoft Access, Microsoft Word, and Microsoft Excel.

client/server model   A model in which multiple user workstations connect to one central server or many different servers with the intention of sharing information. The server manages a common resource, such as a database, and responds to client requests for data from this resource.

clustered index   Determines the physical storage order of the data in a table. There can only be one clustered index in a table, but the index can be made up of multiple columns.

clustering   A technology that allows for recovery from catastrophic network failure. Clustering is managed via the Microsoft Clustering Service (MSCS) that comes native in Windows NT Server Enterprise Edition. MSCS allows for the clustering of two servers and consists of a several options and features.

code page   A database of 256 characters for all IBM PCs that stipulate a common character set.

column   Contains an individual data item within a row; they are called *fields* in traditional programming.

component object model (COM)   The programming model on which several SQL Server and database APIs are based, including SQL-DMO and OLE DB.

composite index   An index using more than one column in a table.

computed column   A virtual column that is not physically stored in the table. It is computed using an expression that uses other columns in the same table.

computer-to-computer installation   Typically used when performing a hardware upgrade simultaneous to the installation of SQL Server. This method allows the administrator to specify a source and a destination system for the upgrade.

consistency   Part of the ACID test, this is the property of a transaction that defines how it manages the state of the database over time. There are three levels of consistency: immediate guaranteed, latent guaranteed, and convergence. *See also* **ACID test.**

constraint   A property that is placed on a column or a set of columns in a table. SQL Server uses CHECK, DEFAULT, FOREIGN KEY, PRIMARY KEY, REFERENCE, and UNIQUE constraints.

control-of-flow structures   A stored procedure that allows you to perform tasks using techniques such as loops or conditional processing on variables that are usually found in programming languages such as Visual Basic or C++.

cursors   Pointers to subsets within a result set. Types of cursors in Microsoft SQL Server are static, dynamic, forward-only, and keyset-driven.

database (DB)   An organization of alphanumeric information designed so that users may easily access and retrieve the information. Databases are organized into objects known as tables, which are groups of data that all have something in common.

database management system (DBMS)   A container for the collection of computerized data files that allows users to perform operations on the files, including appending, editing, generating reports, retrieving, and updating.

database owner (DBO)   Granted at the database level, this account allows for complete access to the database and all its objects. When a user creates a database he/she is automatically the DBO of that database.

database restore syntax   The command line entries that are required in order to recover data from backups and return it to network ready status.

data bus   Connects the network interface card (NIC) to the processor. The data bus provides power, control information, and data to the card.

data definition language (DDL)   The SQL statements used to define all the objects (components), such as tables, queries, forms, and views in a SQL database.

data manipulation language (DML)   The SQL statements used to select, insert, update, and delete data in database objects.

data replication   *See* replication technology.

data type   Specifies what type of data can be stored in a column. Some of the data types include: tinyint, smallint, int, real, float, smalldatatime, datetime, smallmoney, money, and char.

Data Transformation Services (DTS)   A utility native to Microsoft SQL Server 7.0, it allows database administrators to migrate data from several other heterogeneous databases: Access, Excel, SQL, FoxPro, DBase, Paradox, Oracle, Site Server, Index Server, and any ODBC supported data source. Note that you can use VBScript, JScript, or the ActiveX scripting engine to write DTS scripts.

data warehouse   A database that is structured for query and analysis. It usually contains data that represents an organization's business history.

data warehousing   The idea that large amounts of information are stored on physical disks, typically measured in terabytes.

DB-Library   A group of high-level language libraries that provide the application programming interface (API) for the client in a client/server system.

deadlock   Occurs when two applications, which already have locks on separate objects, want a lock on the other's object. This option can be adjusted via the SET DEADLOCK PRIORITY.

default   A value that is automatically used for a column if a user does not insert a value for that column.

denormalize   The act of adding redundancy into a table in order to include data from another table. The other table can then be eliminated. This increases efficiency and performance by reducing complexity.

differential backup   A backup method that only replicates data that has changed since the execution of the previous backup. This is considered a fast method of backing up of data and is commonly used in large enterprise environments.

direct memory access channel (DMA) A hardware configuration that allows for bypassing the CPU of a PC and allow for the operating system to transfer data directly from a given process directly to a peripheral device such as a hard disk controller, a network controller, or a tape backup. The device that controls this process is known as a DMA controller. While the process bypasses the CPU, the transfer of data occurs at a speed one half the CPU's designated optimal running speed.

disk duplexing Exactly like mirroring except that it uses two disk controller cards—one card for each drive in the mirror. This provides redundancy in case one of the controllers fails. *See also* **disk mirroring**.

disk mirroring Used by RAID 1 to duplicate information to another hard disk. *See also* **Redundant Array of Inexpensive Disks (RAID)**.

disk striping This technology allows for data to be placed over multiple physical disks. By allowing for multiple physical drives to maintain data integrity, data fault tolerance is increased. *See also* **Redundant Array of Inexpensive Disks (RAID)**.

Distribution Agent Moves the transactions and snapshot jobs from the distribution database tables to the subscriber servers.

distributor A server that contains the distribution database. It is the responsibility of the distributor to take publications from the publisher and distribute them to the subscriber servers.

domain controller Installed with Windows NT 4.0, the domain consists of a mandatory Primary Domain Controller (PDC) and an optional Backup Domain Controller (BDC). Both can authenticate logins and distribute services as requested by workstations. In the event of a crash of the PDC, the BDC is "promoted" to PDC status.

durability Part of the ACID test, this property refers the to ability of the database to recover if the data is left in an inconsistent state. Once a database reports that a transaction has been committed to the database itself, the transaction is not able to be rolled back.

dynamic link library (DLL)   An executable routine that contains a specific set of functions stored in a .DLL file. It can be loaded upon demand by the program that calls it.

dynamic locking   The process that SQL Server uses to find the most cost-effective locks at any one time.

dynamic memory allocation   The ability to adjust how much disk space is allocated for Microsoft SQL Server 7.0. These values can be adjusted by using the Memory tab in the SQL Server Properties.

dynamic self-management   An automated system new in SQL Server 7.0 that allows the system to monitor how much of its system resources are being consumed by running tasks. Microsoft SQL Server 7.0 can then automatically fit the size of the database to the amount of system resources available to it.

exclusive locks   Used to maintain data integrity during multiple database write attempts. This type of locks is used for INSERT, UPDATE, or DELETE statements.

extent   Consisting of 64KB, or eight contiguous pages, it is the smallest unit of space allocated to indexes and tables. As the need for more memory arises, more extents are allocated to the database.

fault tolerance   The ability of a computer to ensure that data and resources remain functional in the event of an emergency.

filegroup backup   SQL Server allows for filegroups to be backed up. This backup process can be managed via the SQL Server Enterprise Manger interface.

filegroups   Collections of files sharing some common thread. In SQL Server there are three types of filegroups: primary, which contain the data file; user-defined, containing any files the user wishes to create and place here; and, default, which contains the pages for all tables and indexes that did not have a filegroup specified when they were initially created by either the user or the administrator.

file types   Upon creation of a database using Microsoft SQL Server 7.0, three types of files are initially created: MDF (primary files), NDF (non-primary files), and LDF (log files).

fixed database role   Defined at the database level, they exist within each database. In order to be added and granted access to a database, a user must have either an NT login account or a SQL login account. Users are typically added to this role via the SQL Server Enterprise Manager utility.

fixed memory allocation   The option in Enterprise Manager that allows the administrator to set a consistent query memory size for Microsoft SQL Server 7.0. By using this option it prevents the operating system from altering SQL Server memory pages.

foreign key   The column or columns whose values match the primary key in the same or another table. It does not have to be unique.

global temporary table   Prefaced by # #, these tables are available to every client and act as a temporary storage area for work tables and store procedures.

guest user account   A default account created by SQL that allows for anonymous logins to the database.

GUID (globally unique identification number)   A GUID is a binary number that is guaranteed to be unique.

heaps   Tables that are created without a clustered index.

horizontal filtering   Used to restrict the rows that are replicated during the process of data replication. *See* **replication technology.**

implied permission   The ability to manipulate any object for which permission has already been granted. Owners of database objects are the only users capable of receiving implied permissions.

index   A database object that can speed up queries by looking up the data by key values instead of having to scan the entire table. Microsoft SQL Server 7.0 supports clustered and non-clustered indexes.

INSERT statement   Operates much like bcp. This statement can be used to add data from an external OLE DB provider to a SQL Server database in one or more rows.

intent locks   Locks resources in areas lower in the hierarchy of transactions.

Internet Information Services (IIS)   Provides FTP and Web services in Windows NT.

interprocess communication (IPC)   A method of communication between one program and another. Depending on the IPC method being used, this communication can even be across a network. IPC is often used in the client/server environment as a means of communication between the server and the client across the network.

IPX/SPX (Internetwork Packet Exchange/Sequenced Packet Exchange)   Protocol that is primarily used by Novell NetWare networks, but which can be used by other networks (such as Microsoft networks) as a routable protocol or to connect to Novell networks.

isolation   Part of the ACID test, this property defines the level of exposure that data modifications in the current transaction will have to other transactions.

jobs   Tasks that contain steps. Steps are run at intervals and can make certain administrative tasks much more manageable via their ability to automate the network processes.

join   A query that allows users to retrieve data from multiple tables based on logical relationships. Types of joins occurring in Microsoft SQL Server include inner, outer, and cross.

local temporary tables   Prefaced by #, these tables are available to the clients that created them.

locking granularity   Technology that allows Microsoft SQL Server 7.0 to differentiate the efficiency of various locking schemes.

locks   As client applications access data simultaneously, Microsoft SQL Server 7.0 uses locks to prevent concurrent users from reading data that has been changed but not yet written to the database. There are four types of locks used by Microsoft SQL Server 7.0 to restrict access to a resource: shared, update, exclusive, and intent.

log file   Holds all the transaction log information that is used to recover the database. The recommended file extension for all log files is *.LDF*.

Log Reader Agent   Moves transactions that are marked for replication from the transaction log on the publisher sever to the distribution databases.

master server   The server that processes and manages jobs. These jobs are then relayed via SQL Server to the receiving computers known as target servers.

Merge Agent   Moves and reconciles incremental data changes that occurred after the initial snapshot was created. With this agent, data may move in both directions between subscriber and publisher severs.

merge replication   This form of replication enables sites to make independent changes to replicated data. Later, changes are merged at all sites. However, this method does not ensure data consistency at each site.

Messaging Application Programming Interface (MAPI)   A messaging structure that allows for a client graphical user interface in order to send and receive electronic mail. This messaging scheme allows for designing scheduling, calendars, and various personal information managers much like those that exist with Microsoft Exchange and Microsoft Outlook. MAPI also allows for more than one application program to exchange data with several other messaging sources over a wide range of different hardware and software operating platforms.

Microsoft Access   A database that operates as development tool, by using Visual Basic for Applications (VBA) and a database. It differs from Microsoft SQL 7.0 in that Microsoft SQL 7.0 is only a database.

Microsoft Distributed Transaction Controller   A service of Microsoft SQL Server that must run under Windows NT.

Microsoft Distributed Transaction Coordinator (MSDTC)   Installed native with a typical SQL Server installation, this tool allows client (workstation) applications to receive data from multiple servers in a single transaction.

Microsoft English Query interface   Allows users to enter queries such as "What is the relationship of employees to vacation time?" without using Transact-SQL code.

Microsoft Management Console (MMC)   Included within the installation of SQL Server 7.0. This is Microsoft Corporation's strategy to normalize administrative tool interfaces across operating systems and the BackOffice server platform.

Microsoft SiteServer   Microsoft Corporation's internet/intranet commerce server software.

Microsoft System Management Server (SMS)   Part of Microsoft Corporation's "zero administration strategy." SMS allows network engineers to manage software installations, network resource usability, workstation software installations, policies, and profiles, just to name a few. It is designed to exploit the Windows operating systems to their full potential in a network environment.

Microsoft SQL Server Roles   Ways in which SQL Server categorizes groups of users and assigns permissions to group members. The four types of server roles are: fixed server, fixed database, public database, and user-defined.

Microsoft Transaction Server   A server used to store and distribute components. These components are developed using Microsoft's Component Object Model (COM).

Mixed Mode Authentication   Uses both Windows NT Server profile and Microsoft SQL Server authentication. If the user logs into Microsoft SQL Server without an NT login, Windows NT Server will allow its profiles to occur for the user, provided Microsoft SQL Server is set to Mixed Mode.

model database   A SQL Server database used as a template for all new databases created on the system.

multitier client/server architecture   Used for larger enterprises, this scheme of networking splits the logic of the network, allowing the workstation to display data and the business logic or application program(s) to run on the server.

multipublisher   A condition when there is more than one publishing server providing data replication to one or more subscriber servers. As publisher server numbers increase, extra load is placed on the distributor.

multiserver capability   SQL Server allows for this, provided that all servers installed were installed using the same sort orders, Unicode collation, and code pages.

multisubscriber   Exists when there are one or more publishers replicating data to more than one subscriber server. When this occurs, database overhead increases as an extra load is put on the distributor.

multithreading   The capability of an application to start two or more threads of execution, which can then be concurrently processed. SQL Server is written as a multithreaded program.

NetBEUI   Originally written by IBM, NetBEUI runs on all Microsoft operating systems. It is a very fast, yet nonroutable protocol. It is ideally suited to an organization with few computers.

niladic functions   Functions that are built into SQL Server and do not retrieve information from SQL Server. These functions are often used to provide a default data value if one is not supplied during data insertion.

nonclustered index   An index in which the order of the index does not match the stored order of the physical table rows.

non-logged operations   Used to prevent the transaction log from filling up and consuming large amounts of hard disk space.

Northwind database   A sample data set that accompanies many of Microsoft Corporation's database products such as Microsoft Access as well as Microsoft SQL Server 7.0.

NWLink   Microsoft's implementation of Novell's IPX/SPX (Internetwork Packet Exchange/Sequenced Packet Exchange) protocol suite. NWLink is a routable transport protocol for Microsoft networks.

Object Linking and Imbedding (OLE)   A technology standard created by Microsoft Corporation, and adopted by Apple Computers, that allows for data to be shared and automatically updated between running applications. An object (picture, document, etc.) created with one client can be then placed within or called from another client.

object permission   Owners grant specific users the right to access particular objects that they own. Permission is granted at this level to tables, views, and stored procedures.

OLE DB   A set of initialization interfaces required for an OLE DB application to connect to an OLE DB data store. OLE DB is an application programming interface (API) that is based on the Component Object Model (COM).

online transaction processing (OLTP)   A database management system that represents the state of a business function at one point in time. An OLTP database usually has large numbers of concurrent users modifying and adding data.

Open Database Connectivity (ODBC)   Originally conceived by Microsoft, it is now a universal standard to allow heterogeneous database access. Essentially, ODBC is a set of drivers that allow databases, such as Microsoft SQL 7.0 and Microsoft Access, to engage in relational database management. ODBC supports access to all databases for which ODBC drivers are available. *See also* **relational database management system.**

Open Data Services (ODS)   An application programming interface (API) for the server side of a client/server system. It acts as the liaison between the server applications and the network connection.

page   The smallest unit of storage space in Microsoft SQL Server, consisting of 8KB of memory. There are six types of pages: date, text/image, global allocation map, page free space, index, and index allocation map.

performance baseline   The level at which the administrator determines the server is at its optimal level in terms of performance and efficiency. Factors affecting baseline performance include: hardware (CPU speed, amount of RAM, cache, etc); operating system upgrades (in terms of latest Microsoft service pack installed); design considerations on database front-end interface; memory allocation via the setting of page faults; and the number of workstations and users attempting to write and read information from the database.

permissions   Authorization granted to users to access database resources. *See also* **object permission** and **statement permission.**

physical devices   Peripheral hardware machines, typically hard disks and tape drives, that allow for physical backup of mission-critical data.

physical security   The ability to control physical access to servers and peripheral equipment considered vital to the network and database.

point-of-failure   A critical point in data recovery. It is the point at which the network crashed. This is also the point to which adequate backup and restore procedures can quickly return a network to alleviate minimum downtime and loss of data.

port number   The computer address for a specific service such as connection to the internet via a modem or other communications line.

primary data file   The starting point of the database. This file contains pointers to all other files in the database. The recommended naming conventions for SQL Server give this file a file extension of *.MDF*.

primary key   A column or columns that uniquely identify one row from any other row in a table.

Priority-based merge replication   Replication based on custom Common Object Models specific to the network where replication is set to run.

protocol   A set of standardized rules that multiple entities agree to abide by. Computers need a standard set of procedures in order to manage the data packets they send and receive. They must use the same compatible protocol or the communication will not work.

public database role   A special role to which all users belong by default. Users cannot be dropped from the public role as they may from fixed roles. Also, public roles capture all default permissions for users in a database.

Publication Wizard   A graphic user interface that steps the administrator through the procedure of setting up and designating the nature of a particular SQL Server. Through this wizard, an administrator can predetermine if a server is to operate as either a publisher server or a subscriber server.

publisher   The server that makes data available for replication to other servers, known as subscribers. This server is responsible for which data is to be replicated, as well as for which data has changed via late transactions.

pull subscription   A subscription in which the subscriber server is set to request periodic updates of changes from the publisher server.

push subscription   A subscription in which the publisher server propagates the changes to the subscriber without a specific request from the subscriber server.

query   A request for the retrieval, deletion, or modification of specific data.

query governor   The option that allows administrators to conserve system resources by setting restrictions on the duration of a query.

query optimizer   The component that generates the optimum query execution plan.

Redundant Array of Inexpensive Disks (RAID)   A grouping of hard disks connected to a server with the intention of creating mirrored hard disks so that data exists in more than one place on a typical server. RAID levels run from 0 to 5, with 0 stipulating the lowest level of data security and level 5 stipulating complete data redundancy of the disk array.

relational database management system (RBDMS)   An organization of databases that share data, often across multiple networks. Data is sometimes entered into one database and another database can access this data and make it available to users or even to other databases. This system organizes data into related columns and rows.

remote procedure call (RPC)   Used extensively in distributed computing environments, a set of rules and methods for controlling and directing how a process is started and run on a network node foreign from the node/computer that initially requests the process.

remote server   A SQL server on the network that can be accessed from a user's local server.

remote stored procedure   A collection of control-of-flow statements and SQL statements that are stored under a name on a remote server.

Replication Monitor   A graphical tool that can be used for viewing the status of replication agents and troubleshooting potential problems at the distributor. It is found in the SQL Server Enterprise Manager.

replication technology   The Microsoft technology that automatically copies data to multiple locations and can restore and/or move it to multiple locations. This provides a fast and inexpensive way of managing database housed on multiple servers. Note that data can also be replicated to/from other database using ODBC. Microsoft uses several elements to populate its database replication technology including publisher, subscriber, article, and distributor. *See also* **Open Database Connectivity**.

restoration time   The time it takes in order to completely recover a database in the event of a catastrophic hard disk, server, or general network failure.

result set   The set of data returned from a SELECT statement.

roles   Database roles are ways in which users are added to databases and given permission to access those resources.

row   A data structure within a table that contains the complete set of columns. It is called a record in traditional programming.

row aggregate function A function that displays detail and summary rows in one set of results. It does this by generating summary values that appear as additional rows in query results.

rule A database object that is bound to a column, or a user-defined data type that specifies the types of data values that can be used for that column. For example, a rule can be made to make sure that the zip code in a record contains only numbers.

scalability The capability to expand to meet future needs (in other words, to upgrade). It is a characteristic of both software and hardware.

scalar aggregate A function that is applied to all of the rows in a table (which produces one value per function).

secondary data files All data files other than primary data files and log files. Microsoft recommends these data files have an *.NDF* extension.

self-join A join comparing rows within the same table.

select list The expressions or keywords that define the attributes of the columns returned from the specified tables in a query.

server A computer that provides shared resources to network users.

server backup The complete copy and replication of all data that currently exists on the server.

server synchronization The process by which servers in an NT domain, specifically PDC and BDC, are reconciled and brought current to contain identical user databases. In SQL Server it is the synchronization of the primary and standby servers that allows for data replication and mirroring.

shared lock   A lock created by read operations. It allows concurrent database connections to read data. Because reading data does not affect database content, shared locks can be used concurrently with other lock types.

Showplan   A tool used for optimizing queries in Microsoft SQL Server 7.0. It displays the query execution plan for an SQL statement.

side-by-side installation   This method of installing Microsoft SQL Server 7.0 allows the latest version installed to run on the same machine as a previous version of SQL Server, such as Microsoft SQL Server version 6.0 or 6.5.

single publisher   This replication involves a single publisher server providing data information potentially to multiple subscriber servers.

single subscriber   A replication scenario where there typically exist one publisher, one subscriber, and one distributor. This is the most common SQL Server database operating environment.

Snapshot Agent   Prepares the scheme and initial data files of published tables and store procedures. It then stores these snapshots on the distributor server and records information for data synchronization.

snapshot replication   This technique takes a snapshot of the current data on the publisher and replaces all of the data on the subscriber periodically. Snapshot replication provides guaranteed consistency among all servers marked for replication.

spin counter option   Specifies a limit on the attempts a process can make when trying to obtain access to a resource.

SQL Mail   A component of SQL Server that allows for the processing of queries about the status of the server via electronic mail. This service requires the installation of Windows Messaging Service or Microsoft Exchange, in addition to the appropriate Mail Application Programming Interface (MAPI) driver.

SQL Server Agent Installed in a typical SQL Server installation, this tool allows for periodic scheduling of server jobs. It can be configured to respond on demand to activities raised by alerts.

SQL Server Enterprise Manager A graphical user interface used to manage and control users and processes on databases running under Microsoft SQL Server 7.0 and using system resources.

SQL Server Performance Monitor Integration Provides up-to-the-minute performance and activity statistics. It is an integration of SQL Server with Windows NT Performance Monitor.

SQL Server Profiler A graphical tool that allows system administrators to trace problems by monitoring events including deadlocking, server connects and disconnects, login attempts, and other vital server information. In order to achieve this type of information, data is captured in real time as processes run.

SQL Query Analyzer A utility that allows you to enter stored procedures and Transact-SQL statements in a graphical user interface. It also provides the capability to graphically analyze queries.

standard database role Allows the system administrator to set up the correct level of security needed within a database. These roles can contain NT groups and users and other roles that simultaneously occur in other current databases.

Simple Network Management Protocol (SNMP) Part of the TCP/IP suite of protocols, this protocol allows for the management and monitoring of multiple nodes on a network. Two types of SNMP currently exist: SNMP1 and SNMP2.

standard security model Microsoft SQL Server maintains its own security log by requiring the user to authenticate to access the database. This is the most secure model.

statement permission Controls the use of Transact-SQL statements used to create objects within a database. Statement permission can be granted, denied, or revoked.

stored procedure A set of precompiled Transact-SQL statements that execute as an object. The benefit of using stored procedures is that they are precompiled, which translates into faster execution times. Security is more easily enforced because permissions can be set for the object only. Stored procedures that are supplied by SQL Server are called system stored procedures.

Structured Query Language (SQL) Developed by IBM in the 1970s, it is a language used to retrieve information from a database.

subscriber Servers that store data replicated from publishers. Microsoft SQL Server 7.0 allows subscriber servers to update data.

subscription database Database that receives data and tables that are replicated from a publication database.

subquery A SELECT query that returns one value and is nested inside another subquery or a SELECT, UPDATE, DELETE, or INSERT statement.

symmetric multiprocessing (SMP) SMP is the concept that a computer system can support multiple processors, and the processors can balance the load between themselves. If your computer has four CPUs, then they would share the processing work load and each one could participate in executing parts of a single program. Having SMP leads to scalability. *See also* **scalability**.

system administrator Similar to the DBO, but the system administrator has control over the entire server. A built-in feature of Microsoft SQL Server 7.0, this account automatically has control over all databases residing on the server. Note that when you are using mixed-mode security, the system administrator account must be used for the first administrative login.

system catalog   A store of user account information in 13 system tables found in the master database. The user information includes security, ID, passwords, databases, environment tables, system error messages, and system stored procedures.

system stored procedures   A precompiled set of Transact-SQL statements supplied by SQL Server. System stored procedures provide shortcuts for retrieving information from system tables or for updating the tables. The names of system stored procedures begin with *sp_*.

system tables   Tables that are created when the database is created. They store SQL Server configuration information and definitions of the objects, permissions, and users in SQL databases. Initially they consume .5MB of disk space.

table   A collection of data that is stored in multiple rows and columns.

table scan   A scan in which SQL Server starts at the beginning of the table and reads every row to find the rows that meet the search criteria.

TCP/IP (Transmission Control Protocol/Internet Protocol)   An industry standard suite of protocols designed for local and wide area networking. Widely used for Internet communication.

TCP/IP sockets   A library native installed on SQL Server that communicates with Windows 9x workstations. In order to run TCP/IP sockets, a port must be specified. The default number SQL Server uses is port 1433.

TerraServer   A one-terabyte database that is a collection of geographical information collected by Russian and United States satellites.

thread   The smallest unit of code in a process.

time slice option   Used by administrators of Microsoft SQL Server 7.0 to set a limit on the time that a process can be active.

timeoutoption   Sets a predetermined limit on the time that the system will wait for a resource that is currently busy or running.

tool   A SQL Server application with a graphical user interface used to perform common tasks.

Transact-SQL   The standard language used for communication between applications and SQL Server. It allows users to access the database and create and modify the data. In Microsoft SQL Server the four main statements to achieve this are SELECT, UPDATE, DELETE, and INSERT. In SQL Server 7.0, Transact-SQL statements can be used to create a database.

Transaction   A transaction is the smallest logical unit of work for the database. All actions that occur on the database break down into one or more transactions. Transactions consist of the four properties called the ACID properties. Each level of work must contain all of these properties before they are considered transactions. *See also* **ACID test.**

transaction isolation levels   Settings that allow for various levels of data integrity. In Microsoft SQL Server 7.0 there are four different isolation levels: read committed, read uncommitted, repeatable read, and serializable.

transaction log   A serial record of all modifications that have occurred in the database. The log records the start of each transaction, the changes to the data, and enough information to undo the modifications.

transaction processing   A method in which transactions are executed as soon as the system receives them.

transactional replication   Uses the publisher's database transaction log to capture changes that were made to an article's data. The changes are transmitted to the subscribers as incremental changes. When using this method, SQL Server monitors all INSERT, UPDATE, and DELETE statements.

Transfer manager   Part of SQL Server Enterprise Manger in SQL 6.5, this utility allowed administrators to transfer data and objects (triggers, store procedures, etc.) between databases. *See also* **Data Transformation Services (DTS)**.

trigger   A stored procedure that runs when data in a specific table is modified, such as with an update, delete, or insert. Triggers are often used to ensure consistency among related data in multiple tables.

Unicode   Defines a set of numbers, letters, and symbols that SQL Server recognizes in the nchar, nvarchar, and ntext data types. It includes characters for most languages and is related to but separate from character sets.

Unicode collation sequence   Removes language barriers by enabling a 16-bit multilingual character set. A sort order for Unicode data, this utility assists in the deployment of SQL Server using multiple languages within a single server.

UNIQUE constraints   Constraints that ensure a nonprimary key has data integrity.

unique index   An index in which no two rows can have the same index value. This prohibits duplicate key values.

update lock   A lock that is placed on resources, such as rows or tables, that can be updated. These locks are used to prevent deadlocks that occur when multiple sessions lock resources and update them later.

user connection option   A new feature in Microsoft SQL Server 7.0, this function allows for dynamic assignment of system resources as each user establishes a new connection with SQL Server. It is used to specify the maximum number of simultaneous user connections allowed on SQL Server, thus helping to avoid overloading the server with too many concurrent connections.

update statistics   A process of recalculating information about the key value distribution in specified indexes.

user-defined data types   A data type that is based on a SQL Server data type and is created by the user for data storage. User-defined data types can be bound by rules and defaults. *See also* **base data type**.

variable   A defined entity that has a value assigned to it.

vector aggregate   Functions that are applied to all rows with the same value in a specific column, using the GROUP BY clause. The HAVING clause can be used with the GROUP BY clause to produce a value for each group per function.

vertical filtering   Used to specify which rows are replicated during the process of data replication.

view   A display of a table that shows the table's data. A view is a virtual table that retrieves the data with queries, and can contain more than one table. Before the user is able to use the view, they must have permission on the view and on all dependent objects.

Visual InterDev   A suite of Microsoft development products including Visual Basic, Visual C++, Visual J++, Visual FoxPro.

Windows New Technology (NT)   Microsoft's server operating system that is used as an operating platform for Microsoft SQL Server 7.0.

Windows NT Application Event Log   An applet running in Windows NT that tracks all application events. SQL Server writes all events including all SQL Server errors to the Windows NT Event Log.

Windows NT Authentication   Allows users with a Windows NT user account to connect to SQL Server.

wildcard characters   Characters used with the LIKE keyword for matching patterns. The percent (%), brackets ([]), and underscore (_) characters are examples of wildcard characters.

Custom Corporate Network Training

Train on Cutting Edge Technology   We can bring the best in skill-based training to your facility to create a real-world hands-on training experience. Global Knowledge has invested millions of dollars in network hardware and software to train our students on the same equipment they will work with on the job. Our relationships with vendors allow us to incorporate the latest equipment and platforms into your on-site labs.

Maximize Your Training Budget   Global Knowledge provides experienced instructors, comprehensive course materials, and all the networking equipment needed to deliver high quality training. You provide the students; we provide the knowledge.

Avoid Travel Expenses   On-site courses allow you to schedule technical training at your convenience, saving time, expense, and the opportunity cost of travel away from the workplace.

Discuss Confidential Topics   Private on-site training permits the open discussion of sensitive issues such as security, access, and network design. We can work with your existing network's proprietary files while demonstrating the latest technologies.

Customize Course Content   Global Knowledge can tailor your courses to include the technologies and the topics which have the greatest impact on your business. We can complement your internal training efforts or provide a total solution to your training needs.

Corporate Pass   The Corporate Pass Discount Program rewards our best network training customers with preferred pricing on public courses, discounts on multimedia training packages, and an array of career planning services.

Global Knowledge Training Lifecycle   Supporting the Dynamic and Specialized Training Requirements of Information Technology Professionals

- Define Profile
- Assess Skills
- Design Training
- Deliver Training
- Test Knowledge
- Update Profile
- Use New Skills

College Credit Recommendation Program   The American Council on Education's CREDIT program recommends 53 Global Knowledge courses for college credit. Now our network training can help you earn your college degree while you learn the technical skills needed for your job. When you attend an ACE-certified Global Knowledge course and pass the associated exam, you earn college credit recommendations for that course. Global Knowledge can establish a transcript record for you with ACE, which you can use to gain credit at a college or as a written record of your professional training that you can attach to your resume.

Registration Information

COURSE FEE: The fee covers course tuition, refreshments, and all course materials. Any parking expenses that may be incurred are not included. Payment or government training form must be received six business days prior to the course date. We will also accept Visa/MasterCard and American Express. For non-U.S. credit card users, charges will be in U.S. funds and will be converted by your credit card company. Checks drawn on Canadian banks in Canadian funds are acceptable.

COURSE SCHEDULE: Registration is at 8:00 a.m. on the first day. The program begins at 8:30 a.m. and concludes at 4:30 p.m. each day.

CANCELLATION POLICY: Cancellation and full refund will be allowed if written cancellation is received in our office at least six business days prior to the course start date. Registrants who do not attend the course or do not cancel more than six business days in advance are responsible for the full registration fee; you may transfer to a later date provided the course fee has been paid in full. Substitutions may be made at any time. If Global Knowledge must cancel a course for any reason, liability is limited to the registration fee only.

GLOBAL KNOWLEDGE: Global Knowledge programs are developed and presented by industry professionals with "real-world" experience. Designed to help professionals meet today's interconnectivity and interoperability challenges, most of our programs feature hands-on labs that incorporate state-of-the-art communication components and equipment.

ON-SITE TEAM TRAINING: Bring Global Knowledge's powerful training programs to your company. At Global Knowledge, we will custom design courses to meet your specific network requirements. Call 1 (919) 461-8686 for more information.

YOUR GUARANTEE: Global Knowledge believes its courses offer the best possible training in this field. If during the first day you are not satisfied and wish to withdraw from the course, simply notify the instructor, return all course materials, and receive a 100% refund.

In the US:

CALL: 1 (888) 762-4442

FAX: 1 (919) 469-7070

VISIT OUR WEBSITE:

www.globalknowledge.com

MAIL CHECK AND THIS FORM TO:

Global Knowledge

Suite 200

114 Edinburgh South

P.O. Box 1187

Cary, NC 27512

In Canada:

CALL: 1 (800) 465-2226

FAX: 1 (613) 567-3899

VISIT OUR WEBSITE:

www.globalknowledge.com.ca

MAIL CHECK AND THIS FORM TO:

Global Knowledge

Suite 1601

393 University Ave.

Toronto, ON M5G 1E6

REGISTRATION INFORMATION:

Course title _____

Course location _____ Course date _____

Name/title _____ Company _____

Name/title _____ Company _____

Name/title _____ Company _____

Address _____ Telephone _____ Fax _____

City _____ State/Province _____ Zip/Postal Code _____

Credit card _____ Card # _____ Expiration date _____

Signature _____